CW00816452

A.H.M. Jones and the Later Roman Empire

Brill's Series on the Early Middle Ages

(continuation of The Transformation
of the Roman World)

A.H.M. Jones and the
Later Roman Empire

Edited by

David M. Gwynn

BRILL

LEIDEN • BOSTON
2008

Cover Illustration: AHM Jones (1904–1970). Photograph: Walter Stoneman. Courtesy The British Academy (copyright reserved). The editor would like to thank the British Academy for permission to reproduce this image.

This book is printed on acid-free paper.

A Cataloging-in-Publication record for this book is available from the Library of Congress

ISSN 1386-4165
ISBN 978 90 04 16383 6

Copyright 2008 by Koninklijke Brill NV, Leiden, The Netherlands.
Koninklijke Brill NV incorporates the imprints Brill, Hotei Publishing, IDC Publishers, Martinus Nijhoff Publishers and VSP.

PRINTED IN THE NETHERLANDS

CONTENTS

PREFACE

The publication in 1964 of A.H.M. Jones' *The Later Roman Empire 284–602: A Social, Economic, and Administrative Survey* transformed the study of the Late Antique world. As Peter Brown wrote, its appearance marked "the arrival of a steel-plant in a region that has, of late, been given over to light industries". In recognition of Jones and his achievement, a seminar series was held in Oxford in the Spring of 2004 to celebrate the 40th anniversary of his great work. In the course of these seminars, it emerged that very little has been written about Jones or the background to the *Later Roman Empire*. It became apparent that there was much to learn regarding Jones the scholar and his place in the history of Late Antique studies.

The aim of this volume is to fill that void and to provide an insight into the formation and subsequent influence of a work which remains fundamental four decades after it first appeared. The papers presented to the original seminar series in 2004 form the core of what follows. Peter Garnsey began proceedings with an important introduction to Jones and his historical method, and subsequent papers covered the majority of the *Later Roman Empire*'s central themes. Peter Heather and Caroline Humfress discussed respectively the crucial Jonesian questions of Government and the Law. Roger Tomlin took up Jones' presentation of the Late Roman Army, while Luke Lavan assessed his approach to the study of Urbanism and Bryan Ward-Perkins explored his vision of the Economy. My own contribution reconsidered Jones' controversial attitude towards the role of Christianity in the Late Roman Empire, and Averil Cameron, in the final paper of the series, returned to the much-debated question of the 'Decline and Fall' of the Empire in the West. All these papers reappear here, revised to varying degrees in the light of the seminar debates and subsequent reflections.

To those original papers were then added further contributions that extended the volume beyond the limits of the seminar series. Alex Sarantis prepared a biographical outline of Jones' career and its impact upon his work, and compiled the bibliography of his numerous academic writings. Stefan Rebenich provided a valuable insight into Jones' relationship with contemporary continental scholarship, and Michael Whitby examined his presentation of the role of the emperor and the imperial image. Wolf Liebeschuetz, who compiled the index for the original *Later Roman Empire*, composed the volume's Afterword.

Complete uniformity in a volume comprising the writings of multiple authors is neither possible nor necessarily desirable, and the attentive reader will find numerous differences in focus and approach in the papers collected here. Within the parameters of their given subject, each contributor has struck their own balance of emphasis between Jones and his methods on the one hand and developments since Jones on the other. Nevertheless, certain themes do recur. Jones' phenomenal attention to detail and knowledge of the primary sources continue to inspire awe and to make the *Later Roman Empire* an essential work of reference; yet he was also inevitably influenced by the works of earlier scholars, despite his well-known reluctance to refer to modern authors. A number of the contributors similarly highlight Jones' ambivalent attitude towards archaeology, which already in his own time was transforming our knowledge of the Late Roman world. Given the vast advances in Late Antique scholarship that have taken place in the last four decades, however, it is not possible in a single volume to do more than trace briefly the way that subsequent research has built on, or diverged from, the direction that Jones established. This volume is not therefore a 'commentary' on Jones' theories, far less a 'replacement' of his work which remains an essential point of reference on so many subjects. Rather, it offers an aid to academics and students alike to enable them to better understand and exploit the priceless resource that is the *Later Roman Empire*.

The editing and publication of this volume has inevitably incurred many debts. My sincere thanks must go once again to all the contributors and to the audiences who attended the original seminar series. The inspiration for that series came initially from Luke Lavan, and it was organised and chaired by Peter Heather and Bryan Ward-Perkins; I am extremely grateful for all their help and ongoing support. My thanks also go out to the many people with whom I have discussed different aspects of this project for their advice and encouragement, particularly to Peter Brown, Fergus Millar and James Howard-Johnston, and above all to Henry Chadwick, who has supported the publication of this volume just as he supported the publication of the *Later Roman Empire* itself. Marcella Mulder has been an ideal colleague at Brill, and I am grateful alike for her invaluable assistance and her patience as this book gradually took shape.

Finally, on behalf of all the contributors, I must thank A.H.M. Jones. The publication of this volume and the involvement of so many scholars of widely varying interests and backgrounds testifies once again to the sheer scale of his achievement and its enduring significance. The 40th anniversary of the *Later Roman Empire* has passed, and Jones is already exerting his influence on another generation of Late Antique scholarship. If this volume can serve to make his work still more accessible to that next generation, then we will have achieved our aims.

David M. Gwynn
Christ Church
Oxford

LIST OF ABBREVIATIONS

AE	*L'Année Épigraphique*
AJPh	*American Journal of Philology*
BAR	*British Archaeological Reports*
BMGS	*Byzantine and Modern Greek Studies*
BNJ	*Byzantinisch-neugriechische Jahrbücher*
Byz	*Byzantion*
CH	*Church History*
CIL	*Corpus Inscriptionum Latinarum*
CJ	*Codex Iustinianus*
CPh	*Classical Philology*
CPL	*Corpus Papyrorum Latinarum*
CQ	*Classical Quarterly*
CR	*Classical Review*
CTh	*Codex Theodosianus*
DOP	*Dumbarton Oaks Papers*
EcHR	*Economic History Review*
EHR	*English Historical Review*
FIRA	*Fontes Iuris Romani Ante-Iustiniani*
GRBS	*Greek, Roman, and Byzantine Studies*
HThR	*Harvard Theological Review*
ILS	*Inscriptiones Latinae Selectae*
JEA	*Journal of Egyptian Archaeology*
JECS	*Journal of Early Christian Studies*
JEH	*Journal of Ecclesiastical History*
JHS	*Journal of Hellenic Studies*
JRA	*Journal of Roman Archaeology*
JRS	*Journal of Roman Studies*
JThS, NS	*Journal of Theological Studies*, New Series
PBA	*Proceedings of the British Academy*
PBSR	*Papers of the British School at Rome*
REL	*Revue des études latines*
RSI	*Rivista Storica Italiana*
StP	*Studia Patristica*
YCS	*Yale Classical Studies*
ZPE	*Zeitschrift für Papyrologie und Epigraphik*
ZRG	*Zeitschrift der Savigny-Stiftung für Rechtsgeschichte*

LIST OF CONTRIBUTORS

AVERIL CAMERON is Professor of Late Antique and Byzantine History at the University of Oxford and Warden of Keble College. Her recent publications include *Changing Cultures in Early Byzantium* (Aldershot 1996), *Eusebius, Life of Constantine* (with S.G. Hall, Oxford 1999) and *The Byzantines* (Oxford 2006). She is co-editor of volumes XII, XIII and XIV of the *Cambridge Ancient History*.

PETER GARNSEY is Professor of the History of Classical Antiquity at the University of Cambridge and a Fellow of Jesus College. Among his numerous publications are *Ideas of Slavery from Aristotle to Augustine* (Cambridge 1996), *Food and Society in Classical Antiquity* (Cambridge 1999) and *The Evolution of the Late Antique World* (with C. Humfress, Cambridge 2001). He is co-editor of *Cambridge Ancient History* volumes XII and XIII.

DAVID GWYNN is a Junior Research Fellow at Christ Church, Oxford, and now Lecturer in Ancient and Late Antique History at Royal Holloway, University of London. His doctoral thesis was recently published as *The Eusebians: The Polemic of Athanasius of Alexandria and the Construction of the "Arian Controversy"* (Oxford 2007).

PETER HEATHER is a Lecturer in History at the University of Oxford and a Fellow of Worcester College. His publications include *Goths and Romans 332–489* (Oxford 1991), *The Goths* (Oxford 1996) and *The Fall of the Roman Empire: A New History* (London 2005).

CAROLINE HUMFRESS is Reader in History at Birkbeck College, University of London. She has published *The Evolution of the Late Antique World* (with P. Garnsey, Cambridge 2001), "Civil Law and Social Life" in N. Lenski (ed.), *The Cambridge Companion to the Age of Constantine* (Cambridge 2006) 205–225, "Law and Legal Practice" in M. Maas (ed.), *The Cambridge Companion to the Age of Justinian* (Cambridge 2005) 161–184, and most recently *Orthodoxy and the Courts in Late Antiquity* (Oxford 2007).

LUKE LAVAN is a Lecturer in Archaeology at the University of Kent. He has edited a number of conference volumes, including *Recent Research in Late Antique Urbanism* (Portsmouth, Rhode Island 2001), *Theory and Practice in Late Antique Archaeology* (with W. Bowden, Leiden 2003) and *Housing in Late Antiquity: From Palaces to Shops* (with L. Özgenel and A. Sarantis, Leiden forthcoming). He is the series editor for *Late Antique Archaeology*.

WOLFGANG LIEBESCHUETZ is Emeritus Professor at the University of Nottingham. Among his most recent publications are *The Decline and Fall of the Roman City* (Oxford 2001), *Ambrose of Milan, Political Letters and Speeches* (Liverpool 2005) and *Decline and Change in Late Antiquity: Religion, Barbarians and their Historiography* (Aldershot 2006).

STEFAN REBENICH is Professor for Ancient History and Classical Tradition (Alte Geschichte und Rezeptionsgeschichte der Antike) at the University of Berne. His most recent publications include *Xenophon, Lakedaimonion Politeia* (Darmstadt 1998), *Jerome* (London and New York 2002) and *Theodor Mommsen. Eine Biographie* (Munich 2002, 2nd edition 2007).

ALEXANDER SARANTIS completed his doctorate at Oxford in 2006 and his thesis will shortly be published under the title "The Balkans during the reign of Justinian: barbarian invasions and imperial responses". He is currently working for the Central Administration of the University of Oxford and is the editor of *Housing in Late Antiquity: From Palaces to Shops* (with L. Lavan and L. Özgenel, Leiden forthcoming), *Technology in Transition AD 300–700* (Leiden forthcoming) and *The Archaeology of War in Late Antiquity* (Leiden forthcoming).

ROGER TOMLIN is University Lecturer in Late Roman History at the University of Oxford and a Fellow of Wolfson College. His publications include *The Roman Inscriptions of Britain, II: Instrumentum Domesticum* (with S.S. Frere, Stroud 1990–95) and "Christianity and the Late Roman army" in S.N.C. Lieu and D. Montserrat (eds.), *Constantine: History, Historiography and Legend* (London 1998) 21–52. He is the editor of *History and Fiction: Six Essays in Celebration of the Centenary (2003) of Sir Ronald Syme* (London 2005).

BRYAN WARD-PERKINS is a Lecturer in History at the University of Oxford and a Fellow of Trinity College. He is co-editor of *The*

Cambridge Ancient History volume XIV and has published *From Classical Antiquity to the Early Middle Ages: Urban Public Building in Northern and Central Italy, AD 300–850* (Oxford 1984) and *The Fall of Rome and the End of Civilization* (Oxford 2005).

MICHAEL WHITBY is Professor of Classics and Ancient History at the University of Warwick. Among his publications are *The Emperor Maurice and his Historian: Theophylact Simocatta on Persian and Balkan Warfare* (Oxford 1988) and *The Ecclesiastical History of Evagrius Scholasticus* (Liverpool 2000). He is co-editor of *Cambridge Ancient History* volume XIV and has also recently edited *The Cambridge History of Ancient Warfare* (with P. Sabin and H. van Wees, Cambridge 2007).

SECTION I

THE MAN AND THE HISTORIAN

CHAPTER ONE

ARNOLD HUGH MARTIN JONES (1904–1970)

Alexander Sarantis

(i)

Standing on the pavement outside the lecture hall at Mill Lane, a few research students took the opportunity to seek Jones' advice on problems they had encountered in their work. One of them raised a point concerning the political institutions of some Aegean island. Hugo responded by quoting verbatim from memory a few relevant lines in Greek from an inscription, then in mid-sentence, he suddenly stopped and said: "here the stone breaks off"![1]

A.H.M. Jones, Hugo Jones as he was known to his friends, ranks with the greatest Roman historians alongside such illustrious figures as Gibbon, Mommsen, and Bury. His encyclopaedic knowledge of the ancient written sources, literary and epigraphic, and the languages in which they were written, daunted colleagues and frequently left students awestruck. Through the copious books and articles he published during a sparkling academic career, A.H.M. Jones still exerts an important influence. The articles collected in this volume are a tribute to the continued relevance and standing of his work and particularly of his *magnum opus, The Later Roman Empire 284–602: A Social, Economic, and Administrative Survey*.

Arnold Hugh Martin Jones was born in Birkenhead, Cheshire, on 9th March 1904, the son of John Arthur (1867–1939) and Elsie Martin Jones. Jones' paternal grandfather, Dr. Hugh Jones (1807–1919), was a famous Welsh Wesleyan minister and historian and "one of the powerful preachers of his generation".[2] His father was a journalist, who worked at the *Liverpool Post* before being appointed editor of the *Calcutta Statesman* in 1906. In the same year, the Joneses moved to India,

---

[1] Reminiscence of Mostafa El-Abbabi, a student and friend of Jones from 1953 until Jones' death.

[2] 'Dr. Hugh Jones Manuscripts', The University of Wales Bangor at www.archives-networkwales.info, reference code GB 0222 HUGH.

where John Arthur was later awarded a CIE for his public service. In 1910, Jones returned to England with his mother, who registered him at Cheltenham College in September 1913. His academic record at the school, which he attended until July 1922, was outstanding. Top of the year for almost the entire duration of his school career, Jones also picked up prizes for a range of subjects, from Classics and Latin prose, to English literature, chapel reading and Geography. On leaving, he was awarded the Dobson and Jex-Blake scholarship to read Classics at New College, Oxford.

Jones' brilliant academic performance continued at New College and he took a degree with first class honours in *Literae Humaniores* in 1926. His promise had been apparent to his college tutor, Henry Ludwig Henderson, from his first term, at the end of which Henderson scribbled "?fellowship?" next to Jones' name on the relevant page of an exercise book devoted to the progress and performance of his various students.[3] Indeed, the year Jones finished his degree, he was elected to a fellowship at All Souls College, the platform from which he could launch an academic career without having to start teaching immediately or find employment. He was to hold the fellowship until 1946.

This was an age in which the PhD was not a pre-requisite for an academic career, and Jones was able to spend the first three years of his fellowship broadening his intellectual horizons by reading extensively and travelling widely. In March 1927, he married Katherine Freda Mackrell, a medievalist from Somerville College who was to be his life-long companion. During these years, Jones acquired a keen interest in archaeology and took part in a series of excavations, at Constantinople with Stanley Casson in the summer of 1927, and at Jerash in 1928 and 1929. These resulted in his first publications: chapters on inscriptions and coins in the archaeological report from Constantinople in 1928; and two articles on inscriptions from Jerash in 1928 and 1930. Jones also published a letter in *The Times* detailing the excavation of Early Christian churches at Jerash.[4] In 1929, he was appointed Reader in Ancient History at the Egyptian University in Cairo and moved to Egypt with his wife. According to John Crook's biography of Jones, it was the need for money that drove Jones to accept the post in Cairo.[5]

---

[3] New College Archive, reference PA/H3/2/3.
[4] *The Times*, 8th June 1929, page 10, Issue 45224.
[5] Crook (1971) 426.

Having lectured in Egypt for five years, Jones returned to All Souls in 1934 to begin work on the 'Cities' books and produce his first major flurry of publications.

Jones' early experiences of archaeological work, teaching and travelling in the eastern Mediterranean imbued him with an interest in the ancient history of the region, and led him to view it as the centre of the Roman world. In the first instance, it resulted in articles on the history of urbanisation in Palestine and the Ituraean Principality, both published in 1931. These prefaced his first major works: *The Cities of the Eastern Roman Provinces* (1937) and *The Greek City from Alexander to Justinian* (1940).

The Cities of the Eastern Roman Provinces traces the history and configuration of cities based on the Greek model in their political organisation and cultural life throughout the eastern Mediterranean, region by region, from the classical period to the Late Roman era. *The Greek City from Alexander to Justinian* builds upon this work by adopting a thematic approach in analysis of how and why Greek cities sprang up in different regions, their relations with distant governments, internal politics, and the civic services they provided. Its general argument is that increasing centralised control, particularly during the Roman Republic, eroded civic autonomy, patriotism and 'public spiritedness', resulting in the decline of the 'Greek' city.[6] Both books drew on an extensive base of literary texts and epigraphic evidence. In the preface to the second edition of *The Cities of the Eastern Roman Provinces*, published posthumously in 1971, Jones attributed his compilation of this vast historical topography to the energy of youth: "I was young and believed that one man could master the historical topography of an area stretching from Thrace to Cyrenaica over a period of more than a millennium".[7] The ambition that led to the 'cities' books established Jones' wide-reaching approach and willingness to tackle head-on major historical questions.

During the 1930s, Jones also found the time to write more general books—*The History of Abyssinia* and *The Herods of Judaea*, published in 1935 and 1938 respectively.[8] Articles on the architecture and history

---

[6] See in particular *The Greek City* Part V, 'The Achievement of the Cities' 259–304.

[7] *Cities of the Eastern Provinces* (1937), 2nd ed. (1971) v.

[8] Jones is reputed to have co-written *The History of Abyssinia* with Elizabeth Monroe in a frenzied six weeks in the summer of 1935, having been approached at short notice by the OUP who urgently wanted a book on the African state in light of its recent invasion by Mussolini. Jones' contribution of chapters on ancient, dark age and

of New College, All Souls and Worcester College also date from this period. They were later published in the third volume of the *Victoria County History of Oxford*, in 1954. Jones' publications were widely acclaimed, and in 1939 resulted in his appointment to a lectureship in ancient history at Wadham College. This second teaching appointment was, however, immediately interrupted by the outbreak of the Second World War, during which Jones worked for the Ministries of Labour and National Service and for Military Intelligence. The nature of his work for Military Intelligence remains confidential, but in the Ministry of Labour he worked on 'Essential Work Orders' and 'Control of Engagements' acts, which were designed to ensure the stabilisation of labour within the essential war industries.[9] These decrees regulated the provision of manpower to areas such as ship-building, civil engineering, mining and agriculture.[10] As well as restricting workers from leaving their posts save in exceptional circumstances, they prevented managers from dismissing workers without good reason, and meant that the government assumed greater responsibility for the welfare and discipline of workers.

Following the war, Jones returned briefly to his post at Wadham before being elected to the Chair of Ancient History at University College, London, in 1946. Jones presided over something of a golden age in ancient historical studies at UCL, characterised by a generation of excellent students.[11] He delivered a series of lecture courses which had an impact long after he moved to Cambridge. In particular, the special and optional subjects he taught on 'The Principate of Augustus and Tiberius' and 'Administration and Empire', respectively, provided the groundwork for many of the articles later collected in *Studies in Roman Government and Law*, published in 1960.[12] Two of these, 'The Aerarium and the Fiscus' and 'The Imperium of Augustus', appeared in the *Journal of Roman Studies* in the late 1940s and early 1950s. In this period, Jones also re-read the Attic orators and did much of the work

---

medieval history to the first English book on Ethiopian history earned him an invitation from the King of Ethiopia, Haile Selassie, to be his guest at a Royal festival in Addis Ababa in November 1964.

[9] *Ancient Economic History* (1948) 14.
[10] *Ministry of Labour and National Service* 45–52.
[11] Crook (1971) 428.
[12] Wolfgang Liebeschuetz recalls Jones teaching these courses in London (personal communication).

that later contributed to the collection of articles on *Athenian Democracy*, which appeared in 1957.[13]

Jones produced one important work in the late 1940s, *Constantine and the Conversion of Europe* (1948), written for a series of general histories put together by his former colleague at All Souls, A.L. Rowse. Charting the major aspects of Constantine's reign, especially his conversion and attempts at resolving theological controversies, this little book is best known for its conclusion that it was genuine piety that had motivated the great emperor's conversion, rather than political concerns. Jones' inaugural lecture on 'Ancient Economic History', printed in 1948, also had an important influence. As Russell Meiggs recalled, it reminded contemporaries of how little they knew of the precise statistical workings of the Greek and Roman economies.[14] Finally, it was at UCL that Jones began in earnest the research which was to lead to the *Later Roman Empire*. On a less happy note, it was during his time at UCL that Jones became ill, and was treated for a duodenal ulcer at the University of London hospital. He was to suffer with his health for the rest of his life and also to experience periods of crippling depression.

In 1951, Jones exchanged London for Cambridge, succeeding Professor F.E. Adcock to the Chair of Ancient History and becoming a fellow of Jesus College.[15] At Jesus, Jones continued his work on the Late Roman Empire, unleashing a barrage of articles on various aspects of late Roman history, most of which were printed in the *Journal of Roman Studies*. These articles reached some of the principal conclusions that were to underpin the *Later Roman Empire*. For instance, papers on inflation (1953), taxation (1957), over-taxation (1959) and the origins of the *follis* (1959) explored the relationship between the devaluation of silver and copper currencies between the third and sixth centuries, increasing rates of taxation to meet costs, deflated official salaries, corruption, the flight of the peasantry, and the consequent problem of what Jones was to famously term 'idle mouths'. Following on from his inaugural lecture at UCL, Jones examined these developments within the framework of modern economic analysis, highlighting the failure of ancient governments to employ a considered long-term monetary

---

[13] Meiggs (1970) 186.
[14] *Ibid.*
[15] *The Times*, 19th February 1951, page 8, issue 51929.

or currency policy.[16] At the same time, many of his articles explored in greater depth than he had previously attempted intricate facets of the society and economy of the Roman and late Roman period, including studies on the Roman colonate (1958), heretical movements (1959), church finances (1960), the cloth industry (1960) and collegiate prefectures (1964).

In 1964, this spate of publications culminated in the "great work", as Jones referred to it. *The Later Roman Empire 284–602: A Social, Economic, and Administrative Survey* was immediately acclaimed as a successor to the timeless contributions of Gibbon and Bury.[17] Two volumes of text and one of notes in its first printing, it spans more than fourteen hundred pages, and still represents the most extensive study of the Late Roman Empire, mainly founded on an unprecedented analysis of the legislative material. In the preface, Jones explicitly defined his subject matter in opposition to a history of events or ideas.[18] Wars, cultural or intellectual developments and political events were not his main interests. In his mind, these areas had been dealt with by Gibbon and Stein, whose influence upon Jones will be discussed further below. Instead, as his subtitle promises, Jones set out to survey the social, economic and political workings of the Late Roman state. Jones' intricate dissection of all areas of Late Roman society and economy in the *Later Roman Empire*, from the government and central administrative and judicial apparatuses, to the army, the church, cities, education and religious observance, caused quite a stir at the time. Even scholars more interested in the ideological and cultural history of Late Antiquity were impressed by Jones' approach. Momigliano referred to the *Later Roman Empire* as 'the Jones report', pointing out its similarity to a Royal Commission investigation into the health of the state. Peter Brown wrote that the

---

[16] "Inflation under the Roman Empire" (1953) analyses the currency policies of successive Roman governments and the motives behind these.
[17] Heichelheim (1965) called it "a *magnum opus* in the tradition of Bentley, Gibbon, Bury and Baynes". Momigliano (1965) 264 referred to it as a 'great work'; Brown (1967) 343 called it "an irreplaceable chapter in the history of the Byzantine state"; Morris (1964) proclaimed that it was "a decisive book that closes a range of questions that have been arguable for half a century or more and thereby opens a range of new questions"; Browning (1964) 335 was staggered by "its size, its erudition, its systematic and exhaustive treatment of its subject matter, and—may one say—its price".
[18] *Later Roman Empire* (1964) I, v: "This book is not a history of the Roman Empire. It is a social, economic and administrative survey of the empire historically treated".

Later Roman Empire was "an event of the first importance in the study of the Later Roman Empire".[19]

Jones followed the *Later Roman Empire* with an abridged version, entitled *The Decline of the Ancient World*, published in 1966, and wrote articles on 'Asian Trade in Antiquity' (1970), 'The Caste System of the Later Roman Empire' (1970) and 'Ancient Empires and the Economy' (1965, but published in 1970). At the same time, he put together a two-volume collection in translation of source materials from the Republic and the Later Empire, entitled *A History of Rome through the Fifth Century* (1968–1970), and wrote two general books, on *Sparta* (1967) and *Augustus* (1970). These last two books were, by Jones' standards, not a great success. Crook felt that *Augustus* was "a brief book, a little lacking in excitement". *Sparta*, although criticised by Greek historians for what it omits, still displays Jones' ability to write lucidly and logically, and remains a useful introduction to the subject.[20]

The next major project on the horizon was a work on Justinian, which he never lived to complete. Throughout his time at Jesus, Jones had also been busy working on the *Prosopography of the Later Roman Empire*. This collaborative project differed greatly from his regular research, conducted alone in his study, in that it required teamwork to sort, marshal and create order from the written notes of numerous academics, starting with the century-old files of Theodor Mommsen. Jones lived to read the proofs of the first volume.

A.H.M. Jones died from a heart attack on 9th April 1970, during a particularly rough sea journey between Brindisi and Patras. He had decided to spend a sabbatical term in Greece and was on his way to deliver lectures in Athens. He had only one more year of teaching before him. It was a tragic end to an amazingly productive and success-ful academic life. Among the various honours bestowed on him, these stand out: the doctorate in law at Cambridge in 1965 and divinity at Oxford in 1966, the LHD at Chicago in 1969 and an honorary fellow-ship at his *alma mater*, New College, in 1968. He had been the President of the Roman Society between 1952 and 1955, a fellow of the British Academy since 1947, and of the Scottish Academy since 1957.

---

[19] Momigliano (1965) 264; Brown (1967) 327.
[20] Huxley (1968) 90 wrote "I think that we should be grateful that this work has been written; but it is not the work which the Professor's many admirers would choose in order to exemplify the best of his scholarship".

(ii)

In his excellent biography of 1971, John Crook described Jones as "of slight build, with a little stoop or hunch or, almost, prowl, sandy hair, a light tenor timbre of voice, and a crinkly face. He was formidable, mainly because shy".[21] Indeed, according to most accounts, Jones was a serious, private, often distant man who avoided small talk and was most at ease with close friends or relatives, or talking about history, on which he could be inexhaustible. Roger Tomlin looked back on his only meeting with Jones, on a visit to Cambridge to consult the files of the *Prosopography of the Later Roman Empire*:

> Access to these files was controlled by Jones, so I met him for tea at Jesus, in his room over the main gate. I waited here for him, and all I remember is that I was feeling very hungry—I suppose I had missed lunch—when in came this figure in a long, brown mackintosh, looking like a mournful terrier. He produced a brown paper bag from his pocket; it contained two macaroons; he made us a pot of tea, and we ate a macaroon each. Then he drove me to the University Library. I was later told I must have met him on 'one of his bad days'.

Mostafa El-Abbabi, a student and great friend of Jones from 1953, whose father was a colleague of Jones in the department of history at the University of Cairo, recalls that, while in Egypt: "Jones was known to be extremely shy, aloof and considered a most unsociable person who hardly ever exchanged words with either Egyptian or European faculty members". At one international conference, Jones was found wandering alone in the garden holding a cup of tea, while everybody else crowded around the buffet. Joyce Reynolds, a student of Jones at Oxford and colleague at Cambridge, remembered that when being examined by Jones, his shyness limited discussion. A.L. Rowse, Jones' contemporary at All Souls during the 1930s, even referred to Jones as a "dull man" whom he "hardly ever heard say anything of interest".[22]

However, to those who knew him well, Jones was far from dull, and is remembered as a warm and generous friend. His apparently haughty demeanour in formal settings was recognised as an inescapable facet of his academic individuality by friends and students. According to Richard Duncan-Jones, a student of Jones at Cambridge, "Jones was somewhat

---

[21] Crook (1971) 437.
[22] Rowse (1995) 55.

mercurial in temperament, with the dry mannered academic heavily in the ascendant most of the time, perhaps as a result of the gigantic research tasks he imposed upon himself". Nonetheless, Duncan-Jones also recalls that Jones was very hospitable, frequently inviting him to dine with his family. Similarly, on one visit to the Jones residence, Mostafa El-Abbabi was told by Jones' wife, Freda, that he was too unwell to receive guests, only to be promptly invited in by Jones, who assured his wife that he could surely meet a friend. El-Abbabi also remembers Jones singing *The Boar's Head* Carol when celebrating Christmas in Egypt in 1964, and, at other Christmases in Oxford, animatedly leading the way in carefully prepared treasure hunts. Jones could also be witty in his own way. In discussing the very early days of an excavation at Jerash, he once told Duncan-Jones that, after working on some inscriptions, a young colleague had commented: "amazing what a number of people in these parts were called Sebastos".

Although Jones disliked small talk, he enjoyed seminars and colloquia, where he was good at listening, and formidable at debating. In particular, he relished the opportunity seminars afforded him to try new ideas out on his colleagues. However, whereas Jones was in his element in discussions and debates with colleagues, in the lecture theatre his shyness was obvious. Although he enjoyed lecturing, his no-nonsense style was not conducive to large audiences, especially when these consisted of undergraduates, who were in many cases in need of entertainment to retain their interest. Jones' policy was to turn up, reel off the material he had prepared, and then leave.[23] He was known to pace up and down and talk while looking at his feet. El-Abbabi recalls that Jones' first lecture at Mill Lane after moving to Cambridge was packed with students, eager to hear the great ancient historian. However, Jones noticed with great disappointment the rapidly dwindling numbers of students thereafter. His lack of sparkle as a speaker was in fact apparent from a very early stage. A report in *The Cheltonian* magazine on a debate in November 1920 against Rugby School states:

> A.H.M. Jones gave the facts of the case at some length. Unfortunately he was not interesting enough to inspire the speakers from the House to

---

[23] A number of Jones' lectures were converted into first-rate publications. Many of the articles included in *Studies on Roman Government and Law* and *Athenian Democracy* were based on lectures at UCL and Cambridge, while *Sparta* was written on holiday in Alexandria in the summer of 1969 in preparation for a series of lectures he was due to give the following year.

much sound argument. They appeared to have gone to sleep while he was speaking, and it was not entirely their fault. But his exposition was clear and lucid.[24]

Jones retained this ability to speak lucidly, and this, at least, meant that his lectures were extremely beneficial to those sufficiently diligent to pay attention. In the words of Joyce Reynolds, "Jones was not, I think, a good lecturer, but the notes I took were splendid and remained useful to the end of my lecturing career".

For those interested in his subject, Jones was an inspiration. Many illustrious academics, including Joyce Reynolds, Geoffrey de Ste. Croix, John Kent, John Mann, Keith Hopkins, Richard Duncan-Jones and Wolfgang Liebeschuetz, were his students. He was an extremely consci-entious teacher who treated everyone as his equal and disliked the way in which professors on the continent were treated as 'God-like' by their students and not questioned by them. Crook wrote that Jones could daunt undergraduates but at the same time inspire them.[25] Duncan-Jones recalls that Jones' lectures might on occasion "take flight and turn into re-enactments of the past, with his student audience divided into two to recite the Melian dialogue, or to perform other Athenian debates". However, for the most part, he did not need to charm his students by energetic speaking or witticisms, for he could inspire them merely by his vast knowledge and his innovative subject matter. According to Wolfgang Liebeschuetz, who was taught by Jones as an undergraduate at UCL:

> What made a lasting impact was, first, Jones' particular field of interest in Ancient History, that is the topics covered in his classes and in his writ-ings, such as 'government' generally, more particularly the development of cities, problems of administering an empire and an emphasis on social, administrative and economic issues, and second, the skill from which he built up his chosen themes from fragmentary sources.

The extraordinary knowledge of the original literary sources which his students admired played a critical role in Jones' phenomenal productiv-ity. Mostafa El-Abbabi witnessed his writing habits first-hand:

> It was his custom to draw up a detailed outline of the main facts of the subject under discussion sitting on the floor, leaning against a sofa and surrounded by piles of source books. He would write down the full text

---

[24] *The Cheltonian*, November 1920, 22.
[25] Crook (1971) 435.

depending on memory and, finally, would go through the entire text, checking what he had written and adding the necessary footnotes. In this way, he said, he was able to check both text and source.

Jones prided himself on using the earliest editions of the sources, sometimes from the 17th or 18th century, and his skill at translating, absorbing and interpreting Greek and Latin texts was honed during more than a decade of rigorous training in the classics, first at Cheltenham and then at New College. He was able to transmit to paper his familiarity with the original texts as easily as he was able to bring it to bear in debates with colleagues or in seminars with his students. According to Liebeschuetz, "one could not argue with Jones unless one had a comparable knowledge of precisely what the sources said, which I certainly did not have".

Jones' mastery of the primary sources and the languages in which they were written in turn formed the basis of a dogmatic adherence to 'authentication', which became increasingly obsessive later in life. In short, Jones' long experience of studying the classics imbued him with a reverence for original texts, which he felt should lie at the heart of all historical writing. It seems to have been the only point he imposed on students. Wolf Liebeschuetz states: "the influence was one of subject, method and 'scholarly morality', but not of views". Jones' methodology meant that he included very few references to the secondary literature in his publications. This neglect of the secondary material was regularly criticised. Momigliano stated: "in no other country would an author get away with a similar disregard of modern literature on his subject".[26] In the preface to *The Greek City*, Jones insisted that he wanted to provide his reader with easy access to the primary texts rather than making them "consult one or more modern works before getting back to the source of the argument".[27] In the same passage, Jones goes on to explain "how slender is the evidence for many modern theories, which often pass untested on the authority of a great name". Therefore, for Jones, as long as there was evidence of close working from the primary texts, historians had little need to refer to the secondary literature, which was the product of minds situated in the modern world.

It is widely accepted that Jones had a far better knowledge of the secondary works than the paucity of his references suggests. The

---

[26] Momigliano (1965) 264.
[27] *The Greek City* (1940) vii.

numerous book reviews he wrote for the *Journal of Roman Studies* bear
this out. Indeed, it should not be assumed that Jones cut himself off
from the intellectual world and interpreted the primary material with
no care for his contemporaries' views. Momigliano pointed out, in his
review of the *Later Roman Empire* in 1965, that one reason Jones might
not have possessed a detailed list of references to modern works was
that, being ensconced in Oxford and Cambridge for the majority of
his academic life, he would have been able to consult world experts
in person whenever he required an opinion.[28] Time was also a critical
factor. In *The Greek City* he referred to "a lack of space", and in the
Later Roman Empire he claimed "I early realised that if in a field so vast
I tried to read the modern literature exhaustively and keep abreast
of current scholarship I should not have time to read the sources. I
therefore abandoned the former attempt".[29]

This silence on the works of modern scholars also extended to the
evidence of archaeology. In the late 1920s, when only recently married,
Jones had of course taken part in a series of archaeological expedi-
tions, at Constantinople and at Jerash. An immense enthusiasm for
this work is highlighted by A.L. Rowse, who claimed that Jones earned
the nickname 'Jerash Jones': "Returning from his dig at Jerash, he was
astonished to have found the strata of five or six successive civilisations".[30] According to Cordelia Gidney, Jones' daughter, he nearly joined
the Palestinian Archaeological Service in the late 1920s, but eventually
opted for the position of Reader at Cairo University.[31] This early foray
into archaeological research may have been prompted by Rostovtzeff's
monumental *The Social and Economic History of the Roman Empire* of 1926,
which had made ground-breaking use of both archaeological and
written evidence.[32]

With a young family to support, a strong attachment to Oxford and
Cambridge, and, later on, problems with his health, he never seems
to have regained this zeal for archaeological work. Given that Jones
allegedly refused to write upon any region or city unless he had visited
it, it is unlikely that he would have felt comfortable using reports on

---

[28] Momigliano (1965) 264.
[29] *The Greek City* (1940) vii; *Later Roman Empire* (1964) I, vi.
[30] Rowse (1995) 56.
[31] Liebeschuetz (1992) 6.
[32] Momigliano (1954) 91: "We were accustomed to books on ancient history where the
archaeological evidence, if used at all, was never presented and explained to the reader.
Here a lavish series of plates introduced us directly to the archaeological evidence."

material evidence he had not himself worked on. The obituary in *The Times* states that Jones had put off publishing the *Later Roman Empire* "because there were parts of the Roman Empire he was not able to visit until 1958".[33] El-Abbabi recalls Jones' energetic road trips around the East Mediterranean, on which his wife Freda faithfully accompanied him. On one occasion:

> Jones wished to drive from Syria to Alexandretta, in Turkey. At the frontier, he was told that Alexandretta was a military zone and as a foreigner he was not allowed to spend the night in the city. Jones and Freda therefore drove back to Syrian territory, spent the night in the car and in the early hours of the morning, made their entry into Alexandretta.

This restless mania for visiting vast numbers of sites would explain his irritation with the slow moving nature of archaeological work. On one occasion, Jones indicated this frustration to El-Abbabi:

> As a young fellow at All Souls, he once joined an archaeological expedition, headed by Talbot Rice to Turkey. The work on the site required weeks on end just in order to remove the heaps of sand that covered the place. Hugo grew impatient and decided to give up work on archaeology.

Jones was also frustrated by the inaccessibility of the reports generated by archaeological research. In his biography of Rostovtzeff, published in 1952, Jones complained of "indigestible archaeological reports" and a "jungle of archaeological publications".[34] Early in his Cambridge career, despairing of the widely disparate locations of the principal journals and volumes on epigraphy and calligraphy within the University Library, Jones cajoled its librarians into bringing them together in one section. Duncan-Jones describes this as "one of his unsung achievements at Cambridge". Jones was further aggravated by the failure of epigraphers, numismatists and archaeologists to ask what he deemed the 'right' questions of the evidence. His article on "Numismatics and History" (1956) gives an insight into the severe demands he placed on the material evidence. Jones wanted the numismatic evidence to tell him whether the imperial government had an official currency policy, the effects of the progressive debasement of different types of coinage at different times, the location of mints in relation to circulation patterns, and the relationship between coin hoards and significant political

---

[33] *The Times*, 10th April 1970, page 12, issue 57840.
[34] "Michael Ivanovitch Rostovtzeff" (1952) 356–7.

events. More specifically, he wanted to know detailed facts regarding the volume, life and nomenclature of the coins issued, and the sources of bullion from which they originated.[35] Instead, Jones lamented that numismatists sometimes spent their time reading too much into the significance of symbolic decorations depicted on coins or focusing on rare specimens rather than the regular denominations that were more indicative of currency circulation.[36] It may be assumed from such writing that Jones hungered for hard, scientific information with which he could confront the far-reaching problems of understanding the workings of the economy and society of the ancient world.[37] He certainly had little time for the subjective reflections of modern scholars on the possible importance of ideas and images.

(iii)

Given his fervent attempts to avoid the constraints of modern theories, it is perhaps not surprising that identifying the major academic influences behind Jones' work is extremely hard. As a young man, he was certainly influenced by Professor Hugh Last, and in the introduction to his article on "*Capitatio* and *Iugatio*", Jones acknowledged that Last had been the first to encourage him to study the Later Roman Empire.[38] Last had been a fellow of St. John's from 1919, University Lecturer at the same college from 1927, and Camden Professor of Roman history (at Brasenose) from 1936. In the latter post, he gave a series of lectures on his favourite topic, the Roman constitution, which seem to have inspired a whole generation of Roman historians. Brash, outspoken, and, according to the *DNB*, "a man of affairs" who "consciously

---

[35] "Numismatics and History" (1956), esp. 69 on the organisation of mints, sources of bullion and minting techniques and 70–71 on the relative scarcity of different issues. Duncan-Jones, Jones' student, went on to tackle some of these questions: Duncan-Jones (1974), (1990), (1994).

[36] "Numismatics and History" (1956) 62: "Coins commonly bear a brief legend and a type which has a symbolic significance. Numismatists have studied these intensively, and an historian may perhaps be permitted to say in his opinion they have sometimes attached an excessive significance to this".

[37] *Ibid.* 80: "historians would like to know technical data which yield objectively certain results".

[38] "*Capitatio* and *Iugatio*" (1957) 88: "Among the many fields of Roman history which Mr. Last has illuminated the later Roman Empire is not the least, and it was he who first encouraged me to embark on its study".

built an image of himself which he presented to the world",[39] Last's striking and open character meant that he became a natural source of advice for all studying Roman history in 1920s and 1930s Oxford. The famous papyrologist and close friend of Jones, Sir Eric Turner, was one of those who attributed his own choice of career to the great Professor.[40] In terms of precise subject matter, however, it is difficult to pin down Last's influence on Jones. Unlike his student, Last did not publish prolifically and never produced a major work. Nevertheless, his interest in Roman constitutional history could well have helped to inspire Jones' preoccupation with this area at various stages of his career, resulting in the collections of articles *Studies in Roman Government and Law* (1960) and, posthumously, *The Criminal Courts of the Roman Republic and Principate* (1972).

However, the three historians whose works seem to have had the most pronounced influence on Jones were not his acquaintances. One of these was Gibbon. Roger Jones remembers that his father was a great admirer of Gibbon and used to say that it would be extremely difficult to update *The Decline and Fall of the Roman Empire* given that it contained very few mistakes. Another was Stein, whose *Histoire du Bas Empire* greatly impressed Jones in its authoritative narrative reconstructions of ecclesiastical disputes, military history and character sketches of the leading figures of the age.[41] Therefore, Jones chose to adopt a very different focus from these works, while examining the same period. He found his inspiration in Rostovtzeff's *The Social and Economic History of the Roman Empire*, which broke off its detailed discussion in the third century A.D. Despite having never met the Russian émigré, Jones referred to himself as Rostovtzeff's "spiritual pupil", and was driven by a desire to continue Rostovtzeff's work by writing a survey of the society and economy of the later period.[42] In his piece on Rostovtzeff, Jones exalted the Russian's powers of synthesis and imagination, and his courage

---

[39] Fraser (2004) 1.

[40] Crawford (2004) 1.

[41] "Review of Stein" (1953/4) 359: "If the reviewer has said little of the complex ecclesiastical negotiations and nothing of military history, it is because Stein's treatment is so satisfying. The brilliant character sketches of Anastasius, Justinian, Theodora, John the Cappadocian and other leading figures of the age also deserve the highest praise. In short, this is a great book which will for many years remain the standard authority on its period, and a worthy memorial of its lamented author". See Rebenich (ch. 3) 49–53 in this volume for a more detailed discussion of Stein's influence on Jones.

[42] Mostafa El-Abbabi remembers Jones referring to himself as Rostovtzeff's 'spiritual pupil'.

"to formulate broad conclusions and venture bold hypotheses".[43] The wide range of *The Social and Economic History of the Roman Empire* clearly encouraged a young Jones to attempt a similarly broad approach. Jones' principal disappointment with Rostovtzeff's work was its political bias, which he felt "on occasion distorted his vision".[44] This complaint related principally to the Russian's portrayal of the 3rd century crisis as the result of an infiltration of the army by peasantry, keen to bring down and replace the urban bourgeoisie—an argument that stemmed from Rostovtzeff's despair at the Bolshevik revolution, which had driven him from his native land.[45]

Jones appreciated that all historians are to some extent influenced in their writings on the past by their experiences of the present. He argued that this was "not only inevitable, but a necessary condition of progress in historical writing".[46] How far non-academic factors exerted an influence over his own writings is hard to determine, considering that he spent the majority of his life working assiduously on academic projects within the confines of Oxbridge Colleges, and, being a private man, rarely disclosed his political or religious opinions to those around him. A few points may be made, however.

First, in his politics, he was left-wing for the majority of his life. Some of his acquaintances have attempted to play down this side to Jones. Crook made no mention of his political views, and Brunt referred merely to his "mildly socialist leanings".[47] However, Duncan-Jones related that "he always remained a man of the Left", and Rowse commented upon his "unchanging leftist views", which he believed resulted in "a strong disapproval for Julius Caesar's displacing the Senate's authority". According to his son, Roger, "he was a firm believer in the NHS and in the need for progressive taxation". A report from *The Cheltonian* on a debate involving Jones, this time in his last term at Cheltenham, hints at his convictions. It announces that the judges described Jones as having been "too flippant" when arguing against the motion 'Strikes should be made illegal'.[48]

---

[43] "Michael Ivanovitch Rostovtzeff" (1952) 358–9.
[44] *Ibid.*, 361.
[45] *Ibid.*, 359–60; Last (1926) 125–28.
[46] "Michael Ivanovitch Rostovtzeff" (1952) 359.
[47] Brunt (2004) 2.
[48] *The Cheltonian*, May 1921.

Despite having chosen to devote his life to academia, it is unlikely that two World Wars, the Wall Street crash, the rise and fall of totalitarian Fascist dictatorships, the Communist revolution in Russia, the fall of the traditional empires, and the first phase of the Cold War had no impact on Jones. This was a time during which a number of important issues concerning the democracy, administration and economy of Britain and the world were being confronted. In particular, the 1930s was an era during which the academic community of Oxford debated such matters and was, in some quarters, radicalised.[49] Indeed, Jones remained involved in politics whilst at Oxford, serving as secretary to the University Labour Club in 1924 and 1925, and later succeeding A.L. Rowse as its chairman.[50] Although Rowse maintained that Jones did not "waste time on politics", he did express his opinions when he felt it necessary.[51] Generally speaking, he objected to totalitarianism and imperialism, and firmly believed in democracy. Whilst at Jesus College, he signed a petition objecting to the Conservative government's decision to invade Egypt in 1956. On numerous occasions he went out of his way to support the victims of dictatorships—in the main, fellow academics who were unable freely to express themselves. During the war, he accommodated a German Jewish family at his home in Oxford. His sympathy for the victims of Nazi Germany is apparent in his review of *Histoire du Bas Empire*, in which he relates Stein's flight to France, following the German occupation of Belgium.[52] In the mid-1950s, Jones did his utmost to get Moses Finley a fellowship at Jesus College after the latter had fallen foul of the McCarthyist persecution of Marxist intellectuals in the United States. In 1969, he organised visits to Cambridge, and talks, by two academics: from Cluj, Romania, at that time behind the Iron Curtain; and Athens, then under the rule

---

[49] Gaitskell (1967) 6–7; George Woodcock, 'A Trade Unionist at Oxford 1931–1933', 132–37 in Chapter V, 'New College between the two World Wars', in Buxton and Williams (1979).

[50] Rowse (1995) 55.

[51] *Ibid.*

[52] "Review of Stein" (1953/4) 352: "For the next two and a half years Professor and Madame Stein had to live in precarious hiding in occupied France, till in December 1942 they managed to escape to Switzerland; but Professor Stein's health was already seriously undermined, and on 25 February 1945 he died. In these circumstances it is well-nigh miraculous that he managed almost to complete the work".

of the colonels. He was on his way to deliver a reciprocal lecture in Athens on his final journey of April 1970.[53]

Unlike Rostovtzeff, Jones did not allow his politics to overtly influence his work. For a start, he did not employ modern terms with obvious political connotations, such as 'proletariat' or 'bourgeoisie'. In the article "Were the ancient heresies national or social movements in disguise?" he took issue with the notion that late antique provincial religious movements could have been motivated by what he considered to be 'modern' concerns: social consciousness and nationalist sentiment.[54] Nevertheless, Jones' historical writing does sometimes hint at his general approval of local democracies and distaste for centralised bureaucratic regimes. His first two major books, on the 'Cities', essentially argue that the civic autonomy enjoyed by cities in the classical period was slowly replaced by something inferior, as the distant government in Rome gradually impinged upon this freedom.[55] Although this interpretation is toned down in the *Later Roman Empire*, its conclusion partly attributes the fall of the Western Roman Empire to a lack of morale in the provinces, caused not least by the flight of elites from local municipal government to serve in the central bureaucracy.[56] Jones' rose-tinted view of the classical city was presumably in part the result of a traditional classical education in which the *polis* was generally revered, but it seems likely that his belief in 'public spiritedness' also underpinned his conclusions.

Why did Jones modify the generally pessimistic view of the Late Roman administrative machine presented in his earlier works when he wrote the *Later Roman Empire*? Liebeschuetz speculates that Jones' increased awareness of the critical role played by centralised administration in the survival of the eastern half of the empire may have had

---

[53] I am grateful to Jones' children, Eleanor Gidney and Roger Jones, and to Mostafa El-Abbabi for this information on Jones' support for the victims of totalitarian regimes.

[54] "Ancient Heresies" (1959) 295: "Modern historians are, I think, retrojecting into the past the sentiments of the present age".

[55] The preface to *The Cities of the Eastern Provinces* (1937) xiii–xv broadly sets out Jones' theory regarding the gradual decline of civic autonomy as the Greek cities came under the control of a series of distant imperial regimes. Part V of *The Greek City* (1940) 258–304, entitled 'The Achievement of the Cities', discusses in more detail the consequences of this loss of civic independence on the economic, political and cultural bases of the Greek cities. See Lavan in this volume (ch. 8) on Jones and the cities.

[56] *Later Roman Empire* (1964) II, 1058–1059 on 'The Decline of Morale' bemoans the lack of a spirit of public service among the official elites, and puts this in part down to their "self-interested motives" and "a desire to make money".

something to do with his time working as a civil servant during the Second World War.[57] It should certainly be noted that, prior to the war, Jones' work had chiefly comprised articles on inscriptions, urbanisation in the Eastern Mediterranean, the Herods of Judaea and the history of Abyssinia. While the 'Cities' books do consider at length the political, social and economic workings of 'Greek' cities and their various relationships with outside powers, it was only after the war that Jones began to explore in intricate detail the various elements of the economy, administrative structure and society of the Late Roman Empire.

Given that Jones' employment in the Ministries of Labour and National Service and Military Intelligence was his only experience of the world outside academia, it is not surprising that this experience had a pronounced effect upon him, and may have heightened his interest in the day-to-day workings of a large administrative structure, even if this was also influenced by his reading of Late Roman legislative texts. This influence was confirmed in his inaugural lecture at UCL in 1946, in which he discussed how work on 'Essential Work Orders' and 'Control of Engagements' acts during the war had impressed upon him "the close, at times ludicrous, similarity of these wartime orders to the constitutions of the Theodosian Code".[58] He went on: "and I asked myself whether the parallelism did not go deeper". Jones openly admitted to the influence his brief career as a civil servant had had on his interpretation of the past because it had, in his mind, shown him at first hand the practical needs of a state, and the various ways in which these might be met through the manipulation of manpower resources. This was not an ideological influence, more one of subject matter. It would be surprising indeed had the importance of tied labour been the only parallel Jones drew with his keen mind between the wartime administration of Britain and the ancient world.

Gibbon's famous argument that Christianity had had a damaging effect on the Roman Empire also clearly influenced Jones.[59] Any attempt to link Jones' generally pessimistic view of Christianity in the Late Roman period to his own religious leanings, however, is of course extremely speculative. It is true that Jones was not a man of religion, and did not inherit the beliefs of his grandfather, the Wesleyan

---

[57] Liebeschuetz (1992) 6–7.
[58] *Ancient Economic History* (1948) 14.
[59] See Gwynn (ch. 10) in this volume on Jones and religion.

Methodist minister, Hugh Jones. Brunt refers to Jones as an 'agnostic' and his daughter Eleanor Gidney remembers that he styled himself an atheist.[60] According to El-Abbabi, he was "in religion a rationalist and a liberal, perhaps above all he was a humanist in the profound sense of the word". Nevertheless, Jones did appreciate the strength of Christian feeling in the Late Roman Empire,[61] and despite his atheism he was extremely respectful of the views of the devout. His great friend Derwas Chitty was a practising Christian, and Jones supported his local church in Fen Ditton, outside Cambridge, where he had bought an old Jacobean mansion. He apparently doubled the money collected for the church every Christmas and was a founder member of 'The Friends of the Friendless Churches'. He also had an extremely good grasp of the intricacies of Christian doctrine. Professor Barnabas Lindars is known to have once read out from the pulpit Jones' definition of the Trinity, stating that it was the best to be found.[62]

Ultimately, Jones' ability to detach himself from the academic and non-academic contexts within which he worked had a far greater bearing on his work than any of the influences postulated above, and is what he would have wanted to be remembered for. His immense success as a historian stemmed from his choice of subject matter, reflected in a "hankering after the less central and less worked over periods and areas in the ancient world".[63] But this success was also the result of his stubborn adherence to one methodological approach, summed up by John Crook in his preface to *The Criminal Courts of the Roman Republic and Principate*: "it must not be held that Professor Jones did not know those other views; but he quite deliberately put them out of consideration in order to concentrate the laser of his lucid mind on the primary evidence".[64] Jones' single-minded analysis of the sources would explain why, although dated in certain respects, the *Later Roman Empire* still stands today as an essential work on Late Roman history. Had Jones paid closer attention to the writings of contemporaries, concocted grandiose theories based on modern approaches, or stuck closely to a

---

[60] Brunt (2004) 1; Liebeschuetz (1992) 6.

[61] See "Ancient Heresies" (1959), esp. 297, and *Constantine* (1948) 79–102 on 'The Conversion of Constantine' as motivated by strong religious beliefs.

[62] I am grateful to Jones' children, Eleanor Gidney and Roger Jones, and to Mostafa El-Abbabi for this information on Jones' support for the local church and knowledge of Christian doctrine.

[63] *The Times*, 10th April 1970, page 12, issue 57840.

[64] *Criminal Courts* (1972, with a preface by Crook) vi.

series of arguments based on his own prejudices at the expense of writing a detailed source-based account of 'how things worked', the *Later
Roman Empire* would be less relevant. His willingness to let his audience
make up their own minds also made him an extremely gifted teacher,
and many of his students went on to become great ancient historians
in their own right. Hugo Jones had a profound influence on all who
knew him—students, friends and family—who fondly remember him
as a kind, generous and remarkable man.

Acknowledgments

I would like to thank Richard Duncan-Jones, Mostafa El-Abbabi,
Wolfgang Liebeschuetz, Joyce Reynolds, Eleanor Gidney and Roger
Jones for their willingness to answer my questions and share with me
their memories of A.H.M. Jones. I am also very grateful for the help of
Jennifer Thorp and Jill Barlow, the archivists at New College, Oxford
and Cheltenham College, respectively.

Bibliography

(For the works of A.H.M. Jones cited in the preceding pages see the Appendix)

Brown P. (1967) "Review of The Later Roman Empire", *EcHR*, 2nd series, 20 (1967)
    327–43, reprinted in *idem* (1972) *Religion and Society in the Age of Saint Augustine* (London
    1972) 46–73
Browning R. (1965) "Review: Declining Rome Surveyed", *CR*, NS, 15 (1965) 335–39
Brunt P.A. (2004) "Jones, Arnold Hugh Martin (1904–1970)", *Oxford Dictionary of National
    Biography*, article 34223 at www.oxforddnb.com
Buxton, J. and Williams, P. (1979) eds. *New College, Oxford, 1379–1979* (Oxford 1979)
Crawford M.H. (2004) "Turner, Sir Eric Gardner (1911–1983)", *Oxford Dictionary of
    National Biography*, article 60184 at www.oxforddnb.com
Crook J. (1971) "Arnold Hugh Martin Jones, 1904–1970", *PBA* 57 (1971) 425–38
Duncan-Jones R.P. (1974) *The Economy of the Roman Empire: Quantitative Studies* (Cambridge
    1974)
———. (1976) "Review: *The Roman Economy: Studies in Ancient Economic and Administrative
    History* by A.H.M. Jones and P.A. Brunt", *JRS* 66 (1976) 235–36
———. (1990) *Structure and Scale in the Roman Economy* (Cambridge 1990)
———. (1994) *Money and Government in the Roman Empire* (Cambridge 1994)
Fraser P.M. (2004) "Last, Hugh Macilwain (1894–1957)", *Oxford Dictionary of National
    Biography*, article 34413 at www.oxforddnb.com
Gaitskell H. (1967) "At Oxford in the Twenties", in *Essays in Labour History in Honour
    of G.D.H. Cole*, edd. A. Briggs and J. Saville (London 1967) 6–19
Greenslade S.L. (1965) "Review: The Later Roman Empire", *JThS*, NS, 16 (1965)
    220–24

24 ALEXANDER SARANTIS

Heichelheim F.M. (1965) "Review: The Later Roman Empire 284–602: A Social, Economic and Administrative Survey", *JRS* 55 (1965) 250–53

Huxley G.L. (1968). "A Study of Sparta", *CR*, NS, 18 (1968) 88–90

Liebeschuetz J.H.W.G. (1992) "A.H.M. Jones and the *Later Roman Empire*", *Bulletin of the Institute of Archaeology* 29 (1992) 1–8, reprinted in *idem* (2006) *Decline and Change in Late Antiquity: Religion, Barbarians and their Historiography* (Aldershot 2006) XVI

Meiggs R. (1970) "Obituary: Arnold Hugh Martin Jones", *JRS* 60 (1970) 186–87

Ministry of Labour and National Service: report for the years 1939–1946, presented by the Minister of Labour and National Service to Parliament by Command of His Majesty, September 1947 (London 1947)

Momigliano A. (1954) "M.I. Rostovtzeff", *Cambridge Archaeological Journal* 7 (1954) 334–46, reprinted in *idem* (1966) *Studies in Historiography* (London 1966) 91–104

——. (1965) "A.H.M. Jones' The Later Roman Empire", *Oxford Magazine*, NS, 5 (4 March 1965) 264–5, reprinted in *idem* (1969) *Quarto contributo alla storia degli studi classici e del mondo antico* (Rome 1969) 645–47

Morris J. (1964) "Review: The Later Roman Empire", *Past and Present* 29 (1964) 98–104

Powicke F.M. (1956) "The Victoria History of the County of Oxford", *EHR* 71 (1956) 444–47

Rostovtzeff M.I. (1926) *The Social and Economic History of the Roman Empire* (Oxford 1926)

Rowse A.L. (1961) *All Souls and appeasement: a contribution to contemporary history* (London 1961)

——. (1995) *Historians I have known* (London 1995)

The Cheltonian Magazine (Cheltenham 1920 and 1921)

The Times, 10th April 1970 page 12, issue 57840; 19th February 1951, page 8, issue 51929; and 8th June 1929, page 10, issue 45224

CHAPTER TWO

WRITING THE LATE ROMAN EMPIRE:
METHOD AND SOURCES

Peter Garnsey

1. *Introduction*

> A slight wiry man, dogged by ill-health throughout his Cambridge career,
> he was a tireless walker (the only recreation he listed in Who's Who) and
> talker, especially a talker of shop. He had a phenomenal memory and a
> shrewd wit, and behind the façade of austere scholarship, a kindly human-
> ity that revealed itself not only in his warm relations with his students, but
> also in books he wrote for them and for the educated public generally.[1]

So wrote the obituarist of A.H.M. Jones for the Jesus College Report
of 1970. I cannot say that my picture of Jones was ever as rounded as
his, for I had only three fleeting though unforgettable encounters with
him. One transpired a couple of years before his death, when Jones
appeared in my rooms at University College, Oxford, unannounced,
one morning after breakfast. He went straight to the point: "I am
Jones. I want to talk about your article". I had, with the rashness of
youth, questioned his view that the senatorial court in Rome under the
Principate had a basis in law rather than imperial authority. He challenged me to name my source. I stammered out a passage from Tacitus'
Annals. He reached into his pocket, pulled out a match-box, and wrote
the reference down on the back of it. The rest of the conversation has
vanished in the mists of time.

   This little incident is revealing less of Jones' "kindly humanity",
than of his interest in the primary sources. The latter, however, did
not strike me at the time as at all remarkable in the author of *Athenian
Democracy* and the several other works on classical Greece and Rome
that I had sampled as an undergraduate. It did not occur to me then to
connect an interest in (or passion for) the sources with the "phenomenal

---

[1] J.C.C.S. Report (1970) 42–43.

memory" evoked by the obituarist, but an anecdote passed on to me by a colleague (Richard Gordon) makes the link explicit:

> As the Part II Special Subject lecturer, he was a very considerable disappointment: his presentation consisted in reading out, in his very poor voice, the proofs of his little book on Sparta. He never discussed anything, and was too shy to stay and talk. What was incredible however and immensely impressive to us even then, was the fact that he had written the entire book while in Alexandria, from memory, having no books to hand. He simply knew all the sources.

It may be that Jones could have repeated this feat for other areas of ancient history. For his coverage was extraordinary. As P.A. Brunt puts it in the preface of his edition of some papers by Jones: "No other historian in our time has had such a range of familiarity with the evidence for ancient history from Lycurgus of Sparta to Heraclius".[2]

In what Jones himself was prone to term (according to the obituarist) "the great work", which is our present interest, the concentration on the original texts is very conspicuous.[3] It is this concern with the primary sources, linked with an apparent disdain for the scholarly literature, and more broadly, his attitude to history, to his own and other people's history-writing, that will occupy most of my attention in this paper. But first I want to introduce a singular source which became available to me, and has, to a degree, made up for my lack of personal contact with and knowledge of Jones.

Some time ago I came across in the depths of a cupboard in my college office a box of Jones' papers; these were almost entirely notes made for the *Later Roman Empire*. Not all his notes, to be sure, for there must have been a number of boxes. To this day I don't know how this particular box came into my possession. It had probably lain in some kind of dump of former Fellows' papers, and when his widow Freda died—she had served for several years as archivist at the college—someone thought of me. The box sat in my cupboard undisturbed for some time. I was aware of its existence, but did nothing about it. Recently I dug it out, and have been piecing through it, following Jones' lead, one might say, delving into the primary sources.

---

[2] Preface to Jones (1974). Brunt adds: "and none a greater capacity for synthesis and lucid and orderly exposition".

[3] The footnotes take up 345 pages of the *Later Roman Empire*, approaching a quarter of the whole work (and are in smaller print than the text). They consist almost entirely of references and citations from primary sources.

Jones' box is no treasure chest. There are pages and pages of pen-cilled notes taken, yes, from one primary source after another. Letters, chronicles, historical narratives are gutted, one by one. The legal sources are systematically and heavily noted, as are the papyri. Sometimes, but not always, references to papyri are grouped together under a topic. There are a few, very few, notes taken from books and articles. In the case of certain periodicals he had looked through all the issues, for the most part in the search for new documents. The notepaper is frequently reused, having on the other side, typically, old Greek history lectures, or minutes of meetings, or examination papers, usually dated. Headed paper from University College London, where he was Professor of Ancient History from 1946 to 1951, gives another chronological clue, though he might have brought a store of it with him to Cambridge.

The papers are revealing of the method rather than the man. There are a few letters, not enough to interest a biographer, and they are, naturally, almost entirely addressed to him. Two are from Henry Chadwick, then chaplain of Queens College Cambridge. Jones had sent Chadwick two chapters of the *Later Roman Empire*. Chadwick writes (in part), on August 28, 1957:

> Again, on the matter of morality, I think there is clear evidence that on the whole Christians behaved rather better than their pagan neigh-bours, though there were notable exceptions... I was sometimes given the impression that you were ready to take the evidence of sermons and exhortations both ways (heads I win, tails you lose); on the one hand, exhortation to be good may be deemed evidence of the failures of the flock; rebuke is obviously evidence of the same. Are you justified in think-ing sermons virtually passed like water off a duck's back? Your chapter suggests that you have a stronger belief in original sin than I, but I hope it will not seem to you merely facile optimism if I express some measure of cautious doubt on the point.

One letter in the collection was sent to Jones by H.I. Bell, and is dated 12 February, 1952. It includes the following:

> I thought your review of Johnson and West[4] very fair and distinctly more favourable than mine, and the points you made seemed to me clear.... I recognize the research that has gone into it and the acuteness of some observations... but I do feel acutely conscious of some fundamental faults in Johnson's methods. He is dreadfully careless and inaccurate;

---

[4] L.C. West and A.C. Johnson, *Currency in Roman and Byzantine Egypt* (Princeton 1944).

the discovery of many small slips, false references, hasty and mistaken
interpretations and the like gives one an uneasy feeling that one can never
rely on statements which seem unexceptionable unless they have been
checked and verified... The question of the poll tax is a puzzling one.
As you will see from the conclusion of my review, Johnson did rather
shake me on this point, but I was not wholly convinced.

On the matter of the poll tax in Egypt Jones rose to the challenge. He
replied a fortnight later at considerable length with a letter stuffed full
of references to primary sources, mainly legal, for the tax. At this stage
(at the beginning of 1952) he did not know the papyrological evidence,
or did not know it well, because he begins the letter thus:

> Many thanks for your letter. I am glad to be confirmed in my low esti-
> mate of Johnson and West. I am extremely grateful for the information
> on *capitatio* in Egypt, and have postponed a reply till I could look up the
> references (or some of them—it takes hours in the University Library—I
> can vouch for this). As you say, the whole business of *capitatio* is most
> obscure. The latest, as you no doubt know, is A. Déléage, *La capitation du
> Bas-Empire*, which is thorough and mainly sensible. It is clear that *capitatio*
> took different forms in various areas and periods, being a) sometimes a
> money poll tax and b) sometimes an element (with *iugatio*) on the assess-
> ment of *annona*.

At this point Jones rolls up his sleeves and dives into the legal evidence.
The letter concludes with a most revealing sentence:

> If you could return this (with any comments that occur to you), I shall
> be grateful, as I might want to use it myself.

> Yours sincerely,
> A.H.M. Jones.

This last sentence takes us back to a world without computers and
photocopiers; but neither it seems did Jones use typewriter, carbon or
stencil. There is conveyed an acute sense of the unique value of his
references, and a recognition of the time he had taken to accumulate
them. A graduate student of his (Keith Hopkins) was once lent by
Jones a book into which were interleaved two or three pages of notes.
These pages he was unable to return, to Jones' chagrin and his own
acute embarrassment.

Also in the Jones box I came across incomplete versions of papers
subsequently published on the eminent historians Michael Rostovtzeff
and Ernst Stein, preserved on the reverse of pages bearing notes made

on some late antique source or other.[5] Rostovtzeff was something of a polymath, rather like Jones, but perhaps even more so, and he produced three massive works between 1926 and 1941, *A History of the Ancient World* (1926–27), *The Social and Economic History of the Hellenistic World* (1941) and *The Social and Economic History of the Roman Empire* (1926). Stein's *Geschichte des spätrömischen Reiches* of 1928, translated as *Histoire du Bas Empire*, was the last great history of the Late Roman Empire.

The papers on Stein and Rostovtzeff furnish valuable, direct evidence of Jones' own attitudes to history-writing at a formative stage. In them we catch a glimpse of his aims and vision for his own Late Roman Empire project, and his views as to what makes a historian great.

2. *Aims and Vision*

Looking at Jones' discussions of Rostovtzeff and Stein from our vantage point as readers of the *Later Roman Empire* (published more than a decade later), we can see that he was already measuring himself against his predecessors; we can see him resolving to follow their lead, or alternatively to divert from their practice, and acknowledging in advance his own deficiencies where appropriate.

Jones appears to have seen himself as replacing Stein, though there was much that he admired in Stein's work. The obituary/review of Stein begins: "This noble book is a worthy memorial of the great scholar whose last work it was and whose premature death all the learned world mourns".[6]

What improvements on Stein did he seek? Jones had resolved not to write a conventional, narrative history centring on politics, the constitution and wars. The preface of the *Later Roman Empire* begins as follows: "This book is not a history of the later Roman Empire. It is a social, economic and administrative survey of the empire, historically treated". He adds that he has little to say about wars, politics, doctrinal controversies, theology, law, and cultural matters, but *is* concerned with

---

[5] Jones (1952); (1953/4).
[6] Jones (1953/4) 352.

army, church, civil service as institutions, and with the character and
social status of the governing class, the clergy and lawyers.

Let us compare Jones on Stein. He writes: "This book is a history
of the Roman Empire"; and (a little later) continues:

> Its general plan is severe. It is essentially a narrative of events, grouped by
> regions and topics—war and diplomacy, ecclesiastical affairs, administra-
> tion and finance... The strictly narrative form of presentation somewhat
> restricts the scope of the book. In ecclesiastical affairs, for instance, a very
> full account is given of the doctrinal controversies of the age, since they
> gave rise to events. But such topics as the development of monasticism,
> or the growing wealth of the church and the consequent evolution of
> corrupt and simoniacal practices are, because they did not give rise to
> correspondence and councils, completely ignored. Again, administrative
> changes which were carried out by enactments are fully discussed, but
> those which came about by custom are often omitted. Stein probably
> intended to fill these gaps by a series of chapters on various aspects of the
> age of Justinian, but only one, on the golden age of Byzantine literature,
> was written when he died.

In general it seems clear that Jones, in avoiding the Stein model, was
influenced by Rostovtzeff. Writing of Rostovtzeff's two-volume *History
of the Ancient World* (1926–27), Jones says that the author gave "greater
emphasis to the social and economic aspects of ancient history, reducing the narrative of political and military events and omitting most of
the detail of constitutional development".[7] Further, Rostovtzeff, for all
his immense range, had stopped short of the Late Empire. Jones saw
himself as taking up the baton where Rostovtzeff had set it down.[8]

Jones might equally have been talking here of Rostovtzeff's two other
massive works, *The Social and Economic History of the Roman Empire, and
The Social and Economic History of the Hellenistic World.* One may wonder,
however, about the strength of his allegiance to the Rostovtzeffian
model. Jones betrays considerable unease about this choice, and in the
process reveals that he has one foot in the traditionalist camp. Thus,
after heralding Rostovtzeff's opting for social and economic history,
he goes on to say:

> Some will think that he carried the last process too far, particularly in
> Roman history, where such weight is traditionally assigned to constitutional
> law. But though he may have swung away from the traditional presentation

---

[7] Jones (1952) 354.
[8] As is noted by Liebeschuetz (1992) 2.

of ancient history somewhat too violently, he certainly produced a vivid and stimulating book, very different from the jejune compendia of factual information which many professors produce for their students.[9]

These words presage Jones' own preoccupation with Roman legal and constitutional history in his last years, which marked something of a return to the fold of traditional history-writing.

In any case, Jones made a significant concession to the established historiographical tradition, in beginning his *Later Roman Empire* with over 300 pages of narrative. Even his greatest admirers wish he had not done so. John Crook writes:

> He may have been right in deciding that that course was inevitable, but it is a pity, because for a narrative of so vast a period 300 pages was not a large enough canvas to allow for variety and vividness; the effect is too linear and uniform and the sardonic wit so fugitively expressed as to escape the notice of all but the very alert.[10]

Jones was genuinely torn here. As he himself expresses it: "Ideally an historical work should be written chronologically, so as to show not only the development in time of each element in the whole structure but their mutual interaction". His justifications for falling back on what he calls a "compromise" are two. First, he felt that there was too little movement to make possible a chronological approach. As he put it: "In my field this procedure proved practically impossible. In many departments of life conditions were virtually static—or seem to have been so for lack of detailed evidence". He goes on:

> In most departments the movement was so slow that the thread of continuity in each would become imperceptible, if in each decade, reign or even century I discussed the whole field. I have therefore arranged my material by topics, treating each topic chronologically as far as is practicable.

His second reason is that a narrative introduction was necessary if a reader new to the period was not going to lose his way. In the event, Jones wrote quite a substantial narrative introduction.

We might note too, that Jones in reviewing Stein had applauded his treatment of some topics within his admittedly strongly narrative framework:

---

[9] In addition, Jones was already reading the ancient economy differently from Rostovtzeff, emphasizing the importance of agriculture as opposed to trade and industry. See Jones (1940) 164–5; (1948); cf. (1955). He does not raise the issue in the obituary.
[10] Crook (1971) 433.

No scholar has rivalled Stein's intimate knowledge of the intricacies of the Byzantine administrative system, and scattered through the book are admirable sections on this topic. In some other sections, that describing the provincial reorganisation of Justinian, for instance, the reader will find the facts correctly set out for the first time in refreshing contrast to the garbled versions of Diehl and Bury.[11]

My inference is, that if Jones had been writing of a period which saw more rapid change, if he had been writing the history of a more modern period, the result would have looked rather different from the *Later Roman Empire*, with much more narrative and rather less analysis—something more along the lines of Stein's *History*, perhaps.

In any case, Jones regarded Stein's work as an excellent specimen of traditional ancient history writing. Stein was immensely learned in areas in which Jones himself established a mastery, notably, administration. But in addition, Jones much admired his attitude to the sources. Witness this passage from his review:

> Notes at the foot of the page give the authority for every statement, usually the original sources, occasionally a modern work, but only when that work cites the sources in full: and in such a case minor corrections are often made, or additional evidence added. Controversy is not allowed to intrude into the text, minor points being succinctly argued in the notes, more controversial points set out in twenty-five excursuses. Every facility is thus given to the reader to control any single statement.[12]

Here we see clear signs of Jones' own enthusiasm for authentication, and his determination to make accessible to the reader all relevant information.

In sum, Jones decided that a social, economic and administrative history of late antiquity posed a greater challenge than political, military and ecclesiastical history, of which there were in any case already impressive exemplars. But this did not prevent him incorporating the best features of Stein's approach. His choice was not made without tension and self-doubt.

---

[11] Jones (1953/4) 354–5.
[12] *Ibid.*, 352.

3. *The Sources*

In the Preface to the *Later Roman Empire*, Jones confesses to the problems he had encountered in deciding how to marshal and present his material, and then comes clean on the matter of where the material comes from: "It is only fair to tell the reader on what information this book is based and how far I have covered the ground." There follows the notorious statement:

> I early realised that if in a field so vast I tried to read the modern literature exhaustively and keep abreast of current scholarship, I should not have time to read the sources. I therefore abandoned the former attempt.

He continues with a qualification:

> This is not to say that I have not read and profited from many modern books and articles (particularly those whose authors were so kind as to send me offprints), but I have undoubtedly missed much of value, and must have unwittingly reproduced some exploded errors. I must also seem discourteous in failing to acknowledge indebtedness when I have arrived independently at the same conclusion that another scholar had previously reached. In these circumstances it would be dishonest to compile a bibliography, and I have not done so. I have only cited at the beginning of each chapter of notes such general modern works as I have read and found useful, and in the appropriate place in the notes books and articles which treat exhaustively a topic marginal to my theme.

This paragraph must be read alongside the one that follows on the primary sources, which also begins with an admission of inadequacy:

> As I explored the ancient sources I regretfully came to the conclusion that a lifetime would not suffice to read them all; anyone who surveys only the relevant shelves of Migne's *Patrologiae* will understand. I soon decided to abandon theological treatises and commentaries on the Scriptures and secular belles lettres (with obvious exceptions such as Ausonius and Claudian). There are a few grains of wheat in these, but the quantity of chaff (from my point of view) is overwhelming, and many of the best grains have been winnowed by earlier scholars, particularly those of the 17th and 18th centuries, whose editions of patristic literature are a mine of curious information. I next, after reading a fair sample, abandoned sermons, having discovered that most consisted of exegesis of the Scriptures or of vague and generalised moralisation.

This time, however, he comes to his own defence in a more robust way:

> On the other hand I have read secular speeches, even panegyrics… I
> have tried to cover completely all historians, secular and ecclesiastical, in
> Greek, Latin and (where translated) Syriac. I have read and re-read the
> Codes and Novels, the Notitia Dignitatum and similar official documents.
> I have read all collections of letters, whether of laymen or churchmen. I
> have tried to read all contemporary biographies… I have read the Acts
> and Canons of church councils. I can claim to have at least looked at
> every published papyrus of relevant date. I have tried to do the same by
> inscriptions, but my coverage is here much less complete, since many are
> so cunningly concealed in the corpora and periodicals.[13]

Jones goes on to signal a more surprising omission, archaeological evidence. The lacuna is the more surprising in that he placed great weight
upon travel and first-hand experience of the Roman provinces ("I have
visited 94 of the 119 provinces of the Roman empire"). I have been
able to locate only one place in the entire work where archaeological
evidence is explicitly cited. Right at the end of Chapter XX on 'The
Land', he refers to the development of viticulture east of Antioch in the
5th and 6th centuries, with a footnote to G. Tchalenko, *Villages antiques de
la Syrie du nord* (Paris 1953).[14] In this instance Jones might have reached
more plausible conclusions on the prevalence and significance of *agri
deserti* had he extended his coverage of archaeology to other provinces
of the empire and placed less reliance on the literary evidence.[15] Of
course it is above all in the failure to integrate archaeological evidence
into the account that he most conspicuously failed to follow the example
of Rostovtzeff.

To return to the matter of the written sources: let us put Jones' statements cited above from the preface to the *Later Roman Empire* alongside
what he had written about Rostovtzeff more than a decade earlier [the
italics are mine]: "It [Rostovtzeff's work] is of course based—except
for the early oriental history—on a first-hand knowledge of the sources
as well as on an immense range of reading in modern secondary work".[16] And
again: "He seems to have studied and mastered every possible primary
source in his field, *and to have read, criticized, and remembered every modern
publication in all the languages of Europe*".[17]

---

[13] This remark may be taken as a jab at the doyen of epigraphists, Louis Robert, with
whom Jones had had a bad-tempered exchange. See Humfress (ch. 6) 124–5 below.
[14] Jones (1964) III, 1340, n. 119.
[15] See Bowden et al. (2004); Lewit (2004).
[16] Jones (1952) 354.
[17] *Ibid.*, 358.

What follows is interesting:

> How he achieved this result I do not know, but it must have been the fruit of unremitting labour and a vast capacity for organization, aided by a prodigious memory. The results are plain to see in the notes to his great works, which are the wonder and despair of scholars. *In them he corrects and supplements the articles and monographs which he cites,* and where, as often, the evidence had not been previously collected by himself or others, cites it in detail, often with reasoned emendations of the published texts of inscriptions and papyri.

Jones when he wrote these words apparently accepted that he was falling short of the standards set by Rostovtzeff; but there is the clear implication that the latter was superhuman. This is stated openly in the following: "Genius has been, somewhat inadequately, defined as 'an infinite capacity for taking pains.' On this definition Rostovtzeff may without further ado be admitted to have been a genius".

And at the end of the obituary, despite having pulled apart Rostovtzeff's notorious misinterpretation of the third century A.D., he concludes:

> That he was a great historian few would question... There can be little doubt that posterity will esteem him not unworthy to be ranked with Mommsen, Seeck, and the other giants of the nineteenth century.[18]

These words were written, however, in around 1952. By 1963 when he penned his preface to the *Later Roman Empire* it looks as if he had modified his view, at least on the matter of the secondary literature, and probably also on Rostovtzeff. A graduate student (Richard Duncan-Jones) in his first supervision with Jones asked him if he should begin his research with a critical reading of Rostovtzeff's *The Social and Economic History of the Roman Empire,* evidently expecting the answer yes. Instead Jones issued the firm directive that he should go straight into Volume VIII of the *Corpus Inscriptionum Latinarum* (on the North African provinces).[19]

However his attitude to Rostovtzeff evolved in the ten years between the obituary and the preface, Jones clearly felt when he wrote the preface that he was arguing from a position of strength. In any case, Jones had a point in opting for the primary sources at the expense of the

---

[18] *Ibid.,* 361.
[19] In contrast, A. Momigliano once told me that the same work of Rostovtzeff was his bible. And see Momigliano (1954); (1965).

secondary literature.[20] We can say this having witnessed the growth of scholarship in recent decades. A statistical analysis by Walter Scheidel shows that classical scholarship in general produced something in excess of 850,000 items in the 20th century. He writes:

> This figure may be brought into perspective by envisaging a person who spends 50 years of his or her life—say, from age 20 to 70—leafing through all these books and articles for 8 hours a day, every day. Even then this devoted student would have fewer than 9 minutes to spare for each item. The common wisdom that it has long become impossible for a single person to keep up with scholarship is thus true even in the most literal sense.[21]

The figure of approaching a million items is for Classics in general. Each component part of Classics has expanded to a greater or lesser degree. Output in social and economic history, one of the areas favoured by Jones, more than tripled between 1952 and 1992. Ancient history in general registered an increase of 56% in the same period.

There is however more in Jones' elaborate confession than meets the eye. There are two layers of deception. First, it appears that, while giving the impression that his neglect of the secondary literature was primarily a factor of time, he really did undervalue it. This is conceded by both Brunt and Crook, and has been confirmed to me by his pupils Hopkins and Duncan-Jones. Moreover, a careful reading of the *Later Roman Empire* will expose Jones' true attitude. At times he seems to be teasing his audience. In the preface he states, somewhat tongue in cheek, that it would have been dishonest of him to supply a bibliography, since he had not read everything (there is however a catalogue of primary texts). He goes on: "I have only cited at the beginning of each chapter of notes such general modern works as I have read and found useful". If one turns to the footnotes for Chapter XXII, 'The Church', one will find the following: "The most useful and comprehensive book of which I know on the organisation and discipline of the church is Joseph Bingham, *The Antiquities of the Christian Church*, London 1726". That is all.

---

[20] His comments on the secondary literature are provocative, yet he pulls his punches. He says of some of the primary sources, and not of the scholarly literature, that it was mostly chaff, with only a few grains of wheat to be gleaned. And he apologises (if in a rather laboured way) to those scholars who might have felt neglected.

[21] Scheidel (1997) 288.

The second layer of deception lies in the fact that he had in fact read rather more deeply into the secondary literature than he wanted to admit. He embarked on the great work before the Second World War.[22] One of his earlier books, the extraordinary work of synthesis which is *The Greek City from Alexander to Justinian*, contains substantial sections on late antiquity, and it was published in 1940. In the mid-to-late 30s, late 40s and early 50s he must have read everything he could lay his hands on. He would have consumed major works, assorted monographs, especially those introducing him to sources that were at that stage unfamiliar to him. In the review of Stein, there is implicit approval of his occasional citing of modern works in his footnotes *when those works cite the sources in full*. In this category would have fallen, for Jones, for example, A. Déléage, *La capitation du bas-empire* of 1945, which he recommended to H.I. Bell in the letter of February 1952, and which figures in his own footnotes.

Further, there is a revealing parenthesis in the preface, coming just after this sentence: "This is not to say that I have not read and profited from many modern books and articles". It reads: "particularly those whose authors were so kind as to send me offprints". The Professor of Ancient History at Cambridge receives many papers and monographs *ex officio*. If he is a world-figure, his post is the heavier. And that is just the start: the "offprints" of the parenthesis may stand as proxy for the whole range of communication that Jones was involved in with scholars, beginning with colleagues, ex-students and current students. It happens that Jones did not discover the existence of Joseph Bingham's monumental work on the institutional church through the perusal of some dusty bibliography. It was a colleague (Henry Chadwick) who gave him the tip-off.

A glance at Jones' work in Greek history shows that in this area he received (and acknowledged) assistance from other scholars in the field. The essays that make up *The Athenian Democracy* contain numerous references to information derived by word of mouth, correspondence, or from the publications of his pupil G.E.M. de Ste. Croix, and there are more brief notices expressing gratitude, for example, to Mr. R. Meiggs

---

[22] The preface to Jones (1966) begins: "My special interest in the later Roman Empire began before World War II, and this book [a short book on the Decline of the Ancient World] represents some twenty-five years of labour and thought" (vi).

of Balliol and Mr. D.M. Lewis of Christ Church. The scholarly community helped Jones keep up to date, as it helps us.[23]

There was, however, a progressive deterioration in his attitude to the
scholarly literature. Crook, with reference to Jones' last years, talks of
Jones' becoming obsessional in his preference for primary over secondary sources, so that "he did not particularly care whether he was up to
date with the secondary literature on the subject". Brunt agrees: "In
the earlier part of his career he read extensively in modern scholarly
literature, but as time went on, he cared less to know what others had
written".[24]

Crook finds here not arrogance, but "a rather over-rigid adherence
to principle"; while Brunt talks of Jones' confidence "that in setting
out what he saw as certain or probable, on the basis of his mastery of
the original evidence, he would have much to say that was true, which
others had not discerned". He adds:

> This confidence was generally justified. He was indeed fairly criticised for
> relying too often on easily accessible collections of inscriptions rather than
> on the most reliable publications. In no other respect might his scholarship
> be impugned. Ignoring most modern works, he would invariably cite and
> often quote the full evidence on every problem, so that every reader could
> form his own judgement; as he expressly says, this often showed how little
> basis there is for any solution. He could indeed hardly have written so
> much and over so wide a range from personal scrutiny of the evidence,
> if he had not restricted himself as he did. His practice resembled that of
> Fustel du Coulanges, whom he rivalled in his range of knowledge, which
> no contemporary historian of antiquity equalled.

4. *Conclusion*

The *Later Roman Empire* is the *fons et origo* of the extraordinary expansion in late Roman studies that has occurred in the last few decades,
at any rate in the English-speaking world, and its influence continues
unabated (if not always acknowledged). Momigliano, after airing his
doubts about the great work, wrote "we and our sons *and grandsons*
must learn to live with Jones' *Later Roman Empire*" [my italics]. There

---

[23] See Momigliano (1965) 264: "Among classical scholars, Professor Jones is second
only to Mr. R. Meiggs in the art of cross-examining colleagues".
[24] Crook (1971); Brunt (2004).

are some disappointments. The absence of archaeology is conspicuous, and unexpected. Then, one notes his lack of interest in the history of ideas, as opposed to institutions. He was interested in how institutions worked, not in the minds of the men who manned them. This goes for the Christian Church, as much as for the other organisations that come under his scrutiny.[25]

Why did Jones stay with institutions? We should not overlook the formative influence of his long wartime service in the Ministry of Labour (followed by a stretch in military intelligence), at a time when he was already planning his great work. Then, he had a passion for objectivity and authentication. Perhaps he felt that it is harder for a historian of ideas to be impartial than an historian of institutions. In this matter too, Jones' discussion of his predecessors is revealing. Rostovtzeff, he says, "was not altogether a safe historian. He had strong opinions, one might almost say, strong prejudices, and on occasion they distorted his vision".[26] Jones had in mind the civil wars of the third century A.D., which Rostovtzeff read, under the influence of his own experiences in the Russian Revolution, as a confrontation between a red army of peasants and a civilised, liberal urban bourgeoisie. On Stein, Jones commented that his conversion to Catholicism between the first and second volumes of his history had "affected his judgement of the ecclesiastical policy of the emperors".[27] One wonders what he thought of the Marxist superstructure that his pupil Geoffrey de Ste. Croix imposed on his own historical writing.[28] If Jones ever expressed a considered opinion on Edward Gibbon, I do not know of it. Here was another not altogether safe historian.[29] In any case, Jones would not have been attracted by Gibbon's example of combining scholarly

---

[25] Here he left an opening for his younger contemporary, Peter Brown. In Brown (1967), his generous review of the *Later Roman Empire*, Brown assesses Jones' work largely on its own terms. Momigliano (1965) 264–5 is more forthright: "If the Roman Empire were still with us, we should certainly have to do something about the idle Christian mouths, the greedy and hypocritical *curiales* and the corrupt judges who offended contemporary honest men. But how can Jones attribute more importance to these minor complaints than to the revolution in the thought and manners that went together with the dissolution of empire?"

[26] Jones (1952) 361.

[27] Jones (1953/4) 353.

[28] Ste. Croix (1981).

[29] Momigliano (1953/4) 459 writes of Gibbon's "reputation for naughtiness"; cf. 462: "Gibbon, as we know, has written one of his most amusing and naughty chapters about the monks".

erudition with philosophical history. He would have seen eye to eye with
Stein, who in his preface wrote: "I can affirm, with a clear conscience,
that I forced myself to stray not at all from the solid terrain of the
tradition of the sources, and that I have never done violence to those
sources in the service of any idea of philosophic history or conception
of the world".

What we have on display in the *Later Roman Empire* is a vision of the
workings of a huge empire over an extended period of time, presented
in immense detail and yet exemplary lucidity, with, as its hallmark, a
profound familiarity with the ancient sources in all their variety. It is
difficult to find a historical work of the 20th century which is its equal.
It is a masterpiece by a great historian, who was perhaps a genius.

Bibliography

Bowden W., Lavan L. and Machado C. (2004) edd. *Recent Research on the Late Antique
    Countryside*: *Late Antique Archaeology* 2 (Leiden and Boston 2004)
Brown P. (1967) "Review of The Later Roman Empire", *EcHR*, 2nd series, 20 (1967)
    327–43, reprinted in *idem* (1972) 46–73
——. (1972) *Religion and Society in the Age of Saint Augustine* (London 1972)
Brunt P.A. (2004) "Jones, Arnold Hugh Martin (1904–1970)", *Oxford Dictionary of National
    Biography*, article 34223 at www.oxforddnb.com
Crook J. (1971) "Arnold Hugh Martin Jones, 1904–1970", *PBA* 57 (1971) 425–38
Jones A.H.M. (1937) *Cities of the Eastern Roman Provinces* (Oxford 1937), 2nd ed. (Oxford
    1971)
——. (1940) *The Greek City from Alexander to Justinian* (Oxford 1940)
——. (1948) *Ancient Economic History: an inaugural lecture delivered at University College, London*
    (London 1948)
——. (1952) "Michael Ivanovitch Rostovtzeff, 1870–1952", *PBA* 58 (1952) 347–61
——. (1953/4) "Review of E. Stein, *Histoire du Bas Empire, t. 2. De la disparition de l'empire
    d'occident à la mort de Justinien (467–565)*", *Historia* 2 (1953/4) 352–59
——. (1955) "The Economic Life of the Towns in the Roman Empire", *Recueils de la
    Société Jean Bodin* 7 (1955) 161–92, reprinted in *idem* (1974) 35–60
——. (1957) *The Athenian Democracy* (Oxford 1957)
——. (1966) *The Decline of the Ancient World* (London 1966)
——. (1974) *The Roman Economy: Studies in Ancient Economic and Administrative History*, ed.
    P.A. Brunt (London 1974)
Lewit T. (2004) *Villas, Farms and the Late Roman Rural Economy (third to fifth centuries A.D.).
    BAR International Series* 568 (Oxford 2004)
Liebeschuetz J.H.W.G. (1992) "A.H.M. Jones and the *Later Roman Empire*", *Institute of
    Archaeology Bulletin* 29 (1992) 1–8, reprinted in *idem* (2006) *Decline and Change in Late
    Antiquity: Religion, Barbarians and their Historiography* (Aldershot 2006) XVI
Momigliano A. (1953/4) "Gibbon's Contribution to Historical Method", *Historia* 2
    (1953/4) 450–63
——. (1954) "M.I. Rostovtzeff", *Cambridge Archaeological Journal* 7 (1954) 334–46,
    reprinted in *idem* (1966) *Studies in Historiography* (London 1966) 91–104

———. (1965) "A.H.M. Jones' The Later Roman Empire", *Oxford Magazine*, NS, 5 (4 March 1965) 264–5, reprinted in *idem* (1969) *Quarto contributo alla storia degli studi classici e del mondo antico* (Rome 1969) 645–47

Scheidel W. (1997) "Continuity and change in Classical scholarship: a quantitative survey 1924–1992", *Ancient Society* 28 (1997) 265–89

Ste. Croix G.E.M. de (1981) *The Class Struggle in the Ancient Greek World* (London 1981)

CHAPTER THREE

JONES AND CONTINENTAL SCHOLARSHIP

Stefan Rebenich

(i)

On March 4th 1965, a brilliant review of A.H.M. Jones' *Later Roman Empire* was published in *The Oxford Magazine*. The author was Arnaldo Momigliano. He opened his critique with the following remarks:

> This great work is typically English from three points of view. First of all, nowadays only a man educated in a traditional public school is likely to have the necessary command of Greek and Latin (and the stamina) to read such an immense amount of original evidence. Secondly, in no other country would an author get away with a similar disregard of modern literature on his subject. In actual fact Jones is much better informed about recent studies than appears from his notes. The explanation is that oral tradition counts for more in English universities than elsewhere. At All Souls, University College London, Jesus College Cambridge (some of the colleges to which this work is appropriately dedicated), the author could always be certain of finding somebody to interrogate about specific problems (among classical scholars Professor Jones is second only to Mr R. Meiggs in the art of cross-examining colleagues). Finally, the unusual form of this book cannot be explained without the English tradition of Royal Commissions, social surveys, Fabian society pamphlets. A.H.M. Jones is clearly in the direct line of the Webbs and Hammonds, indeed of Booth and Beveridge. His work deserves to go down to future generations as the Jones Report on the State of the Roman Empire (A.D. 284–602).[1]

Indeed, the *Later Roman Empire* seems to be a typically English book. Continental scholars, although acclaiming Jones' outstanding mastery of the primary sources, were especially struck by his obvious neglect of secondary literature. Lellia Cracco Ruggini, for instance, bitterly complained about *un programmatico rifiuto del Jones a dialogare proprio sui suoi problemi con gli altri specialisti viventi di storia tardoimperiale* and bravely

---

[1] Momigliano (1965) 294.

listed a considerable number of books she would have expected to be cited in the *Later Roman Empire*.[2] Johannes Irmscher, classical scholar at the Berlin Academy of the German Democratic Republic, also criticised the selective use of modern literature and emphasised the subjective character of Jones' work which he nevertheless characterised as *eine bedeutende Leistung der progressiv-bürgerlichen Historiographie*.[3] His West-German colleague Gunter Gottlieb was dissatisfied with *die Art und Weise, wie die Sekundärliteratur verwendet und in den Anmerkungen aufgenommen wurde*.[4] André Chastagnol, whose important contributions to the urban prefecture of Rome Jones enumerated only in part, grumbled that *la mention d'auteurs modernes se réduit ordinairement aux ouvrages principaux et aux articles d'A.H.M. Jones lui-même* and concluded *il est dommage que, de ce fait, ce beau livre, synthèse d'importance majeure, ne soit pas en même temps, à cause de ce parti pris voulu, un manuel bibliographique*.[5]

It is, therefore, certainly right to note that secondary literature appears in the *Later Roman Empire* "only subliminally".[6] Jones legitimised his approach in his preface: "I early realised that if in a field so vast I tried to read the modern literature exhaustively and keep abreast of current scholarship, I should not have time to read the sources. I therefore abandoned the former attempt".[7] In his notes he did not engage in much discussion with earlier scholars, although he referred to some works of reference and the principal older studies of O. Seeck, J.B. Bury, A. Piganiol, and E. Stein.[8] Jones' attitude towards modern literature is a marvellous example of academic self-fashioning. As a classicist, he was educated to read Greek and Latin texts and instructed in ancient literature, philosophy and history. He was less interested in methodological questions, and theoretical debates disgusted him. Writing a book on a topic so vast and deep, so multi-faceted and complex as the later Roman empire was an intellectual and cultural exercise and, at the same time, a manifesto against the specialisation and diversification of modern scholarship. Here, Jones was highly influenced by the scholarly literature of the 19th century, both British and continental. Neither Theodor Mommsen in his *History of Rome* and in his *Römisches*

---

[2] Cracco Ruggini (1965) 203.
[3] Irmscher (1970) 769.
[4] Gottlieb (1967) 264.
[5] Chastagnol (1964) 161.
[6] Brown (1967, reprinted in 1972 from which all citations here derive) 49.
[7] Jones (1964) I, vi.
[8] *Ibid.*, III, 2.

Staatsrecht nor Otto Seeck in his *Geschichte des Untergangs der antiken Welt* cared too much about scholarly debates and contradictory views. Jones, too, saw his achievement in collecting, organizing, and analyzing so extensive a range of evidence and drawing conclusions based upon commonsense assumptions about the nature of mankind.[9] Like his predecessors Jones intended to write a work *aere perennius*, centred on his authoritative interpretation of the sources. Current scholarship was de-legitimised by just not referring to it.

Although very few modern scholars are mentioned, and although there is little explicit discussion of their work, I will argue that Jones conducted an intrinsic dialogue not only with his English predecessors Gibbon, Bury and Baynes, but also with the major continental reconstructions of the later Roman empire, especially with Mommsen, Seeck, Rostovtzeff, and Stein, and that Jones, who was a fluent reader of French, German and Italian,[10] had read much more of continental scholarship than he indicated in his footnotes. I will conclude with a brief survey of the prehistory of the *Prosopography of the Later Roman Empire* that also proves Jones' indebtedness to continental scholarship.

(ii)

Jones certainly read the major works of Theodor Mommsen (1817–1903) who, as a historian and as a jurist, had touched upon the later Roman empire and Christian study and, with his great editions, had made accessible the history of late antiquity. Above all, Jones learned from Mommsen's *Römisches Staatsrecht*[11] that a vast amount of material could be organised in a systematic way, and he learned from him the interest in uniform organisations and uniting structures, such as the administration and the army, the law and the government. He reconstructed the institutions of the later Roman empire as Mommsen had reconstructed the institutions of the Roman republic and the Principate. He also absorbed Mommsen's dichotomy between the early and high empire and late antiquity. In contrast to the Principate of Augustus, Mommsen had spoken of the 'Dominate' of the late empire, which he

---

[9] Cf. the acute remarks of Liebeschuetz (1990) 239f.
[10] I owe this information to Roger Jones. I want to thank him for kindly giving me information about his father's contact with continental scholars.
[11] Mommsen (1887/88). Cf. Rebenich (2002) 107–21.

argued began with Diocletian and was characterised by the excessive
oriental veneration of the emperor as *dominus* whose position was no
longer to be defined as a magistrate, but who conducted *ein unbedingtes und
unbeschränktes Herrenrecht über die Personen wie über das Gut aller Unterthanen.*[12]
Although Jones stressed the continuity of historical development from
Augustus to the reign of Justinian, he, like John B. Bury,[13] followed
Mommsen and divided Roman imperial history between those days
"when the emperor had been a republican magistrate" and the time
when "both in the theory and in the practice of the constitution the
emperor's powers were absolute".[14] He only dissented with Mommsen's
description of the Roman empire as an autocracy tempered by the legal
right of revolution: "Whether or not this is a correct definition of the
Principate, it is not true of the later empire".[15]

   Mommsen's pupil Otto Seeck (1850–1921) tried to offer a new explanation for the fall of Rome. His six-volume *Geschichte des Untergangs der
antiken Welt*, first published between 1895 and 1920, stands out particularly for being closely based on the sources, for its impressive wealth
of detail and its superior control of the subject matter. But it aspired
to be more than just a depiction of what had happened: Seeck aimed
to introduce the reader to the laws governing historical processes of
formation and decline.[16] He regarded social, administrative and religious
changes as fundamental to the fall of the empire and constructed an
impressive scenario of decline that culminated in *die Ausrottung der Besten*
("the elimination of the best").[17] His notion of *Ausrottung* referred to a
series of negative choices, whose beginning Seeck dated back to the
time of the Gracchi. The ancient world, according to this argument,
need not have come to an end. The moment of collapse came only
when the most industrious people had become a small minority, thanks
to failures internal to Rome, and when, thanks to the laws of hered-
ity, *angeerbte Feigheit* ("inherited cowardice") and *das moralische Erschlaffen*
("moral weakening") became dominating characteristics of society.
Seeck's work was reprinted several times in quick succession, indicating wide appreciation by a large audience, but in the community of

---

[12] Mommsen (1907) 351.
[13] Bury (1923) I, 5.
[14] Jones (1964) I, 321.
[15] *Ibid.*, I, 326, where Mommsen is characterised as the "greatest constitutional
historian" of the Roman empire.
[16] Seeck (1920–23) I, preface.
[17] *Ibid.*, I, 269–307.

scholars his ideas, shaped by Darwin's theory of the descent of man and the evolutionary biology of the 19th century, remained, however, the phantasm of an outsider. His main thesis, *die Ausrottung der Besten*, met with disapproval among scholars, and Jones, like so many others, just ignored it.[18] Although there is no direct evidence that Jones relied upon Seeck's collection of sources, he might have checked Seeck's references before finishing a chapter. But Seeck's history was more important as a negative model: Jones refused his symbiosis of traditional *Quellenforschung* and obscure biologist theories. The decline of population should not be exaggerated, Jones admonished his readers.[19]

It was another book that proved to be most influential: the epochal *The Social and Economic History of the Roman Empire* of the Russian historian Michael Ivanovitsch Rostovtzeff (1870–1952), published in 1926. Jones is said to have understood his *Later Roman Empire* as a continuation of Rostovtzeff's work.[20] The October Revolution of 1918 had forced Rostovtzeff to leave his country and to flee first to Sweden and then to Oxford. In 1920 he accepted a professorship at the University of Madison, Wisconsin, and in 1925 he moved to Yale. His personal experiences as an immigrant influenced his writing. He regarded late antiquity as a reflection of his own time or, to put it in Jones' words: "Like all creative historians he was influenced in the interpretation of the past by his experience of the present".[21] Rostovtzeff's work is a passionate plea for the social and political significance of a prosperous urban middle class, which had provided the *Imperium Romanum* with its visible splendour and indeed had ruled it. The idealisation of the Roman *bourgeoisie* reflected the political Anti-Bolshevism of the Russian historian. According to Rostovtzeff, the period of crisis for the Roman Empire began in the third century and was accompanied by the decline of the traditional urban economy and a levelling of social classes. He contrasted the enlightened constitutional monarchy of the early Principate with the oriental despotism of late antiquity. The late Roman empire was characterised by coercion and violence, and Rostovtzeff denounced it as a gigantic prison and a slave-state.

---

[18] Cf. my preface to the reprint of Seeck's *Geschichte des Untergangs der antiken Welt* (Darmstadt 2000).
[19] Jones (1964) II, 1044.
[20] As is noted by Liebeschuetz (1992) 2.
[21] Jones (1952) 359.

While Mommsen referred to constitutional principles to describe the late Roman state, Rostovtzeff tried to reconstruct the social and economic conditions of the *Imperium Romanum*. Jones, who began where Rostovtzeff had ended, learned from the classic work of the Russian scholar the significance of social and economic history and thus emphasised the hiatus between the rural peasantry and the urban elite. But Jones was more interested in administration and did not include much archaeological evidence.[22] While the Russian emigrant argued that the wealth of the ruling classes of the cities was based upon commerce, Jones minimised the impact of trade and manufacture in the later Roman empire and propounded his concept of a consumer city whose economic basis was agriculture. "Other historians", Jones wrote with Rostovtzeff in mind, "have attributed the decline of the empire to the gradual elimination of the 'bourgeoisie' or 'middle class', by which term they mean the curial order".[23] He argued that the decline of the local elite was self-imposed since the wealthy civic notables escaped from the civic councils by entering the imperial service or the senatorial order:

> The curiales were not, and never had been, creators of wealth. They were rentiers, landlords, who were often absentees, and did not on the whole, so far as we know, take any active interest in their estates. They were, many of them, men of culture and education, and in so far as they gave their unpaid services to the government and contributed to its cost, fulfilled a social role: but they did not increase the wealth of the empire.[24]

Few producers supported too many idle mouths, as he put it.[25] Jones sympathised with the peasantry and resented the vast and conspicuous consumption of the governing classes.[26] The local elites, too, were parasites, as were the civil servants and the military staff.

(iii)

The works of Max Weber (1864–1920) were of crucial importance for the analysis of the structure of Roman society.[27] In a lecture on the social

[22] Warmington (1965) 58.
[23] Jones (1964) II, 1053.
[24] *Ibid.*
[25] *Ibid.*, II, 1045.
[26] Cf. Liebeschuetz (1990) 240.
[27] Nippel (2000).

reasons for the decline of the Roman empire, first published in 1896, and in his famous study on *Agrarverhältnisse im Altertum*, first published in 1909,[28] Weber identified as reasons for the crisis, *inter alia*, the equal status of slaves and free small-scale tenants, the decline of the cities and of the empire's financial apparatus, the rise of a barter economy and the rapid bureaucratisation of the administration, as well as the restriction of private economic initiative. He addressed, therefore, several topics that would be discussed by scholars in detail over the following years—but, in contrast to Moses Finley, Jones is most likely to have developed his idea of a 'consumer city' without preoccupying himself too much with the sociological theories of Max Weber.

In his early writings, Weber had avoided any tendency to make the study of antiquity part of an analysis of current experience; but by 1909 he had come to regard the late Roman state as a frightening totalitarian vision of the future: *Die Bureaukratisierung der Gesellschaft wird bei uns des Kapitalismus aller Voraussicht nach irgendwann ebenso Herr werden, wie im Altertum.*[29] The pessimistic view of the epoch held during the second half of the nineteenth century had caught up with the social sciences of the twentieth.

Weber's negative perception of the bureaucratisation of society did not affect Ernst Stein's (1891–1945) history of the late empire.[30] The first volume of his *Geschichte des spätrömischen Reiches* was published in Vienna in 1928.[31] Stein, a pupil of the social democrat Ludo Moritz Hartmann and a nephew of the British archaeologist Sir Aurel Stein, was mainly concerned with the systematic reconstruction of administrative structures. The leftist historian, who for some time sympathised with the socialist movement in Austria, ardently defended the democratic character of the late Roman bureaucracy that was meant to be an effective instrument against aristocratic tendencies (*Werkzeug gegen aristokratische Tendenzen*) and integrated social climbers. The administration of the later empire, though deeply corrupt, nevertheless asserted the interests of the State (*Staatsinteresse*) against the class egoism of the senatorial aristocracy, who ruthlessly exploited the state.[32] Stein thought that the

---

[28] Weber (1988) 1–288 and 289–311. Cf. Nippel (2000).
[29] Weber (1988) 278.
[30] Stein (1949/1959).
[31] Stein (1928). Cf. Christ (1982) 186–191; Wiemer (2006) 19–21.
[32] Cf. e.g. Stein (1928) 101 and 342.

bureaukratische Apparat was far more successful in the East than in the West and substantially contributed to the survival of the Byzantine empire.

After 1933, the Jewish scholar categorically refused to continue to publish in German. Hence the manuscript of the second volume, which Stein managed to complete under most difficult conditions as a fugitive, was written in French and posthumously published by Stein's colleague and friend Jean-Rémy Palanque, who also translated the first volume into French. Stein lived in Belgium from 1928 to 1940, but after the German invasion, he had to hide in unoccupied France before escaping to Switzerland, where he died on 25 February 1945.

Jones dedicated the longest review he ever wrote to the second volume of Ernst Stein's *Histoire du Bas-Empire*. He praised the "noble book" of "the great scholar" and accentuated "Stein's intimate knowledge of the intricacies of the Byzantine administrative system", but at the same time criticised many details of Stein's analysis of the administration.[33] Since Stein, in his later years, was converted to the Catholic faith, Jones also felt inclined to mention that "this [...] did not in any way influence his presentation of the facts; he recounts with scrupulous accuracy every sordid detail of the numerous tergiversations of Pope Vigilius. But it has affected his judgement of the ecclesiastical policy of the emperors".[34] Still, Stein's account had a great impact on Jones' writing. It has long been seen that the ten chapters of the narrative part of the *Later Roman Empire* were "divided chronologically more or less along the lines suggested by Stein's chapter headings".[35] Further, Jones' narrative itself is influenced by Stein. Jones often adopted the sequence of events Stein had proposed, abridged Stein's text and presented a more vivid story. Here is just one example from the beginning of both works:

Stein, *Histoire du Bas-Empire*, I, 66f.	Jones, *The Later Roman Empire*, I, 38f.
D'autres dangers étaient encore menaçants en Occident: tandis que la frontière rhénane était troublée par des Alamans, des Francs et d'autres tribus germaniques et que des bandes de pillards saxons	Diocletian [...] appointed a Caesar, Maximian, a military man like himself and an old friend. Maximian was despatched to the West with the special mission of quelling the Bacaudae, the insurgent

---

[33] Jones (1953/4) 352 and 354.
[34] *Ibid.*, 353.
[35] Alexander (1966) 337.

dévataient les côtes de Gaule et de
Bretagne, les masses paysannes de la
Gaule, opprimées et peu romanisées,
que l'on appelait les Bagaudes (terme
celtique qui signifie probablement
'les vagabonds'), s'étaient soulevées
en une effroyable insurrection, pour
secouer, sous la direction de deux
chefs choisis en leur sein, Aelianus et
Amandus, le joug de leurs maîtres et
du gouvernement romain. Dioclétien
ne se chargea pas de restaurer en
personne l'autorité de l'Empire en
Occident; il se contenta de confier
cette tâche à un général capable,
M. Aurélius Maximianus, Pannonien
de la région de Sirmium, manquant
absolument de culture supérieure,
comme tous ces officiers illyriens,
personnalité subalterne de qui
Dioclétien attendait une soumission
complète à ses vues. En nommant
en même temps Maximien César,
sous le nom de M. Aurélius Valérius
Maximianus, il pensait prévenir
une usurpation, sans cela toujours
possible dans la situation de l'époque;
Dioclétien, décidé à garder pour son
propre compte le pouvoir suprême
dans l'Empire tout entier, marquait
expressément cette détermination
en prenant lui-même le surnom de
Jovius et en concédant à son collègue
celui d'*Herculius*: ce qui devait non
seulement effacer l'origine obscure
des nouveaux souverains de la
mémoire de leurs sujets en leur
attribuant cette descendance fictive
de Jupiter et d'Hercule, mais encore
indiquer que leurs rapports mutuels
étaient ceux du père des dieux et
des hommes avec le plus éminent
des héros. Après avoir écrasé les
Bagaudes, Maximien fut élevé au
rang d'Auguste, le 1ᵉʳ avril 286. […]

peasants of Gaul, who had raised
a regular revolt under two leaders,
Amandus and Aelianus. Next year,
on 1 April 286, Maximian was raised
to the rank of Augustus. He thus
became constitutionally the equal
of Diocletian, who only claimed
superior authority as Senior
Augustus. In actuality the
relationship of the two is better
expressed by the divine names which
they assumed, Iovius and Herculius.
Diocletian was the representative
and vice-gerent upon earth of Jupiter
Optimus Maximus, king of gods and
men; Maximian of Hercules, his
heroic agent in rooting out the evils
which oppressed the world.

More striking than these formal consonances, however, are the resemblances between Jones and Stein in their assessment of the positive function of the late Roman bureaucracy. I would argue that Jones, who was certainly left of centre,[36] is not only in the direct line of the Webbs and the Hammonds, of Booth and Beveridge, as Momigliano noticed, but also in the direct line of Stein. Both scholars strongly believed in the bureaucratic foundation of a welfare system. As historians of the late empire they clearly recognised and stigmatised, many administrative abuses, but they shared the conviction that the East survived because of its efficient bureaucracy. Already in 1949 Jones was fascinated by the Byzantine administration: "It is easy to poke fun at the Byzantine bureaucracy, but cumbersome and corrupt as it was, it served some useful purposes".[37] In the *Later Roman Empire* Jones continued to reconstruct the administrative system of this period and followed up a tradition that had been founded by Mommsen who had taught Ludo Moritz Hartmann, Ernst Stein's academic teacher. But the liberal politician Mommsen mistrusted the late Roman state and its despotic government. Stein instead praised the bureaucratic reforms of Diocletian and his administrative system that defended the interests of the government against individual interests:

> *Das weströmische Reich ist daran zugrunde gegangen, daß es unter die Botmäßigkeit eines großgrundherrlichen Adels geraten war, der sich selbst gab, was des Staates war, so daß diesem die Machtmittel fehlten, deren er zum erfolgreichen Widerstand gegen den Ansturm der Germanen bedurft hätte. [...] In den Kernlanden der partes Orientis aber hat es keinen solchen Adel gegeben; die Verwaltung wurde daher nicht zum Werkzeug einer bureaukratisch maskierten Standesherrschaft, sondern blieb die Hüterin der Staatsinteressen, und das ermöglichte die Rettung des oströmischen Reiches.*[38]

Jones' remarks in the final chapter of the *Later Roman Empire* seem to be reminiscent of Stein's conclusion:

> These great noblemen [in the West] were naturally tender to the interests of their own class, and were on the whole inefficient administrators. In the East, on the other hand, hereditary nobles did not dominate the administration, and the highest posts were often filled by men who had risen by ability, and being dependent on the emperor's favour, gave priority to the interests of the government.[39]

---

[36] Liebeschuetz (1992) 4.
[37] Jones (1949) 55.
[38] Stein (1922) 72f.
[39] Jones (1964) II, 1066.

The *Later Roman Empire* is a very different book from those of Mommsen, Seeck, Rostovtzeff, and Stein. J.M. Wallace-Hadrill is certainly right in saying:

> Less passionate than Mommsen, more discerning than Seeck, not at all obsessed, as was Stein, by the urge to say something about everything, Jones covers the ground of his choice with a terrible eye and in majestic calm.[40]

But Jones must be read—and understood—in the context of the continental representations and interpretations of the late Roman empire. Like Mommsen in the *Staatsrecht*, Jones concentrated in the *Later Roman Empire* on the state and the administration, but was less constructivist; unlike Seeck, Jones is not interested in 'decline and fall', but in the functioning of the empire and its public machinery; like Rostovtzeff he is concerned with economic and social phenomena, but disagreed on the nature of the ancient city and argued that the elites destroyed the empire; and like Stein he believed in the public profit of administrative professionalism.

(iv)

Throughout the *Later Roman Empire* there is evidence that Jones exploited books and articles not cited to present a new image of the late Roman empire. This is not surprising. During his lifetime, Jones read and reviewed, commended and criticised quite a few books on late antiquity. He must have excerpted them and used some of the extracts for his *Later Roman Empire*. Some examples may suffice.

In 1951, the Italian scholar Santo Mazzarino published his important work on *Aspetti sociali del quarto secolo*.[41] Two years later, Jones wrote a favourable review.[42] He followed the latter's reconstruction of the military conscription and adopted his interpretation of *CTh* 14.4.10 from which Mazzarino had deduced that the number of persons entitled to pork rations was 120,000 in 419. Jones praised this "ingenious"

---

[40] Wallace-Hadrill (1965) 789.
[41] Mazzarino (1951).
[42] Jones (1953).

deduction in his review, and reproduced it in the *Later Roman Empire*, but he did not mention Mazzarino by name.[43]

Jones derived much profit from Paul Petit's book on Libanius and the municipal life in Antioch,[44] which he reviewed in 1957 and to which he only once referred in the *Later Roman Empire*.[45] Since there was no comparable study for the western part of the empire, Jones' remarks on the city in the West are rather scanty.

One wonders whether Jones had not been influenced by Karl Ferdinand Stroheker's seminal investigation into the senatorial aristocracy of late Roman Gaul which helped to overcome the juridical definition of the senatorial aristocracy Mommsen had advanced.[46] Had Jones read the book, or heard of Stroheker's groundbreaking study, as Momigliano may have conjectured?

The collected studies of the French historian Ferdinand Lot, posthumously published, did not find Jones' approval: "The editors of this volume have done a doubtful service to M. Lot's memory in publishing these products of his declining years. But having decided to publish they should at least have read the proofs. The book abounds in misprints, mainly in the Latin... and in figures".[47] But Jones accepted Lot's emendation in the text of the Table of Brigetio. Under the regulations of the law dated to 311 veterans gained immunity for four *capita*, i.e. the man himself, his wife, and parents. Jones followed Lot's reading in an article on *capitatio* and *iugatio*[48] and reiterated the emended version in the *Later Roman Empire*, where Lot's name is not to be found.[49]

Finally, Jones in the *Later Roman Empire* revised his dating of the *Laterculus Veronensis* proposed in an article published in 1954,[50] and argued that this manuscript list of provinces "seems to be, apart from a few later glosses and textual errors, an accurate account of the empire as it was between 312 and 314".[51] Of crucial importance for his reconsideration was the inscription *CIL* VIII 18905 according to

---

[43] Mazzarino (1951) 228f.; Jones (1953) 115; Jones (1964) II, 702 and III, 219–20.n.35.
[44] Petit (1955).
[45] Jones (1957a) and Jones (1964) III, 225.
[46] Stroheker (1948).
[47] Jones (1957c) 257.
[48] Jones (1957b) 90.
[49] Jones (1964) II, 635 and III, 195.n.62.
[50] Jones (1954).
[51] Jones (1964) III, 381; cf. I, 43.

which the province of Numidia had been reunited in 314.[52] Jones had not discussed this piece of epigraphic evidence in his article. Now he just added it to his argument—and proposed a new date. It seems most likely that Jones shifted his opinion after having read the study of Hans-Georg Kolbe on *Die Statthalter Numidiens von Gallien bis Konstantin* (1962), where the inscription is discussed and the redaction of the list dated between 312 and 314.[53] Kolbe's book is nowhere mentioned in the *Later Roman Empire*.

(v)

After 1000 pages of historical narrative and systematic description, Jones gave a survey of various explanations for the decline of the Roman empire. Hardly any scholars were identified, and so one may conclude that Jones' "attitude amounts to mystification where he establishes his own view on a controversial problem against the background of previous discussions by scholars whom he does not name".[54]

In his final chapter, he distanced himself from monocausal attempts at explanation of the fall of the *Imperium Romanum*.[55] Thus, he was not captivated by Oswald Spengler's cyclical interpretation of history, for whom the rise and fall of Rome stood as a paradigm for the present. Jones did not believe in Karl Julius Beloch's theory that the Roman occupation of Greece destroyed the Hellenic culture and was the beginning of a long period of decline for the ancient world. He refuted Guglielmo Ferrero's idea that the destruction of senatorial power and aristocratic authority caused the disintegration of the Roman empire, and he ignored the racist speculations of Tenney Frank. At the same time, Jones dissociated his work from post-war historiography of late antiquity. He did not follow Pierre Courcelle, who, in 1948, published his *Histoire littéraire des grandes invasions germaniques*, in which numerous passages depended upon reference to the recent past. The account is divided into *invasion, occupation*, and *libération*. The Vandal Huneric sets up a *camp de concentration* for rebellious Catholics, and Hilderic pursues

---

[52] *Ibid.*, III, 4.
[53] Kolbe (1962) 65–71; cf. Chastagnol (1965) 162.
[54] Alexander (1966) 340.
[55] Jones (1964) II, 1025–1068.

intermittently a *politique d'appaisement*.[56] And Jones was critical too of André Piganiol's *L'Empire chrétien*, written during the German occupation of France and first published in 1947, who considered the Germanic invaders as the destructive element responsible for the decline of the Roman empire. Piganiol made the famous point, *la civilisation romaine n'est pas morte de sa belle morte. Elle a été assassinée.*[57] Arnaldo Momigliano referred to this aptly as a *"cri de coeur* of a valiant Frenchman against *boches* and collaborationists".[58] This kind of re-enactment of the past was not Jones' model. He just remarked "that the simple but rather unfashionable view that the barbarians played a considerable part in the decline and fall of the empire may have some truth".[59] Instead, Jones analyzed interacting factors and took into account the crisis of the economy and the tax burden, the decrease in population and the shortage of workers, the orientation of Christian teaching towards the afterlife and the bureaucratisation of the administration, the barbarisation of the army and the invasions by the Germanic tribes. He accurately examined the evidence and developed his argument *senza lasciarsi fuorviare da impostazioni teoriche e da giudizi apodittici.*[60]

(vi)

Jones' most influential reassessment of the late Roman elites and his recovery of the new imperial nobility of service demanded prosopographical research. Stroheker had already demonstrated how important this method would be for any research into late Roman society.[61] One of Jones' lasting achievements, therefore, is the *Prosopography of the Later Roman Empire* that provided a new basis for Roman social history. At the end of the 1940s, he, together with a group of scholars from the British Academy, made the initial preparations for a secular prosopography of late antiquity. At the same time, Henri-Irénée Marrou and Jean-Rémy Palanque, with their colleagues at the Sorbonne, tackled a Christian

---

[56] Courcelle (1948) 183 and 195.
[57] Piganiol (1972) 466.
[58] Momigliano (1969) 646.
[59] Jones (1964) II, 1027.
[60] D'Elia (1967) 356.
[61] Stroheker (1948) esp. 137–227 ("Anhang: Prosopographie zum senatorischen Adel im spätantiken Gallien").

prosopography.[62] At the first International Congress for Classical Studies held in Paris in August 1950, Jones and Marrou agreed upon a close co-operation. This joint venture was supported by the *Kommission für spätantike Religionsgeschichte* of the Berlin Academy that decided on 16 May 1951, after a long debate, to allow the planned Anglo-French project to use its extensive collection of prosopographical material. 14 years later, on a summer evening in 1965, 151 boxes, full to the brim with excerpts, left the *Akademie der Wissenschaften* of the German Democratic Republic and were shipped to England. Already in April 1965, the British and Berlin academies concluded a contract prescribing that the collection would be placed at the disposal of the planned *Prosopography of the Later Roman Empire* for three years, with the additional possibility of an extension of the loan period by mutual agreement. The British side promised to cite the material in the bibliography, in accordance with scholarly practice, and to provide, free of charge, a copy of the completed prosopography.

Where did the Berlin collection come from? It was initiated by Mommsen, in collaboration with the protestant church historian Adolf Harnack. At the very beginning of the 20th century, Mommsen planned to continue the *Prosopographia Imperii Romani saec. I.II.III* for the period from 284 until the death of Justinian, in order to free, as Harnack wrote in a circular letter to his colleagues, the fourth to the sixth centuries from the neglect in which they lie. This large-scale interdisciplinary project, which sought to create a *Prosopographia Imperii Romani saec. IV.V.VI.*, i.e. a fundamental work of reference for theologians, philologists and historians of late antiquity, was financed by the *Kirchenväterkommission* of the Berlin Academy and supported by more than fifty German and Austrian scholars who eagerly excerpted Christian and non-Christian sources and entered on cards prosopographical information of ecclesiastical and secular dignitaries. Mommsen himself took in hand the editing of the secular part of the prosopography and extracted Ammianus Marcellinus, Zosimus, the letters of Athanasius, and the *Codex Theodosianus*. Adolf Jülicher, church historian at Marburg University, was assigned the position of general editor and director of the ecclesiastical part.

Mommsen and Harnack recognised the outstanding importance of a prosopography of late antiquity. The project integrated the interests

---

[62] Cf. Rebenich (1997a) 247–326 and Rebenich (1997b).

of various specialists and was based upon the assumption that for a
period during which Christianity was penetrating into the highest social
levels, and during which more and more members of the traditional
regional and imperial elites moved into the ecclesiastical hierarchy, only
a prosopography that embraced the Christian as well as the secular
sphere could provide a research instrument suitable for interdisciplinary purposes.

Mommsen, however, underestimated the complications that resulted
from the immense mass of Christian literary sources and from the lack
of critical editions, as soon became obvious. He also greatly underestimated the difficulties that would arise in drawing up episcopal *fasti*.
Nevertheless, the undertaking that the eighty-four-year-old Mommsen
had inaugurated appeared to make good progress. After his death
on 1 November 1903, Otto Seeck stepped into his place. Hundreds
of Patristic texts were excerpted, and thousands of files compiled. In
the following years, Jülicher, as general editor, tried to systematise the
excerpts and prepare them for publication. But the outbreak of the
First World War interrupted the scheduled continuation of the work.
In fact, the completion of the secular prosopography stagnated, since
Seeck concentrated all his efforts on his own research, for which, as
editor, he made use of the collected material, but he decided not to
promote the prosopography as a whole since he declined from looking
at the multiplicity of chronological, textual and historical problems. The
actual state of the secular prosopography, which was seen after Seeck's
death on 29 June 1921, caused the *Kirchenväterkommission* to terminate
the work on this part of the *Prosopographia Imperii Romani saec. IV.V.VI.*

The ecclesiastical prosopography, that Jülicher himself had tirelessly
supported, also stood under an unlucky star. After 1918, the unfavour-
able political and economic circumstances hindered the enterprise.
Then Jülicher had to request, because of his badly suffering eyesight,
to be released from his duties. At its meeting on 24 February 1928,
the commission decided to put at rest any question of further work on
the prosopography. An attempt at the beginning of the 1930s to reac-
tivate the project was not successful. No one knew how complete and
reliable the excerpts were, since there was no comprehensive index of
the extracted sources. The *Kirchenväterkommission* of the Berlin Academy
therefore decided in December 1933 to cease work.

This decision meant the end of the *Prosopographia Imperii Romani saec.
IV.V.VI.* 75,000 *lemmata* were not published. The plan for an extensive
prosopography of late antiquity, which had been started with great

confidence and was funded with large financial expenditures for nearly thirty years, failed because of a goal placed too far in the distance, because of methodological difficulties and organisational shortcomings, and finally through war and its aftermath.

The collection of files survived the Second World War nearly intact; only thirty boxes got lost. The remaining 151 boxes were brought to Cambridge in 1965. Seventeen years later, in August 1982, forty-five boxes containing the excerpts of the secular prosopography were returned. It is difficult to say to what extent the editors of the British *Prosopography of the Later Roman Empire* used the Berlin excerpts. Jones and his collaborators might have recognised soon that Otto Seeck and his colleagues had already published the most interesting extracts in their articles on important persons in the *Realencyclopädie der classischen Altertumswissenschaft*. These proved to be the greatest help, along with other relevant publications of Seeck.[63] Jones' assessment of the remaining extracts corresponded, perhaps, with that of the *Kommission für spätantike Religionsgeschichte* in 1951; then it was decided that the prosopographical material was of only limited value. Nevertheless, the British permitted the French group to have the ecclesiastical material for their *Prosopographie chrétienne du Bas-Empire*. Charles Pietri and his other colleagues finally returned the remaining boxes to Berlin at the beginning of the 1990s.

Jones initiated the *Prosopography of the Later Roman Empire*, "secured the finance for it, assembled the team of scholars for it, guided and supported it through all the preliminary stages of slips and filing, drafted the articles on *viri illustres* for Volume I, and had checked the final proofs of that volume before he died" in 1970.[64] And he had realised how demanding and laborious such an enterprise would be. Looking at the failure of the Berlin project he, from the very beginning, decided to divide the task into two separate projects to secure a realistic schedule so that he could finish what he had started.[65]

---

[63] Cf. Jones, Martindale and Morris (1971) v.

[64] Crook (1971) 429.

[65] There is an insider's account of the evolution of the *Prosopography of the Later Roman Empire* by one of Jones' co-editors in Martindale (2003), while for a survey of scholarly reactions to the publication of the work see Mathisen (2003).

(vii)

Jones preferred to explore the sources, but he did, as he himself admitted, read and profit from many modern books and articles, particularly those whose authors were so kind to send him offprints.[66] Indeed, the *Later Roman Empire* was not a *creatio ex nihilo*. Jones adopted and advanced different models which were developed on the continent to describe the Roman empire in late antiquity. His approach helped to supersede Mommsen's *Staatsrecht*, which tried to define the *proprium* of the Roman state by the abstract construction of a constitutional law, and Seeck's *Untergang der antiken Welt*, which amalgamated political history and Darwinist speculation. At the same time Jones followed Rostovtzeff's emphasis on social and economic questions and was truly fascinated by Stein's positive assessment of the late Roman bureaucracy. Of course, Jones' perception of the scholarly discourse was not exhaustive, since he wrote a social, economic and administrative survey of the later Roman empire and did not compile a comprehensive bibliography of the subject. But he had read—and heard of—many modern contributions to his subject which he integrated in his argument. It seems that although few modern scholars are mentioned by name, "not much of importance has escaped his notice".[67] Jones' achievement was based upon an intimate knowledge of primary evidence and secondary literature alike. But he did not care much about documenting scholarly discourse and dissent and providing access to current and retrospective positions in scholarship. Long bibliographies and winding debates in footnotes were meant to be tedious and appeared to be a privilege of continental, especially German and Italian scholarship. Jones proposed a fresh look at the sources instead, which promised originality to the reader and gave authority to the author. Jones' opening statement that he abandoned the attempt to keep abreast with modern scholarship[68] is a striking example of academic self-fashioning.

---

[66] Jones (1964) I, vi.
[67] Browning (1965) 336.
[68] Jones (1964) I, vi.

Bibliography

Alexander P.J. (1966) "Review of A.H.M. Jones, *The Later Roman Empire*", *AJPh* 97 (1966) 337–50

Brown P. (1967) "The Later Roman Empire", *EcHR*, 2nd series, 20 (1967) 327–43, reprinted in *idem* (1972) *Religion and Society in the Age of Saint Augustine* (London 1972) 46–73

Browning R. (1965) "Review: Declining Rome Surveyed", *CR*, NS, 15 (1965) 335–39

Bury J.B. (1923) *A history of the Roman empire from the death of Theodosius to the death of Justinian*, 2 vols. (London 1923)

Chastagnol A. (1964) "Review of A.H.M. Jones, *The Later Roman Empire*", *REL* 42 (1964) 159–65

Christ K. (1982) *Römische Geschichte und deutsche Geschichtswissenschaft* (Munich 1982)

Courcelle P. (1948) *Histoire littéraire des grandes invasions germaniques* (Paris 1948)

Cracco Ruggini L. (1965) "Review of A.H.M. Jones, *The Later Roman Empire*", *RSI* 77 (1965) 201–11

Crook J. (1971) "Arnold Hugh Martin Jones, 1904–1970", *PBA* 57 (1971) 425–38

D'Elia S. (1967) *Il basso impero nella cultura moderna dal quattrocento A.D. oggi* (Naples 1967)

Gottlieb G. (1967) "Review of A.H.M. Jones, *The Later Roman Empire*", *AA* 30 (1967) 263–66

Irmscher J. (1970) "Review of A.H.M. Jones, *The Later Roman Empire*", *Deutsche Literaturzeitung* 91 (1970) 766–69

Jones A.H.M. (1948) *Constantine and the Conversion of Europe* (London 1948)

——. (1949) "The Roman civil service (clerical and sub-clerical grades)", *JRS* 39 (1949) 38–55, reprinted in *idem* (1960) *Studies in Roman Government and Law* (Oxford 1960) 151–175

——. (1952) "Michael Ivanovitch Rostovtzeff, 1870–1952", *PBA* 58 (1952) 347–61

——. (1953) "Review of S. Mazzarino, *Aspetti sociali del quarto secolo. Richerche di storia tardo-romana*", *CR*, NS, 3 (1953) 113–15

——. (1953/4) "Review of E. Stein, *Histoire du Bas Empire, t. 2. De la disparition de l'empire d'occident à la mort de Justinien (467–565)*", *Historia* 2 (1953/4) 352–59

——. (1954) "The Date and Value of the Verona List", *JRS* 44 (1954) 21–29, reprinted in *idem* (1974) 263–79

——. (1957a) "Review of P. Petit, *Libanius et la vie municipale à Antioche au IVe siècle après J.C.*", *CR*, NS, 7 (1957) 252–54

——. (1957b) "*Capitatio* and *Iugatio*", JRS 47 (1957) 88–94, reprinted in *idem* (1974) 280–92

——. (1957c) "Review of F. Lot, *Nouvelles recherches sur l'impôt foncier et la capitation personnelle sous le Bas-Empire*", *JRS* 47 (1957) 256–57

——. (1964) *The Later Roman Empire 284–602: A Social, Economic, and Administrative Survey*, 3 vols (Oxford 1964), reprinted in two volumes with continuous pagination (Oxford 1973)

——. (1974) *The Roman Economy: Studies in Ancient Economic and Administrative History*, ed. P.A. Brunt (Oxford 1974)

Jones A.H.M, Martindale J.R. and Morris J. (1971) *The Prosopography of the Later Roman Empire I, A.D. 260–395* (Cambridge 1971)

Kolbe H.G. (1962) *Die Statthalter Numidiens von Gallien bis Konstantin* (Munich 1962)

Liebeschuetz J.H.W.G. (1990) *Barbarians and Bishops. Army, Church, and State in the Age of Arcadius and Chrysostom* (Oxford 1990)

——. (1992) "A.H.M. Jones and the *Later Roman Empire*", *Institute of Archaeology Bulletin* 29 (1992) 1–8, reprinted in *idem* (2006) *Decline and Change in Late Antiquity: Religion, Barbarians and their Historiography* (Aldershot 2006) XVI

Lot F. (1955) *Nouvelles recherches sur l'impôt foncier et la capitation personnelle sous le Bas-Empire* (Paris 1955)

Martindale J.R. (2003) "*The Prosopography of the Later Roman Empire*, Volume I: A Memoir of the Era of A.H.M. Jones", in *Fifty Years of Prosopography: The Later Roman Empire, Byzantium and Beyond*, ed. Averil Cameron (Oxford 2003) 3–10

Mathisen R.W. (2003) "*The Prosopography of the Later Roman Empire*: Yesterday, Today and Tomorrow", in *Fifty Years of Prosopography: The Later Roman Empire, Byzantium and Beyond*, ed. Averil Cameron (Oxford 2003) 23–40

Mazzarino S. (1951) *Aspetti sociali del quarto secolo. Richerche di storia tardo-romana* (Rome 1951)

Momigliano A. (1965) "A.H.M. Jones' The Later Roman Empire", *Oxford Magazine*, NS, 5 (1965) 264–5, reprinted in *idem* (1969) 645–47

———. (1969) *Quarto contributo alla storia degli studi classici e del mondo antico* (Rome 1969)

Mommsen Th. (1887/88) *Römisches Staatsrecht*, 3 vols. in 5, 3rd edition (Leipzig 1887/1888)

———. (1907) *Abriß des römischen Staatsrechts*, 2nd ed. (Leipzig 1907)

Nippel W. (2000) "From agrarian history to cross-cultural comparisons: Weber on Greco-Roman antiquity", in *The Cambridge Companion to Weber*, ed. St. Turner (Cambridge 2000) 240–55

Petit P. (1955) *Libanius et la vie municipale à Antioche au IVe siècle après J.C.* (Paris 1955)

Piganiol A. (1972) *L'Empire chrétien (325–395)*, 2nd ed. (Paris 1972)

Rebenich St. (1997a) *Theodor Mommsen und Adolf Harnack. Wissenschaft und Politik im Berlin des ausgehenden 19. Jahrhunderts* (Berlin and New York 1997)

———. (1997b) "Mommsen, Harnack und die Prosopographie der Spätantike", *StP* 29 (1997) 109–18

———. (2002) *Theodor Mommsen. Eine Biographie* (Munich 2002)

Rostovtzeff M.I. (1926) *The Social and Economic History of the Roman Empire* (Oxford 1926)

Seeck O. (1920–23) *Geschichte des Untergangs der antiken Welt*, 6 vols., rev. ed. (Stuttgart 1920–1923)

Stein E. (1922) *Untersuchungen über das Officium der Prätorianerpräfektur seit Diokletian* (Wien 1922)

———. (1928) *Geschichte des spätrömischen Reiches*, vol. i: *Vom römischen zum byzantinischen Staate (284–476)* (Vienna 1928)

———. (1949/1959) *Histoire du Bas-Empire*, vol. i: *De l'état romain à l'état byzantin (284–476)*, èdition française par Jean-Rémy Palanque (Paris 1959); vol. ii: *De la disparition de l'empire d'occident à la mort de Justinien (467–565)*, publié par Jean-Rémy Palanque (Paris 1949)

Stroheker K.F. (1948) *Der senatorische Adel im spätantiken Gallien* (Tübingen 1948)

Wallace-Hadrill J.M. (1965) "Review of A.H.M. Jones, *The Later Roman Empire*", *EHR* 80 (1965) 785–90

Warmington B.H. (1965) "Review of A.H.M. Jones, *The Later Roman Empire*", *History* 50 (1965) 54–60

Weber M. (1988) *Gesammelte Aufsätze zur Sozial- und Wirtschaftsgeschichte*, 2nd ed. (Tübingen 1988)

Wiemer H.-U. (2006) ed. *Staatlichkeit und politisches Handeln in der römischen Kaiserzeit* (Berlin and New York 2006)

SECTION II

THE LATER ROMAN EMPIRE

CHAPTER FOUR

THE ROLE OF THE EMPEROR

Michael Whitby

1. *Jones and his Successors*

There are plenty of emperors in Jones' *Later Roman Empire*, especially in the narrative chapters which are organised by individual reigns or groups of reigns, but little discussion of the position of the emperor: the index contains only one relevant entry, for 'emperor, office and powers'.[1] Other possible entries, which would almost certainly appear in a contemporary study of late Roman imperial government, such as ceremonies, court, panegyrics do not appear; even palaces are absent, and the hopes raised by the sub-heading 'imperial residence' under such places as Antioch, Milan, Nicomedia, Ravenna, Sirmium, and Trier are not realised, since these relate to the use of such cities as short-term imperial bases rather than to the appearance or organisation of the physical residence there (of which little, in fact, is known). The Great Palace of Constantinople, the most important imperial seat and the subject of extensive scholarly speculation and occasional archaeological investigation during the past century and more, is not accorded an entry. This, of course, in part reflects Jones' conception of his project as outlined in his Preface (p. v), with its focus on organisation and structures rather than specific individuals.

Jones' single passage on the emperor (321–9) opens Chapter XI, 'The Government', and hence launches the descriptive second part of *Later Roman Empire*, an appropriate recognition of the supremacy of the emperor over the system which is about to be dissected. After noting that the emperor's powers were absolute in theory and practice, and that they survived the transition from divine status among the Olympian gods to terrestrial representative of the Christian God (321), Jones embarks on his first significant topic, that of imperial succession

---

[1] Jones (1964) III, 1490.

(322–5), with the overlapping alternatives of the hereditary principle, co-option by a current emperor, selection by a powerful general, and election in which the interests of army, senate and senior administrators might be considered. It is noticeable that, after a very brief reference to the nominal involvement of the people in conferring power at the point of succession (322), there is then no mention of the role of the people in the Hippodrome, or of the circus factions as articulators of popular views and, increasingly, supporters of particular rulers: thus the eastern successions of the late fifth century are discussed (325) without the physical spaces in which these events occurred being considered.[2] Jones then goes on to examine three issues related to succession, the predominance throughout Late Antiquity of multiple rulers and the nature of the relationship between these (325–6), the threat of usurpation as an alternative to orderly succession (326), and finally the type of men chosen for imperial office on those occasions when inheritance did not dictate the succession, with comments on their relative obscurity (326–9).

The appearance of emperors in the narrative chapters in Part I of the *Later Roman Empire* does not add much to this narrow constitutional treatment. These chapters follow a fairly standard pattern, with a succinct survey of the relevant source material, then coverage of the major events of the reign, in particular internal and external wars, and any specific aspects of the succession, before turning towards major themes which anticipate the chapter headings in Part II: administration, finance, army, the Church. Relations between emperors and their senior officials and military commanders are covered, but the narrative focuses on changes to administrative, military and ecclesiastical structures.[3] Emperors do occasionally intrude as people with characters, when Jones adopts the habits of a historian like Ammianus to insert a comment, usually mordant, on the ability and achievements of an individual: Constantine was impulsive and ambitious, with a violent temper (78), whose considerable achievements must be weighed against his ruinous increases in expenditure (111); Constantius II is presented explicitly through the eyes of Ammianus (116), while Theodosius I's title of 'the Great'

---

[2] In the narrative section, Jones does mention that some of the events of 518 occurred in the Hippodrome (267), but this is not recognised in relation to Anastasius (230) or earlier accessions.

[3] Jones' narrative was deliberately more focused than the accounts in Bury (1923) and Stein (1949–59).

is questioned because of financial extravagance, irresolute responses to external military threats, and fanatical piety (169). With regard to Theodosius' feeble descendants, Jones alludes to the benefits which a legitimate emperor, however weak, could bring to their subjects (173), but this interesting suggestion is not pursued. Emperors who attempted to reduce taxes and remove other administrative burdens receive the most favourable comment, specifically Valens (147) and Justinian (269), though in neither case is the praise left unqualified.

It is interesting to contrast the general treatment of the emperor in Bury's *Later Roman Empire*, the most authoritative statement in English before Jones and a passage which Jones naturally knew well: if the joint use of Mommsen's aphorism about monarchy as 'an autocracy tempered by the legal right of revolution' is unsurprising, granted its pithy force,[4] the common citation of Valentinian III's statement of 429 (*CJ* I.xiv.4) about the relationship of ruler to law suggests that Jones was responding to his predecessor's formulation, especially as in this case he assigned the dictum less weight than Bury had. Bury naturally covered the same key topics, succession, inheritance versus co-option, appointment or election, and usurpation, but he also ranged more widely. Perhaps because his chronological horizons extended across the Byzantine period, Bury remarked on the significance of appearances (purple), symbols (the diadem), terminology (*basileus*), and ceremonies (*adoratio*); he noted the increased contribution of the Constantinople patriarch to succession arrangements, and devoted space to the role of the Augusta in conferring legality through marriage as well as exercising power on occasion.[5] The breadth of Bury's approach is more in tune with the priorities of modern scholars than the narrow focus of Jones.

A striking example of the difference in treatment of the emperor a generation after Jones is provided by the two Late Antique volumes of the extended *Cambridge Ancient History*.[6] Each volume contains a chapter in which the emperor looms large: in volume XIII, Christopher Kelly's 'Emperors, Government and Bureaucracy' (138–83), of which a bit

---

[4] Bury (1923) 5–18. Mommsen: Bury (1923) 15, Jones (1964) I, 326; Valentinian III: Bury 13–14, Jones 321.

[5] Bury (1923) 8–10; by contrast Jones devoted less than a paragraph to empresses (1964: 341), and was far more interested in generals as wielders of power over the throne.

[6] Cameron et al. (1998); Cameron et al. (2000).

over half is devoted to the emperor; in XIV Michael McCormick's 'Emperor and Court' (135–63) where the court is little more than the physical extension of the emperor. The constitutional issues on which Jones had focused are simply assumed as non-controversial. Kelly's most important theme is 'Perceptions of Power', an investigation of how the imperial image was enhanced and propagated through ceremonies, panegyrical literature, and acclamations to create an ideology which reinforced the main military and administrative forces for imperial unity (139–50). Bureaucratic centralisation, which both underpinned but also threatened emperors' scope for action (150–6), leads to the question of 'The Limits of Rule' (157–62), a section which opens with a plain reversal of Jones' belief in imperial omnipotence.[7] McCormick's agenda is differently arranged, but covers analogous topics as well as adding others. McCormick begins with 'The Physical Context of Power' (136–42), a brief survey of the spaces within which the eastern empire was controlled from Constantinople. The next section on 'The Emperor' (142–5) covers titulature, duties, the mechanics of loyalty, and the differing backgrounds of western and eastern rulers. His longest section, on 'The Court: the human element' (145–56), tackles the important issue of which people apart from emperors wielded influence at court, with particular attention paid to imperial families and especially to empresses who are too often overlooked in studies of the functioning of the state. The last two sections on 'Court and Ceremony' (156–60), and 'Court and Culture' (160–3), deal with some of the issues of image which predominate in Kelly's chapter in *CAH* XIII.

The most important difference is that serious attention is devoted to understanding how emperors projected their image. Although Jones was writing when politicians appreciated and exploited the benefits which the right image might bring, for example 'Supermac' Harold MacMillan's 'You've never had it so good' slogan from the 1959 UK General Election campaign, or highlighted the weaknesses of adversaries, as in the 'Tricky Dicky' image of dark-shadowed Richard Nixon which emerged from the televised debates with the 'clean' John F. Kennedy in the 1960 US presidential contest, this was still an age before media advisers, image make-overs and spin-doctors. Contemporary experience ensures that we pay at least as much attention to the creation and sustenance of a political image as to what that individual might do. In Late Antique

---

[7] This discussion is reprised, at considerably greater length, in Kelly (2004).

terms this entails devoting serious consideration to imperial panegyrics, occasions for public interaction between the powerful and their public, and all aspects of the trappings of power. We also live in a world in which powerful figures are seen as elements within interlocking networks of influence and patronage, so that it matters where the person of power operates, with whom they interact regularly, and how effectively they can implement their policies and preferences. It is accepted that even the most powerful of individuals, or states, cannot always achieve everything they want, so that methods of securing action and the compromises which have to be made on occasion must be noted. In the Late Antique world this means that emperors are unlikely to be seen as omnipotent, but as people operating within families, in consultation with advisers at court, possessing particular agendas but also susceptible to influence by the preferences of others, and dependent on a far-flung network of subordinates to secure the implementation of any actions on which they might decide.

Between Jones and the recent *CAH* volumes certain key publications have influenced how the role of the emperor in Late Antiquity is now approached. Alan Cameron's *Circus Factions* (1976), an investigation of the general context which underlay his earlier more detailed study of charioteer monuments and careers in *Porphyrius* (1973), focused attention on the shifting relationship between the emperor and his people which was repeatedly played out in the Hippodrome to the accompaniment of chariot races and chanting orchestrated by the Blue and Green circus factions. Cameron effectively disposed of grander hypotheses about their alleged political and religious roles, and, even if some of his conclusions about the impact and importance of the factions are too negative,[8] he highlighted the significance of this symbiotic relationship. Through his study of *Claudian* (1970), Alan Cameron also contributed decisively to enhancing appreciation of panegyrics and illustrating how sensitive analysis of a corpus of material could reveal the political and cultural dynamics at a particular royal court. Subsequently rhetoric has been a significant area of study, with important work devoted to the Latin panegyrics by Nixon and Rodgers (1994), while in *Barbarians and Politics* (1993) Alan Cameron, in collaboration with Jacqueline Long, did for the court of Arcadius what *Claudian* had achieved for his brother Honorius; Peter Brown's *Power and Persuasion in Late Antiquity* (1992)

---

[8] See, for example, Whitby (2006).

pulled together many emerging ideas about the roles of rhetoric in the developing Christian society. But with regard to the significance of panegyric for understanding imperial behaviour, pride of place goes to Sabine MacCormack's *Art and Ceremony in Late Antiquity* (1981), a work which integrated the study of text, image and event in the analysis of the imperial image: the mechanics of a ceremony along with the rhetoric which decorated it, and the artefacts which recorded and diffused its messages, were all marshalled to chart the evolution of imperial representation as the Late Antique world evolved into a Christian society. Another important work which built on the advances in *Circus Factions* and *Art and Ceremony* is Michael McCormick's *Eternal Victory* (1986); this examined the enduring significance of the triumph in the image-building of rulers, and how Roman traditions were transmuted through the Late Roman period into the practices of the Byzantine and early medieval western states.

A different set of approaches to the emperor has been opened up by works which have tackled the practicalities of how, with whom, through whom, and for whose benefit particular people operated. Of fundamental importance here has been the production of the three volumes of the *Prosopography of the Later Roman Empire*,[9] a project which was initiated by Jones and seen through, in considerably expanded form, to improvement and completion by John Martindale. An early demonstration of how a perceptive investigator might exploit this raw material was provided in John Matthews' *Western Aristocracies* (1975) which weaves it into a much richer study of interactions between emperors, courts and aristocracies, both central and local, to examine how the balance of power and the religious identity of the elite shifted over a period of two generations.[10] Matthews' next major work, *The Roman Empire of Ammianus* (1989), further demonstrated how sensitive reading of historical sources could open up the complexities of politics, wars, social change and much more in the mid-fourth century; it contains illuminating chapters on 'The Office of Emperor' (XI) and 'The Character of Government' (XII). Another work to focus on the practicalities of how the world worked is Fergus Millar's *The Emperor in the Roman World*, a volume which explicitly covered rulers through to Constantine and, in practice, brought in material from later in the fourth

---

[9] Jones et al. (1971); Martindale (1980); Martindale (1992).
[10] For a more recent example, see Lenski (2002) 56–67, on the reign of Valens.

century.[11] Millar's reconstruction of imperial activities was anchored very closely in the evidence, primarily textual, and elucidated how emperors interacted with their household, entourage, and other constituencies such as the Senate, Provinces and increasingly the Church. This is now complemented by his study (2006) of the extensive evidence for relations between Church and State during Theodosius II's reign.[12]

2. *The Imperial Image*

In most of the above works it is possible to detect the influence of Jones' *Later Roman Empire*, if only in its establishment of the structures of Late Antique political and administrative arrangements within which scholars can pursue their own investigations. It is interesting, however, that MacCormack did not cite the *Later Roman Empire* in her bibliography,[13] a reflection of the extent to which her agenda and focus had transcended Jones' approach. The imperial image, therefore, is a reasonable topic with which to start a survey of the role of emperors in the post-Jonesian world.

A prime resource for investigating the changing public image of different emperors are the surviving panegyrics—reasonably numerous, even though they represent a very small fraction of what was a regular mode of communication. Jones, of course, was familiar with these and exploited them as far as they might contribute to his agenda, but somewhat impatiently: he refers to the 'few flowery and uninformative panegyrics on Constantius by Themistius' (115), and is only slightly less uncomplimentary about his speeches for Valens and Theodosius 'which though panegyrical in character contain some factual information' (154); the primacy of fact is also clear in his comments on the collection of Tetrarchic panegyrics which are 'not very informative, but contain some useful allusions to contemporary events and institutions' (37). Jones has not been alone in his search for factual information: for example, many complaints about Procopius' *Buildings* are based on the assumption that a panegyrical text should be presenting the whole truth

---

[11] Millar (1977; second ed. with afterword, 1992).

[12] For the application of Millar's principles to the late empire see also Errington (2006).

[13] The only item by Jones to be cited is his 1962 study of Odoacer and Theoderic.

and nothing but the truth, so that errors or misrepresentations must be held against the author's competence or knowledge.[14]

One prime achievement of panegyrics was to present rulers in a suitably intellectual light. Although some late Roman rulers were well educated, Julian famously, Gratian unfortunately for himself, but Anastasius more effectively, others such as Diocletian and his colleagues, Valentinian I, Zeno or Justin I were soldiers whose rural background had precluded the acquisition of an educated patina. All rulers, however, had to interact with educated elites who did much of the ruling in the empire, whether senators, senior courtiers and administrators, or representatives of provincial cities, and such people might be quick to sneer at an illiterate ruler such as Justin I, 'who was completely ignorant of letters, and "alphabetless" as the saying goes' (Procopius, *Secret History* 6.11). The elaborate language, historical and literary allusions and metaphorical constructs in the speeches helped to embrace emperors, whether educated or not, within the common *paideia* which united the civilian elites.[15] Emperors, especially unfamiliar new arrivals, had to be brought into the fold and panegyrists contributed to alleviating possible tensions. The principles of imperial praise were well known, being analysed in the late third century by Menander Rhetor,[16] whose handbook served as a flexible frame which speakers adapted to new ceremonies and changing circumstances; the absence of Menander from Jones' index reflects his distaste for this aspect of imperial power.

The most sustained expression of this intellectual representation of emperors occurs in the 'flowery' works of Themistius, who set out to construct for himself the image of a philosopher who offered frank advice to emperors; their toleration of such free speech and apparent appreciation of its literary subtleties then enhanced their image. He maintained a position of prominence in the eastern empire for forty years, with the only blip occurring during the reign of Julian, the emperor closest to him in terms of intellectual interests and religious affiliation. Themistius' comments have been interpreted literally so that he emerges as a principled orator, prepared to give advice which was not always to the liking of his imperial master,[17] but this reflects

---

[14] Criticisms in Croke and Crow (1983); Cameron (1985); some defence in Whitby (1986a, 1987).

[15] See Rees (2002) for discussion of Tetrarchic panegyrics, especially ch. 5.

[16] Ed. and trans. Russell and Wilson (1981).

[17] Vanderspoel (1995) ch. 1.

his success as imperial spin-doctor: throughout his public career his sentiments converged with a succession of imperial priorities, and it is reasonable to view him as an advocate of policies and images which had already been determined.[18] Themistius' speeches benefit from close attention to what themes were excluded as well as included on a particular occasion. Sensitivity to location and context has revealed the agenda of his 357 speech, delivered to Constantius in the Senate at Rome; Themistius was leading a delegation from the Senate in Constantinople, which was still junior in status and numbers. It emerges that Themistius, on behalf of the emperor, was softening up the senior Senate for a dramatic expansion in the size of its eastern counterpart, which would involve the allocation to Constantinople of those members of the Roman Senate whose estates lay in the east, and a rise in status to equal that of Rome. Constantinople would also benefit from an upsurge in building activity in the last five years of Constantius' reign as he set about establishing it as the acknowledged centre for the eastern empire. We live in a world in which major political announcements are regularly trailed in advance, with a forthcoming announcement in fact becoming a newsworthy item, so we are attuned to detect such tactics in the ancient world; these subtleties cannot be extracted by a reader concerned to identify simple nuggets of information.

Themistius is but one example of how this once despised category of literature has enriched our understanding of imperial policies and behaviour. Another instance is Justin II, whose reign Jones narrated briefly with most emphasis placed upon the failures, his mental balance being characterised as never very stable.[19] This is an accurate reflection of our sources, most of which were written after the unfortunate consequences of Justin's foreign initiatives had become clear and when his descent into madness appeared to give divine support to the natural desire of his successors to attribute blame for problems to a suitable predecessor. By contrast, the panegyric of Corippus on Justin's accession articulates the optimistic image of the early years when doctrinal reconciliation seemed possible, an assertive attitude in foreign relations practical, and financial munificence affordable.[20] All this had been a

---

[18] Heather and Moncur (2001) ch. 1. Note the convergent presentation in Symmachus 2 and Themistius 10 of the frontier works of Valentinian and Valens along the Rhine and Danube respectively.

[19] Jones (1964) I, 304–6.

[20] Summary of the poem's context in Averil Cameron (1976) 4–7.

calculated and welcome change from the situation towards the end of Justinian's reign, when imperial debts were left unpaid, foreign embassies appeared to secure what they wanted at whatever cost to the Roman state, and the Aphthartodocetist initiative had threatened the Chalcedonian hierarchy with chaos. Justin is a case of a ruler whose historiographical image has been largely shaped by the criticisms which unpopular policies and failures attracted.[21] The inversion of the panegyric, the *psogos* or defamation, is exemplified by Gregory of Nazianzen's posthumous speeches against Julian, Synesius of Cyrene's *De Regno* which attacks Arcadius and his ministers, and, most famously, Procopius' *Secret History* whose vitriol is difficult to ignore when assessing Justinian's reign.[22] Rhetorical presentations of emperors, negative as well as positive, deserve serious attention, since, if their conventions are not understood, their insights on the Late Antique world and impact on the historiographical record will be overlooked.

Corippus' poem on Justin has been identified as a work which transformed panegyric from an account of deeds and virtues into a description of ceremony; if credit should be shared with Paul the Silentiary's *Ekphrasis* on S. Sophia, which formed part of the celebrations for its rededication at Christmas 562, the linkage between imperial praise and imperial ceremonies is still valid.[23] Jones did touch on accession ceremonies as evidence for the constitutional process of ratifying a new ruler (322), but he did not probe ceremonial developments during Late Antiquity for evidence of particular innovations. His lack of sympathy for ceremony emerges from passing comments in the narrative: Julian 'swept away the ostentatious splendour of the court' (136), reversing developments to which Constantius, who 'was evidently fond of pomp and circumstance' (105), had significantly contributed through his desire to enhance the glamour of imperial service with grandiloquent titles; *adoratio* and the seclusion of the ceremonial court are characterised as poor defences against revolt (40). Our understanding has been very considerably advanced by MacCormack, in particular of the ways in which the accession, a ceremony with a primarily military significance, came to be adapted to a settled urban location in which the increasingly influential church hierarchy carved out a prominent role.

---

[21] Averil Cameron (1977).
[22] For the impact of this material on historians, see Tinnefeld (1971).
[23] MacCormack (1981) 6–7; Mary Whitby (1985).

These ceremonies were of sufficient interest to be recorded by contemporaries at great length, with verbatim quotations of different acclamations, and to survive to appear in Constantine Porphyrogennitus'
compilation *De Caerimoniis*. As a result, at Constantinople we can detect
the emergence of the excubitors as the most important military representatives after the venue moved from the extra-mural Hebdomon
to the Hippodrome, and the shifting concerns at different proclama-
tions, e.g. the chant in 491 that the Augusta Ariadne select 'a Roman
emperor for the *oikoumene*' in succession to the Isaurian Zeno.[24] The
development of the *adventus*, the other ceremony discussed in detail
by MacCormack, illumines an aspect of the transition from the
essentially mobile emperors of the third and fourth centuries to their
capital-based successors in the fifth and sixth, with one response to
the loss of contact with provincial populations being the adaptation
of the ceremony from the arrival of the ruler in person to that of a
statue or icon.[25] Later emperors were not completely confined to the
capital, but their travels rarely took them beyond suburban palaces
and the immediate hinterland of the Sea of Marmara, to places such
as Selymbria or Pylae; a journey to Aphrodisias such as Theodosius II
undertook in 443, or slightly further to the Church of the Archangel
Michael at Germia, which Justinian visited in 563, was very rare. The
reception of imperial laws in provincial cities, a process which should
have interested Jones, had similarities to the new *adventus*, with inhabitants being assembled in the theatre or other suitable space to listen to
the rhetorical preamble, whose arguments to justify the forthcoming
change might well coincide with the themes of imperial panegyric,
and then the actual law.[26] Another frequent ceremony which reflected
the theatricality of imperial power was *adoratio* in which a privileged
minority was permitted to enter the imperial presence and adore the
purple, i.e. kneel and kiss the emperor's robe, often on appointment
to official position, sometimes as a public demonstration of continued
imperial favour (e.g. Ammianus 15.5.18–19).[27] Jones noted Diocletian's

---

[24] Contrast the bald treatment of these events in Jones (1964: I, 325).

[25] MacCormack (1981) ch. 1, with discussion of Procopius of Gaza's account of the
arrival of a statue of Anastasius at 68–70; see also MacCoull (1988) 72–6 for Dioscorus
of Aphrodito's celebration of the arrival in Antinoe of Justin II's image.

[26] For the whole process, see, for example, Matthews (2000) ch. 7.

[27] Jones subsequently acknowledged that *adoratio* might be an honour (1964: I, 337),
but did not pursue this angle with the sensitivity of, for example, Matthews (1989)
244–7.

introduction of *adoratio* in a sentence coloured by the hostility of Aurelius Victor, Eutropius and the Augustan History to this abandonment of earlier simplicity (40). The traditional triumph adapted to changing imperial needs, in particular the switch from mobile to sedentary rulers.[28] Down to the death of Theodosius I, almost all late Roman rulers commanded armies in the field and so had the chance to win victories, or at least to be physically present when victories were being won. After 395, emperors campaigned very rarely,[29] and none could claim personal credit for victory until Heraclius campaigned against the Persians in the 620s, but this did not stop the development of triumphal celebrations. These were often focused on the Hippodrome, though services in church are also attested (Theophylact 6.8.8) and the most dramatic imperial victory, Khusro II's overthrow in 628, was announced from the pulpit of S. Sophia in a detailed report which opened with Biblical celebrations (*Chronicon Paschale* 727–37). This is an aspect of the intertwining of imperial image and the ecclesiastical hierarchy which Jones did not pursue in his treatment of Church and State.

Triumphs and accessions were major events whose ceremonial elaboration is not surprising, but of equal interest from the perspective of relations between rulers and their immediate populace in the capital city is the way in which a calendar of processions and other celebrations developed at Constantinople during the fourth and fifth centuries as the 'liturgical dimension of public life' evolved.[30] Processions celebrated the arrival and deposition of relics, saints' days and other church feasts were observed at the appropriate church, deliverance from natural disasters was commemorated, and symbolic events such as the imperial inspection of the public granaries conducted. Details of the different ceremonies were recorded, to be preserved by Constantine Porphyrogennitus, and such was the expectation on emperors to participate that on 26 January 457 Marcian struggled to undertake the seven-mile walk to the Hebdomon on the anniversary of the destructive earthquake of 447; Marcian prided himself on making the journey on foot, and the patriarch Anatolius had felt obliged to follow his example, but on this occasion the emperor could not complete the event and

---

[28] Full discussion in McCormick (1986) chs. 2–3; neither *adventus* nor triumph merits an entry in Jones' index.
[29] Minor exceptions noted in Whitby (2005) 368–9.
[30] Croke (2001) 116–24.

died back in the palace on the next day.[31] The appearance in public of the emperor without his normal ceremonial attendants could be used as a sign of great urgency.[32]

An important aspect of any public event was, of course, how it was received by the audience. A procession which went wrong, such as that of Maurice to the church of the Virgin at Blachernae to celebrate the Feast of Candlemas in 602, when stones were thrown, a man who resembled the emperor placed on a donkey, and insults chanted,[33] was a public relations disaster which might encourage unrest in other places. The most obvious gauge of public opinion were acclamations, and emperors paid attention to these. Jones was aware of their significance as a medium of communication, since his discussions of the reception by the Roman Senate of the Theodosian Code (1964: 331), and of a provincial assembly at Oxyrhynchus (1964: 722–3), noted how standard expressions of loyalty could be interspersed with specific requests, but he did not probe their role as a mechanism of government. Acclamations were often manufactured or led, as Jones, following Libanius, observed with regard to the theatre claque at Antioch (1964: 723), but that does not mean that what was said had no significance. Excavations at Aphrodisias have permitted Charlotte Roueché to analyse a sequence of inscribed acclamations in favour of one prominent citizen, the *clarissimus* Albinus, and place the event which generated them in its broader social context:[34] what is abnormal about the Aphrodisias acclamations is that they have survived at length. It is likely that in other cities local benefactors were accorded similar treatment, with scapegoats or enemies such as Bishop Ibas at Edessa receiving the opposite.[35] Acclamations chanted in provincial cities were of sufficient interest for Constantine in 331 to instruct that they should be transmitted to the emperor by the public post (*CTh* 1.16.6).

The increasing role of the circus factions in capital cities is now much better understood thanks to the work of Alan Cameron, who probed the symbiotic relationship between an emperor and his people in the Hippodrome: games could not occur without imperial support, but

---

[31] Croke (1978).
[32] Paul the Silentiary, *Ekphrasis* 255–61, with discussion in Mary Whitby (1987).
[33] Theophylact 8.4.11–5.4; Theophanes 283.12–24.
[34] Roueché (1984, 1989).
[35] German translation of the Syriac record, with clear attention to structure, in Wiemer (2004) 66–73.

emperors also benefited from the vociferous displays of support which a
faction could generate. This service led to the factions obtaining increasing prominence in other areas of ceremonial during the sixth century, so
that they retained a major role in imperial routine after entertainments
in the Hippodrome declined in regularity and importance in the seventh
century. Cameron's overall thesis was that during Late Antiquity their
main function was to focus attention on entertainment and distract the
populace from more serious issues, with the exception being the very
occasional disputed succession which briefly gave them great influence.
This minimalist interpretation of the factions' political significance has
been challenged on the basis that, although our evidence inevitably
focuses on moments of imperial drama, there are some indications of
the involvement of factions in wider issues and with a range of non-
imperial patrons.[36] Even on Cameron's limited view the crisis of the Nika
Riot in 532 demonstrated the serious consequences of an emperor's
failure to manage relations with the factions, while Anastasius' public
offer to resign in 512 (Malalas 16.16, esp. pp. 407.21–408.1 [Bonn]),
an even more extraordinary incident, illustrates the potential impact of
popular opinion which the allegiance of a faction might defuse.

It has been suggested that the factions contributed significantly
both to emperors' authority over their court and aristocracy, a continuation of a tradition of emperors playing off popular enthusiasms
against senatorial ambitions which can be traced back to Augustus,
and to the promotion of imperial authority in the provinces; these
were powerful reasons why their excesses had to be tolerated, within
limits.[37] Cameron had proposed that there was a major overhaul of
the organisation of entertainment throughout the empire's cities in the
early fifth century, which led to much wider involvement in supporting events. This suggestion can be associated with a rearrangement of
the factions' seats in the Constantinople Hippodrome by Theodosius
II, which was designed to place his preferred faction, the Greens,
opposite the imperial box; the new configuration was then replicated
in provincial hippodromes throughout the East (Malalas 351.5–352.7).
This development ensured that in the major provincial cities, which
they no longer visited, Constantinopolitan emperors had a group of
supporters whose existence depended on the financial support provided

[36] Liebeschuetz (1998), (2001).
[37] Whitby (2006).

by the state for the running of games; after the Church, this was the most widely-spread civilian organisation in the state. The factions knew that their chants would be reported to the emperor, and this link to the imperial centre gave them clout and permitted them to behave with less restraint outside as well as inside sporting venues. Whereas the empire in the West was disintegrating under the mutually reinforcing challenges of tribal invasion and local warlords whose defence of their region detracted from imperial authority, Theodosius stumbled on a solution which ensured that in every city emperors were celebrated as much as any local grandee like Albinus. At the very least, the circus factions deserved to be considered in Jones' analysis of the contrasting fates of the eastern and western empires in Chapter XXV.

3. *Location*

Location was a central aspect of imperial ceremonies with their attendant panegyrics and acclamations, whether a single place such as the imperial box in the Hippodrome or a route along which a procession passed; the detailed report of one such event, the return to Constantinople of Justinian in August 559 after supervising building works near Selymbria, has been explicated by Brian Croke in order to place his journey in its full monumental context.[38] Jones did not pay much attention to the physical context of power. His chapter on 'Rome and Constantinople' (XVIII) allocated less than a couple of pages to the growth of Constantinople, one of the most important developments in relation to the exercise of imperial power, and most of the chapter is devoted to issues of authority, law and order, food supply, education and entertainments: all these issues are significant, but no sense emerges of the shape of the city which ensured the survival of Roman imperial authority. To achieve that would have required engagement with physical evidence, which was not a priority for Jones; in any case our understanding of the imperial development of Constantinople, if still far from perfect, has advanced very considerably since the publication

[38] Croke (2005) 60–67.

of Janin's *Constantinople byzantine* (second edition) in the same year as Jones' *Later Roman Empire*.[39]

The mobile emperors of the third and fourth centuries had to make do with whatever facilities were available, but cities such as Antioch, Trier, and Milan were well appointed with palaces, audience halls, and hippodromes or other arenas for public events. Rome, still the most lavish of imperial settings, was rarely visited, although when an emperor did see the physical spaces he might be impressed by their grandeur, as Constantius II was in the famous account by Ammianus Marcellinus of his triumphal entry in 357: "on every side to which his eyes turned he was amazed by the close array of marvellous sights... But when he came to the Forum of Trajan... he stood still in astonishment as he mentally embraced the colossal structure" (16.10.13–17). This Roman experience stimulated Constantius to develop Constantinople, where he had spent little time during the first two decades of his reign. Alongside the aggrandisement of the senate to equal that at Rome (noted above), he launched a decisive expansion of the city's public amenities which took over half a century to see through to completion as successive emperors competed to demonstrate favour to their capital city. As a result, grand spaces such as the Fora of Theodosius and of Arcadius were created, and these then provided settings for imperial monuments such as the Arch of Theodosius, whose fragments indicate its elaborate decoration without revealing its overall iconographic programme, or the Column of Arcadius, demolished as dangerous in the 18th century but fortunately recorded in detail by visitors.[40] The spiral reliefs on Arcadius' column celebrated the expulsion of Gainas and his Gothic followers in 400 as a manifestation of divine favour and occasion of imperial unity between East and West, in all a monumental counterpart to the panegyrics and acclamations which will have accompanied both the initial success and the completion of the monument in 421. A similar interweaving of monument and ceremony is evident in the reliefs on the base of the Theodosian obelisk in the Hippodrome, where the emperor and his orderly bodyguards and court oversee the elevation of the obelisk, which rises above them, and view the races, which will have marked its completion, as well as receive suppliant barbarians.[41]

---

[39] Janin (1964); Dagron (1974); Mango (1985, rev. ed. 1990); Mango and Dagron (1997); Bardill (2004).
[40] Liebeschuetz (1990) 273–8.
[41] Kiilerich (1998).

The centre of imperial power in the East was the Great Palace, whose complex structure remains debated, although meticulous analysis of brick stamps collected at various sites over the past century has produced greater understanding of some developments.[42] Apart from the initial siting of the palace by Constantine, which was largely determined by the location of the Severan Hippodrome as well as the fact that the best situation, the Acropolis of Byzantium, was occupied by several functioning temples, the major development of this central part of the city occurred under Justinian, when the emperor took advantage of the widespread destruction of the Nika riot in 532 to reshape the central monumental complex: bronze-roofed entrance to the imperial palace with attendant guard and reception rooms, formal public square with imperial equestrian statue, impressive even if a reused statue of Theodosius, and, most importantly, the Great Church of S. Sophia. Hints of the lavish appearance of parts of the palace at the end of the sixth century are provided by the grand hunting mosaic,[43] but it is the massive S. Sophia which, in spite of damage and adaptations over the centuries, illustrates how Justinian created an imperial complex which impressed visitors to the same extent that Rome had struck Constantius II. It is also likely that S. Sophia was intended to contribute to the on-going competition for honour, and hence authority, between emperor and aristocracy: the comment attributed to Justinian on first entering S. Sophia, "Solomon, I have surpassed you", has plausibly been interpreted as a response to the grand church to Polyeuctus completed a decade earlier by Anicia Juliana, a woman whose ancestry embraced both western and eastern rulers and whose husband Areobindus had been in danger of being acclaimed emperor in 512.[44]

The physical location of the emperor has been identified as one way in which the western and eastern emperors parted company during the fifth century.[45] When Honorius moved the western court from Milan to Ravenna in winter 402/3 to evade the growing Gothic threat, he based the court in a small city whose inaccessibility was one of its main attractions. Visitors, however, commented on its poor water supply, an essential aspect of civilised life whose delivery to Constantinople required

---

[42] Bardill (2004); see also Mango (1958).
[43] Talbot Rice (1958); Bardill (2004) 134–47 for date.
[44] *Narratio de aedificatione templi S. Sophiae* (T. Preger, *Sciptores Originum Constantinopolitanarum*) 105; Harrison (1989) 36–41.
[45] E.g. Whitby (2005); Hunger (1986).

massive investment as channels and aqueducts were extended across Thrace,[46] and it is clear that western emperors lacked the spectacular setting for imperial ceremonies, and in particular diplomatic encounters, which their eastern counterparts possessed in the Great Palace, whose impact on Attila's ambassador, Edeco, is attested by Priscus (fr. 11.23–6). The western empire also lacked the single centre of power which Constantinople provided for the East through its combination of imperial residence, focus for senators, leadership of the eastern church, and apex of military command. In the West, Rome was the base for both the Pope and Senate, except for individual senators eager to advance themselves in imperial service. Even more importantly the army was stationed elsewhere, often near Milan, so that even when emperors briefly returned to Rome during the 440s and 450s they were still cut off from the crucial source of their power and could not pretend to control king-makers such as Ricimer. Thus, physical location helped to ensure that the shift in imperial behaviour in 395 affected the two parts of the empire very differently.

4. *Duties and Actions*

The motto for Millar's study of pre-Constantinian emperors is that 'the emperor was what the emperor did', with the role conceptualised in an essentially passive manner as most major actions were triggered by requests from subjects or suggestions from governors or other officials.[47] Military security, relations between earth and heaven, adjudication and responses to other requests were key areas where emperors were expected to act. With regard to warfare, Jones was naturally aware of the change in 395, but did not attach much significance to it, with, for example, there being no discussion of this as a possible reason for decline in Chapter XXV; by contrast Millar, in his surveys of early imperial diplomacy and foreign relations recognised this development as significant, if "mysterious".[48] Although the emperor, as *imperator*,

---

[46] Crow and Bayliss (2004).

[47] Millar (1977) ch. 1 for the general thesis, though note some significant qualifications in the after-word to the reprint: (1992) 636–52.

[48] Millar (1988) 377; cf. also Millar (1982). Discussion in Whitby (2005) 368–81. It is surprising that this question is not considered in Millar (2006), though the material

had always been a military figure, the importance of personal military ability and involvement had varied from reign to reign, often depending as much on the individual ruler's personality and reputation as the threats to imperial stability. The upheavals of the third century and then the contest for power in the early fourth had inevitably privileged successful command, but the increasing stability and prosperity of the fourth century had reduced this so that there are signs of shifting priorities even before 395. What the inhabitants of the empire wanted was security, and if an emperor could provide this, or at least maintain a plausible image of doing so, it was of less importance who actually commanded the relevant forces as long as successful commanders preserved their loyalty to their imperial master: even in the days of campaigning emperors (apart from Diocletian's Tetrarchy), there had often been one or more frontiers which had to be entrusted to a non-imperial general whose actions would be carefully monitored, as happened to Ursicinus under Constantius II, to ensure that he both achieved the expected successes but did not develop ideas above his station. The East had the relevant resources and structures to manage the transition, the West did not—and, partly as a consequence, it also had to face more serious challenges. It is noticeable, however, that the return to personal campaigning in the early seventh century produced as much adverse reaction as its abandonment had in the early fifth. One conclusion to be drawn from these developments was that emperors were expected to behave in certain ways, and that breaks with recent precedent were unsettling.

One way in which imperial duties changed dramatically in Late Antiquity was with regard to religion. Down to Constantine the emperor, or one member of an imperial college, was *pontifex maximus*; as such he was head of the various priestly colleges, nomination to which he could exploit as a useful patronage tool, and participated in the central rituals of the Roman state. Emperors with their priestly colleagues were expected to provide answers to questions on sacred issues, for example about the movement of corpses, but an emperor could respond with the confidence that his wishes would be implemented as completely as in the secular sphere. Even before Constantine's conversion Christians

---

under discussion there suggests possible answers in terms of the efficiency and cohesion of the administrative system.

had been prepared to place contentious issues before an emperor, as
when the church at Antioch petitioned Aurelian about Paul of Samosata
(Eusebius, *HE* 8.30.19), probably in connection with his continued
occupation of ecclesiastical property after deposition,[49] but the nature
and complexity of issues confronting rulers and the ramifications of
imperial decisions changed significantly. Constantine accepted in his letter to Aelafius that divine favour for the empire depended on his ability
to ensure that everyone worshipped God through the correct Catholic
rites, for which reason he attempted to coerce the Donatists back into
communion with the African Catholics (Optatus, Appendix 3). Within
a decade of his conversion, however, Constantine had to accept that
he could not enforce his will in ecclesiastical matters when confronted
with obdurate resistance; in his letter to the African Catholics in 321
he counselled patience and restraint, qualities which are not often
found in late Roman legislation (Optatus, Appendix 9). Nestorius self-
confidently proclaimed the same linkage of human and divine affairs
when, in his first sermon as patriarch of Constantinople in 428, he
promised Theodosius II "Give me the earth purged of heretics and I
will give you heaven in return. Destroy the heretics with me and I will
destroy the Persians with you" (Socrates, *Eccl.Hist.* 7.29.5); in normal
circumstances this would have seemed unexceptional, but the boast
became notorious once Nestorius emerged as the arch-heretic.

The progress of the Nestorian dispute reveals what emperors could
and could not achieve with regard to the Church. The first Council of
Ephesus in 431 was convened by Theodosius II to allow Nestorius to
rebut accusations concerning his Christology, but the determination of
Cyril of Alexandria, in collaboration with Pope Celestine and his representatives, managed to turn the tables and have Nestorius condemned
in spite of the presence of an imperial commissioner.[50] Theodosius
took some time to accept this rebuff, but in due course he became a
staunch promoter of Cyrilline doctrine and acted to remove supporters of Nestorius, such as Theodoret of Cyrrhus, but he was unable
to control the doctrinal allegiance of Flavian of Constantinople, with
whom he broke off communion during a protracted stand-off over the
archimandrite Eutyches. Theodosius ignored papal remonstrations and

---

[49] Ste. Croix (2006a) 215, 219.
[50] For a clear review of the complicated evidence for developments down to Second
Ephesus, see Millar (2006) esp. Appendices A and B.

gave full support to Dioscorus of Alexandria in a campaign against all
fellow-travellers of Nestorius which culminated in the second Council
of Ephesus (449), but the emperor's sudden death in 450 changed
the doctrinal landscape: his successor Marcian married the Augusta
Pulcheria, they shared Pope Leo's concerns, and Marcian summoned
another Ecumenical Council, eventually held at Chalcedon in 451, to
resolve the issues. Marcian left nothing to chance at this meeting, since
control of proceedings was entrusted to the *magister militum praesentalis*
Anatolius, one of the most powerful men in the empire and a long-
standing supporter of Theodoret.[51] The expected disciplinary and
doctrinal decisions were reached, including the formulation of a new
Creed at Marcian's insistence even though the overwhelming majority of bishops had initially rejected this as unnecessary. This triumph,
duly celebrated in acclamations which likened the imperial pair to
Constantine and Helena, was far from the end of the affair, since in
many of the eastern provinces the Council decisions were rejected as
the work of the devil, and the dispute rumbled on until Justinian's
attempts to impose a solution led to the emergence of a separate anti-
Chalcedonian Church hierarchy.

These discussions represented a massive investment of thought,
money and prestige by a succession of emperors who attempted to
corral independent provincial bishops and monks into line; the only
precedent before Constantine for such a diversion of imperial energy
were the relatively brief sacrifice campaigns and resultant persecution
under Decius and Valerian. It is unlikely to be a coincidence that it
was during this extended struggle, when his decisions provoked resistance in much of the diocese of Oriens, that Theodosius intervened
to consolidate his connection with the Green faction and demonstrate
his preference throughout the empire (see above). Chalcedon showed
that very few church leaders, while exploiting all possible avenues to
influence an emperor, were prepared to resist direct imperial demands.
Open defiance was more likely to come from a prominent, though
probably non-establishment, Christian than anyone else: the dealings
between Ambrose of Milan and Theodosius I are well known, but
may not have been quite so confrontational as the ecclesiastical sources
would want us to believe;[52] at Constantinople there was a comparable

---

[51] For the significance of Anatolius, see Ste. Croix and Whitby (2006).
[52] McLynn (1994) ch. 7.

show-down involving the stylite Daniel who descended from his column at Anaplus to enter the city and curse the usurper Basiliscus, who
eventually prostrated himself, in company with the Patriarch, before the
saint in S. Sophia (*Life of Daniel* 72–84).[53] If Theodosius and Basiliscus
were caught at moments of weakness, the same cannot be said for the
encounter of Justinian and Theodora with the Amidan ascetic Mare
the Solitary (John of Ephesus, *Lives of the Eastern Saints* 36): Mare
visited Constantinople to reproach the emperor over his treatment
of anti-Chalcedonians, and such was his contempt and rudeness that
John thought it better not to record the details of the exchanges; but
at the end of the interview when Theodora attempted to placate him
with a gift of 100 pounds of gold which he might use for charitable
works Mare amazed the audience by throwing the money away and
further cursing the empress—the gesture ensured that the meaning of
his words, which might have been softened in translation from Syriac,
was not lost.[54]

Millar's early Roman emperor was a man constantly responding to
requests, and the work-rate of later emperors did not slacken: the anecdote from Dio (59.6.3) about a woman reproaching Hadrian for being
too busy to be emperor, with which Millar opens his work—and which
already had a long pedigree as he notes—was adapted to Heraclius
in Nicephorus (ch. 4), though here it is the emperor's bodyguard who
attempt to prevent the woman from pressing her petition. There was a
constant stream of correspondence and petitions which required attention, to the extent that Julian could comment to his uncle that he was
having to write the letter himself since it was late evening and all available secretaries were already occupied (*Letter* 9, Wright); while writing to
Libanius in the early stages of the Persian expedition Julian remarked
on the number of letters he had signed and the papers, things which
followed him like his own shadow (*Letter* 58, Wright). In 447 Theodosius
II used the continuous duties of state to explain his failure to transmit

---

[53] On Daniel, see Lane Fox (1997); the abbot Marcellus also emerged from his
monastery to prophesy in the Hippodrome (*Life of Marcellus* 34). A less confrontational
event occurred in 431 when the archimandrite Dalmatius left his monastery for the
first time in 48 years to urge Theodosius II to condemn Nestorius (Nestorius, *Bazaar
of Heraclides* pp. 272–3 [Driver-Hodgson]).

[54] Millar (2006) 97 doubts the use of languages other than Greek and Latin in public exchanges, but Syriac is attested at Theodoret, *HR* 13.7 and *Life of Daniel* 28; the
turbulent Barsauma is another Syriac speaker who had various dealings with important
people, from the empress Eudocia down.

legislation to his western colleague Valentinian III more promptly (*Novel Theod.* 2). With regard to legal matters, Jones paid more attention to the administrative impact of imperial legal decisions than to their composition and propagation, but these processes are now more fully understood thanks to the work of Honoré, Harries, and Matthews.[55] The central role of communication in the empire's operations has been re-emphasised by Millar in his analysis of the well-documented reign of Theodosius II.[56] Emperors, even energetic individuals with a keen interest in administrative matters such as Justinian, did not compose every word in their edicts or other legal pronouncements, and there will have been occasions when legal decisions were taken with scant involvement of the ruler, but the public presentation of laws through their rhetorical preambles was an important part of the construction and dissemination of the imperial image and this material will have been tailored to the current image. Codification of the law was a very substantial undertaking which rulers, both Roman and post-Roman in the West, expected to redound to their eternal credit, rightly so.[57]

Not all requests required legal solution, since many approaches to emperors were for tax relief, gifts after disasters and other demonstrations of imperial munificence, but all such requests, if successful, would have generated the same sort of imperial letter of instruction which underlies the law codes. The emperor sat at the apex of the patronage pyramid and ultimately determined the allocation of offices and other rewards to a wide range of people; most appointments would have been determined well below the level of emperor, but it was always possible for a determined individual to take a particular case to the emperor, as Abinnaeus did when his military command in Egypt was threatened by a rival claimant.[58] Gifts to individuals might take the form of money, in coin whose image and slogans propagated the donor's image,[59] or in more spectacular objects such as the silver Missorium of Theodosius in which the emperor with his sons Arcadius and Honorius is shown presenting symbols of office to a kneeling dignitary: the scene provides

---

[55] Honoré (1978; 1994; 1998); Harries and Wood (1993); Harries (1999); Matthews (2000).
[56] Millar (2006).
[57] On legal developments in the West, see Charles-Edwards (2000).
[58] Bell et al. (1962) 6–12.
[59] See Lenski (2002) 28–32 for Valens' *concordia* coinage which complemented the contemporary rhetoric of Themistius.

a solid and valuable reflection for aspects of Themistius' panegyrics.[60] Earthquakes and enemy invasions were major occasions for the display of imperial generosity: Antioch received 200 pounds of gold after the fire of 526, and a further 500 pounds after the massive quake of 527, with additional help being provided by Justinian when he came to the throne. It is interesting to chart the change in the nature of petitioners. At Autun in 311 a well-educated local councillor stood up, with some trepidation, to welcome Constantine and ask for tax relief; at Antioch in 387 after the Riot of the Statues the educated Libanius and illiterate monks presented alternative arguments for clemency and the preacher John Chrysostom predicted dire consequences, while Bishop Flavian pleaded at court with the help of a choir which serenaded the emperor with the Antiochenes' own laments for their misfortune (Sozomen 7.23.3); in 446/7 it was Bishop Theodoret who requested tax relief for Cyrrhus, and in 526 Patriarch Euphrasius who petitioned Justin for assistance for Antioch.

Generosity was a crucial part of the imperial image, and failure to meet expectations could lead to damaging accusations: Maurice was regarded as avaricious, especially in contrast to the lavish Tiberius whose gifts had emptied imperial treasuries; when Maurice attempted to rationalise military pay in 588, mutinous soldiers tore down imperial images and taunted the emperor as a shopkeeper (Theophylact 3.2.8), while in 602 the Constantinople mob chanted that he was a Marcianist (Theophylact 8.9.3), an allusion to a heresy which rejected normal standards of Christian charity. Julian's failures to conform to expectations prompted condemnation, even from the normally positive Ammianus (22.7): he failed to observe proper behaviour at the celebrations for the start of the consular year, and 'forgot who he was' during a session of the senate in his enthusiasm to greet the philosopher Maximus. The proclamation of the usurper Procopius in 365 was marred by the lack of a proper purple cloak and other problems, so that the occasion became a ludicrous disgrace and symbolised his unsuitability for rule (26.6.15–16). Successful exercise of imperial duties had always involved a substantial element of public performance, as is clear from the criticisms of Claudius' lack of bodily control. Constantius, no favourite of Ammianus, is yet praised for preserving the *cothurnus*, which means 'tragic buskin', of imperial majesty, with the word nicely capturing the

---

[60] Discussion in MacCormack (1981) 214–20.

performative nature of the position (Ammianus 21.16.1). Historians such as Ammianus and Malalas gave attention to the personal characteristics of rulers, with some reason.

5. *Powers and Limitations*

Although Jones categorised emperors as possessing absolute powers (321), he also accepted some limitations, which might be personal, so that the descendants of Theodosius I could be said to have "reigned rather than ruled the empire" (173), or structural in the form of "powers behind the throne" (341–7). Jones fully recognised that even the most engaged of emperors acted within a particular human context, so that the close entourage was of considerable significance in determining imperial decisions; he reviewed at some length (344–6) two famous instances of influence from the early fifth century, the petition about attacking pagans from Porphyry of Gaza who managed to circumvent the reluctance of Arcadius with the help of a eunuch chamberlain, the empress Eudoxia and the man carrying the infant Theodosius II after his baptism, and the schedule of bribes expended by Cyril of Alexandria in winning over senior officials, their wives, and the staff of the bedchambers of Theodosius and Pulcheria to support his doctrinal position in the aftermath of First Ephesus.[61]

Empresses and other female members of the imperial family were clearly figures of considerable importance, and their role might be highlighted by those keen to castigate the spectre of female domination, but it is worth reflecting on quite how great their influence was. Theodosius II is portrayed as a classic weak ruler, with his palace dominated by the pious ladies in an image approved by the church historians Socrates and Sozomen, but first his wife Eudocia succumbed to scandal and withdrew to Jerusalem, and then his sister Pulcheria lost out in competition for influence with the chamberlain Chrysaphius. Theodora is believed to have been able to support anti-Chalcedonians despite Justinian's religious preferences, but it appears that Justinian made no change to her arrangements after her death. Even Sophia, briefly *de facto* ruler during the insanity of Justin II, could not sustain this position and within a year had to accept the elevation of Tiberius as

---

[61] Cf. also Kelly (2004) ch. 4, esp. 165–81.

Caesar. Determined women could be obstacles, as Lupicina Euphemia was to Justinian's plan to marry Theodora or Sophia over the presence in the palace of Tiberius' wife, but emperors could usually manipulate rivalries among their closest entourage, including their womenfolk, to stay in charge.

Eunuch power was an extension of that of palace women, and attracted the same sort of criticism.[62] Ammianus mordantly observed that Constantius II had considerable influence with his eunuch chamberlain Eusebius (18.4.3), while Eutropius, the dominant power at Arcadius' court for three years, was attacked by Claudian at Rome and, after his fall, by John Chrysostom in S. Sophia.[63] Although eunuchs owed their prominence, in part, to their lack of family connections, they may have been harder to dislodge by a reigning emperor—but at the same time they were particularly vulnerable at times of succession, when a new ruler might settle old scores, as Marcian did with Chrysaphius, and Justin I with Amantius.

Beyond their immediate entourage an emperor had to dominate the senior administrators and the bureaucracy. There has been much discussion of administrative corruption,[64] which Jones identified among the causes of imperial decline (1053–8), and officials could prevent accurate information from reaching the emperor, as the unfortunate inhabitants of Tripolitania discovered when attempting to report problems to Valentinian I (Ammianus 28.6).[65] It was impossible for emperors to control what happened at lower levels, but they could ensure that senior figures paid attention to their wishes through the regular turn-over of personnel and through maintaining the empire as a polycracy of competitive positions, with themselves as the ultimate arbiters of success and failure.[66] Since official duties were not firmly delimited it was possible for emperors to reward loyal service with a *de facto* expansion of duties, thereby occasioning the sort of administrative rebalancing which John Lydus bemoaned as the judicial responsibilities of the Praetorian Prefecture, in which he served, were eroded.[67] This

---

[62] On eunuchs, see Hopkins (1978); Scholten (1995) esp. ch. 6.

[63] Matthews (1989) 274–77; Liebeschuetz (1990) ch. 7–9; in general, Scholten (1995).

[64] At length and negatively: MacMullen (1988); recently and more sensitively: Kelly (2004) esp. ch. 2, 4.

[65] See Matthews (1989) 383–7.

[66] Kelly (1998) 150–5, 169–75; Barnish, Lee and Whitby (2000) 200–3.

[67] Summary of his career in Kelly (2004) ch. 1.

could work provided that the emperor retained a pool of compliant individuals in the capital, and the only ruler who seems to have managed to destroy this resource of support was Phocas during a reign marked by repeated plots and extensive purges of senior officials and courtiers. At any time the fall from power of a dominant figure, such as Cyrus of Panopolis in 441, and John the Cappadocian in 541, would have provided a potent reminder to others of the fragility of their position and dependence upon the emperor; John, indeed, who had already experienced one dismissal during the Nika riot, seems to have attempted to safeguard his position by striking up an alliance with the Green Faction, but this did not preserve him.

A key issue for emperors was how to ensure that their commands passed through the immediate entourage at court and across the considerable geographical extent and diversity of the empire to achieve the intended impact. It is known that there were areas where the emperors' writ did not run, for example mountainous Isauria until, perhaps, Anastasius at last brought this within imperial control, or the war-torn Balkans in the late sixth century, but even in settled areas local powers might attempt to circumvent instructions, as appears to have occurred in the dispute over Aphrodito's tax privilege of *autopragia*.[68] The bureaucracy itself might be reluctant to implement imperial wishes, as Anastasius suspected when arranging the termination of the Chrysargyron tax, which he believed officials would reinstate at the first opportunity because of the financial opportunities it presented (Evagrius 3.39). Repetition of legislation has been seen as one indication of the limits to imperial power, and there are certainly occasions when emperors did fail to impose their wishes, as the sequence of recruitment legislation relating to senatorial estates issued by Honorius indicates (*CTh* 7.13.12–14), but it has also been argued that repetition is a sign that legislation was working, since individuals were concerned to clarify its impact.[69]

An ideal for emperors was a fusion of the ambitions and interests of provincial elites and the imperial centre. Emperors had to maintain influence over such people, as western emperors spectacularly failed to do in the early fifth century; a Justinianic law about private armed forces

---

[68] Bell (1944); cf. also the troubles of Abinnaeus: Bell et al. (1962) 6–12.
[69] Harries (1999) ch. 4.

in the province of Honorias reflects a similar threat in the East.[70] The existence in the West of the ancient Senate created a serious challenge, even if the body did not wield real power: it embraced the major land-owners and possessed a strong corporate identity which tended to dissuade many of its members from sustained engagement in the imperial administration—office was a diversion from other business.[71] In the East the rapid expansion of the new Constantinopolitan Senate in the fourth century was achieved through imperial patronage, so that new arrivals owed loyalty to the emperor as well as provided links between centre and periphery. By the sixth century, when two centuries of operation might have been weakening these bonds, even though it is difficult to identify many senatorial families with membership across several generations, Justinian seems to have exploited the device of honorific titles such as patrician to attach to himself the more ambitious and wealthy of his subjects. This process may have made actual office holding less attractive, since equal status could be obtained without the labour, but the benefits to the emperor outweighed this possible danger.

Conclusion

Jones deliberately adopted a narrow view of what mattered for imperial power and action. He was concerned to investigate the structures of empire rather than the personal performances located within those structures; as a result, his *Later Roman Empire* does not attempt to capture the nature of imperial action. Jones' all-powerful ruler sat at the apex of the administrative pyramid whose lower operations constituted the focus of his analysis; even under weak emperors, who 'reigned rather than ruled', the system remained the same with the imperial position simply being appropriated by a general or, occasionally, official. By contrast, subsequent studies assume a regular circulation of power with the emperor as one among several competing elements. Emperors, even the most dynamic and successful, have to work hard at wielding power, bolstering their position with theatrical ceremonies and splendid surroundings, disseminating their preferred images through panegyrics,

---

[70] Feissel and Kaygusuz (1985).
[71] Matthews (1975).

correspondence, icons and coins, and restraining potential competitors by the turnover of appointments, the occasional spectacular disgrace, and active exploitation of patronage networks, which included the noisy circus factions whose prominence is one of the distinctive features of the later fifth and sixth centuries. As a result, the range of issues to be considered in relation to the emperor, and the diversity of material which needs to be brought to bear, make the topic much more interesting and challenging.

The narrowness of Jones' vision is undoubtedly a weakness, which, for example, constrains his analysis of the decline of the empire (Chapter XXV): the power of the imperial image and the ideology of a Roman empire are significant factors in explaining why it was that the bishop of Nisibis reported that the emperor Constantius had been seen patrolling their walls during the Persian siege of 350 (*Chronicon Paschale* p. 358), whereas at Thessalonica in 479 the citizens tore down imperial statues and handed the city keys to their bishop when they suspected that Zeno was about to quarter Gothic troops in their city (Malchus 20.1–19). However, the broader perspectives which Bury had noted in his 1923 passage on the emperor, and which have subsequently been developed, would have distracted Jones from the aspects of his project to which he could bring unparalleled strengths, namely the evaluation and interpretation of literary evidence, and in particular the close reading of legal texts. As a result, the project would have produced a very different volume, and perhaps one that would not have proved so influential or stood the test of time so well. It is most unlikely, in the absence of Jones' investigation of the structures of empire in *Later Roman Empire*, that the successor scholars who have advanced our understanding of the emperor's position and role, even MacCormack who does not acknowledge the debt, would have been able to develop their ideas so effectively.

Bibliography

Bardill J. (2004) *Brickstamps of Constantinople* (Oxford 2004)

Barnish S., Lee D. and Whitby Michael (2000) "Government and Administration", in Cameron, Averil et al. (2000) 164–206

Bell H.I. (1944) "An Egyptian Village in the Age of Justinian", *JHS* 64 (1944) 21–36

Bell H.I., Martin V., Turner E.G., and van Berchem D. (1962) edd. *The Abinnaeus Archive, Papers of a Roman Officer in the Reign of Constantius II* (Oxford 1962)

Bury J.B. (1923) *History of the Later Roman Empire from the Death of Theodosius I to the Death of Justinian* (London 1923)

Brown P. (1992), *Power and Persuasion in Late Antiquity: towards a Christian Empire* (Madison 1992)

Cameron Alan (1970) *Claudian* (Oxford 1970)

—— (1973) *Porphyrius the Charioteer* (Oxford 1973)

—— (1976) *Circus Factions, Blues and Greens at Rome and Byzantium* (Oxford 1976)

Cameron Alan and Long, J. (1993) *Barbarians and Politics at the Court of Arcadius* (Berkeley 1993)

Cameron Averil (1976) *Flavius Crescontius Corippus, In Laudem Iustini Augusti minoris* (London 1976)

—— (1977) "Early Byzantine *Kaiserkritik*: two case histories", *BMGS* 3 (1977) 1–17; reprinted in *idem* (1981) *Continuity and Change in Sixth-century Byzantium* (Aldershot 1981) IX

—— (1985) *Procopius* (London 1985)

Cameron Averil, and Garnsey P. (1998) edd. *Cambridge Ancient History XIII,* 2nd ed., *The Late Empire: A.D. 337–425* (Cambridge 1998)

Cameron Averil, Ward-Perkins B. and Whitby Michael (2000) edd. *The Cambridge Ancient History XIV,* 2nd ed., *Late Antiquity: Empire and Successors A.D. 425–600* (Cambridge 2000)

Charles-Edwards T. (2000) "Law in the Western Kingdoms between the Fifth and the Seventh Century", in Cameron Averil et al. (2000) 260–87

Croke B. (1978) "The Date and Circumstances of Marcian's Death", *Byz* 58 (1978) 5–9; reprinted in *idem* (1992), *Christian Chronicles and Byzantine History, 5th–6th Centuries* (Aldershot 1992) VIII

——. (2001) *Count Marcellinus and his Chronicle,* (Oxford 2001)

——. (2005) "Justinian's Constantinople", in *The Cambridge Companion to the Age of Justinian,* ed. Maas, M. (Cambridge 2005) 60–86

Croke B. and Crow J. (1983) "Procopius and Dara", *JRS* 73 (1983) 143–59

Crow J. and Bayliss R. (2004) "Water for the Queen of Cities: a review of recent research in the Byzantine and early Ottoman water supply of Constantinople", *Basilissa* 1 (2004) 28–49

Dagron G. (1974) *Naissance d'une capitale: Constantinople et ses institutions de 330 à 451* (Paris 1974)

Errington R.M. (2006) *Roman Imperial Policy from Julian to Theodosius* (Chapel Hill 2006)

Feissel D. and Kaygusuz I. (1985) "Un Mandement impérial du VIᵉ siècle dans une inscription d'Hadrianoupolis d'Honoriade", *Travaux et Mémoires* 9 (1985) 397–419

Harries J. (1999) *Law and Empire in Late Antiquity* (Cambridge 1999)

Harries J. and Wood I. (1993) edd. *The Theodosian Code. Studies in the Imperial Law of Late Antiquity* (London 1993)

Harrison M. (1989) *A Temple for Byzantium* (London 1989)

Heather P. and Moncur D. (2001) *Politics, Philosophy and Empire in the Fourth Century. Select Orations of Themistius* (Liverpool 2001)

Honoré T. (1978) *Tribonian* (London 1978)

——. (1994) *Emperors and Lawyers* (Oxford 1994)

——. (1998) *Law in the Crisis of Empire, 370–455 A.D.: The Theodosian Dynasty and its Quaestors* (Oxford 1998)

Hopkins K. (1978) *Conquerors and Slaves* (Cambridge 1978)

Janin R. (1964) *Constantinople byzantine: développement urbain et répertoire topographique,* 2nd ed. (Paris 1964)

Jones A.H.M. (1962) "The Constitutional Position of Odoacer and Theoderic", *JRS* 52 (1962) 107–32, reprinted in *idem* (1974) *The Roman Economy: Studies in Ancient Economic and Administrative History,* ed. P.A. Brunt (Oxford 1974)

——. (1964) *The Later Roman Empire 284–602: A Social, Economic, and Administrative Survey*, 3 vols (Oxford 1964), reprinted in two volumes with continuous pagination (Oxford 1973)

Jones A.H.M, Martindale J.R. and Morris J. (1971) *The Prosopography of the Later Roman Empire I, A.D. 260–395* (Cambridge 1971)

Kelly C.M. (1998) "Emperors, Government and Bureaucracy", in Cameron, Averil et al. (1998) 138–83

——. (2004) *Ruling the Later Roman Empire* (Cambridge, Mass. 2004)

Killerich B. (1998) *The Obelisk Base in Constantinople: Court, Art and Imperial Ideology* (Rome 1998)

Lane Fox R. (1997) "The *Life of Daniel*", in *Portraits: Biographical Representation in the Greek and Latin Literature of the Roman Empire*, edd. M.J. Edwards and S. Swain, S. (Oxford 1997) 175–225

Lenski N. (2002) *Failure of Empire. Valens and the Roman State in the Fourth Century A.D.* (Berkeley 2002)

Liebeschuetz J.H.W.G. (1990) *Barbarians and Bishops. Army Church and State in the Age of Arcadius and Chrysostom* (Oxford 1990)

——. (1998) "The Circus Factions", *Convegno per Santo Mazzarino, Roma 9–11 maggio 1991, Saggi di Storia Antica* 13 (1998) 163–85

——. (2001) *The Decline and Fall of the Roman City* (Oxford 2001)

MacCormack S. (1981) *Art and Ceremony in Late Antiquity* (Berkeley 1981)

MacCoull L.S.B. (1988) *Dioscorus of Aphrodito, his Work and his World* (Berkeley 1988)

MacMullen R. (1988) *Corruption and the Decline of Rome* (New Haven 1988)

Mango C. (1958) *The Brazen House: A Study of the Vestibule of the Imperial Palace of Constantinople* (Copenhagen 1958)

——. (1985; rev. ed. 1990) *Le Développement urbain de Constantinople* (Paris 1985)

Mango C. and Dagron G. (1997) *Constantinople and its Hinterland* (Aldershot 1997)

Martindale J. (1980) *The Prosopography of the Later Roman Empire II, A.D. 395–527* (Cambridge 1980)

——. (1992) *The Prosopography of the Later Roman Empire III, A.D. 527–641* (Cambridge 1992)

Matthews J.F. (1975) *Western Aristocracies and Imperial Court A.D. 364–425* (Oxford 1975)

——. (1989) *The Roman Empire of Ammianus* (London 1989)

——. (2000) *Laying Down the Law: A Study of the Theodosian Code* (New Haven 2000)

McCormick M. (1986) *Eternal Victory. Triumphal Rulership in Late Antiquity, Byzantium, and the Early Medieval West* (Cambridge 1986)

——. (2000) "Emperor and Court", in Cameron Averil et al. (2000) 135–63

McLynn N. (1994) *Ambrose of Milan, Church and Court in a Christian Capital* (Berkeley 1994)

Millar F. (1977; reprint with afterword 1992) *The Emperor in the Roman World* (London 1977)

——. (1982) "Emperors, Frontiers and Foreign Relations, 31 B.C. to A.D. 378", *Britannia* 13 (1982) 1–23

——. (1988) "Government and Diplomacy in the Roman Empire during the First Three Centuries", *International History Review* 10 (1988) 345–77

——. (2006) *A Greek Roman Empire. Power and Belief under Theodosius II, 408–50* (Berkeley 2006)

Nixon C.E.V. and Rodgers B.S. (1994) *In Praise of Later Roman Emperors: The "Panegyrici Latini"* (Berkeley and Los Angeles 1994)

Rees R. (2002) *Layers of Loyalty in Latin Panegyric A.D. 289–307* (Oxford 2002)

Roueché C. (1984) "Acclamations in the Late Roman Empire: new evidence from Aphrodisias", *JRS* 74 (1984) 181–99

——. (1989) *Aphrodisias in Late Antiquity, JRS* Monograph 5 (London 1989)

Russell D.A. and Wilson N.G. (1981) *Menander Rhetor* (Oxford 1981)

Scholten H. (1995) *Der Eunuch in Kaisernähe: zur politischen und sozialen Bedeutung des praepositus sacri cubiculi im 4. und 5. Jahrhundert n. Chr.* (Frankfurt 1995)

Ste. Croix G.E.M. de (2006a) "Heresy, Schism and Persecution in the Later Roman Empire", in *idem* (2006b) 201–29

—— (2006b) *Christian Persecution, Martyrdom and Orthodoxy*, edd. Michael Whitby and J. Streeter (Oxford 2006)

Ste. Croix G.E.M. de and Whitby Michael (2006) "The Council of Chalcedon", in Ste. Croix (2006b) 259–319

Stein E. (1949/1959) *Histoire du Bas-Empire*, vol. i: *De l'état romain à l'état byzantin (284–476)*, èdition française par Jean-Rémy Palanque (Paris 1959); vol. ii: *De la disparition de l'empire d'occident à la mort de Justinien (467–565)*, publié par Jean-Rémy Palanque (Paris 1949)

Talbot Rice D. (1958) *The Great Palace of the Byzantine Emperors. Second Report* (Edinburgh 1958)

Tinnefeld F. (1971) *Kategorien der Kaiserkritik in der byzantinischen Historiographie von Prokop bis Niketas Choniates* (Munich 1971)

Vanderspoel J. (1995) *Themistius and the Imperial Court: Oratory, Civic Duty, and Paideia from Constantius to Theodosius* (Ann Arbor 1995)

Whitby Mary (1985) "The Occasion of Paul the Silentiary's *Ekphrasis* of S. Sophia", *CQ*, NS, 35 (1985) 215–28

—— (1987) "On the Omission of a Ceremony in Mid-sixth Century Constantinople: Candidati, Curopalatus, Silentiarii, Excubitores and Others", *Historia* 36 (1987) 462–88

Whitby Michael (1986) "Procopius' description of Dara *(Buildings* II.1–3)", *BAR International Series* 297 (1986) 737–83

—— (1987) "Notes on some Justinianic Constructions", *BNJ* 23 (1987) 89–112

—— (1999) "The Violence of the Circus Factions", in *Organised Crime in Antiquity*, ed. K. Hopwood (London 1999) 229–53

—— (2005) "War and State in Late Antiquity; some economic and political connections", in *Krieg—Gesellschaft—Institutionen. Beiträge zu einer vergleichenden Kriegsgeschichte*, edd. B. Meissner, O. Schmitt and M. Sommer (Berlin 2005) 355–85

—— (2006) "Factions, Bishops, Violence and Urban Decline", in *Die spätantike Stadt*, edd. J.-U. Krause and C. Witschel *(Historia Einzelschrift* 190, Stuttgart 2006) 441–61

Wiemer H.-U. (2004) "Aklamationen im spätrömischen Reich. Zur Typologie und Funktion eines Kommunikationsrituals", *Archiv fuur Kulturgeschichte* 86 (2004) 27–73

CHAPTER FIVE

RUNNING THE EMPIRE:
BUREAUCRATS, CURIALS, AND SENATORS

Peter Heather

A.H.M. Jones' account of central and local governmental institutions, of their interaction, and of the men who ran them is to be found scattered across three and a half chapters of the *Later Roman Empire*—XII, XV, XVI, and part of XIX—altogether about one hundred and fifty pages of text. These come fully equipped with the normal, highly dense, body of supporting evidence, sometimes including further discussion in the relevant notes in Volume III.[1] Trying, in one short paper, to discuss Jones' collected thoughts on bureaucrats, curials, and senators has thus an epic summarise-Proust type quality. But, for all the scale and apparent disparity of the task, its sub-topics are deeply interrelated and form one core element in Jones' understanding of the late imperial period. For that reason they are worth treating together, even if full justice cannot be done to every interpretative nuance.

1. *The* Later Roman Empire

In Chapter XII of his epic work, Jones set himself the task of exploring the nature and quality of the central administrative body of the late Empire. His sub-headings were 'Centre', 'Provinces', 'Tenure of Offices', 'Choice of Officers', 'Suffragium', 'Salaries and Extortion', 'Centralisation', and, finally, 'Efficiency'. They give a clear indication not only of the shape of his treatment, but also of some of the key pillars of his overall interpretation. The first two sections are essentially descriptive, analyzing the evidence for the developing functions of the different administrative bureaus by which the Empire was run in the

---

[1] Chapter XII comprises 44 pages, XV another 39, XVI a further 38, and 22 pages of Chapter XIX are devoted to *curiales*. The relevant notes occupy a further 75 pages of Volume III.

centre and out in the provinces. At the centre, the tasks of the *Quaestor* and *Magister Officiorum* attracted Jones' particular attention, together with those of the new style Praetorian Prefecture denuded in the late Empire of its active military functions, though it still retained responsibilities for army supply, and charged with the responsibility of overseeing provincial administration. The corresponding section on the provinces has two themes: gathering and analyzing the evidence for the process by which provinces were steadily fragmented into smaller units in the late Roman period, and charting the accompanying demilitarisation of the gubernatorial office.[2]

The task of description complete, Jones then attempted to build up a picture of the general character of the late Roman bureaucracy, in a series of sub-sections whose approach was substantially more analytical. He began by looking at the length of tenure of office enjoyed by top-level administrators. For many bureaus, surviving information is far too incomplete to offer much insight, but the few jobs where relatively complete *fasti* can be reconstructed, together with all the other available evidence of a more qualitative kind, overwhelmingly suggest that tenures of office were short: often no more than a year or so. This led Jones to the conclusion that those in charge of the running of the Empire were surely not expert administrators, carefully schooled in their tasks. This rather negative judgment sets the tone for the remainder of the chapter, whose subsequent sub-sections marshal the evidence to show that top administrative careers were not open to men of talent, but drew almost exclusively from aristocratic circles, that the corrupt buying and selling of office was rife thanks to the institutionalisation of payments for preferment (*suffragia*), that administrative salaries were low and the tendency for officers to engage in extortion correspondingly high, and that the whole edifice was highly—indeed overly—centralised.[3]

The chapter culminates in a discussion of administrative efficiency which draws together the evidence Jones had surveyed to make a series of damning observations. Social order was maintained, justice administered, and taxes were raised—the three great tasks of the bureaucracy—but only just! Inefficiency and incompetence dogged the entire administrative process. The whole bureaucratic edifice, he stresses,

---

[2] Jones (1964a) II, 366–77.
[3] *Ibid.*, II, 377–83 (lengths of tenure); 383–90 (choice of officers); 391–6 (*suffragium*); 396–401 salaries and extortion; 401–6 (centralisation).

was not rationally planned. There were no clear lines of authority and jurisdiction which meant that officers were always interfering in one another's business. Aristocratic amateur officers, holding their jobs for no more than a year at a time, were incapable of fulfilling their tasks properly. Pathetically small salaries could not but generate 'low standards of public morality', as demonstrated by extortion and *suffragium*.

And, overall, a ridiculous degree of centralisation combined with these other faults to create a kind of sclerotic chaos:

> In the judicial sphere the central courts of appeal were congested with business, and the long delays and heavy expenses imposed on the appellants proved a virtual denial of justice to any but the wealthy. In finance and general administration centralised control imposed serious delays and demanded an ever-increasing bulk of paper work and a corresponding increase in the number of clerks to deal with it. The machine tended always to work more slowly and to become more expensive to run. Moreover more and more routine work was piled on the central ministers and above all on the emperor himself. It would have been impossible for the most conscientious emperor to read all the papers that he was expected to sign, and he was thus placed at the mercy of his ministers and clerks, who, as many imperial constitutions testify, unscrupulously exploited their opportunities to obtain his signature for documents contravening the regulations which he had himself enacted.[4]

In all of this, Jones makes not the slightest reference to the origins of the frame of reference by which he was judging the late Roman bureaucratic edifice. Given his own life experience as a wartime bureaucrat, however, there can be little doubt that he had the British civil service of the mid-twentieth century firmly in mind, without us needing to suppose that Jones thought this later structure entirely devoid of the problems he identified in its earlier Roman counterpart.[5]

Having looked at the overall pattern of late Roman administration and the nature of its top officials in Chapter XII, Jones eventually turned his attention in Chapter XVI to the civil service: the men filling the bulk of the posts in the administrative hierarchy—central and provincial—and their capacity to undertake the tasks they faced. Although physically separate from it, the two chapters are very much counterparts, and have the same basic structure. As with Chapter XII, Jones begins

---

[4] *Ibid.*, 406–10; the quotation is from 410.
[5] See the papers of Sarantis (ch. 1) 20–1 and Garnsey (ch. 2) 39 earlier in this volume.

Chapter XVI with analytical description. After a brief discussion of its origins, he launches first into an analysis of the growth and tasks of the different offices of the central administration: the *comitatus* gathered around the Emperor. A first section deals with the Sacred Bedchamber, before moving on to the Palatine ministries: the notaries, the *scrinia*, the *agentes in rebus*, the *largitionales* and the *privatiani*. He then does the same job with provincial administration. He begins, quite naturally, with the office of the Praetorian Prefect and its separate financial and judicial sub-sections, before moving on to the rather anomalous Urban Prefects of Rome and Constantinople, and then finally to that great workhorse of imperial government in the localities: the offices of the provincial governors. The latter answered directly to their relevant Praetorian Prefecture and, like them, comprised separate financial and judicial officials.[6]

Again directly following the approach of Chapter XII, Jones then turns his attention to more general issues of interpretation, seeking to establish the general character of this Roman civil service. And for Jones, this was no small question. Having established to his own satisfaction that the later Empire was deeply (indeed irrationally) centralised, it clearly mattered how well the instrument of that centralisation—the imperial bureaucracy—handled its tasks. He makes all this entirely explicit at the start of Chapter XVI:

> The later Roman Empire was before all things a bureaucratic state. Civil servants played a vital role in all departments of government, in the drafting and circulation of laws and ordinances and the administration of justice, in the recruitment and supply of the armies, and above all in the operation of the vast and complicated fiscal machine... Without its civil servants the whole complicated machine of government which held the vast empire together would have collapsed.[7]

The implicit sub-headings he uses to establish whether the late Roman bureaucracy was fit for its purpose are 'entrance payments', 'numbers', 'absenteeism', 'pay and corruption', and 'efficiency'. As is immediately apparent, they are the same as—or directly mimic—the headings he used to provide a frame of reference for interrogating the capacities of the top level of the bureaucracy, and he is essentially asking the same

---

[6] Jones (1964a) II, 563–6 (origins); 566–72 (sacred bedchamber); 572–86 (palatine ministries); 586–92 (Praetorian and Urban Prefects); 592–601 (offices of provincial governors).

[7] *Ibid.*, II, 563.

big question. To what extent was the late Roman bureaucracy staffed by competent professionals, well-trained to perform sensible tasks?

Just like the senior administrators, the lower levels of the governmental machine are found deeply wanting. Too many of its cadres got their jobs because they paid for them or had influential friends, rather than because they had the necessary abilities. There was a structural tendency for the numbers of bureaucrats to keep on growing, not because they were required for the tasks in hand, but because the perquisites of office were highly desirable. Absenteeism was rife, pay low and corruption high, and the overall structure was thoroughly unprofessional and highly inefficient. As Jones himself put it in a famous summing up:

> The Roman civil service suffered from all the faults of an overripe bureaucracy. It was intensely conservative. It preserved curious old titles and grades, going back to the Principate and even the Republic... [John Lydus'] resistance to change is typical of the service. The service was also... excessively devoted to forms and much addicted to 'papyrasserie'... and revelled in files, daybooks, indices and the like... The multiplication of paper work undoubtedly choked the administrative machine, and greatly increased the cost of justice... The service was riven by departmental jealousies, mainly concerned with their jurisdictional privileges and with the allocation of work—and the fees which it brought... The service was excessively rigid in structure, allowing for no transfers of misfits or promotion by merit.[8]

In short, the resources of the empire were being wasted in supporting a governmental machine that did not do its job well and was staffed by a multiplicity of 'idle mouths'.[9]

If Chapters XII and XVI form the bulk of Jones' explicit account of the late Roman imperial governmental machine, parts of Chapters XV and XIX are also relevant. Chapter XV is devoted to 'Senators and *Honorati*', charting the evolution of marks of status at the top end of society.[10] Much of it addresses other concerns, but there is one central theme which is entirely relevant to this paper. For what Jones documents with total clarity is a fundamental change in the nature of the senatorial order in the late imperial period. Towards the end of the

---

[8] *Ibid.*, II, 601–2.
[9] *Ibid.*, II, 601–6.
[10] The sub-headings used in Chapter XV are: aristocratic ideal (523–4); *ordo equester*, *comitiva* and senate (525–30); admission and precedence (530–5); privileges and burdens (535–42); value of rank (543–5); social composition (545–52); geographical origins (552–4); wealth (554–7); *otium* (557–62).

third century, senatorial status still largely remained the preserve of an hereditary caste of landowners concentrated around the city of Rome. By the year 400, this had changed out of all recognition. For one thing, a parallel senate had been established for Roman elites of the eastern Mediterranean in the new imperial capital of Constantinople, and, from sometime in the mid-fourth century, which of the two senatorial bodies an individual would belong to was decided on purely geographical grounds. If your *origo* lay in the east, you became a member of the Senate of Constantinople, if in the west the Senate of Rome. In other words, from this point on the bodies were being treated as exact equals.

Even more important than this major development, however, was the revolution which transformed how an individual qualified for senatorial status. Here Jones put together the developing story largely from evidence collected from the law codes, supplemented to some extent by fourth-century letter collections. As the central bureaucracy expanded, emperors looked to reward their servants with appropriately significant grants of high status. From Diocletian onwards, the top grade of equestrian rank—the *perfectissimate*—became very widely used as a reward for top civil servants. Constantine's creation of the *comitiva* took the process further and grade inflation set in, so that, by the second half of the fourth century, senatorial rather than even top equestrian status became the award generally granted to leading civil servants: upon retirement, if not during actual service. A key moment, as Jones carefully documented, was a law on precedence drawn up by Valentinian and Valens in 368 which systematised all the previously separate strands of high status into one trajectory towards greatness, all of which culminated in grants of senatorial rank.[11]

The result of these processes by the end of the fourth century was a new senatorial elite. Descendents of old senatorial families continued to acquire senatorial status by descent, but, in each generation, many new men were acquiring it by bureaucratic service. And, in fact, there were now so many senators of one kind or another that the rank itself had to be sub-divided into three (the law of Valentinian and Valens again), and it quickly became the case that the top two grades (*spectabilis* and *illustris* ranks) could only be acquired by active office-holding. Even the

---

[11] This key piece of legislation survives in a series of fragments in the Theodosian Code: 6.7.1; 9.1; 11.1; 14.1; 22.4; cf. Jones (1964a) I, 142–4.

grandest of familial origins would now bring only the inferior *clarissimus* rank. As to the source of these new senators, many came from old provincial curial stock, motivated both by "the common human desire to have a handle to one's name and take precedence over one's neighbours" and an increasing determination to escape the burden of curial duties. At the same time, there is evidence that some top civil servants emerged from really obscure social origins. Jones summarised his findings thus: "The new hierarchy effectively transformed the aristocracy from one of birth into one of service".[12]

The final pieces of the jigsaw are given full treatment in Chapter XIX, devoted to the *curiales*, members of the town councils who ran the city territories, the characteristic unit of local government in the late Empire. This chapter again has many themes, but bears on the subject matter of this paper because former curials provided many of the recruits for the burgeoning offices of the central civil service. A particular concern of this chapter, therefore, is to explore the motivations behind this transfer of allegiance, picking up a topic that had already been explored to some extent in Chapter XV. Chapter XIX again mentions all the opportunities open to the curial who found his way into the imperial civil service, but puts the emphasis much more on the deteriorating conditions facing the curial class. Here Jones was analyzing the huge amount of legislation about so-called 'curial flight', collected particularly in book 12, chapter 1 of the Theodosian Code:

> From this tangled mass of legislation, two points emerge clearly, that the imperial government considered the maintenance of the city councils essential to the well-being of the Empire, and that many members of the city councils strongly disliked their position.

For Jones, the key points were that imperial government was heaping an increasing number of more onerous tasks on the curial class, particularly in the field of tax collection, while at the same time overseeing a process which saw them progressively lose social status, especially in relation to the *honorati*, the new elite of top equestrian and senatorial civil servants. For Jones, it was not at all surprising, therefore, that curials should have sought to escape their status, a process which only made the general situation worse. Richer curials were better able, through their wealth and connections, to escape council membership, leaving a poorer

---

[12] Jones (1964a) II, Chapter XV. The quotations are from 543 and 529.

rump to shoulder the burdens. The situation deteriorated further when senatorial rather than equestrian rank became the customary prize of bureaucratic office. For equestrians were exempt from curial duties only for their own lifetimes, whereas senators of Rome or Constantinople passed on hereditary exemptions to their descendents.[13]

In the pages of these four chapters, therefore, Jones carefully constructs a composite picture of how the late Empire was run, and what made it different from its predecessors. Above all, it was a much more centralised state, in which the autonomy of local city government had been deeply eroded. This necessitated recruiting and rewarding a large body of civil servants, which undermined the status of the old curial elites of the Empire. At the same time, salaries were so low, procedures so cumbersome, and lines of authority so muddled, that there was huge room for corruption and inefficiency at every level of the system. Jones, one gets the feeling, was both impressed and appalled by what his research and analysis had brought into view. But how did his picture of how the late Empire was run compare to what had gone before?

2. *The* Later Roman Empire *in Context*

To set Jones' achievement properly in context, the true measure of greatness is where did he find the subject area and where did he leave it. Peter Brown's long review of 1967 provides an excellent point of departure. As Brown observes, understandings of the later Roman Empire before Jones were dominated by a set of 'big' ideas which had achieved pretty much canonical status. Equally important, these idea sets had achieved their status via what were really interpretative essays rather than on the basis of full-scale, thoroughly professional pieces of historical research. Many of the same ideas can even be found in the only 'big' work on the later Roman Empire which we know Jones to have admired, that of Ernest Stein.[14]

Before Jones, there were in fact no full-scale analytical works devoted to the late imperial period in English or any other language. Decent narrative histories were to be had, and these obviously had analytical

---

[13] *Ibid.*, II, Chapter XIX. The main topics of relevance are: civic finance (732–4); the *curiales* (737–57); the decline of the councils (757–63). The quotation is from p. 748.

[14] Brown (1967). On Jones and Stein, see the papers of Garnsey (ch. 2) 28–32 and Rebenich (ch. 3) 49–53 above.

points to make, but if you wanted an interpretative overview, racy but rather insubstantial essays dominated the bill of fare. Pre-eminent among these was Rostovtzeff's *The Social and Economic History of the Roman World*, first published in 1926. This was in overall terms hardly an insubstantial piece of work, but Rostovtzeff's thoughts on the late Empire were a postscript to the main focus of his book. They were not based on the same depth of research and were profoundly influenced by the author's responses to the upheavals of his own adult lifetime. Otherwise, interpretative overview chapters could be found in the first editions of the first volume of *The Cambridge Medieval History* and the last volume of *The Cambridge Ancient History*, the former published in 1911, the latter in 1939.[15] Between them, these treatments created an overarching framework within which the later Empire was understood. Several key elements of this structure were directly relevant to the subject of this paper.

Perhaps above all, every one of these works shared the view that the self-governing city state was the great institution of the ancient world, and hence the institution whose health or otherwise most needed to be considered and measured. A great theme running through the essays on late Roman history of the early twentieth century was to highlight the evidence suggesting that the period had seen a substantial decline in the fortunes of the curials, sometimes rather misleadingly labelled the urban middle class or bourgeoisie. Since, in this worldview, they were the key component of the most important institution of antiquity, a seeming decline in their fortunes, whatever the cause, was sufficient to cast a pall of doom and gloom over understandings of the period. Most assumed that economic problems were at the heart of this decline, although it could also be argued that the destruction of paganism played a substantial role in undermining the unity and coherence of the old urban communities.[16]

Operating in parallel to this much-lamented decline of the city, the early twentieth-century commentators were convinced that the obviously

---

[15] The works I have used to form some estimate of the state of the discipline prior to Jones are: Bury (1923); Rostovtzeff (1926); Stein (1959); Vinogradoff (1911) and Reid (1911) from vol. 1 of the first edition of *The Cambridge Medieval History*; Ensslin (1939a), (1939b) and Oertel (1939) from vol. 12 of the first edition of *The Cambridge Ancient History*.

[16] Economic decline of bourgeoisie: Rostovtzeff (1926) echoed in Oertel (1939); paganism: Vinogradoff (1911). Very similar is the relevant introductory analytical section of Stein (1959) 2–3.

larger central imperial bureaucracy of the late Roman period was the product of a carefully conceived plan: a response, indeed, to the cities' decline. On page one of his narrative, for instance, J.B. Bury asserted that Diocletian and Constantine realised "that a new system, more centralised and uniform, was required if the Empire was to be held together": precisely because the weakened cities could no longer do the job. Other commentators agreed, and pretty much everyone was confident that Diocletian and Constantine had carefully assessed the problem and consciously multiplied the number of central bureaucratic organs of government accordingly to keep the now struggling Empire together in adversity. The cheerful prosperity of the early Empire, where healthy self-governing cities had been the basis of the greater whole, had now had to be replaced with constant supervision and iron discipline, but the emperors' plans did at least put some extra life into the tottering structure.[17]

All were equally agreed, however, that this new life came at a considerable price. Again, Rostovtzeff set the tone, emphasising the extent to which the new bureaucratic structures of Empire were corrupt, oppressive, and inefficient. For him the *agentes in rebus* in particular represented a network of "thousands of police agents". Vinogradoff, in *The Cambridge Ancient History*, was happy enough that the collapse of the city meant that the new bureaucracy was absolutely necessary, but equally had no doubt that it basically did a lousy job. Already evident in these essays was the idea that the lack of clear hierarchies hamstrung the bureaucracy's operations, and some of them liked to give it all an extra, sinister twist.[18] The long-standing dominance and governmental skills of the urban bourgeoisie of the Mediterranean world was thus replaced by a grasping, inefficient, and oppressive imperial machine, which recruited from much lesser men. And this indeed was the final strand of interpretation. The imperial bureaucrats were recruited from the lower orders of society, new men replacing the old wealthy and

---

[17] See e.g. Stein (1959) 67–9 (on Diocletian: his main purpose being seen as minimizing the possibility of revolt) and 111 ff. (Constantine). For similar discussions of the 'plan', see Bury (1923) esp. 25–34; Rostovtzeff (1926) 459–60; Reid (1911); Vinogradoff (1911) 554; Ensslin (1939b) 389–96.

[18] E.g. Rostovtzeff (1926) 460 "utterly corrupt"; Bury (1923) esp. 32–4; Reid (1911) esp. 32 on lack of hierarchies and 52–4 on its oppressiveness; Ensslin (1939a) 376–82.

cultured families who had run the self-governing cities of the Roman Empire in their—and its—heyday.[19]

When Jones is compared to these predecessors, the real question is where to begin. Late Roman history prior to the *Later Roman Empire* is so slight—depending upon a minimal evidential base and a great deal of prior assumption—that it would be easy to spend endless pages doing nothing else but listing a myriad detailed points. Jones it was, for instance, who demonstrated conclusively that it was a wild anachronism to view the *agentes in rebus* as an early version of an internal intelligence service. A few particular individuals in the service of Constantius II aside, it was a bureaucratic corps, like any other, with set if evolving duties and remuneration. And, as so many of the papers in this volume have emphasised, all of Jones' arguments were constructed not on the traditional wing and a prayer, but upon a bedrock of references which had been tirelessly gathered from a vast range of primary sources. To my mind, the single most illuminating vignette of the effort this required of such a pathfinder in a world without prosopographies, indices, or even photocopiers is provided by the letter discussed by Peter Garnsey, in which Jones asked *the recipient* to return the list of source references to their author after perusal.[20] And as a result, for every topic relating to late Roman government, the place to begin remains Jones' footnotes and the careful commentary which accompanies them. Given that over forty years have now gone by, this is an extraordinary achievement.

But as Peter Brown noted back in the 1960s, and many of the contributions to this volume have re-emphasised, Jones' historical achievement amounts to a great deal more than a lengthy series of minor adjustments and corrections, based on a closer reading of a greater quantity of evidence. For in the process of sifting all the evidence, Jones also liberated himself from many of the canonical pillars of interpretation so characteristic of the essayists who preceded him. One of the first big ideas to hit the historical dustbin was the view that Diocletian and Constantine had between them conjured up a massive late Roman bureaucracy virtually from scratch. Refracted through Jones' lens, it becomes clear that the later Empire's governmental machine emerged by a process of gradual evolution from the central imperial apparatus of the Principate. No sudden plan brought it into existence. Some

---

[19] E.g. Stein (1959) 69; Bury (1926) 19–20; Vinogradoff (1911); Ensslin (1939b).
[20] Garnsey (ch. 2) 28.

of its fourth-century patterns betray their evolutionary origins and it
continued to evolve. Thus Jones was the first scholar that I am aware
of to stress the continuing importance of the equestrian order. Well
into the fourth century, many imperial bureaucrats continued to hold
equestrian rather than senatorial rank, as so many of their predecessors of the Principate had done. None of the essayists even mentioned
that the order continued to exist. And not only was the bureaucracy
not the result of imposing a sudden cunning plan, but, in part at least,
there was no plan at all. Again it was Jones who first gathered all the
evidence to show how much of the process of bureaucratic expansion
was entirely outside emperors' control.[21]

A similarly fresh breath of air permeates the *Later Roman Empire*'s
account of the fate of cities and their ruling elites in Chapter XIX.
These topics are dealt with more fully elsewhere in this volume, but
it is certainly to the point of this paper, too, to note that Jones completely overturned Rostovtzeff's account of the third-century crisis
as the revolutionary triumph of the peasant masses over a civilised,
urban bourgeoisie. Jones continued to argue, of course, that the local
governmental institutions of the city were transformed almost beyond
recognition in the late Roman period, but showed that the process was
evolutionary.[22] The city remained a key cog in the imperial machine
and had not suddenly disappeared. The same was also true of the land-
owning families by whom the cities had traditionally been run. In the
canonical tradition, these curial families perished along with their cities
in the third century. Jones showed that the status of the curial order
came under pressure in the late imperial period, and that old certain-
ties were being shaken. But, again, there is no sign of an entire class
meeting its destruction in the third century, and he was able to show
that some elements of it even prospered. At city level, some manoeu-
vred themselves into the still attractive status of *principalis*, members of
the core inner group of curials who found ways still to run the city for
their benefit. Further up the administrative scale, many other curials,
Jones was clear, found their way into the burgeoning imperial bureaucracy. Jones of course knew Libanius' famous diatribe against some of
the administrative officers of Constantius II, which emphasised their

---

[21] Equestrians and evolution: 525 ff.; lack of planning: e.g. 377 "The whole administrative system was something of a patchwork. It was not rationally planned....".

[22] A considerable amount of this argumentation was already in place in Jones
(1937).

obscure and generally sordid social origins. It was this, indeed, which underlay the essayists' vision of the average late Roman bureaucrat as a vengeful, uneducated peasant on the make. But having immersed himself so fully in the primary sources, Jones was also aware of a vast body of other evidence which showed that many of the Empire's new bureaucrats had much more 'respectable' origins, being drawn precisely from the old curial classes.[23]

In one further area, too, Jones' analyses took the traditional accounts of late Roman government into entirely new territory. In his overall judgment of the bureaucracy he did not, as we have already seen, deny its inefficiencies and propensity for corruption. As in the traditional view of things, he saw the lack of clearly defined lines of responsibility as a serious problem; different departments were always interfering in each other's business and hampering the governmental process. He also fully analyzed all the evidence for what we might call 'structural corruption' for the first time: arguing that low salaries combined with the selling of office to generate a need among office holders to recoup on their initial investments by making money out of their time in office. Corruption had long been part of the picture, but had usually been seen as the natural outcome of appointing men of low birth. Jones showed that financial trafficking was deeply rooted in the nature of the whole bureaucratic system.[24]

Aside from doing the corruption job properly, Jones also evolved a substantially different overall take on the business of government. In general terms, the *Later Roman Empire* is much less sure of the overwhelming historical importance of the self-governing city as a force for the general good of mankind, and much more sympathetic to the efforts of the central administrators. This represented, in fact, an evolution in his own thinking. In the introduction to *Cities of the Eastern Roman Provinces* of 1937, he wrote of the early Roman period:

> The life of the cities was fostered by the establishment of orderly government, and in such backward districts as were still organized on a tribal or village basis the development of city institutions proceeded apace, stimulated by the general peace and prosperity, and sometimes directly promoted by the imperial government. On the other hand, bureaucratic administration was often retained in districts which had been so governed before annexation, in the hope that the newly created imperial civil service

---

[23] *Principales*: 757 ff.; social origins of bureaucrats: 383–90; cf. 757–63.
[24] Largely under the wonderful sub-heading of 'salaries and extortion': 396–401.

would prove capable of running it successfully. This hope was rarely realized, and in most of the bureaucratically administered provinces the principle of local responsibility had sooner or later to be recognized by the institution of city government.[25]

This was very much the traditional view: cities good, bureaucracy bad. By the *Later Roman Empire*, it is not that Jones necessarily thought that the central bureaucracy was any more efficient, but he had become more sympathetic to its efforts, and much less sanguine about the willingness of cities to govern their populations efficiently and in the Empire's interests. As others in this volume have also concluded, Jones' late Roman state may not add up to a bundle of human joy, but it is a much less grisly place of doom and gloom than it had normally been thought to be—even by himself—before he produced the magnum opus.

3. *Beyond the* Later Roman Empire

What follows has no pretensions to be anything other than brief and selective, but it does aim to give some impression of some of the major areas in which Jones' great work has inspired successors and the kinds of discussion that have continued since its publication. Not, of course, that there haven't been studies moving right away from the topic areas with which Jones was concerned. As Michael Whitby's paper explores, for instance, the non-administrative functioning of the imperial court and its bureaus as a setting for orchestrated ceremonies has been brought to the fore since Jones wrote. He was aware of this dimension of late Roman government, but was interested in neither its role nor its significance.[26] Much other research on central and local government in the late Empire, however, has continued along more recognisably Jonesian lines.

Not least, our understanding of the continued development over time of the late Roman bureaucracy, moving entirely beyond the older visions of the cunning plan of Diocletian and Constantine, has continued to grow. Jones himself carried on contributing manfully—and determinedly—in this area before his untimely death: above all in the cheerful challenge match he carried on with all-comers over whether

---

[25] Jones (1937) xi–xii.
[26] Whitby (ch. 4).

there had ever been such a thing as a collegiate Praetorian Prefecture in the late Roman administrative system.[27] More recent work has also seen highly fruitful debates on precisely how the new type of non-military, regionally-based Praetorian Prefects emerged in and around the courts of the Tetrarchs and Constantine.[28] On other topics, the years since the *Later Roman Empire* was published have seen important—particularly but not solely French—monographs on the evolution of particular branches of the *comitatus*, and on the related theme of the evolution of the Senate of Constantinople. From this work and others—not least Jill Harries' major piece on the office of the Quaestor—Jones' vision of the slow emergence of the late Roman bureaucracy, with larger, more numerous and more specialist central bureaus, from its earlier imperial predecessors has been greatly developed, with the time frame for its major developments being steadily increased.[29] The backdrop to the late Roman system is now also better known. Thanks to the work notably of Fergus Millar, amongst many other possible candidates for explicit mention, our understanding of the earlier imperial apparatus from which the Jones world emerged is much more firmly grounded.[30] All of these contributions, it can reasonably be said, have been following firmly in Jones' footsteps: advancing knowledge and understanding much further along lines that he had himself set down.

There has, alongside this, been a volume of work on what might be termed the internal politics of the imperial bureaucracy: how its different departments functioned and competed. Jones was aware of the dimension of bureaucratic development, but it was not something he dwelt on at length, even though he did note the adverse effects of confused lines of responsibility. Most recently, Chris Kelly has explored how the bureaucracy could in fact act as a block on the exercise of the imperial will, the different departments acting as pressure groups to intrude their own competitive agendas into the governmental process. This kind of vision of bureaucratic politics obviously also has considerable implications for governmental efficiency, another of Jones' presiding concerns in the relevant chapters of the *Later Roman Empire*. It was also Jones who first demonstrated that the late Roman bureaucracy was not only not

---

[27] Jones (1964b).
[28] Corcoran (2000) with refs.
[29] Dagron (1974); Vogler (1979); Teitler (1985); Harries (1988); Delmaire (1989), (1995).
[30] Millar (1992).

a sudden creation of Diocletian and Constantine, but also a process
which went far beyond the capacity of individual emperors to control.
From this perspective, it is hardly surprising that the resulting edifice
should not simply have been an instrument of imperial power.[31]

On the characteristic institution of local government—the city—work
has also continued apace.[32] Thanks, perhaps above all to the work of
Claude and Liebeschuetz, we have a much clearer idea of the continued
evolution of local government at city level. By the late fourth century,
the old-style large city councils were disappearing, with administrative control now in the hands of restricted groups of richer curials,
sometimes called *principales* in our sources. By the sixth century, formal
curial government had disappeared almost entirely in the east ('natural'
development in the west having by this time been cut off by the end
of the western Empire), being replaced by a more informal body of
local grandees, often including now the bishop, who between them ran
local affairs and distributed the key administrative positions of *curator*
and *pater*. Jones had already sorted much of this out himself, but the
pattern of evolution is now better understood, and on its outlines there
is now basic consensus.[33]

There is overall consensus too that the two halves of the process that
have emerged—a considerable rise in the scale and complexity of the
central governmental machine matched by a considerable decline in the
number of landowners apparently involved in the operation of local
government—were intimately linked in terms of actual people. The
older literature was profoundly influenced by that famous speech of
Libanius on the socially inferior origins of some of the key administrators of the Emperor Constantius II. When looked at in detail, however,
the mass of the fourth-century evidence, from law-codes to letter collections, makes it entirely clear that the overwhelming majority of the
new bureaucrats were in fact recruited from the curial classes. Even the
evolving educational patterns of the fourth century were largely about
fitting former curials for these new careers.[34] The rise of the bureau-

---

[31] Kelly (2004) but see too the earlier work of Carney (1971) amongst other contributions.

[32] I will be considering the town here purely as the characteristic unit of local
administration. For consideration of work on the economic and other aspects of town
life, see the paper of Luke Lavan elsewhere in this volume (ch. 8).

[33] Claude (1969); Liebeschuetz (1972), (2001).

[34] Heather (1994) drawing heavily on the literature cited at note 29; with Kaster
(1988) on adjustments to the educational curriculum. Emerging consensus: e.g. Wickham
(2005) 68–9, 155–68.

cracy, therefore, was the mirror image of the same process which saw the decline of the curiae, and the two—everyone now agrees—must be discussed together. Where there is much less agreement, however, is the overall significance to ascribe to the wider evolutionary pattern visible in late Roman government which Jones first established and others have rounded out. How big a transformation did all this represent in the government of the Empire, and did it affect the Empire's overall operation for good or ill?

Jones himself offered parallel but contrasting lines of explanation for the shifting career patterns of the former curial classes. On some pages, he carefully documents the attractions of attaching oneself to the ranks of the new imperial bureaucracy. On others, he catalogues equally carefully the declining status and economic fortunes of most of those who remained curials, and, while being more optimistic than the essayists who preceded him, did also think that the economic situation was generally becoming worse for the land-owning classes from the third century onwards. I am aware of no passage where he considered these positive and negative motivations alongside each other and came to a balanced judgment as to their relative importance, although I suspect this was because he thought it obvious enough that the negative motivations were paramount.[35]

Since Jones wrote, however, as Ward-Perkins' chapter points out, general estimates of the late Roman economy have been moving steadily upwards. There is no sign of widespread economic crisis at all in the late Roman countryside, problems at most being confined to a relatively few localities. In general landowners were doing fine, and perhaps even profiting further from an ability to sell into a vigorous market.[36] In this context, the decline of curial numbers and the corresponding shift of landowners into the bureaucracy looks to have a more specific kind of motivation than economic collapse, and a convincing one, to my mind, has emerged more clearly since Jones was writing. By the fourth century, the central state had in fact confiscated all the profits of the revenue sources that the cities used to enjoy in earlier periods: their landed endowments combined with local tolls and taxes. As Liebeschuetz showed so clearly for Antioch, curial officers still had to levy these funds,

---

[35] Positive motivation: 383 ff.; negative motivation: 757–63.

[36] Ward-Perkins (ch. 9). On the possibility of market specialisation and higher profits, see now, e.g., Ward-Perkins (2001); Sarris (2006) and Wickham (2005) 155–68, 708 ff. Disagreement continues only over the extent of market-led exchange. Sarris (2006) represents a maximalist position.

but all the profits were handed over to central government. And in the fourth century, as Liebeschuetz has again convincingly argued against Durliat, only limited amounts of these funds—one third at best—were ever returned to the councils. In short, the city council now had all the work of collecting the money but none of the fun of spending it, and, to make matters worse, was also given major new responsibilities when it came to collecting central imperial taxes as well.

All spending was now in the hands of imperial bureaucrats, and this, together with the latter's growing social status, generated a huge magnetic force which bent landowners' career patterns into a new shape. And as the legislation of the Theodosian Code shows so clearly, the process of late Roman bureaucratic expansion was in fact quickly taken over by former curials demanding, winning, and protecting positions within it. Once again, the essayists were substantially mistaken. Emperors were barely in control of bureaucratic recruitment, not implementing a careful plan. Such a view also suggests a different take on the balance of motives behind the shift. It was the product of the negative force of public economic loss in the form of confiscated city revenues—but not private economic loss in terms of low rents and profits from their own landholdings—combined with the very positive attractions of the benefits of bureaucratic status, which continued to grow as the fourth century progressed. Specifically, it rapidly became the case that serving a short spell in the bureaucracy became the new route to dominance in local city-based society, since retired bureaucrats—*honorati*—came to be given all the best jobs in local government too, such as running tax reallocations and sitting with the provincial governor in court.[37] So much, I think, is accepted now by most people. But how big a change did this shift in elite career patterns represent, and was it, in overall terms, a good or a bad thing—or neither—for the government of the Empire? This, of course, is the point at which this chapter potentially intersects with discussions of overall Roman imperial collapse.

---

[37] Liebeschuetz (1972), (2001); contra Durliat (1988), (1990). That emperors were not in control of bureaucratic expansion is the overall message of *CTh.* 12. 1, where apparently fierce orders that curials-turned-bureaucrats should return to their councils are interspersed with—sometimes within the same law—amnesties allowing those already in possession of a bureaucratic post to remain there. On the subsidiary issue of when the city's funds were confiscated; Jones assumed it happened under the Tetrarchy but there is no explicit evidence to this effect in any source, and it may well have been earlier: Heather (1994) 22–4 with refs.

Jones himself, as we have seen, stepped back from pre-existing empha-ses on the decline of the self-governing city as self-evidently a disaster for the overall quality of public life in the Empire. He did not think the imperial bureaucracy necessarily a good thing, but the *Later Roman Empire* is less certain that it was so much worse than the world of more independent cities which preceded it. He certainly did not identify the transformation of government as a major cause of imperial collapse in the work's famous final chapter.[38] After Jones, vigorous debate on this hugely important topic has continued. One strand of thought remains highly suspicious of the overall effect of this alteration in the balance of power between central and local governmental structures. Ramsay MacMullen, for instance, famously devoted a major book to catalogu-ing the many and varied corruptions of late Roman bureaucrats, and argued that the resulting inefficiency was a major contributory factor to imperial collapse: a return to the thought world of the old essayists, but this time based on historical research of a professional standard. For Wolf Liebeschuetz likewise, following up and developing much further lines of thought already present in his monograph on Antioch, the erosion of city autonomy generated a type of public life in the later Empire which was profoundly inferior to that which had prevailed in its earlier counterparts. It stimulated much less in the way of genuinely intellectual culture, amongst many other drawbacks, but also removed the kind of restraints on the behaviour of the powerful which the smaller political societies of the old cities had helped keep in place. The overall effect on landowners' loyalty to the Roman imperial enterprise was profoundly damaging.[39]

But the effects of governmental transformation can also be construed quite differently. Since Jones wrote, the unearthing of the *Lex Irnitana* has made it possible to think in more detail about the spread of the self-governing city in the early Roman period. On one reading, the process was all about the spread of Mediterranean civilisation across the Roman Empire. The details of its organisation make it equally possible to read the process, however, as one where pre-existing local oligarchies organised themselves to win the legal and financial privileges that came with a grant of such a constitution: Roman citizenship for

---

[38] The basic message of Chapter XXV is that outside 'barbarian' pressure was the cause of the over-taxation which, in Jones' view, prompted over-centralisation and a slow but noticeable population decline amongst other associated ills.

[39] MacMullen (1988); Liebeschuetz (2001).

the top office holders of their 'city' (i.e. themselves), and the right to gather and spend certain revenues.[40] In this view, the later adjustment in the balance of control between central bureaucracy and city council might not have had very profound consequences. Throughout imperial history, the centre was so distant from most of its constituent localities that, revenue raising for the state apart, the latter were essentially autonomous. Otherwise, the centre intruded itself into localities only in so far as factions within local land-owning elites employed its powers in their own battles. Whether it was by winning the right to run their locality as a self-governing city in the first to the third centuries, becoming a retired ex-bureaucrat (an *honoratus*) in the fourth and fifth centuries, or by participating in the more informal gatherings of notables in the sixth, it was always the same kind of men, if certainly in new guises, who were running localities throughout imperial history.[41] What seem like major changes merely mark moments where the old game was being recast according to some new rules, but the basic nature of the game itself never changed.[42]

These and related issues are far from resolved, but they do all share something in common. Jones' *Later Roman Empire* was a self-proclaimed survey of social, economic, and administrative developments. And thanks to Jones, and the further work he has stimulated, we understand much better the administrative and also the social side of the developing relationship between central and local government in the late Roman period. The new archaeological evidence that has become available since Jones wrote, arguably, has also massively increased our understanding of its economic context. What Jones did not cover in any detail, and what this subsequent debate is all about, really, is the *political* significance of these social, administrative, and economic devel-

---

[40] The *Lex Irnitana* was published and translated by Gonzalez (1986).

[41] E.g. Heather (1994), (1998); Whittow (1990). For an application of the 'de facto local autonomy' model, see some of the recent literature on Christianisation: Bradbury (1994); Brown (1995) chs. 1–2; Heather and Moncur (2001) ch. 1.

[42] The subsidiary question of whether the sixth-century elite were the direct descendents of the third-century elite or whether the shift from curial to bureaucratic careers allowed the rise of a new set of local oligarchs remains under discussion. Banaji (2001) and Sarris (2006) assume so, but Banaji's 'new' *honorati* landowners of late fourth- and fifth-century Egypt could easily be the descendants of the third-century landowners, who had added imperial offices to their portfolio of assets. If so, Jones' summing up that an 'aristocracy of service' was created in the fourth century (above note 12) would be only a half truth; rather, the landowners were adding service, often pretty virtual service in fact, to their list of attributes.

opments. Any comparison with large medieval states, which depended upon broadly similar levels of governmental and logistic technology, underlines that the key issue in imperial longevity is keeping constituent local elites 'interested' in the enterprise. What happens when you fail to do so shows up dramatically in recent perspectives on Carolingian collapse, for instance, which stress that local elites started to ignore the centre when the centre ran out of a credible mixture of blandishment and threat.[43]

In the case of the later Roman Empire, there is no clear answer yet as to the overall political significance of the substantial adjustment to the relationship between centre and locality which undoubtedly unfolded from the second half of the third century onwards and which it has been the purpose of this paper to chart. I have argued elsewhere that you might view the tying in of local landowners of the eastern Mediterranean to the imperial bureaucracy and new Senate of Constantinople in the fourth century as representing a much-improved level of integration: one of overall benefit, in other words, to the internal workings of the Empire. This was directly inspired by the pioneering work of John Matthews focused on the way in which western senatorial and provincial elites operated the political potentials of the new system, as it had started to bed down by the second half of the fourth century.[44] But an integrative strategy that worked in the fourth century, when provincial elites had only just joined the Senate of Constantinople, could conceivably cease to work so well two centuries later, if the Senate became a body sealed off from its provincial roots, and if local landowners became fewer in number and richer as some have recently argued. It is also the case that larger oligarchies often have to behave better than smaller ones, as Liebeschuetz had firmly in mind when writing his great book on the fall of the ancient city. But these are all still possible arguments, and not certain ones. A.H.M. Jones set out for us the administrative and social transformation of governance in the late Roman period. He left it to his successors to try to work out its political consequences.

---

[43] On the process of Carolingian collapse, see e.g. Reuter (1985), (1990); Dunbabin (1985); with the overall results that show up so clearly in the varying but marked degrees of regional autonomy surveyed by Hallam (1980).

[44] Heather (1994); after above all Matthews (1975). But see also Matthews (1970), (1971), (1974).

Bibliography

Banaji J. (2001) *Agrarian Change in Late Antiquity: Gold, Labour and Aristocratic Dominance* (Oxford 2001)
Bradbury S.A. (1994) "Constantine and anti-pagan legislation in the Fourth Century", *CPh* 89 (1994) 120–39
Brown P. (1967) "The Later Roman Empire", *EcHR*, 2nd series, 20 (1967) 327–43, reprinted in *idem* (1972) *Religion and Society in the Age of Saint Augustine* (London 1972) 46–73
——. (1995) *Authority and the Sacred: Aspects of the Christianisation of the Roman World* (Cambridge 1995)
Bury J.B. (1923) *History of the later Roman empire from the death of Theodosius I to the death of Justinian (A.D. 395 to A.D. 565)* (London 1923)
Carney T.F. (1971) *Bureaucracy in Traditional Society: Romano-Byzantine Bureaucracies Viewed from Within* (Kansas 1971)
Claude D. (1969) *Die byzantinische Stadt im 6 Jahrhundert* (Munich 1969)
Cook S.A., et al. (1939) edd. *The Cambridge Ancient History XII*, 1st ed. (Cambridge 1939)
Corcoran S. (2000) *The Empire of the Tetrarchs: Imperial Pronouncements and Government, A.D. 284–324* (Oxford 2000)
Dagron G. (1974) *Naissance d'une capitale: Constantinople et ses institutions de 330 a 451* (Paris 1974)
Delmaire R. (1989) *Largesses sacrees et res privata: l'aerarium imperial et son administation du I^{ie} au VIe siecle* (Rome 1989)
——. (1995) *Les institutions du Bas—Empire romain de Constantin à Justinien*, vol. 1, *Les institutions civiles palatines* (Paris 1995)
Dunbabin J. (1985) *France in the making, 843–1180* (Oxford 1985)
Durliat J. (1988) "Le salaire de la paix sociale dans les royaumes barbares (V^e–V^{ie} siecles)", in *Anerkennung und Integration: Zu den wirtschaftlichen Gundlagen der Volkerwanderungszeit (400–600)*, Denkschriften der Osterreichischen Akademie der Wissenschaften, Phil-Hist. Kl. 193, edd. H. Wolfram and A. Schwarcz (Vienna 1988) 21–72
Durliat J. (1990) *Les finances publiques de Diocletien aux Carolingiens (284–889)* (Sigmaringen 1990)
Ensslin W. (1939a) "The End of the Principate", in Cook et al. (1939) 353–82
——. (1939b) "The Reforms of Diocletian", in Cook et al. (1939) 383–407
Gonzalez J. (1986) "The *Lex Irnitana*: a New Copy of the Flavian Municipal Law", *JRS* 76 (1986) 147–243
Gwatkin H.M. and Whitney J.P. (1911) edd. *The Cambridge Medieval History I*, 1st ed. (Cambridge 1911)
Hallam E.M. (1980) *Capetian France, 987–1328* (London 1980)
Harries J. (1988) "The Roman Imperial Quaestor from Constantine to Theodosius II", *JRS* 78 (1988) 148–72
Heather P.J. (1994) "New Men for New Constantines?: Creating an Imperial Elite in the eastern Mediterranean", in *New Constantines: The Rhythm of Imperial Renewal in Byzantium, 4th–13th Centuries*, ed. P. Magdalino (London 1994) 11–33
——. (1998) "Senators and Senates", in *Cambridge Ancient History XIII*, 2nd ed., *The Late Empire: A.D. 337–425*, edd. Averil Cameron and P. Garnsey (Cambridge 1998) 184–210
Heather P.J. and Moncur D. (2001) *Politics, Philosophy, and Empire in the Fourth Century: Select Orations of Themistius*, Translated Texts for Historians (Liverpool 2001)
Jones A.H.M. (1937) *Cities of the Eastern Roman Provinces* (Oxford 1937), 2nd ed. (Oxford 1971)

———. (1964a) *The Later Roman Empire 284–602: A Social, Economic, and Administrative Survey*, 3 vols (Oxford 1964), reprinted in two volumes with continuous pagination (Oxford 1973)

———. (1964b) "Collegiate Prefectures", *JRS* 54 (1964) 78–89, reprinted in *idem* (1974) *The Roman Economy: Studies in Ancient Economic and Administrative History*, ed. P.A. Brunt (London 1974) 375–95

Kaster R.A. (1988) *Guardians of Language: The Grammarian and Society in Late Antiquity* (Berkeley 1988)

Kelly C.M. (2004) *Ruling the Later Roman Empire* (Cambridge, Mass. 2004)

Liebeschuetz J.H.W.G. (1972) *Antioch: City and Imperial Administration in the Later Roman Empire* (Oxford 1972)

———. (2001) *The Decline and Fall of the Roman City* (Oxford 2001)

MacMullen R. (1988) *Corruption and the Decline of Rome* (New Haven 1988)

Matthews J.F. (1970) "Olympiodorus of Thebes and the History of the West (A.D. 407–425)", *JRS* 60 (1970) 79–97, reprinted in *idem* (1985) VI

———. (1971) "Gallic Supporters of Theodosius", *Latomus* 30 (1971) 1073–1099, reprinted in *idem* (1985) IX

———. (1974) "The Letters of Symmachus", in *Latin Literature of the Fourth Century*, ed. J.W. Binns (London 1974) 58–99, reprinted in *idem* (1985) IV

———. (1975) *Western Aristocracies and Imperial Court A.D. 364–425* (Oxford 1975)

———. (1985) *Political Life and Culture in late Roman society* (London 1985)

Millar F. (1992) *The Emperor in the Roman World*, 2nd. ed. (London 1992)

Oertel F. (1939) "The Economic Life of the Empire", in Cook et al. (1939) 232–81

Reid J.S. (1911) "The Reorganisation of the Empire", in Gwatkin and Whitney (1911) 24–54

Reuter T. (1985) "Plunder and Tribute in the Carolingian Empire," *Transactions of the Royal Historical Society*, 5th series, 35 (1985) 75–94

———. (1990) "The End of Carolingian Military Expansion", in *Charlemagne's Heir: New Perspectives on the Reign of Louis the Pious*, edd. P. Godman and R. Collins (Oxford 1990) 391–405

Rostovtzeff M.I. (1926) *The Social and Economic History of the Roman Empire* (Oxford 1926)

Sarris P. (2006) *Economy and Society in the age of Justinian* (Cambridge 2006)

Stein E. (1949/1959) *Histoire du Bas-Empire*, vol. i: *De l'état romain à l'état byzantin (284–476)*, èdition française par Jean-Rémy Palanque (Paris 1959); vol. ii: *De la disparition de l'empire d'occident à la mort de Justinien (467–565)*, publié par Jean-Rémy Palanque (Paris 1949)

Teitler H.C. (1985) *Notarii and Exceptores* (Amsterdam 1985)

Vinogradoff P. (1911) "Social and Economic Conditions of the Roman Empire in the Fourth Century", in Gwatkin and Whitney (1911) 542–567

Vogler C. (1979) *Constance II et l'administration imperiale* (Strasbourg 1979)

Ward-Perkins B. (2000) "Specialised production and exchange", in *The Cambridge Ancient History XIV*, 2nd ed., *Late Antiquity: Empire and Successors A.D. 425–600*, edd. Averil Cameron, B. Ward-Perkins and M. Whitby (Cambridge 2000) 346–91

Whittow M. (1990) "Ruling the Late Roman and Early Byzantine City: A Continuous History", *Past and Present* 129 (1990) 4–29

Wickham C. (2005) *Framing the Early Middle Ages: Europe and the Mediterranean, 400–800* (Oxford 2005)

CHAPTER SIX

LAW AND JUSTICE IN THE *LATER ROMAN EMPIRE*

Caroline Humfress

1. *Introduction*

Jones took a significant decision in the *Later Roman Empire* to give his thematic chapter on Roman law a very specific title: 'Justice'. A clue as to why Chapter XIV was not entitled 'Postclassical Law' (for example) is provided in the very first paragraph of his preface: "I ignore the two major intellectual achievements of the age, theology and law...".[1]

What *would* Jones have written about law, one of his twin "major intellectual achievements" of the late empire, had he chosen to face the challenge directly?[2] Would he have limited Late Roman law's "major intellectual" achievement to the *renovatio* achieved during the age of the sixth-century emperor Justinian—or would he have allowed for a more positive assessment of law as an intellectual enterprise between 284 and 531? Max Kaser's *Römische Rechtsgeschichte*, a textbook of Roman law first published in 1950, had already opened the way for a more positive assessment of intellectual legal development in the fourth and fifth centuries; however there are no direct footnote references to Kaser in Jones. In a preliminary paragraph to his footnotes on Chapter XIV Jones hints that he had consulted many modern Roman law textbooks, but characteristically signals only one general history in particular: "Of the many histories of Roman law I have found H.F. Jolowicz, *Historical Introduction to the Study of Roman law*, Cambridge 1952, the most useful from my standpoint."[3] Herbert Felix Jolowicz was Professor of Civil Law and a contemporary of Jones at Oxford; both were fellows of All Souls College. Jolowicz himself, moreover, is generally acknowledged as one of the most historically minded legal scholars of Roman law—hence no doubt Jones' preference for his work. The only other Roman law

---

[1] Jones (1964) I, v.
[2] Jones (1960) and (1972) focus on the Republic and the Principate.
[3] Jones (1964) III, 132.

bibliography mentioned explicitly is M.A. von Bethmann-Hollweg's volume of 1886, *Der Römische Civilprozess*, which Jones describes as "...still the most comprehensive work". The fact that Jones directs his readers to the most exhaustive, monumental late nineteenth-century tome on Roman civil procedure underscores his very particular historical approach: Jones was interested in Roman law as action, not Roman law as abstraction. With his statement that he has "ignored" the major intellectual achievement of law, Jones is firmly reminding his audience that he is not to be taken for a historian of ideas.

When Jones' *Later Roman Empire* was published in 1964 it was noted by the leading Italian journals of Roman law, *Labeo* and *Iura*. Both of these periodicals, however, signalled the existence of Jones' volumes under 'general history' rubrics.[4] In other words, the individuals who were responsible for commissioning the reviews for these major Roman law journals did not note any particular contribution of Jones' 1964 volumes to Roman legal history *per se*. The *Zeitschrift der Savigny-Stiftung für Rechtsgeschichte (Romanistische Abteilung)*, on the other hand does not seem to have noted the publication of the *Later Roman Empire* at all. Taking Jones' own characterisation of his work seriously, perhaps, his contemporary scholars of Roman law classed the *Later Roman Empire* as "...a social, economic and administrative survey of the empire, historically treated".[5]

There is no discussion of substantive late Roman law in the *Later Roman Empire*: there is no sense given of how late Romans would divide their inheritances up, how they would stipulate clauses in a private agreement or how they would argue a case concerning free status, for example. Neither does Jones provide us with any sense of how postclassical legal principles developed or diverged from their classical foundations, aside from a throwaway line that law remained "obscure and uncertain" down to Justinian's great reforms and was "riddled with arcane technicalities".[6] Instead, Chapter XIV of the *Later Roman Empire* is divided into seven sub-sections, beginning with a short explication of the sources of late Roman law. Notwithstanding Jones' opening salvo that: "It is unnecessary for the purposes of this book to discuss the

---

[4] *Labeo* 10.2 (1964) 324 under the heading 'Storia Economica, Storia Politica'; *Iura* XVI.2 (1965) 656–57 under the heading 'Studi di Storia Generale'.
[5] Jones (1964) I, v.
[6] *Ibid.*, I, 470.

ultimate sources of the law", he devotes over three pages of detailed analysis to them.[7] The chapter then moves on to a complex structural analysis of judicial practice, focused especially on the relationship between the various courts of the late empire and the officials engaged in administering their business. In fact, if we return to Jones' preface to the whole volume (quoted above) we can see that he deliberately prepares his audience for this focus: "I ignore the two major intellectual achievements of the age, theology and law, but discuss the organisation and finances of the church, the administration of justice, and the social status of the clergy and of lawyers". Here Jones provides us with a tantalising glimpse of his methodology, together with a fundamental recognition that late Roman legal structures and processes cannot be analysed apart from ecclesiastical and religious developments.

2. *Jones on Law: Sources and Methodology*

The primary sources for Jones' Chapter XIV on 'Justice' reached far beyond those used by either Jolowicz or Bethmann-Hollweg. One striking example of Jones' use of source material in discussing legal practice will suffice: in a sub-section of Chapter XIV entitled 'The Judges' Jones uses a vignette from the writings of a sixth-century Christian ascetic to make an astute and methodologically aware point about late Roman access to justice:

> Governors were, it is true, directed to hear petty cases informally (*sine scriptis*, without the written record which formed a large part of the cost) and even to give free justice to the poor. It may be doubted however whether these directions were often obeyed. Joshua the Stylite tells of one Alexander, governor of Osrhoene in 496, who put up a box outside his official residence in which complainants could drop their petitions, and sat every Friday in a church administering justice free to all comers. But this was a very exceptional case, worthy of record in a chronicle, and the result was that Alexander was besieged by suitors seeking redress for old wrongs, some dating back forty years, which they had never been able to bring into court hitherto.[8]

---

[7] *Ibid.*, I, 470–74.
[8] *Ibid.*, I, 499.

Jones' footnote reference for this passage cites Joshua the Stylite's *Chronicle* (section 29), alongside two other textual sources: a Justinianic *Novel* and the papyrological report of a trial proceeding. Jones thus combined late Roman Christian texts with a variety of legal evidence to shed light on processes and practises in action. In his careful analysis of the protocols of church synods he equally demonstrated the impact of Roman legal practices on the Christian Church.

On page vi of his general preface to the *Later Roman Empire*, however, Jones frankly confessed that he ditched theological treatises and commentaries on the scriptures and secular *belles lettres*, as "...many of the best grains have been winnowed by earlier scholars, particularly those of the seventeenth and eighteenth centuries, whose editions of patristic literature are a mine of curious information". Next, he tells us that he abandoned his reading of late Roman sermons, before emphasising the fact that he "...read *and re-read* (my italics) the Codes and Novels"—as well as staking a claim "...to have at least looked at every published papyrus of relevant date". Jones also notes that he tried to do the same for inscriptions, but he was frustrated in his attempts: "...many are so cunningly concealed in the *corpora* and periodicals". This reference to the 'cunning concealment' of epigraphical evidence was in fact an oblique reference to Jones' row with the leading epigraphist Louis Robert—a spat that Jones referred to again in the second edition of his *Cities of the Eastern Roman Empire* (published posthumously in 1971). In the introduction to this second edition Jones wrote:

> It is thus clear that in so far as the second edition is better than the first, the credit is entirely due to my collaborators and I thank them heartily for all the work, much of it tedious and unrewarding that they have put into it. I also owe much to the reviewers and critics of the original book, notably Monsieur Louis Robert, but his corrections were made in such an offensive manner that I find it hard to thank him.

Jones' objection to Robert, aside from the personal animosity implied in the quotation above, was that he published inscriptions found in out of the way places in out of the way journals—hence the reference to the 'cunning concealment' of inscriptions in the 1964 *Later Roman Empire* preface. The recent work of Denis Feissel, amongst others, has highlighted the extent to which the discovery of a relevant inscription can change the way in which historians understand late Roman law: not only in terms of reconstituting legal texts from the inscribed evidence, but also with respect to illuminating the particular processes that lay behind the promulgation and permanent display of individual impe-

rial constitutions in a given locality.[9] Jones had recognised the potential
value of inscriptional evidence to the legal historian forty years earlier,
however, he felt that Louis Robert had personally thwarted him in his
attempts to exploit this material effectively. Jones' difficulties in locat-
ing the epigraphic evidence, and his decision not to dig at the cliff
face of the theological material, had a significant effect on his general
interpretation of the late Roman legal system and judicial practice.
There is no doubt that Jones did indeed 'read and re-read' the *Codex
Theodosianus* and the *Codex Justinianus*, alongside the *Novels* (the 'new laws'
issued by Theodosius II and later emperors including Justinian himself,
that survive outside the two official late Roman imperial *Codes*). We
should remember that the *Theodosian Code*, the *Novels* and the Justinianic
Corpus Iuris Civilis (*Digest, Code* and *Institutes*) are major sources for the
'narrative chapters" in Part I of the *Later Roman Empire*. We are also
told by Jones at the end of his 1964 preface that the Regius Professor
of Civil Law at Cambridge had read through Chapter XIV and that
J. Martindale had checked all the dates and footnote references to the
Codes and *Novels*—an accomplishment that would surely qualify as a
worthy contender for the thirteenth labour of Hercules. Although not
a Roman lawyer himself, Jones took the sources of late Roman law
very seriously indeed.

Jones' surviving unpublished papers—in particular the notes that
record his preparatory research for the *Later Roman Empire*—illuminate
his own working methodology in approaching the late Roman law
codes.[10] These unpublished papers include one hundred or so pages
of hand written notes on the constitutions of the *Codex Theodosianus*
(covering all sixteen books, rubric by rubric), together with a further
thirty handwritten pages or so on Justinian's *Codex*. Not surprisingly,
perhaps, the constitutions that seem to have interested Jones the most
were those on legal status, legal privilege, the development of the late
Roman appeals procedure and taxation abuses. Next, Jones re-ordered
his most important or relevant notes thematically onto separate sheets,
headed by titles such as 'Advocates' and 'Objections to Imperial Law
by Churchmen'. A particularly revealing title in these sheets reads

---

[9] Feissel (2000) and (2004); see also Roueché (1984), Corcoran (2002) and Crawford
(2002). New epigraphic research relevant to late Roman law is noted annually in
L'Année épigraphique.
[10] See the paper by Peter Garnsey in this volume (ch. 2) 26–7—with thanks to him
for allowing me to consult Jones' unpublished notes whilst writing this paper.

'Popular v. Roman law', followed by three words in Jones' handwriting: "not much here". It is easy to imagine Jones mining these thematically structured handwritten pages when he was frantically writing his endnotes—and Sir Basil Blackwell rolled the rest of the book off the printing press. As Jones candidly admits in his preface, the text of the *Later Roman Empire* went off first, and the footnotes followed later.[11] With regard to the editions of the legal sources that Jones consulted, he cites the standard texts: the 1905 Berlin edition of the *Codex Theodosianus* by Theodor Mommsen and Paul Krüger's 1877 Berlin edition of the *Codex Justinianus*.[12] However, this reliance on the standard editions has recently laid Jones open to a criticism that would be barely credible in any other context than late Roman law: namely that Jones did not pay enough attention to source criticism.

In a 2003 review article entitled "Sacred Letters of the Law; The Emperor's Hand in Late Roman (Literary) History", Mark Vessey has traced the lineage of three recent 'British' monographs on late Roman law back to Jones' particular bureaucratic conception of it:

> When A.H.M. Jones's three volumes on *The Later Roman Empire* appeared in 1964, a friendly reviewer [Momigliano] compared them to a report by a British Parliamentary commission. Only a British historian, he quipped, would treat the Roman empire as if it were still in working order... Treating *The Later Roman Empire* as a kind of formative anomaly, we can distinguish two lines of development. One impulse has been towards giving expression to the voices, not all of them subaltern, that clamour at the gates of Jones's stately edifice. Most brilliantly exemplified by Peter Brown, this broadly recuperative strain of late Roman history brings to life whole areas of human experience excluded or downplayed by the official transcripts of empire... Another complementary movement in British late Roman studies follows an almost opposite path. Instead of expanding the interstices of Jones's text, historians of this slant reoccupy the space of his notes. Theirs is still an "imperial" history, but one that now includes the media and archives of empire itself. Three recent studies afford an opportunity to take stock of it.[13]

The three "recent studies" which, according to Vessey, "reoccupy the space" of Jones' endnotes are Tony Honoré's 1998 *Law in the Crisis of Empire 379–455 A.D.: The Theodosian Empire and its Quaestors*, Jill Harries' 1999 *Law and Empire in Late Antiquity* and John Matthews' 2000 *Laying*

---

[11] Jones (1964) I, ix.
[12] *Ibid.*, III, 396, under the abbreviations *CTh* and *CJ* respectively.
[13] Vessey (2003) 345–46.

Down the Law: A Study of the Theodosian Code. Vessey argues for a geographical as well as an intellectual connection between A.H.M. Jones and these recent monographs: a geographical connection in the sense that all four had, or currently have, Oxford associations, and an intellectual connection in that each is focused on the 'Emperor's hand' and its bureaucratic reach in late Roman legal history. Vessey also contends, however, that there is a difference between Jones' approach to the late Roman legal source material and that of Harries, Honoré and Matthews. Jones took the texts of the major late Roman legal sources for granted:

> Of all the abbreviations studding those oddly readable pages [of notes to the *Later Roman Empire*], the most frequent by far are *CTh* and *CJ*. Yet despite their overwhelming importance for Jones's enterprise, the legal collections denoted by these letters receive scant attention in the text... Any questions that might be raised about the composition of imperial laws and law codes had already been answered. The majority of the population of the late empire may have thought little of the Roman law, but modern historians knew what they meant by *CTh* and *CJ*.[14]

In contrast to Jones, however, the monographs under review by Harries, Honoré and Matthews refuse to take the late Roman *Codes* at face value. According to Vessey, this more recent research treats the late Roman laws and *codes* as historical texts in need of (literary) analysis, rather than as a canonical body of authoritative 'literature':

> Forty years after the publication of *LRE* [Jones' *Later Roman Empire*], mainly as a result of the work of other British scholars, that unwritten historiographic "Law of Citations" has been abrogated. Laws and Codes that once formed the invisible bedrock of our histories are now objects of historical description and narrative. It is not just a matter of making room on the library shelf for new and longer prolegomena and appendices. The history of late Roman legal documents is giving rise to a new late Roman history.[15]

Whether we agree or not with Vessey's suggestion that a 'new' history is beginning to be written on the basis of a critical approach to the late Roman legal sources, we should accept his judgement that Harries, Honoré and Matthews are indeed each consciously concerned with how the imperial *codes* came to be composed and how we now come

---

[14] *Ibid.*, 346.
[15] *Ibid.*

to read them. It is also certainly the case that all four historians, not-withstanding the almost forty year publication gap between Jones and the others, are focused on the emperor and the structures of empire as the most important indicators of late Roman law and the judicial system. Besides this focus on the emperors and their bureaucrats, how-ever, Jones was at the same time well aware that asking questions about late Roman justice demanded reaching out beyond the authoritative letter of the imperial *Codes*. Jones (as we shall see) would have agreed with the premise that late Roman law was bigger than the emperors, their quaestors and their imperial texts.[16] If we wish to understand late Roman justice, we have to focus on legal practice 'on the ground'. It is this emergent bottom-up, rather than top-down, perspective on Roman law that is currently provoking challenging questions concerning both classical and late Roman legal history.[17] Jones himself had already arrived at the beginnings of this perspective in 1964, when he took the decision to frame Chapter XIV as a discussion of "justice" rather than the law(s) of the emperors.

Before expanding on this idea, however, it is worth challenging Vessey's view that Jones himself was not overly troubled by source criticism questions with respect to late Roman law. Vessey's comments about Jones were made by way of an introduction to his review essay of Honoré, Harries and Matthews—he does not claim to be provid-ing a historiographical examination of A.H.M. Jones himself. I would maintain, however, that Vessey has underestimated the extent to which Jones was consciously aware of the complexities surrounding the legal source material and its transmission. In his preface to *The Later Roman Empire* Jones states:

> The abundant legal material presents many difficulties of interpretation. There are some technical problems. The dates of many laws are wrong in the Codes; one often cannot tell from the address whether a given enactment was a general circular applicable to all the empire (or rather to that part of it which the emperor who issued it ruled), or special to a particular diocese or province, whether it represented general policy or was evoked by a particular scandal.[18]

---

[16] Garnsey and Humfress (2001); Humfress (2006) and (2007, forthcoming).
[17] For example Nörr (1998); Meyer (2004); Metzger (2004); and Du Plessis (2004).
[18] Jones (1964) I, viii.

These three brief sentences outline an agenda that most historians interested in late Roman legal sources have had to confront at some point, whether explicitly or not. The technical problems concerning the addressees (and hence the intended application) of late Roman imperial constitutions, for example, have been a subject of source criticism since the legal humanists in the sixteenth century. Jones offers a brief working formula for getting a handle on this technical difficulty on pages 472–74 of the *Later Roman Empire* and it still remains the subject of significant debate today.[19] Epigraphy has also become very important here (as noted above)—thinking, for example, of Simon Corcoran's careful work on reconstructing the various and different local inscriptions recording Constantine's edict *de accusationibus*.[20] Similarly with the much vexed topic of how to spot and identify fourth and fifth-century imperial constitutions with a 'general' rather than a 'specific' character: the scholarly debate over *leges generales* is touched on briefly by Jones on pages 471 and 472 in his discussion of rescripts and edicts, without any direct reference to the secondary literature that he had undoubtedly read. Once again this issue has been repeatedly revisited in scholarly debates over the last forty years; although it is tempting to still agree with Jones that any attempt "...to draw a distinction between general and special laws is not very illuminating".[21] From the perspective of a legal historian interested in practice and forensic activity, any attempt to divorce 'general' from 'case-specific' in late Roman constitutions misses the point that the one constantly fed into the other. Finally, the question of whom or what prompted the issuing of imperial constitutions—discussed by Jones in the *Later Roman Empire* on pages 504 and 505—remains very much on the scholarly agenda today. We can thus conclude that Jones was more than aware of the complexity of the legal sources he was handling, even if he chose not to be unduly delayed by it.

---

[19] See in particular the painstaking reconstructions of individual constitutions and their transmission in Matthews (2000): 200–53.

[20] Corcoran (2002).

[21] Jones (1964) I, 472, with particular reference to Valentinian III's attempt to define *edicta* in 426. For recent debate see Maggio (1995); Harries (1999) 20–25; Corcoran (2000) 11–12; and Matthews (2000) 16–18 and 65–70.

3. Jones and Late Roman Legal Practice

In Chapter XIV Jones painstakingly analysed the legal source material, combing through every book of the *Codex Theodosianus* and the *Codex Justinianus*—as well as bureaucratic documents such as the Notitia Dignitatum—in an attempt to illuminate practice and evaluate the effectiveness of late Roman imperial government. A fundamental concern of Jones in Chapter XIV, however, was to judge whether the inhabitants of the later Roman Empire got rough justice, and he seems to have been left in no doubt that they did and, moreover, that they paid dearly for the privilege. To borrow a metaphor from John Pocock, Jones' methodology in approaching the legal source material was to use the microscope first and the telescope second.[22] The *Later Roman Empire* does indeed rely heavily upon, what Vessey terms, the 'official transcripts of empire' for its microscopic detail.[23] In Chapter XIV, however, the 'microscopic detail' is frequently lost amidst Jones' bold, sweeping and evaluative generalisations. Hence the most memorable and oft quoted Jonesian one-liners on late Roman law and the legal system: "The excellence of the Roman Law is justly extolled: but it may be doubted whether under the later Roman empire its virtues were obvious to the majority of the population".[24] Under a sub-section entitled "*Praescriptio fori*" Jones summarises his complex and detailed thoughts on the workings of the imperial courts in a single inimitable sentence:

> The intricate web of jurisdictions would have been tangled enough if litigants, the courts and the government itself had kept to the already complicated rules, but confusion was worse confounded by the inveterate propensity of all parties to by-pass the rules.

To which he adds the laconic statement that "Justinian made some rather half-hearted attempts to clear up the mess".[25] Pithy one-liners such as those quoted above give us the Jones we tend to remember from Chapter XIV: the stress on bureaucratic confusion and corruption; the repeated insistence on the obscurities and uncertainties of the late Roman legal system and its excessively slow, inefficient and venal administration. The chapter ends by vibrantly portraying the horrors of

---

[22] Pocock (2004) 542 (describing the methodology of Quentin Skinner).
[23] Vessey (2003) 345.
[24] Jones (1964) I, 470.
[25] *Ibid.*, I, 493.

criminal justice under the late empire, with an especially unforgettable and damming dismissal: "Roman criminal justice was in general not only brutal but inefficient".[26] These are the 'telescopic' views of the late Roman legal system that readers tend to take away from Jones' Chapter XIV: focused on the emperors, their over-bureaucratised judicial system and its legislative brutality.

Whilst acknowledging Jones' damning general evaluations of the late Roman judicial system there is another Jones in Chapter XIV—if we read between the lines. This other Jones reveals himself in a more positive 'bottom-up' analysis of forensic practice. Let us take Jones' discussions of late Roman advocacy as an example. The section of Chapter XIV entitled 'Lawyers' (spanning pages 507–16) focuses on the structure of the profession of advocacy, the numbers and social origins of advocates, their distribution and professional attachment to particular courts, their salary, and their avenues for career advancement. Jones seems to say nothing about what advocates actually did in the courtroom, apart from a playful aside that Postumianus (one of the characters in Macrobius' *Saturnalia*), was represented as being so busy with his forensic practice that he was unable to accept an invitation to dinner. Jones, however, does touch upon forensic activity in the courtroom at particular points elsewhere in the chapter—albeit without ever pulling his comments together into a coherent analysis. Two instances will suffice to demonstrate Jones' nascent bottom-up perspective on late Roman advocates.

First, Jones' discussion of the celebrated (so-called) 'law of citations': a constitution issued by the Western emperor Valentinian III in 426.[27] Jones notes that this 426 'law of citations' reaffirmed the primary authority of the jurists Papinian, Paul, Ulpian and Modestinus and also raised Gaius (described by Jones as "the author of a hitherto not much regarded textbook") amongst their number. Jones then carefully specifies that Valentinian III's 426 constitution also allowed authority to earlier jurists whom the "great five" (namely Papinian, Paul, Ulpian, Modestinus and now Gaius) quoted, provided that the texts were verified by the collation of different copies. Jones goes on to explain that the 426 law also specified a rubric for judges and legal practitioners to use, if they had to resolve conflicts of authority between any of the

---

[26] *Ibid.*, I, 520–21.
[27] *Ibid.*, I, 471.

jurists named. The 'majority' opinion was to be followed; if opinion was equally divided then the jurist Papinian had to prevail; only if Papinian offered no guidance on the subject at hand and the other jurists were equally divided, was the judge to use his own discretion. Jones thus concludes: "This rule has been justly regarded as the low-water mark of Roman jurisprudence", repeating a value judgement which can be found in all the standard Roman law textbooks. Jones, however, immediately adds a caveat to this modern assessment of the 426 'law of citations' as the nadir of Roman jurisprudence. Jones states that Valentinian's 'law of citations': "... did at least allow a diligent barrister to tell his client what the law was—unless a more ingenious opponent could produce an imperial constitution which affected the issue". Seen from the bottom up, the law of citations did not restrict or curtail forensic debate: according to Jones it perhaps made it easier. Here Jones hints at the ingenuity and resourcefulness of late Roman advocates in pleading the cases of their clients. The 'law of citations' may have been a low-water mark for Roman jurisprudence, but Jones' assessment of its implications also hints at a vigorous and lively forensic culture.

Our second example of a more positive Jonesian view of legal practice occurs during his discussion of the legal implications of the administrative division between East and West.[28] Jones begins his analysis with a series of simple statements:

> Further confusion was caused by the divisions of the empire. Theoretically, all laws were issued by the college of emperors, and were, if *leges generales*, valid throughout the empire. Actually, the laws of each emperor were promulgated only in the part of the empire which he ruled.

Jones could have left his analysis here, with the stress on theoretical confusion tempered by effective pragmatism, but once again he adds a caveat:

> Though, however, in the ordinary way the courts of one emperor ignored the legislation of his colleague or colleagues, it was always open to an *enterprising barrister* [my italics] to produce a law issued in the other half of the empire, and the courts could not refuse to admit its validity.

Here again, Jones' gives us a telescopic picture of legal and jurisdictional confusion, balanced by a microscopic assessment that an "enterprising

---

[28] *Ibid.*, I, 472–73. For a recent treatment of the relationship between legislation issued in the 'Eastern' and 'Western' halves of the empire see Lepore (2000).

barrister" could work this 'confusion' to their clients' advantage. Jones was also well aware that advocates were not only for the rich—although he astutely notes that if you could pay more, you could employ a better one. Jones cites two papyri dated 340 and 350, one recording a case before the *defensor* of Arsinoe and the other a case heard by the *iuridicus* of Alexandria.[29] Both papyri record disputes undertaken between citizens of (to quote from Jones) "a fairly modest degree" and all of the parties employ advocates. Jones concludes that:

> Both these records give a favourable impression of the way in which justice was administered in these lowly courts. The procedure is informal. The advocates of both parties—all employ counsel—are allowed to have their say; the judge, prompted from time to time by the advocates, endeavours to elicit the facts by questioning the parties or their witnesses. At Arsinoe there is an interpreter to translate for peasant witnesses who know no Greek. On the face of it there appears to be an honest attempt to elicit the truth and make a fair judgement.

Justice on the ground *could* function fairly in the later Roman Empire, even according to A.H.M. Jones.

A more concentrated microscopic focus on day-to-day legal practice can also open the way for a revision of Jones' more damning indictments of late Roman bureaucratic justice. An argument that runs throughout the thematic chapters of the *Later Roman Empire* is that the continual repetition of imperial laws should be interpreted as a sign of the weakness of late Roman government. Jones even throws down a historiographical gauntlet on this topic in his 1964 preface:

> Many modern historians, it seems to me, have too readily assumed that Roman citizens obeyed the law, and that everything was done as the imperial government directed. My own impression is that many, if not most, laws were intermittently and sporadically enforced, and that their chief evidential value is to prove that the abuses which they were intended to remove were known to the central government. The laws, in my view, are clues to the difficulties of the empire, and records of the aspirations of the government and not the achievement.[30]

On Jones' reading the emperors were forced to continually reissue legislation on the same subjects and were under few illusions about the extent to which their subjects took any notice. This argument has

---

[29] Jones (1964) I, 517.
[30] *Ibid.*, I, viii; compare Honoré (2004) 26, citing Gaudemet (1972) 693 and 713–15.

in turn been used in recent scholarship to support the related ideas of *lex scripta* as a (rhetorical) mode for articulating power, and late Roman legal codifications as 'prestige projects'. Whilst there are good reasons to support an understanding of the compilation of late Roman law codes as exercises in imperial theatrics, this should not obscure the fact that they were (at the same time) practical texts designed to be used in litigation. Adopting a microscopic reading, we can see that there is in fact virtually no literal repetition of laws in the Theodosian or Justinianic *Codes*. Even when a new imperial constitution directly refers to a previous imperial law and restates the latter's authority or repeats its text, there is almost always some new applicability specified or some new variation laid down. In fact a text of the third-century jurist Modestinus (included in Justinian's *Digest* at Book I, title 4, section 4) lays out the relevant principle of forensic interpretation: Modestinus states that later imperial constitutions repeal earlier ones, to the extent that they are inconsistent with them; in other words, later constitutions repeal earlier ones *to the extent that they conflict with them or add something to them*. Rather than simply seeing the continual repetition of laws—and the inclusion of those repetitious texts in the law codes—as a weakness of government, we should perhaps interpret it as part of a legislative and forensic culture that was used to referring to the past in order to make sense of the present.

On balance, of course, any reader of Chapter XIV would be correct to take away the overall impression that, according to Jones, the functioning of late Roman justice was confused and corrupt. However, as Jones' asides on the actual practice of advocates illustrate, there is another story that can be told if we focus on legal practice on the ground. This angle has recently come much more to the fore in late Roman scholarship. For example, Traianos Gagos and Peter van Minnen's *Settling a Dispute. Toward a Legal Anthropology of Late Antique Egypt* (1994) and the final two chapters of Jill Harries' *Law and Empire in Late Antiquity* both focus on law as dispute settlement, using perspectives informed by recent debates in the field of anthropology. Significantly, Jones' Chapter XIV says nothing about dispute settlement out of court, nor about the particular practices of formal arbitration that existed outside of imperial jurisdiction. I would suggest nonetheless, however, that Jones' interest in legal practice and justice has prepared the way for a new emphasis on the activity of 'doing law' in the late Empire.

4. *After Jones: New Perspectives on Late Roman Law*

Few of the following 'new perspectives' are entirely new; a story could be told for virtually all of them which would trace their development back to late nineteenth and early twentieth-century Roman lawyers, or to those elusive seventeenth and eighteenth-century scholars of patristic and ecclesiastical texts whom Jones alludes to in his preface or indeed even further back, to the great early modern humanist scholars Cujas and Godefroy. It would likewise be misleading to imply that Jones' 1964 *Later Roman Empire* had a major impact on either Anglophone or Continental Roman lawyers (as opposed to historians interested in law). Jones' determination, however, to treat the later Roman Empire as a coherent period in its own right has certainly encouraged both modern Roman lawyers and historians alike to approach postclassical law on its own terms. Late Roman law is no longer treated simply as a codicil to classical jurisprudence.

A major development in scholarship over the last forty years has been the publication of secondary literature that takes developments in substantive late Roman law seriously. In other words, legal historians and Roman lawyers alike no longer necessarily work within the previous dominant paradigm of jurisprudential 'decline' from an early imperial high to a late Roman low (with an Indian summer occurring during the age of Justinian).[31] There are now textbooks dedicated to late Roman law—a remarkable historiographical advance in itself.[32] There are also recent studies that seek to understand late Roman changes in particular areas of substantive law within the context of a development out of, rather than a deviation away from, classical principles.[33] Legal periodisation is also being rethought: lawyers and historians now speak of an 'epi-classical' period of Roman law, sandwiched between the end of the 'classical' period of Roman jurisprudence and the 'postclassical' period proper (namely from roughly A.D. 223 and the death of Ulpian, until about 310).[34] Finally, the intellectual quality of

---

[31] For discussion see Honoré (1998) and Humfress (2007, forthcoming). This perspective is already evident in Continental scholarship on late Roman law published before 1964.

[32] De Giovanni (1999); see also Kaser and Hackl (1996) 517–644.

[33] For example Sargenti (1994), Barone-Adesi (1998) and Pulitanò (1999).

[34] Corcoran (2000) 2–3; Liebs (1987), (1989), (2000) 258–259 and (2002); Johnston (2005) and in general Wieacker (1988).

postclassical jurisprudence itself is being cautiously re-evaluated.[35] As David Johnston comments in his 1999 *Roman Law in Context*:

> It seems that the postclassical law schools of the fourth and fifth centuries A.D., once blamed for wholesale onslaughts on the texts [of existing jurisprudence], actually approached them with restraint; their intervention is likely to have been confined to writing glosses on the texts, some of which, it is true, may have been absorbed into them. There is, however, some evidence of substantial additions to works that were used for teaching in the law schools... the works of the great Severan jurists, Ulpian, Paul and Papinian, are more likely to have been subject to much reworking, in the course of regular new editions.[36]

That regular new editions of the great Severan jurists *were* being produced in late Roman law schools is of course an important recognition in itself. An interest in postclassical jurisprudence has also been accompanied in recent scholarship by sustained attempts to stabilise late Roman legislative texts by situating them in the contexts in which they were first drafted and posted. We have already discussed the works of Honoré, Harries and Matthews in this respect. The publications and conferences held under the auspices of the *Accademia Romanistica Costantiniana* are part of an ambitious project that aims to reconstruct the entire corpus of late imperial *leges*.[37] The *Accademia Romanistica Costantiniana* itself was founded in 1973, with a detailed mission statement drafted by Mario De Dominicis, Jean Gaudemet, Francesco de Martini and Manlio Sargenti. The stated aims of the *Accademia* are twofold: first to produce a collection of all the material necessary for a reconstruction of law in late antiquity and second "... to promote the critical study of imperial constitutions, their style and their content, with particular reference to determining their efficacy in time and space, and identifying their intended audience".[38] Manlio Sargenti's explanation of the rationale behind the project brings to mind Vessey's criticism of Jones and his legal sources: Sargenti states that "Students today are too often satisfied by the information furnished from the edition

---

[35] See Bianchini (1990) and Wieling (2000).

[36] Johnston (1999) 22.

[37] The *Accademia Romanistica Costantiniana* supports a well-established monograph series, published by Giuffrè Editore, Milan; their annual conference proceedings are published by Edizioni Scientifiche Italiane, Naples.

[38] Quoted from the "Mission statement of the *Accademia Romanistica Costantiniana*", at http://www.telediritto.it/acca/atti_di_convegni.htm (accessed on 05/04/2004).

of Mommsen and the *Regesten* of Seeck".[39] This concern with stabilis-
ing the sources and the complex transmission of late Roman imperial
constitutions also forms the backbone of an important British project:
Projet Volterra I, Law and Empire A.D. 193–455.[40] It is worth quoting the
rationale and aims of the *Projet Volterra I* (as summarised by its principal
researcher, Simon Corcoran) in some detail:

> Given that the general aims of the *Projet Volterra* are to promote the study
> of Roman legislation, the area of Roman imperial legal pronouncements
> was identified as one in which current scholarship was less than adequately
> served in terms of *Regesten, repertoria* and bibliographical aids. Within this
> field the area of later imperial legislation was felt to be particularly poorly
> exploited by scholars in general. It was decided that access to the material
> would be most satisfactorily facilitated by the production of a database
> in an electronic medium which would act not only as a Regest but also
> contain the basic texts of imperial legal pronouncements (where the
> *ipsissima verba* of the issuer(s) survive) from whatever provenance, be it an
> epigraphic, papyrological, juristic or literary source, details relating to each
> text's transmission (including their fate during successive codifications),
> the texts of ancient scholia upon them and an annotated bibliography of
> relevant modern scholarly output. While in no sense providing entirely new
> editions, the text of laws included in the database are critical, including
> the checking of original manuscript readings where appropriate.[41]

The *Projet Volterra I* electronic database thus heralds a radical change in
research on late Roman law, through the exploitation of newly available
information technologies; these encompass digitalised texts, computer-
ised *palingenesia* and internet resources in general.[42] Forty years on from
Jones, we thus have incomparably better resources with which to tackle

---

[39] Quoted from the "Mission statement of the *Accademia Romanistica Costantiniana*", at
http://www.telediritto.it/acca/atti_di_convegni.htm (accessed on 05/04/2004).

[40] See http://www.ucl.ac.uk/history/volterra/pv1.htm—the *Projet Volterra I* is based
at University College, London and was initially funded by the British Academy, then
by the Arts and Humanities Research Board until its principal completion in 2004.
It has subsequently been adopted as a *British Academy Research Project*, thus ensuring
the maintenance and updating of its electronic database. A second five-year phase of
the project, funded by the *Arts and Humanities Research Council* and based at University
College, London, is now underway. *Projet Volterra II, Law and the End of Empire* is focused
on the early medieval period; for details and a full description see http://www.ucl.
ac.uk/history/volterra/pv2.htm

[41] http://www.ucl.ac.uk/history/volterra/pv1.htm#intro (accessed on 06/06/
2006).

[42] For digitalised texts of Roman law see the *Projet Volterra I* database itself at the
stable URL http://www.ucl.ac.uk/history/volterra/perl/volterra.htm; for computer-
ised *palingenesia* of imperial legislation see the disks that accompanied Honoré (1994)
and (1998), both of which are now also available via the *Projet Volterra I database*; Ernst

the complex questions surrounding the transmission of legislative texts
and their source criticism.

A further major 'perspective shift' in recent legal history encompasses
scholarship that seeks to recover the 'actors' and the individuals within
late Roman legislative and legal processes. If we begin with the drafters
of late Roman imperial legislation, Tony Honoré's 1998 monograph
*Law in the Crisis of Empire 379–455 A.D.: The Theodosian Empire and its
Quaestors* summarises decades of research on the office of the *quaestor*,
a bureaucratic official whose importance came to the fore in the mid
to late fourth century A.D. As Honoré explains in chapter 6, entitled
"Understanding the Theodosian Code":

> An important aim of this book is to persuade those who study the laws
> of the Theodosian era to read them, when possible, as part of the output
> of the quaestor who composed them. As we saw in chapter 1, quaestors
> varied in their literary, political and juristic capacity. Nor did all conceive
> their role in the same way...These differences should be borne in mind
> in reading Code texts. A modern court interprets a will drawn up by a
> lawyer differently from a home-made will. Similar discrimination is called
> for in reading the laws of the later empire. Contemporaries were aware
> of this. As the *interpretationes* to the Code show, some laws were thought
> to need interpretation, while others spoke for themselves.[43]

Detlef Liebs, on the other hand, has focused on the identification of
individual late Roman *iurisperiti* (legal experts or jurists) and in doing so
has made an invaluable contribution to the reassessment of provincial
legal culture.[44] John Crook has blazed the trail for a similar identification process that individuates late Roman advocates within their forensic
contexts.[45] This recent focus on 'actors' and individuals within late
Roman legal processes has also been accompanied by the publication
of monographs dedicated to exploring institutions or procedures that
were either established or developed significantly in the late Roman
period. For example, in the *Later Roman Empire* Jones devoted a brief
descriptive paragraph to the late Roman institution of the *defensor civitatis*,
stating that it was "...the first radical improvement at the bottom end
of the scale".[46] This late Roman official is now the subject of an entire

---

Metzger's "Roman Law Resources" web-site provides an excellent introduction to the
wider internet resources for late Roman law: http://www.iuscivile.com/

[43] Honoré (1998) 134.
[44] Liebs (1987), (1989) and (2001).
[45] Crook (1995).
[46] Jones (1964) I, 479.

monograph by Robert Frakes, entitled *Contra potentium iniurias: the defensor civitatis and Late Roman Justice*.[47] Likewise for the thematic subject of the appeals structure of late Roman bureaucratic courts: Jones concluded that the late Roman appeal mechanism amounted to "...the weighing of the scales of justice in favour of the rich" and Federico Pergami has now published an entire monograph that explores the complexities of the late Roman appeals procedure and reassesses its social impact.[48] Newly discovered papyrological and epigraphic evidence, or re-assessments of existing finds, have also contributed to this uncovering of a (provincial) legal world on the ground.[49]

A further aspect of recent research in late Roman legal practice focuses on changes in the documentation of court records after the accession of Diocletian—thus continuing and developing a distinctly Jonesian 'social and administrative' perspective. A 1985 monograph by Hans Carol Teitler on *notarii* and *exceptores* (shorthand writers) in the late Roman imperial and ecclesiastical bureaucracy, highlights a series of post-Diocletianic developments in official record-keeping.[50] Elizabeth Meyer's 2004 monograph *Legitimacy and Law in the Roman World. Tabulae in Roman Belief and Practice* underscores the importance of these changes for legal practice and procedure in particular:

> Over time, and especially after A.D. 284, these court records came to include fuller (if not entirely complete) accounts of everything that went on and what the protagonists and witnesses said...Large segments of court records came to be regularly reread in subsequent cases, as a way of accurately reconstructing what had happened, and of checking current testimony against previous acts or words. Concomitantly, court-records became a regularly referred-to type of "proof" in non-legal settings..."[51]

As Meyer goes on to argue, these changes in notarial and procedural practices became particularly important in the context of religious disputes (for example Augustine's use of trial records in his polemic against North African Donatists or the recitation of courtroom and synodal records in Church councils). As already noted above Jones' *Later*

---

[47] Frakes (2001).
[48] Jones (1964) I, 481–82 and Pergami (2000).
[49] For a recent relevant papyrological discovery see D'Ippolito and Nasti (2003) and in general Purpura (1995).
[50] Teitler (1985), in Dutch with a summary in English.
[51] Meyer (2004) 243. See also Lévy (1999), not cited by Meyer.

Roman Empire, published exactly forty years earlier, took it for granted that late Roman legal structures and processes could not be analysed apart from ecclesiastical and religious developments.

In conclusion, Jones' primary focus was on the bureaucratic structures and the efficacy and equity (or otherwise) of the administration of justice, in so far as they are exposed by the official legal documents. However, his remarkable familiarity with a diverse body of source material, including papyrology and Christian literature, gave him access to the workings of the law (and forensic practitioners) in mundane provincial settings and in the back-woods of empire. Jones' encounter with legal activity *on the ground* leaves its mark on both his narrative and analysis, and to some extent undermines his own summary judgements on the nature of the legal culture and the quality of the law experienced by Rome's subjects in the late Empire. Jones may have intended to studiously ignore Law (and theology) as 'intellectual achievements'—but a careful reading of his ideas on 'Justice' reveals an understanding of Roman law, its setting and its impact, which is broader, more subtle and more influential than a concentration on the main themes of Chapter XIV would suggest.

Bibliography

Barone-Adesi G. (1998) *Ricerche sui 'corpora' normativi dell'impero romano. 1—I 'corpora' degli 'iura' tardoimperiali* (Turin 1998)

Bianchini M. (1990) "Sulla giurisprudenza nell'Italia tardoantica", *Labeo* 36 (1990) 85–115

Corcoran S. (2000) *The Empire of the Tetrarchs*, 2nd revised ed. (Oxford 2000)

——. (2002) "A Tetrarchic inscription from Corcyra and the *Edictum de Accusationibus*", *ZPE* 141 (2002) 221–30

Crawford M. (2002) "Discovery, autopsy and progress: Diocletian's jigsaw puzzles", in *Classics in Progress: essays on Ancient Greece and Rome*, ed. T.P. Wiseman (Oxford 2002) 145–64

Crook J. (1995) *Legal Advocacy in the Roman World* (London 1995)

De Giovanni L. (1999) *Introduzione allo studio del diritto romano tardoantico* (Naples 1999)

D'Ippolito F.M. and Nasti F. (2003) "Frammenti Papiracei di un'Opera della Giurisprudenza Tardo Imperiale", *Studia et Documenta Historiae et Iuris* 69 (2003) 383–98

Du Plessis P. (2004) "Review of Meyer, E.A. (2004) *Legitimacy and Law in the Roman World*", *Edinburgh Law Review* 9(2) (2004) 338–40

Feissel D. (2000) "Une constitution de l'empereur Julien entre text épigraphique et codification (*CIL* III 459 et *CTh* 1.16.8)", in *La Codification des lois dans l'antiquité*, ed. E. Lévy (Paris 2000) 315–37

——. (2004) "Un rescrit de Justinien découvert à Didymes (1er avril 533)", *Chiron* 34 (2004) 285–365

Frakes R.M. (2001) *Contra potentium iniurias: the defensor civitatis and Late Roman Justice* (Munich 2001)

Gagos T. and van Minnen P. (1994) *Settling a Dispute. Toward a Legal Anthropology of Late Antique Egypt* (Ann Arbor 1994)

Gaudemet J. (1972) "Recherches sur la legislation du Bas-Empire", *Studi Scherillo* 2 (1972) 693–715

Harries J. (1999) *Law and Empire in Late Antiquity* (Cambridge 1999)

Honoré T. (1994) *Emperors and Lawyers*, 2nd ed. (Oxford 1994)

——. (1998) *Law in the Crisis of Empire 379–455 A.D.: The Theodosian Empire and its Quaestors* (Oxford 1998)

——. (2004) "Roman Law A.D. 200–400: From Cosmopolis to Rechtstaat?", in *Approaching Late Antiquity, The Transformation form Early to Late Empire*, edd. S. Swain and M. Edwards (Oxford 2004) 109–132

Humfress C. (2005) "Law and Legal Practice in the Age of Justinian", in *Cambridge Companion to the Age of Justinian*, ed. M. Maas (Cambridge and New York 2005) 161–84

——. (2006) "Civil law and social life", in *Cambridge Companion to the Age of Constantine*, ed. N. Lenski (Cambridge and New York 2006) 205–25

——. (2007, forthcoming) "Law in Practice", in *A Companion to Late Antiquity*, ed. P. Rousseau (Oxford 2007)

Johnston D. (1999) *Roman Law in Context* (Cambridge 1999)

——. (2005) "Epiclassical law", in *The Cambridge Ancient History Vol. XII* 2nd ed., *The Crisis of Empire A.D. 193–337*, edd. A. Bowman, P. Garnsey and Averil Cameron (Cambridge 2005) 200–207

Jones A.H.M. (1937) *Cities of the Eastern Roman Provinces* (Oxford 1937), 2nd ed. (Oxford 1971)

——. (1960) *Studies in Roman Government and Law* (Oxford 1960)

——. (1964) *The Later Roman Empire 284–602: A Social, Economic, and Administrative Survey*, 3 vols (Oxford 1964), reprinted in two volumes with continuous pagination (Oxford 1973)

——. (1972) *The Criminal Courts of the Roman Republic and Principate*, with a preface by John Crook (Oxford 1972)

Kaser M. (1950) *Römische Rechtsgeschichte* (Göttingen 1950)

Kaser M. and Hackl K. (1996) *Das Römische Zivilprozessrecht* (Munich 1996)

Lepore P. (2000) "Un Problema Ancora Aperto: I Rapporti Legislativi tra Oriente ed Occidente nel Tardo Impero Romano", *Studia et Documenta Historiae et Iuris* 66 (2000) 343–98

Lévy J.-P. (1999) "L'insinuation 'apud acta' des actes privés dans le droit de la preuve au Bas-Empire", in *Mélanges Fritz Sturm* edd. J.-F. Gerkens, H. Peter, P. Trenk-Hinterberger and R. Vigneron (Liège 1999) 311–26

Liebs D. (1987) *Die Jurisprudenz im spätantiken Italien (260–640 n.Chr.)* (Berlin 1987)

——. (1989) "Römische Jurisprudenz in Africa im 4. Jh. n. chr.", *Zeitschrift der Savigny-Stiftung für Rechtsgeschichte (Romanistische Abteilung)* 106 (1989) 201–17

——. (2000) "Roman law", in *The Cambridge Ancient History Vol. XIV*, 2nd ed., *Late Antiquity: Empire and Successors A.D. 425–600*, edd. Averil Cameron, B. Ward-Perkins and M. Whitby (Cambridge 2000) 238–59

——. (2002) *Römische Jurisprudenz in Gallien (2 bis 8 Jahrhundert)* (Berlin 2002)

Maggio L. (1995) "Note critiche sui rescritti postclassici. 1. Il c.d. processo per rescriptum", *Studia et Documenta Historiae et Iuris* 61 (1995) 285–312

Matthews J.F. (2000) *Laying Down the Law: A Study of the Theodosian Code* (Yale 2000)

Metzger E.A. (2004) "Review of Meyer, E.A. *Legitimacy and Law in the Roman World*", *Irish Jurist* 39 (2004) 370–72

Meyer E.A. (2004) *Legitimacy and Law in the Roman World: Tabulae in Roman Belief and Practice* (Cambridge 2004)

Nörr D. (1998) "Römisches Zivilprozesrecht nach Max Kaser: Prozesrecht und Prozespraxis in der Provinz Arabia", *Zeitschrift der Savigny-Stiftung für Rechtsgeschichte (Romanistische Abteilung)* 115 (1998) 80–98

Pergami F. (2000) *L'appello nella legislazione del tardo impero (AARC, materiali per una palingenesi delle costituzioni tardo-imperiali, serie terza 2)* (Milan 2000)

Pocock J.G.A. (2004) "Quentin Skinner: The History of Politics and the Politics of History", *Common Knowledge* 10.3 (2004) 532–50

Pulitanò F. (1999) *Ricerche sulla 'bonorum possessio ab intestato' nell'età tardo-romana* (Turin 1999)

Purpura G. (1995) *Diritto papiri e scrittura* (Turin 1995)

Roueche C. (1984) "Acclamations in the Later Roman Empire: New Evidence from Aphrodisias", *JRS*, 74 (1984) 181–99

Sargenti M. (1994) "Le 'res' nel diritto del tardo Impero", *Labeo* 40.3 (1994) 309–24

Teitler H.C. (1983) *Notarii en exceptores: een onderzoek naar rol en betekenis van notarii en exceptores in dienst van overheid en kerk in de Romeinse keizertijd (tot circa 450 A.D.)* (Utrecht 1983)

Vessey M. (2003) "Sacred Letters of the Law: The Emperor's Hand in Late Roman (Literary) History", *Antiquité Tardive: Revue Internationale d'Histoire et d'Archéologie* 11 (2003) 345–58

Wieacker F. (1988) *Romische Rechtsgeschichte* (Munich 1988)

Wieling H. (2000) "Rechtsstudium in der Spätantike", *Juristische Schulung* 40.1 (2000) 10–15

CHAPTER SEVEN

A.H.M. JONES AND THE ARMY OF THE FOURTH CENTURY

Roger Tomlin

1. *Introduction*

'The history of the later Roman army falls into two distinct chapters', the fourth century and the sixth, divided by an obscure period in the mid-fifth century, when the Western army disintegrated and the Eastern army evolved into something markedly different.[1] But in the *Later Roman Empire* Jones gives the army, like other institutions, just one chapter, not two, and two-thirds of it to the well-documented army of the fourth century, the army of Ammianus Marcellinus, the Notitia Dignitatum and the Theodosian Code.[2]

As usual this is a social, economic and administrative survey: "I have therefore little to say about wars, but much about the organisation, recruitment and conditions of service of the army".[3] Topics include the types of unit, the difference if any between *comitatenses* and *limitanei*, the recruitment of soldiers, their pay, rations, conditions of service, their promotion and discharge, morale and discipline, the *protectores* and other officers, and lastly numbers. Jones was apparently not much interested in military equipment and battle tactics, for example cavalry against infantry, Romans against barbarians, nor in grand strategy, a concept which has interested his successors more than it may have done the Romans.[4] They have also studied Roman military intelligence and 'the face of battle', unlike Jones, despite his own wartime service in

---

[1] Jones (1964) II, 607.
[2] *Ibid.*, II, 607–54, to which add II, 679–86 (army numbers), and most of Appendix II, 'The Notitia Dignitatum' (in III, 347–80). Also relevant are I, 52–60 (Diocletian), I, 97–100 (Constantine), I, 149 (Valentinian) and I, 156 (Theodosius).
[3] *Ibid.*, Preface, first two sentences.
[4] Luttwak (1976) "has done for Roman historians what they have not done for themselves" (Yavetz), but compare Mann (1979) and Millar (1982). See also Nicasie (1998) 117–84.

Intelligence at the War Office, after an experience of the Ministry of
Labour which he later claimed had not been useless to the historian of
the Roman empire.[5] But like Eric Birley, whose own wartime service
reinforced the fascination, he made himself expert in the Roman order
of battle. This is well summarised in Appendix II and Map IV.

2. *Sources*

Jones excavated in Istanbul and Jerash before the War, but he candidly
admits his "most lamentable gap" is the archaeological material.[6] Thus
he cites none of the "ample archaeological and epigraphic evidence
for [Diocletian's] activity in building strategic roads and fortresses".[7]
A law of 409 which mentions the *fossatum Africae* prompts him to cite
the French aerial survey of that ditch-system, but he could also be as
vague as Gibbon: "The forts of the *limitanei* are depicted in the illus-
trations [...] in the Notitia and the ruins of many still survive".[8] But
unlike Gibbon, he had seen some of them for himself, and even if he
neglected excavation reports, he could have taken a short cut through
the Proceedings of the Frontier Congresses which began in 1949.[9] Since
then, of course, forts and frontiers have been much studied.[10]

Jones famously over-states his neglect of ancient moralists and modern scholarship, but his three principal sources were inevitably written,
secular and ancient. The first is Ammianus Marcellinus, who describes
himself as a former soldier and a Greek; he was a *protector domesticus* who
experienced the Persian siege of Amida (359) and Julian's disastrous
invasion of Mesopotamia (363), before retiring to Rome in the 380s
where he wrote the long Latin history whose surviving books provide
much the most detailed and powerful narrative of the years 353–78.
Jones, like Gibbon, rightly praises him as a great historian, "a man

---

[5] Jones deserves to echo Gibbon here, but in fact he only claimed it was "of some
academic profit" (Crook (1971) 428). For 'the face of battle' in Ammianus, see Matthews (1989) 279–303, citing earlier treatments. For Intelligence, see Lee (1993); Austin
and Rankov (1995).
[6] Jones (1964) Preface.
[7] *Ibid.*, I, 55.
[8] *Ibid.*, III, 192.n.51. Baradez (1949) is the "recent archaeological surveys" of Jones
(1964) II, 652, the note to which (III, 201.n.103) quotes the whole of *CTh* 7.15.1
(409).
[9] Birley (2002).
[10] See, for example, Johnson (1983); Isaac (1992); Elton (1996b).

of penetrating intelligence and of remarkable fairness".[11] Next is the
Notitia Dignitatum, an extraordinary bureaucratic survival, an illustrated
list, or rather two lists, of important military and civil offices in the
East and West dating from about 395, when the Empire was divided
between the sons of Theodosius. The military officials are generals of
the various 'mobile' and frontier armies, and 'at their disposal' are all
the Empire's military units, which are listed by name in the 'mobile'
armies, and by name and station in the frontier armies. Jones devotes
an appendix to this fascinating but rebarbative document, the most
lucid contribution from the years between Seeck's edition (1876) and
Hoffmann's *Bewegungsheer* (1969). After analysing its complex history, he
tabulates it in detail.[12] Lastly the Theodosian Code is a sixteen-book
collection of dated extracts from imperial legislation, ranging by topic
from the year after 312 when Constantine became western emperor,
to the year before its issue by Theodosius II in 438. The army is the
subject of Book VII, a mass of legislation aimed at all sorts of ingenious abuses which regulates the lives of soldiers in minute detail, but
omitting strategy, tactics and specific operations. Its perspective may
have been congenial to Jones, who was reputed to quote it extensively
from memory, a reputation his notes confirm, but characteristically he
comments: "Many modern scholars, it seems to me, have too readily
assumed that Roman citizens obeyed the law, and that everything was
done as the imperial government directed".[13]

Jones' sources for the army ranged far more widely than this trinity:
over inscriptions and papyri, notably from Oxyrhynchus and Panopolis
(the two Beatty papyri) to the Fayyûm (the Abinnaeus archive), as well as
technical writers such as the anonymous *De Rebus Bellicis* and Vegetius'
Epitoma rei militaris. Vegetius he dates to the reign of Valentinian I
(364–75), surely by oversight, since he would have known the reference
to Valentinian's son and successor, 'the deified Gratian', who died in
383.[14] He also exploited litterateurs such as Symmachus, Synesius, the
Latin panegyrists, Themistius and Libanius, and the other historians
such as Aurelius Victor, Orosius and Zosimus (Eunapius). Emperors of
the second and third centuries are the subjects of biographies in the

---

[11] Jones (1964) I, 116. See now Matthews (1989).
[12] Jones (1964) III, 347–91.
[13] *Ibid.*, Preface.
[14] *Ibid.*, II, 642, "writing under Valentinian" [i.e. Valentinian I, *ibid.*]. But see Vegetius i.20, *divus Gratianus*.

style of Suetonius known collectively as the Augustan History, which is poor compensation for the loss of contemporary historians. Jones even forty years ago was somewhat reactionary in dating it to Constantine and accepting its multiple authorship, perhaps with the misgivings found in the *Prosopography* he inspired. Thus he cites its "authors" for the rigid discipline of Pescennius Niger, but instead of naming the spurious historian Flavius Vopiscus, he cites "the author of the *vita Numeriani*".[15]

Jones credits previous scholars with winnowing a "few grains of wheat" from the 'chaff' of Migne's *Patrologiae*. Perhaps the metaphor was unconsciously suggested by Ammianus, who reports an ill-omen which preceded Julian's Persian Expedition, the collapse of a great stack of chaff, crushing fifty foraging soldiers.[16] But it was disingenuous, since "even while convalescing after a critical operation for a gastric ulcer his recurring demand was for volume after volume of Migne's *Patrologia*".[17] He knew Socrates and the other church historians very well, and confidently uses martyr-acts and the lives of saints, for example those of Hilarion of Gaza, Ambrose and Martin, and even the sad tale of Euphemia's marriage to the Goth, mobile soldier and bigamist. In discussing recruits and promotion, he quotes Jerome's exhaustive list of the grades in a cavalry unit which separated 'recruit' from 'tribune', something he may have found at second-hand in 'the standard work on the later Roman army'.[18] But later, in his detailed account of the levy and issue of military clothing, he does not cite another of Jerome's extraordinary asides, his reference to the long linen shirt worn by soldiers because it made for easy movement, the *camisa* or *camisia* (whence French 'chemise').[19] A comprehensive collection of military *Realien* in late-Roman theological writers would be a godsend to students of the army, a thought which brings us to the first Christian emperor, and what Jones has to say about him.

---

[15] Jones (1964) II, 644; III, 195.n.64 (where the wording is a doublette with I, 53).

[16] *Ibid.*, Preface (p. vi). Amm. 23.2.8.

[17] Meiggs (1970). Strictly speaking, it was only "theological treatises and commentaries on the Scriptures" that Jones abandoned.

[18] Jerome, *contra Iohannem Hierosol.* 19, quoted by Grosse (1920) 108, but already known to Mommsen and Dessau (note to *ILS* 2803). Jones cites Grosse at the head of his notes to Chapter XVII (in III, 181).

[19] Jones (1964) II, 624–5. Jerome, *ep.* 64.11, now cited by d'Amato (2005) 8. Since Jerome glosses it as a 'Vulgar' term, this passage has interested philologists, but not James (2004) 59–60, or Bishop and Coulston (2006) 224–5.

3. *Constantine and the* Comitatus

"Constantine appears to have been the innovator who created the army of the fourth century."[20] This judgement repeats the last paragraph of the chapter on Constantine: despite his "extravagant expenditure and reckless fiscality", he had many great achievements to his credit, including the organisation of "an efficient mobile army".[21] Scholars may differ as to the extent of this innovation, but they would agree that it existed. Essentially they follow an early pagan critic, Eunapius as mediated by Zosimus, who contrasts the strategies of Diocletian and Constantine:

> By the forethought of Diocletian, the frontiers of the empire everywhere were covered with cities, garrisons and fortifications which housed the whole army. Consequently it was impossible for the barbarians to cross the frontier because they were confined at every point by forces capable of resisting their attacks. Constantine destroyed this security by removing most of the troops from the frontiers and stationing them in cities which did not need assistance, thus both stripping of protection those being molested by the barbarians and subjecting the cities left alone by them to the outrages of the soldiers, so that henceforth most have become deserted. Moreover, he enervated the troops by allowing them to devote themselves to shows and luxuries. In plain terms, Constantine was the origin and beginning of the present destruction of the empire.[22]

This comparison is justly famous, but it is prejudiced and perverse. Jones more temperately calls it "too absolute...for there were under Diocletian, and almost certainly had been before him, mobile forces under the immediate command of the emperor, which, since they accompanied him on his movements, were called the *comitatus*".[23] This is Jones' term for the mobile army, which he took from the epitaph of a Diocletianic soldier who was promoted from the Eleventh Legion to be a 'lancer in the sacred *comitatus*'.[24] This inscription had already been cited by Grosse, who was careful to distinguish the *comitatenses* (soldiers of the mobile army) from the *comitatus* (the imperial entourage).[25] It is true that soldiers served 'in the *comitatus*', a phrase also found in two

---

[20] Jones (1964) II, 608.
[21] *Ibid.*, I, 111.
[22] Zosimus. *Historia Nova* 2.34 (trans. Ridley).
[23] Jones (1964) I, 52 (on Zos. ii 34).
[24] *ILS* 2781, *lectus in sacro comit(atu) lanciarius*.
[25] Grosse (1920) 60.

martyr-acts of the Great Persecution; and since Jones wrote, another inscription has been found which was dedicated by an *optio age(n)s sacru comitatu*.[26] Thus recruits for the mobile army were sent 'to the *comitatus*'.[27] But Jones was misled by this ambiguity of language. The *comitatus* was the emperor's entourage, the imperial court. Thus Abinnaeus, addressing Constantius II, recalls that as a senior NCO (*ducenarius*) he escorted foreign envoys to "the sacred feet of your piety" in 336, was then promoted *protector domesticus*, and "returned to your sacred *comitatus*" three years later; on both occasions he is referring to the imperial court that 'accompanied' the emperor.[28] Four other *protectores* journeyed to "the most sacred *comitatus*" in 398, "to adore the divine purple of Our Lords" at Easter.[29] But the same language was used by civilians. 'Palatine' civil servants, although they seem to have preferred the term *in palatio*, also served 'in the *comitatus*'; thus an archivist (*adiutor memoriae*) was granted rations "while returning to the sacred *comitatus* of Maximianus Caesar" [Galerius] in 293.[30] So the mobile army was not the *comitatus*, but only part of it. Jones' misnomer was soon pointed out by Hoffmann, but it has been retained by Southern and Dixon.[31] Yet Jones had already defined the *comitatus* correctly as "the group of ministries which were attached to the emperor's person and formed the central government", and he evokes it vividly:

> When in transit the *comitatus* must have presented a formidable spectacle. The roads must have been packed for miles with thousands of troopers of the guard and clerks of the ministries (who were appropriately rated as troopers and drew fodder allowances), and choked with trains of wagons piled with boxes of files (*scrinia*) and sacks of coin and bars of gold and silver.[32]

Again since Jones wrote, a remarkable tombstone has been found, that of the wife of Aurelius Gaius, a soldier in this mobile army of

---

[26] Jones (1964) I, 52–53, quoting the Acts of Maximilian, 2.9 (now Musurillo (1972) 246) and Optatus, Appendix I; Speidel (1979) (*AE* (1979) 535).

[27] *P. Abinn.* 19, explicitly contrasted with local service.

[28] *P. Abinn.* 1, dated by Barnes (1985).

[29] *CPL* 267.

[30] Rea, Salomons and Worp (1985), *proficiscenti...in sacrum comitatum. Comitatus* even became a place-name, apparently at Rome, since it is the burial-place of four martyrs honoured locally (*Chron. Min.* I, 72); perhaps therefore Albanum, or the cemetery of the Equites Singulares Augusti.

[31] Hoffmann (1969) 3. Southern and Dixon (1996) 16–17, despite citing Hoffmann on the previous page.

[32] Jones (1964) I, 366 and 367.

Diocletian and Maximian.[33] Gaius details his own career at great length: first service in legions on the Danube and Rhine, then entry into the cavalry as a mounted 'lancer', followed by successive promotions until he became an *optio* of the *Comites*: this was probably a detachment of the old *Equites Singulares Augusti*, and during the fourth century it was the most senior mobile cavalry regiment.[34] During his military service, he visited 23 provinces or groups of provinces, 4 cities, and crossed the frontier five times—to 'Germany', 'Carpia' and 'Sarmatia'. Evidently he served with Maximian in Mauretania, with Diocletian and Galerius on the Danube. "After these many labours", he writes, "I came to my home in Galatia where I was brought up, to the village of Cotiaeum".

Gaius, like Kipling's legionary who had marched from the Indus to Spain, illustrates the mobility of service *in comitatu*, a soldier in the imperial entourage at the end of the third century, one of the new *comitatenses*. Jones notes that this term first appears in a law of 325, but he rightly thinks it was used earlier.[35] He opts for 312, when Constantine mobilised only one-quarter of his army for the invasion of Italy, but he overlooks two inscriptions, both in Dessau. The first is from Noricum, and is a dedication by the commander of the *Equites Dalm(atae) Aquesiani Comit(atenses)* for an imperial victory dated 27 June 310.[36] The second is the tombstone of a junior officer (*exarcus*) called Valerius Iuventinus who died aged 40 after serving 20 years in the (cavalry) vexillation of the *Equites Dal(matae) Comit(atenses) Ancialitana*.[37] His name is pre-Constantinian, but his tombstone cannot be closely dated. Both these units of *Equites Dalmatae* are named after their station, the first being one of the many bathing-resorts called Aquae, the second Anchialus in Thrace, so they can hardly be 'mobile' units. The location of the first inscription, in Noricum, confirms this. But they also bear the title of *comitatenses*, which must mean that they had been detached from the *comitatus*. It is likely that the term was originally informal: as Jones noticed, when Diocletian confirms veterans' privileges, he refers not to *comitatenses* but to soldiers discharged from "a legion or a vexillation".

---

[33] *AE* (1981) 777 (Aurelius Gaius).
[34] Speidel (1987). For a contemporary *optio* of the *Comites*, see *P. Oxy.* I 43, listing units of Diocletian's expeditionary force in Egypt.
[35] *CTh* 7.20.4. Jones (1964) I, 97.
[36] *ILS* 664.
[37] *ILS* 2792.

As late as the Brigetio Tablet (311), the reference is still to "legionary soldiers and cavalrymen organised in Illyrian vexillations".[38]

These documents all indicate that, despite Zosimus, there was a 'mobile army' before Constantine. Jones was well aware of this, even if he thought "the *comitatus* [by which he meant the mobile army] seems to have been a very small body under Diocletian".[39] He gives two good reasons for thinking this: in the Notitia lists, which go by seniority, only the most senior mobile units are Diocletianic; and there is literary and documentary evidence to show that when Diocletian and his colleagues mobilised an expeditionary force, "it was formed in the manner habitual in the second century by assembling detachments drawn from the frontier legions and auxiliary troops".[40] This is quite true, but arguably he underestimates the size of the permanent mobile force, and by implication ignores the ill-documented evolution of the third century which anticipated the Constantinian revolution.

4. *Before Constantine*

In this earlier period, Jones comments, "there is virtually no evidence for changes in the military establishment after the reign of Alexander Severus... even for the Severan period our information is incomplete".[41] Of Gallienus he notes that senators were excluded from military commands, but only adds: "Attempts to make [Gallienus] into a hero are not very convincing, but he must have had some good qualities to reign eight years".[42] This is too general: the same might be said of President Bush. But Jones makes a more apposite comment in the very last chapter: its professional officer-corps was one respect in which the later Roman army was superior to that of the Principate.[43] This can be traced back to Marcus Aurelius, but Gallienus and his new *protectores divini lateris* deserve much of the credit.[44] After Gallienus,

---

[38] Jones (1964) I, 55, with III, 7.n.35, quoting *CJ* vii 64.9 (293/305); *CJ* x 55.3 (286/93) and *FIRA* I² 93, *tam legionarii milites quam etiam equites in vexillationibus constituti Inlyriciani*.

[39] *Ibid.*, I, 54.

[40] *Ibid.*

[41] *Ibid.*, I, 56.

[42] *Ibid.*, I, 24–25.

[43] *Ibid.*, II, 1037.

[44] Christol (1977).

Jones refers to "the Dalmatian and Moorish cavalry which appear to have been part of Aurelian's mobile field army", citing Zosimus and the Notitia.[45] Here he misses an extraordinary fragment of the Greek historian Dexippus, Eunapius' predecessor, which actually names this army: Aurelian received a German delegation in front of "the standards of the select army, golden eagles, imperial images, and the names of units picked out in golden letters".[46] This elite, the 'select army', was the shining weapon with which the great 'Illyrian' emperors of the later third century worked a military miracle.

Most of the evidence was available to Jones, and it had already been exploited. For the cavalry, Ritterling had pointed out sixty years before that Greek sources, unlike the Latin, paint a positive picture of Gallienus; and in particular they credit him with a 'cavalry army' under unified command which was then used by his Illyrian successors.[47] Later scholars have deduced that late-Roman cavalry units were called 'vexillations' [detachments], not because they used the cavalry flag or *vexillum*, as Vegetius thought, but because they were 'detached' from the larger units of this cavalry army. Thus the various *Equites Dalmatae* go back to the 'Dalmatian' cavalry mentioned in literary sources. As Jones himself noticed, the 'reactionary' Diocletian distributed much of this cavalry among the frontier armies, where it would still be available for campaigns. Constantine increased the numbers *in comitatu* by recalling many of these detachments, and by skimming others which were reduced to *cunei*.[48]

For the infantry, Maria Alföldi in 1959 published important coin evidence. This was five years before *The Later Roman Empire* was published, and Jones devotes much space to third-century coinage, but only as an index of inflation. Alföldi showed that the coinage of Gallienus honours 17 legions, from the Rhine and Danube, in *c.* 260. At this date he did not control these frontiers, so the explanation must be that his 'legions' were only detachments based in northern Italy.[49] The same system, on a smaller scale, is later found in the 'legionary' coinage of Carausius from

---

[45] Jones (1964) I, 55.

[46] Dexippus, fragment 6.2.

[47] Ritterling (1903). For a detailed assessment of the Greek sources for the third-century Roman army and how they differ from the Latin tradition see Bleckmann (1992).

[48] Jones (1964) I, 55 and I, 99–100, but analysed by Hoffmann (1969) 211, 253–60.

[49] Alföldi (1959).

Britain and northern Gaul.[50] These vexillations formed an improvised field army, like the legionary detachments which had already fought for Septimius Severus and his successors. Typical of his generals is Iulius Septimius Castinus, legate of the German Legion *I Minervia*, and "*dux* of detachments drawn from the four German legions against traitors and rebels".[51] Their use by Gallienus in the 260s was nothing new, as Jones knew, and it was continued by Diocletian.[52] Alföldi's insight is supported by a scatter of epigraphic evidence. For Britain there is the engraved bronze roundel now in Paris, but deriving perhaps from north Italy, which shows detachments of the Second Legion *Augusta* and the Twentieth *Valeria Victrix* 'brigaded' under a single commander, watching a wild-beast show.[53] At Sirmium likewise, there is a dedication for the well-being of Gallienus and "the soldiers of the German and British legions with their auxiliaries".[54]

The largest group of relevant inscriptions was not available to Jones: these are the tombstones re-used in the walls of Apamea in Syria, which commemorate legionaries, notably from the Second *Parthica*, who died during the eastern campaigns of Caracalla, Severus Alexander and Gordian III.[55] This legion is central to the evolution of the late-Roman army: it was raised by Septimius Severus, but was not committed to frontier defence; instead he based it near Rome, at Albanum, and with his much enlarged Praetorian Guard (now an elite drawn from the Danubian legions) and the old *Equites Singulares Augusti* (a mounted elite drawn from auxiliary cavalry), it gave him the powerful nucleus of an expeditionary force.[56] It was also the premium paid by the Empire to insure against Septimius Severus himself, another provincial general marching on Rome.

The use of detachments is the key to understanding the evolution of the late-Roman mobile army. How they were actually formed is illustrated by two inscriptions from Rome, one available to Jones in Dessau, the other only published in 1981, in which the Second Legion *Parthica* makes two dedications for the safe return from the East of Gordian III and then of Philip, both of them without avail. The first is dated

[50] Casey (1994) 92–3.
[51] *ILS* 1153. This and the other evidence is collected by Cooper (1968) ch. 7.
[52] Jones (1964) I, 54.
[53] *RIB* II.3, 2427.26*.
[54] *ILS* 546.
[55] Balty (1988); Balty and van Rengen (1993).
[56] Birley (1969).

24 July 242, and names the legionaries who joined in 216 and were now being discharged; they were commanded by the deputy Praetorian Prefect (indicating the link between the Guard and this 'mobile' legion), and by their own 'reserve commander' (*praefectus reliquationis*).[57] The other dedication is dated 23 July 244, and names the recruits of 218 who were now being discharged.[58] It follows from both inscriptions that when the legion went on campaign, potential veterans, the men already in their 40s, were left behind. In other words, 'field-service' units were formed from soldiers who were young and fit.

The Praetorian Guard of Septimius Severus and his Second *Parthica* were the ancestors, in strategic terms, of Diocletian's famous *Ioviani* and *Herculiani*, which are listed by the Notitia as the senior pair of mobile legions. Their seniority is confirmed by the Arch of Galerius at Thessalonica, where the shields of soldiers attending the Emperor on his Persian campaign carry the devices of a standing Hercules or an eagle, just like the *Ioviani* in the Notitia.[59] But Jones with some reservation followed Seeck in seeing them as detachments of the frontier Legions I *Iovia* and II *Herculia*.[60] This idea was suggested by Diocletian's practice already mentioned of forming expeditionary forces from legionary detachments, and it supports his view that Diocletian's *comitatus* (his permanent establishment) was small, but it goes against Vegetius' statement that they were 6,000-strong legions from Illyricum armed with the *mattiobarbulus* [the weighted dart which superseded the *pilum*].[61] Even if their size is wrong—other new legions at this date were much smaller—Vegetius is surely correct in seeing them as separate and entire. As it happens, we know of detachments drawn from both these frontier legions, and they kept their parent's name: the *legio prima Iovia Scythica* of Aurelius Gaius, and *leg(ionis) II Herculiae co(ho)r(tes) X et VII* which accompanied Maximian to Mauretania.[62]

---

[57] *AE* (1981) 134.

[58] *ILS* 505, whose provenance of Rome (not Albanum) is now confirmed by the discovery of *AE* (1981) 134.

[59] *Not. Dig. Or.* 5.3 (*Ioviani iuniores*); *Occ.* 5.2 (*Ioviani seniores*); the device by implication antedates the division of the legion into *iuniores* and *seniores*. Laubscher (1975) pls. 38.1 and 56.2 (Hercules); 32.1 and 42.1 (eagle).

[60] Jones (1964) I, 53; compare Seeck (1876) 309.

[61] Vegetius i.17.

[62] *AE* (1981) 777 (translating the Greek); *ILS* 4195 (with Speidel 1982). Further argument in Hoffmann (1969) 215–8.

The *Ioviani* and *Herculiani* were named after the gods of Diocletian
and Maximian, and are thus parallelled by two other very senior
legions, the *Solenses* and *Martenses*, which were evidently named after the
gods of Diocletian's two junior colleagues, Constantius and Galerius.[63]
Diocletian, like Septimius Severus, was raising 'mobile' legions which
were not committed to frontier defence. Jones overlooked the parallel,
but he used the same argument to date another legion with a pagan
name, the *Dianenses*, which he thought was earlier than Constantine.
They were, as it happens, but for another reason. Their name derives,
not from the goddess directly, but from the place-name Ad Dianam on
the Via Egnatia, where they must have been previously stationed. They
were typical of the hinterland garrisons 'mobilised' by Constantine.[64]
The same is true of another unit (this time of cavalry), the *Equites
Crispiani*, which Jones twice calls "certainly Constantinian".[65] He was
thinking of Crispus Caesar, who died in 326, but their name is better derived from Crispiana, a station on the road from Sirmium to
Carnuntum. This is one of eleven listed by the Antonine Itinerary,
two others of which also contributed to the Notitia armies, Antianis
the *Antianenses*, and Cimbrianis the *Milites Cimbriani*.[66]

Late-Roman unit-titles can be difficult. Jones deduces from a law
of 344 which privileges *fabricenses* and *calcarienses*, that there may have
been "imperial boot factories" at this time, as well as arms factories.[67]
Evidently he derives *calcariensis* from *calceus* (a boot, although its cognate
caliga might have been better in this context), but actually it derives
from *calx* (lime) and means 'limeburner'. There is even a unit of *milites
calcarienses* at Sirmium; not 'limeburners', as it happens, but deriving
their name from one of the places called Calcaria ('the lime kilns'),
one of them in Britain.[68]

---

[63] Hoffmann (1969) 173. Their exact seniority is obscured in the Notitia, since they
have been posted to armies commanded by regional *magistri militum*, but the *Solenses*
were the first-ranking legion in Thrace (*Not. Dig. Or.* 8.34) and the *Martenses* the second
in Oriens (7.40).
[64] Jones (1964) I, 59. See Hoffmann (1970) 4.n.149.
[65] Jones (1964) I, 58 (but not named) and I, 99; *Not. Dig. Occ.* 40.20.
[66] *Itin. Ant.* 266.14, *item a Sirmio Carnunto.* Crispiana is 267.9; Antianis is 267.4 (compare *Not. Dig. Occ.* 5.112 = 262); Cimbrianis is 267.8 (compare *Not. Dig. Occ.* 5.155 =
7.145).
[67] Jones (1964) II, 625, citing *CTh* 12.1.37.
[68] *Not. Dig. Occ.* 32.49. *Itin. Ant.* 468.5 (near York); Rivet and Smith (1979) 288–9
note others in Gaul and Lower Germany.

5. *The New Army of Constantine*

Jones may have exaggerated the contrast between Diocletian and Constantine, and played down the third-century evolution, but these are questions of emphasis where scholars will differ. Essentially he is right to see Constantine as the creator of the mobile army we find in Ammianus and the Notitia. It consisted of 'vexillations', a term now restricted to cavalry, 'legions' old and new and old, and a new type of unit recruited from non-Romans, the *auxilium*. The earliest *auxilia* were pre-Constantinian, but he much increased their number. Some of the legions are 'new' like the *Ioviani* and *Herculiani*, others originate from 'old' legions, former detachments often with numerical titles like *Primani* and *Octavani*. The clearest instance of Constantine's permanent 'mobilisation' of frontier detachments is the pair of legions which follow the *Ioviani* and *Herculiani* in the Notitia, the very senior *Divitenses* and the *Tungrecani*.[69] The origin of the *Divitenses* is certain, as Jones knew, for there are Tetrarchic tombstones of men from the so-called *legio II Italica* 'of the *Divitenses*'.[70] Clearly it was a detachment from the old garrison of Noricum, Marcus Aurelius' Legion II *Italica*, which was posted to the Cologne bridgehead fort of Divitia (*castrum Divitensium*) built "in the land of the Franks in the Emperor's presence" after their defeat by Constantine.[71] Brigaded with them in the fourth century are the *Tungrecani*, not a cohort of Tungrians re-named, but the former garrison of the *civitas Tungrorum* (Tongres), a key point on the strategic road leading west from Cologne. They were thus like the *Dianenses* and *Equites Crispiani* already mentioned. The same may have happened in Britain. Here the archaeological evidence suggests that the outpost forts of Hadrian's Wall were abandoned at about this date, and it is tempting to link this with a visit by Constantine, attested only by coins which mark his *adventus*, when he may have withdrawn units from Britain for his impending campaign against Maxentius in 312.[72]

Constantine's new army was commanded, not by the praetorian prefects, who now lost their military authority, but by two new generals, the *magister peditum* and the *magister equitum*. Like the progressive transfer of frontier armies from provincial governors to professional

---

[69] *Not. Dig. Occ.* 5.145–8.
[70] Jones (1964) I, 97–8, with III, 14.n.43. See further, Hoffmann (1969) 177–9.
[71] *ILS* 8937.
[72] Casey (1978).

soldiers (*duces*), this completed what Jones calls the "growing cleavage between the civilian and military careers".[73] There is, however, a small scatter of evidence that in emergency, or in special circumstances, civilians might take command. In 354, for example, Isaurian brigands converged on the provincial capital of Cilicia, which was then held by three legions. The legions made a sortie but, despite morale being good, their officers decided not to risk battle, in Ammianus' words "because walls were not far away, which could safely protect them all". They stood siege instead and were rescued by forces collected by the Count of the East, a civilian.[74]

These Cilician legions were *limitanei*, the 'immobile' counterpart of Constantine's strategic reserve. The frontier armies were now a bewildering mosaic of old and new legions, old auxiliary cohorts and *alae*, new units of *equites* and *milites*. They garrisoned forts along the frontiers and in areas of internal insecurity like the borders of Isauria. Whether deliberately or not, they also acted as police, a role best illustrated by the correspondence of Abinnaeus who, after his two visits to the *comitatus*, was promoted to command a cavalry garrison in the Fayyûm. The history of these frontier army-lists in the Notitia is very complicated. There are actually two Notitias, East and West, which were separated in about 395, but their contents are often earlier in date. In Britain, for example, the Duke's chief of office-staff is drawn in alternate years from the offices of the *magistri militum praesentales*.[75] This tactic of centralisation is not found in the Eastern Notitia, so it may be attributed to Stilicho, that is, after 395. But within the same chapter, the famous list *per lineam valli* of Hadrian's Wall forts and garrisons contains nothing which is demonstrably later than the mid-third century, in spite of numismatic evidence that the forts were occupied until the end of the fourth century. Likewise the Eastern Notitia includes units which we know from Ammianus were lost at the siege of Amida in 359. They would all seem to be bureaucratic 'fossils'.

Jones postponed a problem which had exercised his predecessors, the difference between *comitatenses* and *limitanei*. Only after surveying Diocletian and Constantine in detail does he remark that he draws "no radical distinction" between *comitatenses* and *limitanei*, despite "the

---

[73] Jones (1964) I, 101.
[74] Amm. Marc. 14.2.15–20. See further, Tomlin (1976).
[75] *Not. Dig. Occ.* 40.58.

generally accepted view" that only the *comitatenses* were regular soldiers, whereas *limitanei* were "a kind of hereditary peasant militia". The positive evidence is "very slender", the Augustan History's *Life of Severus Alexander* in fact. But, he continues: "the whole Life is a fantasy, a portrait of the ideal emperor painted for the edification of the monarch to whom it was dedicated, who is stated to be, and probably was, Constantine".[76] The negative evidence by contrast is overwhelming. The Code shows that service in the *limitanei* was not hereditary; that by issuing rations and granting land on discharge, the government recognised that *limitanei* were not already cultivating land. The Notitia shows that *limitanei* might be 'mobilised' as *pseudocomitatenses*.[77] Jones might have added anecdotal evidence from Ammianus that Julian, for example, drew on the frontier forces of Osrhoene for his invasion of Persia.[78] Hoffmann has since noted the numbers of cavalry involved in fourth-century campaigns, for example at the battle of Mursa; they are too large for the *comitatenses* alone to have provided, and it is likely that Magnentius and Constantius drew on frontier units as well.[79] However, not all contemporaries believed that mobile service was superior. Abinnaeus received a begging letter from a clergyman: his nephew, the son of a soldier, had been conscripted; but he was his widowed mother's sole support, so get him released, or "if he must serve, please safeguard him from going abroad with the draft for the *comitatus*".[80]

6. *Recruitment, Equipment and Numbers*

Jones incidentally says that recruits were "branded", but in fact they were tattooed.[81] The source of these recruits has been much discussed. Jones notes that "Constantine has been charged with barbarising the Roman army"; and "The Roman government has been strongly criticised for enlisting Germans in such profusion into its armies".[82] Independent-minded as usual, he refutes these charges: in Ammianus'

---

[76] Jones (1964) II, 649, citing *Alex.* 58.
[77] *Ibid.*, II, 650.
[78] Amm. 24.1.2.
[79] Hoffmann (1969) 193–4.
[80] *P. Abinn.* 19.
[81] Jones (1964) II, 617, with III, 185.n.19. He cites Vegetius i.8, but tattooing is explicit: *punctis signorum scribendus est tiro*. See also C.P. Jones (1987) 149.
[82] Jones (1964) I, 98 and II, 621.

detailed narrative, there is hardly an instance of individual German soldiers proving 'unreliable'. In fact "the danger was not very serious", Jones comments, because Germans served in mixed units under Roman or romanised German officers; there was no pan-German sentiment, and the Germans were cut off from their roots. Much the same pressures applied in the army of the Principate, when it was quite exceptional—say among the Batavians in 69—for auxiliary regiments to be disloyal. Jones illustrates this process by the usurpation of Silvanus, a Frankish general who could not appeal to his native people; he might have added a telling detail, also in Ammianus, that the Frankish tribune of a *schola*, Malarichus, protested that he and his colleagues were 'men devoted to the Empire'.[83] What is interesting is that Ammianus implicitly agrees with them. The old idea of his *Antigermanismus* has since been exploded by Demandt, but there is no sign that Jones shared it.[84] It would be more true to say that Ammianus was indeed prejudiced against Germans, but only when they were not serving Rome.

Even if Jones read less archaeology than he should have done, he did the archaeologists a good turn by defining *laeti* and *federati* for them. French and German archaeologists, when they found late-Roman inhumations with weapons, would label them as the graves of *laeti* or *federati*, as if the two terms were interchangeable.[85] Ammianus confuses the issue by referring to *laeti* once as a raiding tribe, but in fact they were, in Jones' words, "barbarians from outside the empire settled on land in Gaul and Italy, who were, with their descendants, liable to military service".[86] *Federati*, on the other hand, were "contingents furnished under treaty by tribes in alliance with the empire and serving under their own tribal leaders".[87] They are rare until the disaster of Adrianople in 378, which compelled desperate measures to make good the irreversible loss of battle-trained Roman infantry.

If Jones had read more archaeological reports, he might also have described the army's arms, armour and equipment. He is aware of arms factories (*fabricae*), since they concern the Code. Incomplete evidence from Dura Europus would have been available, and he might have used famous images like the porphyry Tetrarchs at Venice and

---

[83] Amm. 15.1.6, *homines dicatos imperio*.
[84] Demandt (1965) 31–9. Contrast Ensslin (1923) 30–33.
[85] MacMullen (1963).
[86] Jones (1964) I, 60.
[87] *Ibid.*, II, 611.

the Arch of Galerius at Thessalonica. But much of the evidence has been collected since.[88] Military hardware may now be the province of re-enactment buffs, but it had important implications for the Empire's organisation and economy. The army absorbed a large proportion of 'industrial' production. The late-Roman helmet, for example, instead of being hand-forged in one piece, was now made of two iron plates riveted together under a ridge: it was heavier, but effective and cheaper to make. Multiple lances and the *mattiobarbulus* replaced the legionary *pilum*, again cheaper expedients, which also increased the 'firepower' of the infantry before hand-to-hand fighting. In technology the late-Roman army was far superior to its barbarian opponents, a point already well made by E.A. Thompson, who warns against assuming "that wars are won simply by the superiority of weapons, armour and reserves".[89] But new weapons imply different tactics: the longsword largely replaced the short, stabbing *gladius*; a smaller, oval shield replaced the old rectangular *scutum*; these might imply a looser, less disciplined fighting order. There is also the question of whether Vegetius is right to blame the army's defeats by the Goths on its abandonment of body-armour and helmets.[90] There is no positive evidence for this, and it was not a factor at Adrianople, but the issue is emotive, as we have seen in Iraq. And there is the question raised by the anonymous *De Rebus Bellicis*, of whether the Roman high command was consciously innovative and even anxious to save manpower by primitive 'mechanisation'.

"One of the most important and most difficult questions, that of numbers", in Jones' words, "has been left to the last". When quantifying the Notitia's order of battle, he assumed an establishment of 1,000 for legions, 500 for other units, but these figures are surely too high.[91] He expected, for example, that Diocletian's frontier legions "remained at two-thirds or half their original strength", without considering the well-preserved and accessible site of Kaiseraugst on the Swiss Rhine. This fortress built for Diocletian's new legion, the First *Martia*, was only 3.6 hectares in area, less than one-fifth of an old legionary fortress like Caerleon (20.5 hectares). Comparable figures have since

---

[88] James (1988); Southern and Dixon (1996) 89–126; Bishop and Coulston (2006) 200–52.

[89] Thompson (1965) 109–49, adapted from Thompson (1958) quoted at 22.

[90] Vegetius i.20.

[91] Jones (1964) II, 679–84. See further, Duncan-Jones (1990); Coello (1996); Tomlin (2000).

been published for other new fortresses. In 359 Ammianus notes that eight 'legions' were trapped in Amida, but the total number, which included refugees and the civil population, was only 20,000.[92] In 398, three mobile legions including the *Ioviani* and *Herculiani*, and four crack *auxilia*, totalled only 5,000 men.[93] This was the expedition which sailed to Africa against Gildo, a force comparable with the 3,500 men available to Count Theodosius at a crucial moment twenty-five years earlier, when he campaigned in Africa against Gildo's brother Firmus. By the standards of the Principate, expeditionary forces seem rather small: in 360, Constantius II ruled that when a legion was on the march, it should have a maximum of two wagons of the *cursus publicus* to carry its invalids.[94] The legionaries must have been very fit—or the wagons very large—if they numbered even 500.

As for auxiliary units, Jones thought there was "no reason to believe that their establishment had ever been altered, and it may be presumed to have been the same in the later empire". His only direct evidence is that the Notitia still specifies some units as 'milliary', but he did not consider the archaeological evidence for the reduction in size of old forts, the signs of less intensive occupation, the presence of civilians, all of which point to a reduction in unit-strength.[95] Instead he used the two Beatty Panopolis Papyri, published by Skeat in 1964, but already available. They are extensive fragments of the archives of an Egyptian deputy-governor, the *strategus* of the Panopolite nome, which contain orders for the issue of pay and rations to various military units in 298 and 300. "The starting-point", Skeat noted, "is the brilliant observation of Professor A.H.M. Jones that, without exception, all the amounts of the donatives are divisible by 625".[96] But this is not the donative, only a unit of account deriving from the 25 *aurei* of 25 *denarii* each which were used apparently to calculate much earlier donatives, and it leaves unanswered the difficult question of differentials according to the

---

[92] Amm. 18.9.3, but only four have 'legionary' names. The total of 20,000 was less than Persian losses of 30,000 (19.2.14, 19.9.9).

[93] Claudian, *Bellum Gildonicum* I.418–19, with Orosius, *Historia adversus paganos* 7.36.6.

[94] *CTh* 8.5.11.

[95] Duncan-Jones (1990) 214–7.

[96] Skeat (1964) xxvii, which Crook (1971) notes as an example of Jones' *felicitas*. The figures are tabulated in Jones (1964) III, 187–8.n.31, and with minor corrections in Duncan-Jones (1990) 218–9.

recipient's rank.[97] The excellence of Skeat's edition notwithstanding, the subject is safe only for mathematicians, although Jones' pioneering analysis has since been much refined.[98] In fact the papyri merit further study, but only one detail will be considered here, Jones' conclusion that an auxiliary cavalry regiment, the *ala I Hiberorum*, numbered about 360 men.

This unit features in both papyri, being the only one for which we have figures, both of barley (for the horses) and wheat (for the men) issued in 298, and of *denarii* for pay (*stipendium*) and in lieu of rations (*annona*) issued in 300.[99] It can thus be compared with a much earlier regiment, the *ala Sebosiana*, which was at Carlisle towards the end of the first century. In three days the latter's horses consumed 630 bushels (*modii*) of barley, its men 267 bushels of wheat; a ratio of about 10: 4.2.[100] The *ala I Hiberorum* in 298 was issued with 2,610 bushels of barley, and the equivalent of 1,030 bushels of wheat, for a period of two months; a ratio of about 10: 4. This near-coincidence inspires confidence in both sets of figures.[101] They tell us that in one day, the Carlisle regiment consumed 210 bushels of barley and 89 bushels of wheat; the Egyptian 43.5 bushels of barley and 17 bushels of wheat. Evidently the *ala I Hiberorum* was no more than one-fifth the strength of the old *ala Sebosiana*. In fact the latter was not quite up to strength, since consumption per troop (*turma*) was not uniform, but varied slightly; but even if we assume a high figure of 480 men, this would give the *ala I Hiberorum* just over 90 men, or rather, men-rations. The actual number of horsemen would have been lower still, since after Diocletian's reforms, when rations became the major part of a soldier's regular pay, officers and NCOs received multiple rations; they would also have had

---

[97] See, for example, Tomlin (2006).

[98] Duncan-Jones (1990).

[99] The unit is named only in *P. Beatty Panop.* ii 37, which like the contemporary *P. Oxy.* 2953 locates it at Thmoö, still its station in the Notitia (*Or.* 31.46); but Skeat followed by Duncan-Jones (1990) 107) convincingly identifies it with "the soldiers under the prefect Papias, stationed in the fort of Thmoö" (*P. Beatty Panop.* i 392).

[100] Tomlin (1998) 36–51. This is actual consumption, and compares quite well with our only other figure for the (projected) consumption of barley by an *ala*, in Egypt in 187, which was 90,000 bushels a year, or 750 for three days.

[101] Duncan-Jones (1990) 107–8 works from a wheat figure of only 128 7/8ths *artabas* [580 *modii*] for the *ala*, as in *P. Beatty Panop.* i 395–8, by excluding the next letter in "same form and date" (i 399) which adds another 100 *artabas*. But his argument for doing so, which entails a barley / wheat ratio of 9:2, is not really convincing.

remounts.[102] The effective strength, in men and horses, would have been less than 90. Archaeologically this conclusion is borne out by a well-preserved contemporary fort, Diocletian's *castra Praetorii Mobeni*, Qasr Bshir in Jordan, where the stabling comprises 21 rooms, each with 3 mangers; in other words, enough space for 63 horses.[103]

This impression is reinforced by the figures for pay. On 1 January 300, the *ala I Hiberorum* received 73,500 *denarii* in pay (*stipendium*) and 23,600 *denarii* cash in lieu of four months' rations (*annona*). Since the papyrus prices gold at 60,000 *denarii* to the pound, this would notionally have been 97 *aurei*. If we take the two payments to be the Diocletianic equivalent of the first of the three annual pay-instalments received by soldiers in the late first century, which then included the cost of food before deduction, and if we assume that 480 troopers of the *ala Sebosiana* were each being paid the same as a legionary, that is 100 *denarii* (or 4 *aurei*) three times a year, we can say that on 1 January 100, the men of *ala Sebosiana* would have received 1,920 *aurei*. This is almost twenty times what the *ala I Hiberorum* received two centuries later. An exact comparison is not possible since we are ignoring the (multiple) pay received by the officers of the *ala Sebosiana*, otherwise assumed to be at full-strength, and ignoring the regular donatives received by *ala I Hiberorum*, and the whole question of whether Diocletianic 'pay' (even including rations and donatives) had kept pace with inflation. But even so, it would be surprising if the *ala I Hiberorum* were as much as one-tenth the size of the old *ala Sebosiana*. In fact it was now commanded by a decurion, the implication being that it approximated towards an old-style *turma* of 30 men.[104]

But these are points of detail, too much detail perhaps. In spite of occasional limitations, whether self-imposed or simply due to the shortness of human life, Jones contributed more to the study of the late-Roman army than any other English-speaking scholar. Eric Birley called him 'Imperial Jones', and he deserves a royal panegyric for his knowledge of the primary sources, the extraordinary lucidity of his presentation, the common-sense and independence of mind, virtues we take for granted in the *Later Roman Empire*. Forty years on, its chapter

---

[102] Jones (1964) II, 626–30. For remounts, compare *CTh* 7.22.2: two horses for even quite a junior officer, the *circitor*.

[103] Kennedy (2004) 148–51.

[104] *P. Beatty Panop.* ii 37. This may have been a temporary expedient, just as in *P. Oxy.* 2953, where a centurion seems to have been responsible.

on the army remains the essential starting-point, and still quite often has the last word.[105]

Bibliography

Alföldi M.R. (1959) "Zu den Militärreformen des Kaisers Gallienus", in *Limes-Studien: Vorträge des 3. Internationalen Limes-Kongresses in Rheinfelden/Basel 1957* (Basel 1959) 13–18

Austin N.J.E. and Rankov N.B. (1995) *EXPLORATIO: Military and Political Intelligence in the Roman World from the Second Punic War to the Battle of Adrianople* (London 1995)

Balty J.C. (1988) "Apamea in Syria in the Second and Third Centuries A.D.", *JRS* 78 (1988) 91–104

Balty J.C. and van Rengen W. (1993) *Apamea in Syria: the winter quarters of Legio II Parthica* (Bruxelles 1993)

Baradez J. (1949) *Fossatum Africae: recherches aériennes sur l'organisation des confins sahariens à l'époque romaine* (Paris 1949)

Barnes T.D. (1985) "The career of Abinnaeus", *Phoenix* 39 (1985) 368–74

Birley A.R. (2002) "Fifty years of Roman frontier studies", in *Limes XVIII: Proceedings of the XVIIIth International Congress of Roman Frontier Studies held in Amman, Jordan (September 2000)*, edd. P. Freeman, J. Bennett, Z.T. Fiema and B. Hoffmann (Oxford 2002) 1–11

Birley E. (1969) "Septimius Severus and the Roman Army", *Epigraphische Studien* 8 (1969) 63–82, reprinted in *idem* (1988) *The Roman Army: Papers 1929–1986* (Amsterdam 1988) 21–40

Bishop M.C. and Coulston J.C.N. (2006) *Roman Military Equipment: from the Punic Wars to the Fall of Rome*, 2nd ed. (Oxford 2006)

Bleckmann B. (1992) *Die Reichskrise des III. Jahrhunderts in der spätantiken und byzantinischen Geschichtsschreibung: Untersuchungen zu den nachdionischen Quelle der Chronik des Johannes Zonaras* (Munich 1992)

Casey P.J. (1978) "Constantine the Great in Britain—the Evidence of the Coinage of the London Mint, A.D. 312–14", in *Collectanea Londiniensia: Studies in London and Archaeology presented to Ralph Merrifield* edd. J. Bird, H. Chapman and J. Clark (London 1978) 180–93

——. (1994) *Carausius and Allectus: the British Usurpers* (London 1994)

Christol M. (1977) "La carrière de Traianus Mucianus et *l'origine des protectores*", *Chiron* 7 (1977) 393–408

Coello T. 1996 *Unit Sizes in the Late Roman Army* (Oxford 1996)

Cooper P.K. (1968) *The third-century origins of the 'New' Roman Army* (Unpublished DPhil thesis, Oxford 1968)

Crook J. (1971) "Arnold Hugh Martin Jones, 1904–1970", *PBA* 57 (1971) 425–38

d'Amato R. and Sumner G. (2005) *Roman Military Clothing* (London 2005)

Demandt A. (1965) *Zeitkritik und Geschichtsbild im Werk Ammians* (Bonn 1965)

Duncan-Jones R. (1990) "Pay and numbers in Diocletian's army", in *idem* (1990) *Structure and Scale in the Roman Economy* (Cambridge 1990) 105–17, 214–21

Elton H. (1996a) *Warfare in Roman Europe, A.D. 350–425* (Oxford 1996)

——. (1996b) *Frontiers of the Roman Empire* (London 1996)

---

[105] Witness the footnotes of Lee (1998), which shares these virtues. Also to be recommended are Elton (1996a), Nicasie (1998), and now Lee (2007).

Ensslin W. (1923) *Zur Geschichtsschreibung und Weltanschauung des Ammianus Marcellinus* (Leipzig 1923)

Grosse R. (1920) *Römische Militärgeschichte von Gallienus bis zum Beginn der byzantinischen Themenverfassung* (Berlin 1920)

Hoffmann D. (1969–1970) *Das spätrömische Bewegungsheer und die Notitia Dignitatum*, I and II (Dusseldorf 1969–1970)

Isaac B. (1992) *The Limits of Empire: the Roman Army in the East* (Oxford 1992)

James S. (1988) "The fabricae: state arms factories of the Later Roman Empire", in *Military Equipment and the Identity of Roman Soldiers: Proceedings of the Fourth Roman Military Equipment Conference*, ed. J.C. Coulston (Oxford 1988) 257–331

——. (2004) *The Excavations at Dura-Europos conducted by Yale University and the French Academy of Inscriptions and Letters 1928 to 1937. Final Report VII: The Arms and Armour and other Military Equipment* (London 2004)

Johnson S. (1983) *Late Roman Fortifications* (London 1983)

Jones A.H.M. (1964) *The Later Roman Empire 284–602: A Social, Economic, and Administrative Survey*, 3 vols (Oxford 1964), reprinted in two volumes with continuous pagination (Oxford 1973)

Jones C.P. (1987) "*Stigma*: Tattooing and Branding in Graeco-Roman Antiquity", *JRS* 77 (1987) 139–55

Kennedy D. (2004) *The Roman Army in Jordan*, 2nd rev. ed. (London 2004)

Laubscher H.P. (1975) *Der Reliefschmuck des Galeriusbogens in Thessaloniki* (Berlin 1975)

Lee A.D. (1993) *Information and frontiers: Roman foreign relations in late antiquity* (Cambridge 1993)

——. (1998) "The Army", in *Cambridge Ancient History XIII*, 2nd ed., *The Late Empire: A.D. 337–425*, edd. Averil Cameron and P. Garnsey (Cambridge 1998) 211–37

——. (2007) *War in Late Antiquity: A Social History* (Oxford 2007)

Luttwak E.N. (1976) *The Grand Strategy of the Roman Empire: from the First Century A.D. to the Third* (Baltimore and London 1976)

Mann J.C. (1979) "Power, Force, and the Frontiers of the Empire", *JRS* 69 (1979) 175–83, reprinted in *idem* (1996) *Britain and the Roman Empire* (Aldershot 1996) 85–93

Matthews J. (1989) *The Roman Empire of Ammianus* (London 1989)

Meiggs R. (1970) "Obituary: Arnold Hugh Martin Jones", *JRS* 60 91970) 186–87

Millar F. (1982) "Emperors, Frontiers and Foreign Relations, 31 B.C. to A.D. 378", *Britannia* 13 (1982) 1–23

Musurillo H. (1972) ed. and trans. *The Acts of the Christian Martyrs* (Oxford 1972)

Nicasie M.J. (1998) *Twilight of Empire: the Roman Army from the reign of Diocletian until the battle of Adrianople* (Amsterdam 1998)

Rea J.R., Salomons R.P. and Worp K.A. (1985) "A ration-warrant for an *adiutor memoriae*", *YCS* 28 (1985) 101–13

Ritterling E. (1903) "Zum römischen Heerwesen des ausgehenden dritten Jhs.", *Festschrift Hirschfeld* (1903) 345–9

Rivet A.L.F. and Smith C. (1979) *The Place-Names of Roman Britain* (London 1979)

Seeck O. (1876) ed. *Notitia Dignitatum: accedunt notitia urbis Constantinopolitanae et Laterculi provinciarum* (Berlin 1876)

Skeat T.C. (1964) ed. *Papyri from Panopolis in the Chester Beatty Library, Dublin* (Dublin 1964)

Southern P. and Dixon K.R. (1996) *The Late Roman Army* (London 1996)

Speidel M.P. (1987) "The Later Roman Field Army and the Guard of the High Empire", *Latomus* 46 (1987) 375–9, reprinted in *idem* (1992) *Roman Army Studies II* (Stuttgart 1992) 379–84

Thompson E.A. (1958) "Early Germanic Warfare", *Past and Present* 14 (1958) 2–28

——. (1965) *The Early Germans* (Oxford 1965)

Tomlin R.S.O. (1976) "Notitia dignitatum omnium, tam civilium quam militarium", in *Aspects of the Notitia Dignitatum*, edd. R. Goodburn and P. Bartholomew (Oxford 1976) 189–209

———. (1998) "Roman Manuscripts from Carlisle: the ink-written tablets", *Britannia* 29 (1998) 31–84

———. (2000) "The legions in the Late Empire", in *Roman Fortresses and their Legions*, ed. R.J. Brewer (London 2000) 159–78

———. (2006) "The Owners of the Beaurains (Arras) Treasure", in *Constantine the Great: York's Roman Emperor*, edd. E. Hartley, J. Hawkes, M. Henig with F. Mee (York 2006) 59–64

CHAPTER EIGHT

A.H.M. JONES AND "THE CITIES" 1964–2004

Luke Lavan

1. *Introduction*

A.H.M. Jones' chapters on 'Rome and Constantinople' and 'The Cities' in the *Later Roman Empire* of 1964 remain seminal for the topics they cover. However, assessing this work is no easy task. The latter chapter represents the compression of a great deal of research that he had undertaken earlier in his career. Indeed, until the publication of the *Later Roman Empire*, Jones could be characterised primarily as an urban historian, having published his first two great works on the *Cities of the East Roman Provinces* (henceforth *Cities*) in 1937 and *The Greek City from Alexander to Justinian* (henceforth *The Greek City*) in 1940. Most of what he said about the cities in the *Later Roman Empire* can in fact be found in the pages of *The Greek City*.[1] Significantly, Jones seems to have changed his general views on later urban history very little between 1940 and 1964, although he avoids starker formulations in the *Later Roman Empire*. His historical method is also already apparent in his earlier works: a mastery of the literary and epigraphic sources accompanied by a determination to present clearly the evidence he cites and to make transparent and 'fair' interpretative judgments, with very few references to secondary literature. Such references dwindled to almost nothing by the time of the *Later Roman Empire*. Archaeological texts are cited in his further reading list in the *Cities*, but he does not use archaeology in the *Later Roman Empire*, with two exceptions to which I shall return.

---

[1] Jones, *The Greek City*: Spread of cities, foundation etc. 85–94; finances, relations with governors, justice, defensors, taxes 147–155; decline of curial order 192–210; finances and services, including games 251–58; economic aspects of the city 267–69; administrative achievement 275–76; decline in civic patriotism 303–304.

2. *Before Jones*

Before the *Later Roman Empire*, very little had been written on Late
Roman cities. Tentative syntheses had been attempted for the East on
the transition to the Byzantine City,[2] whilst for the West the late 1950s
had seen an awakening of interest in the Early Medieval city.[3] However,
there was very not much scholarship available on the Roman city of
the 4th to 6th centuries A.D. Prior to Jones' earlier books there was
almost nothing, apart from a few syntheses of urban administration
that included the late empire and so touched on cities. Liebenam's
Stadtverwaltung im römischen Kaiserreiche (1900) covers many topics of
interest to Jones, and although its focus is mainly earlier it includes a
short section on decline. Another book that stands out is Abbot and
Johnson's *Municipal Administration of the Roman Empire* (1926), the only
work in English that I have found which seriously deals with topics
such as the decline of the curial order, the growth of the power of
governors over councils, and later curial finance. Both of these scholarly
tomes must have been read by Jones as an undergraduate at Oxford.
He does cite them once in *The Greek City* (359) in explaining why a
lengthy treatment on civic estates is necessary—because even "repu-
table works" such as Abbot and Johnson and Liebenam have glossed
this subject incorrectly.

Jones thus acknowledged some debt to earlier scholars, but he preferred to present his evidence directly rather than point to the footnotes
of others. He believed that the reader should be able to see where an
interpretation came from, and not have to rely on authority (*The Greek
City* viii). It seems that Jones saw his task as to make a *tabula rasa* for the
later city, as in so many other domains, and to begin afresh, without
reference to earlier literature. This is an impression that students of
Jones have confirmed to me, noting that he was not really influenced
by books of his time (such as Petit on Libanius), developing his own
opinions directly from the sources. On the other hand, he did respect

---

[2] E.g. by Ostrogorsky (1959), Kirsten (1959) and Dölger (1962), with AAVV (1961).
See Ostrogorsky (1959) 48 for some very early bibliography on (mainly Medieval)
Byzantine cities, including discussions of the 1950s in Russian, which were prefigured
by a lone and largely ignored Russian pioneer of the early 20th century: Rudakov
(1917) 71f.

[3] AAVV. (1958a), (1958b), (1966).

good research, referring the reader to Petit Antioch (*Later Roman Empire* 1295) and to Chastagnol on Rome (*Later Roman Empire* 1282).[4]

Although he avoided repeating the theories of others, Jones' work does reflect the general scholarly priorities of his age. By the mid-20th century, Roman historians had gradually descended the political hierarchy, from studying emperors, then governors, to studying cities, whilst some were even touching on late cities.[5] The bibliographies of Claude (1969), Février (1977) and Liebeschuetz (2001) reveal a general intellectual trend developing in many different scholarly circles, although Jones was one of the first to publish. Lallemand's text on *L'administration civile de l'Egypte* (1964), covering the 4th century, and published in the same year as the *Later Roman Empire*, contains a large chapter on "Les cités" with much of direct relevance to Jones. Yet the similarity of Jones' interests to those of earlier scholars such as Liebenam, Abbot and Johnson also has a more prosaic origin. It depends in large part on their reliance on the legal codes as a guide to the institutional history of the period—thus reflecting the priorities, gripes and lacunae of these sources. Here Jones and many other historians had been practicing what Collingwood called "scissors and paste history"—the re-arrangement of sources according to obvious headings, often suggested by the material itself.[6] This is especially obvious in the works of Jones, as he sought to keep close to his sources, rather than construct wordy interpretative paradigms.

From the late perspective on Jones' career that the *Later Roman Empire* affords, his main interest appears not to be cities but rather administration. Indeed, in the foreword to his *History of Rome* vol. 2 (1972) Jones regarded the art of government as "the greatest achievement of the Roman empire", rather than say cultural integration, economic complexity or technological innovation. In doing so he reflects one of two key beliefs common in his milieu which influenced his work on cities. First, and perhaps most important, were his well-documented social democratic convictions, confident of the power of efficient administration and the value of the recently erected welfare state in underwriting human prosperity.[7] A second belief, admittedly not documented, seems

---

[4] Petit (1955); Chastagnol (1960).
[5] Lepelley reveals that Pflaum had precisely this hierarchical attitude in relation to the former's study of *curiales*: Lepelley (2006) 36.
[6] Collingwood (1993) 257–61.
[7] Liebeschuetz (1992) 4–6.

to be a somewhat English notion that small-scale democratic participatory bodies such as Oxford colleges and town councils, regulated by constitutions and procedures, were an ideal form of government, and that the replacement of these bodies by unaccountable centralised institutions might result in a world not worth living in. These two beliefs were probably responsible for his history of the later city being an administrative survey in which movement away from past constitutional norms was to be regretted.

3. *Jones Prior to the* Later Roman Empire: *What He Thought*

As I have indicated, much of what is presented in 'The Cities' chapter of the *Later Roman Empire* had appeared already in *The Greek City*, though the chapter on 'Rome and Constantinople' is new. Already in *The Greek City* we see much of the same source material laid out, with the conclusions that the city of the "Byzantine" (i.e. Late Roman) period, whilst still "the symbol of civilisation" (147), had sunk to become "an organ of local administration" (155). Confiscations of civic revenue by Constantius and Valens had the result "that the cities abandoned even their most essential services", though some restitutions were made, initially to allow for repairs to fortification walls (149). The civic services that survived these cuts depended on the initiative of governors, as city councillors were now "greatly reduced in number and wealth" (148), being "continually subject...to leakage and attrition" (204). Civic patriotism had died and could not be revived by the extensive efforts of the emperors, who recognised that cities were still more effective at tax collection than imperial officials (147–48). Yet the city was paradoxically "still in Justinian's day of some importance" (155), with some "normal services—salaries, games, the heating of baths, the purchase of corn and public works" still covered by civic revenues (257–58), although city councils as an executive body had ceased to exist with the reforms of Anastasius.

How does this account in *The Greek City* compare with the *Later Roman Empire*? Quite closely, it would seem, not just in points of detail and evidence cited, but in interpretative judgment, as exemplified by the following remark: "As the councils lost their richest and most enterprising members, as their revenues were curtailed, and as civic patriotism decayed, the cities lost initiative and vitality" (*Later Roman Empire* 757). The chief suspects for the demise of the city in *The Greek City* are the

imperial government and the Church. Liebeschuetz has suggested a
more positive tone is present towards the Late Roman imperial government in the *Later Roman Empire* than *The Greek City*, but this appears
not to be the case as regards cities.[8] In fact, Jones noted in *The Greek
City* that it was the early and middle provincial administration that had
weakened the cities (303), whilst Justinian sought to keep them alive.
In the *Later Roman Empire* this view does not re-appear: rather at one
point (756) Jones notes that the decurions were "helpless victims of
the imperial bureaucracy". Jones also does not seem to have changed
his attitude towards the influence of the Church. He is very hard on
Christianity in *The Greek City*, and his view is not notably different in
the *Later Roman Empire*. However, his conclusions are presented more
starkly in the earlier book; he finished *The Greek City* by claiming that
Christianity (as a religion of escape from the world) undermined
motivation for the support of cities, by providing no political doctrine
equivalent to ancient municipal loyalty (303–304). This is a judgement
which, although not repeated, was not retracted in the *Later Roman
Empire*, despite his survey of church administration in the latter work.
Elsewhere in the *Later Roman Empire*, his talk of "idle mouths" (1046)
and of the drain of honest capable men into the Church (1063) suggests
that his views had changed little between 1940 and 1964.

4. *Jones in the* Later Roman Empire: *What He Said*

The two chapters on cities in the *Later Roman Empire* essentially comprise
an administrative survey based on textual sources. The overall picture
that Jones paints of the Late Roman city is of an institution under
severe pressure, suffering loss of finance and personnel and experienc-
ing general demoralisation, with the imperial government desperate to
maintain it, but unable to accept the real reasons for its weakness with
sincerity. Yet like Gibbon, Jones has to continue his narrative long after
his declining subject ought to have completely expired, chasing civic
institutions and *curiales* into the 8th century A.D.

Chapter XVIII 'Rome and Constantinople' (687–711) discusses the
following topics: 'Rome an anachronism' (687–88), Constantinople: its
foundation and the deciding factors in its greatness (688–89), the Urban

---

[8] Liebeschuetz (1992) 6–7.

Prefect and other officials in Rome (689–92), the Urban Prefect at
Constantinople (692–93), the nature of the Urban Prefects' power and
police forces (693–95), the supply of food and drink (aqueducts, bread,
pigs, wine) (695–70), baths and games (705–707), higher education
(707–708), public building (708–709), finances (709–10), the expansion
of Constantinople and the contraction of Rome (710–11).

Chapter XIX 'The Cities' (712–66) can perhaps be divided into four
sections: i) the nature of cities, ii) the constitutional elements of cities, iii)
the workings of civic administration, and iv) the curial order. The first
section (712–22) covers the definition of the city, non-city administrative
units, the economic nature of cities, differences in the sizes of cities,
regional variations, new urban foundations, and civic status. The second
section (722–31) discusses the people, the council, its magistrates, the
curator, the *defensor*, elections, and the internal structure of the council
(including the sequence of offices and the *principales*). The third section
(732–37) discusses civic finances and municipal services, including building projects. The fourth section (737–63) discusses the curial order—its
membership, variations, attempts of members to escape, the decline of
the councils (especially in relation to the power of the governor) and
imperial attempts to prevent this. The chapter finishes (763–66) with
a section on provincial assemblies—set a little uncomfortably here, as
part of civic rather than provincial government.

How much of this is new? As I have already observed, earlier
scholars had passed along the same path as Jones, drawing similar
conclusions about cities based on the same material. Yet *Later Roman
Empire* Chapter XVIII included the first balanced administrative survey of Constantinople, pre-figuring Dagron's exhaustive *Naissance d'une
capitale* (1974). It was also the first time that the eastern capital had
been compared with Rome in a comprehensive manner, as two cities
in the same empire, rather than as the representatives of two different civilisations. Obviously, much of what is said about Rome can be
found in Chastagnol's 1960 study *La préfecture urbaine* and some earlier
works, whilst Janin's *Constantinople byzantine* of 1950 uses some of the
same sources, to different ends.[9] But the study of both cities benefited
from Jones' 'new broom', at a time in his career when he was at the
height of his powers. He swept everything away and reinterpreted the

---

[9] Earlier works with discussions of some similar topics to Jones included Gregorovius
(1886f.) and Grisar (1911).

sources afresh, based on his wide experience of analysing Late Roman administration, and the city in particular. Perhaps most original was his bold statement that Rome was now an anachronism (687). This unsettling claim is typical of Jones' style.

Chapter XIX on 'The Cities' also treats many themes which are obviously not new, the decline of the curial order being perhaps the most obvious. However, Jones does go later than most scholars had done previously, trying to track down the real end of the curia and of the *curiales* in both East and West. His discussions of the role of governors and the significance of the *principales* are new, whilst his attempt to understand late Roman civic finances was the most thorough treatment in English down to his time. He is the first to suggest that *metropoleis* were more prosperous than other cities, at least in terms of their resident elite (765).

5. *Assessing Jones*

i) *General Remarks*

Jones' chapters are a model of both clarity and economy, leaving the reader crystal clear as to what the evidence for late antique civic life can tell us. Through this method one is transformed from being the admirer of a *grande maître* into being his enabled companion. What sets Jones' treatment of cities apart is his use of the sources. In addition to the law codes, which others had quarried, he extensively employs inscriptions, papyri and cross references to patristic sources which had not previously been exploited in such a systematic way. His use of examples is not only rich but vivid. But he only uses archaeology twice, in very general allusions to the revival of the East during the later 5th to 6th century (763) and to spolia, which he believes must indicate inferior building: "work was done on the cheap reusing blocks" (736). At first glance this seems surprising, as important archaeological information on later urbanism was available at this time, for Africa, Macedonia, Syria and elsewhere,[10] and was used by Claude in his synthesis of the 6th century

---

[10] Salona: Gerber et al. (1917–39); Dyggve (1951). Timgad: Ballu (1903). Djemilla: Ballu (1926). Dougga: Poinsot (1958). Sufetula: Merlin (1911). Tipasa: Duval (1946). Philippi and Macedonia: Lemerle (1945). Corinth: Scranton (1957) and other vol-

city, published in 1969 as *Die byzantinische Stadt*, and by Kurbatov in his
little-read Russian synthesis of 1971. Yet up to the 1970s most work on
late Roman and early medieval cities had been text-based, as a 1977
survey article by Février reveals.[11] Jones stuck to the sources he knew,
and left the challenge of archaeology to others.

As has often been noted, Jones' historical method is somewhat 'commonsense'. He presents an argument supported by pertinent evidence,
but refuses to ignore material which apparently contradicts the broad
flow of the argument he has constructed: he does not try to tie-up all
loose threads. In his work on cities this occasionally leads to inconclusive
arguments that can somewhat perplex the reader, giving the impression
that he avoided really thorny problems which might have revealed the
limitations of his sources. Thus Jones' account of civic finances does not
really resolve the issue: somewhat conflicting evidence is presented but
it is unclear what Jones really thinks or what impression he wishes to
carry forward into the subsequent pages. More obviously, his account of
the internal politics of city councils is perhaps not fully coherent—did
leading members use their position to oppress junior members with
difficult services whilst helping potential senators to escape? If so were
they not at some financial risk from poor councillors who might default
on their obligations? Perhaps they thought that having a local senator
actually raised the status of the city, by providing a powerful patron.
Some such senators remained engaged with their city, still sitting in
council sessions to offer patronising advice, like Libanius: this situation
was eventually recognised by the government through the involvement
of 'notables' in running civic administration.[12]

ii) *Distortions of bias*

Perhaps most importantly, it can be argued that Jones misrepresented
the institutional changes of late antiquity by describing those changes
in largely negative terms, as a result of his admiration for the traditional political forms of the classical city. He was not positive about the

---

umes in this series. Antioch: Elderkin and Stillwell (1934–41). Bostra: Brunnow and
Domaszewski (1909), Butler (1914).
   [11] Février (1977).
   [12] This is also suggested by legal codes and Libanius' own gripes on the behavior of
others: *honorati* with only honorary codicils not to be seated during meetings of curiae:
CTh 12.1.4 (A.D. 317); former *curialis* of Antioch has honorary codicils and now struts
around the council chamber: Libanius *Or.* 98.11–13.

development of an empire-wide governing class at the expense of the city councils. In this he was closely reflecting his principal sources, but also their conservative prejudices, a common trait of classical scholars produced by the humanist tradition. Part of the problem comes from relying too much on a straightforward reading of the codes and on Libanius' rather dishonest discourse about the difficulties of a city council which he wished his own son to escape from.[13] But equally important is that Jones, despite his social democratic background, appears to be somewhat sympathetic to institutional conservatives (notably Libanius, or the moralising writers of late Roman law) who saw contemporary developments in negative terms. These authors reinforced what I suspect was his own feeling that participatory Greek city government was a model to be celebrated and that its demise was to be regretted.[14]

Probably Jones would have produced a stronger account of institutional change if he had considered the distortion of perspective that the socio-political conservatism of his sources had produced. Throughout Roman history, established (rather than emerging) elites had always tended to be ill at ease with new developments in imperial society. In one age they railed against luxury, wealth from trade and rich freedmen, and in another against powerful eunuchs, lawyers and the flight of the *curiales*. The problem, as MacMullen noted, is that some such commentators believed the Roman State to have been in decline from the 2nd century B.C., something which no modern institutional historian can take seriously.[15] In late antiquity, as in earlier times, the values of the established elites left a heavy imprint on the literary culture which produced our sources. Regardless of the truth about one's past, it was necessary to embrace these values to consolidate one's status in the civilian elite.

Did Jones' tendency to reflect the worries of traditionalists seriously distort his account? Not in the detail of administration, that is clear; he is also quick to identify evidence for survival or positive reforms where it can be detected. But his overall assessment is rather one-sided: he does not dare to say that the eclipse of city councils and the lessened prestige of civic life may have been the necessary price to pay for the creation of a strong and stable central imperial state. But it was the

---

[13] Lib. *Or.* 49.8, *Ep.* 959 (390).
[14] A measured admiration for Athenian democracy is of course present in Jones' book of 1957.
[15] MacMullen (1988) 1.

army and court society at Constantinople, not the provincial cities, which now provided the effective political basis for Mediterranean prosperity. The army underpinned Mediterranean peace by competently guarding the frontiers, and the court linked the provinces to the capital through widespread senatorial membership, constituting a system arguably more stable than that of the Principate. A new and larger world was coming into being, in which the division between conqueror and conquered was entirely removed, and in which there was a great deal of cultural, religious and political unity. Can the political eclipse of the city not therefore be seen in positive terms? On a human level, probably obvious to residents of Constantinople, imperial society was arguably more emotionally satisfying, less parochial and more fun than life in most cities, where the social scene must have seemed tedious in comparison. The Empire's political glue was made from such feelings.

In sympathising with the cities rather than the empire, Jones takes the perspective of Libanius, rather than that which a senator at the court might have taken. But the perspective of Libanius was surely extreme—this was a man who was not prepared to use Latin to the point of refusing to employ well-established technical terms which had passed into Greek and who had fled from Constantinople to Antioch for cultural reasons. Jones also fails to fully probe the difference between the rhetoric and the behaviour of individuals like Libanius, which can be explained less as moral failing and rather as a reaction to the growth of imperial society.[16]

One might also suggest that Jones' emphasis upon the decline of traditional institutions led him to neglect the significance and nature of later civic government from the later 5th and 6th century onwards—the notables, with the *pater civitatis, sitona* and other officers, led by the bishop. It may have also led him to miss the significance of the urban institutions of the Church and its capacity for local leadership. Today, this looks like a deliberate choice by Jones. But it is probably explained by an unconscious classicising reflex, that well-planned porticoes, theatres and baths provided more utility than the charitable and religious buildings of Christianity.

Finally, Jones arguably over-emphasised the total political significance of the city. "It is scarcely an exaggeration to say that the history of

---

[16] On understanding 'corruption' see Kelly (2004).

Greco-Roman civilisation is the history of cities" (*Cities* 299). What Jones seems to be implying here is that there was no civilisation without the political structures of the *civitas/polis*. Ancient authors might have agreed, but was it true? One might equally assert that there was no Roman civilisation without the army, or without the imperial bureaucracy, or without long-distance trade, or without Christianity. Once we take civilisation to mean 'complex societies', or even 'urban societies', the fate of the political institutions of the classical city seems to fade in importance.

iii) *The omission of archaeology*

Whilst Jones' omission of archaeology in the *Later Roman Empire* was not surprising, given the nature of ancient history in 1964, it is disappointing. He had actually excavated at Gerasa and knew archaeologists working in the East. As an admirer of Rostovtzeff, one might have hoped that he would extend the latter's use of urban archaeology to the late empire, but this was not to be so.[17] Yet the significance of Jones' non-use of archaeology is clear from a reference he does make to it concerning Gerasa (763). Here his conclusions regarding the health of the city based on a study of its monumental building are striking:

> To take one instance, Gerasa, a largish city of Arabia, which had flourished greatly in the second century A.D., evidently fell on evil days in the third and shows little or no sign of revival in the fourth or early fifth. But from the latter part of the fifth century a dozen churches, many of them of some architectural pretentions, were erected and several public buildings repaired or re-erected. This activity went on uninterrupted down to the Arab conquest, the last church being dedicated under Phocas.

These comments do not fit at all well with Jones' picture of the institutional and economic decline of cities based on texts, and it seems very odd that these remarks did not cause him some unease. If Jones had made more use of Mediterranean urban archaeology, such as the

---

[17] See Rostovtzeff (1926) 629.n.6 for his only use of archaeology in a brief consideration of developments under the late empire. Despite Rostovtzeff's negative views, based largely on the codes, he allows depictions of villa life on Late Roman African mosaics to let him conclude that "agriculture on the large estates was not in any way decaying". This seems to be his sole use of 'archaeology' for the late period, though he had used it extensively for earlier times.

results then available from excavations in Bostra, Antioch or Africa, he might have concluded that the decline of the curia was no more than an institutional re-arrangement.[18] He might also have been able to improve his regional impressions, which are not very accurate: for example, he missed the prosperity of 4th century African cities, despite guide books and syntheses being available that could have served to correct the impressions he had obtained from the legal codes. The use of archaeology does of course present a whole new series of problems. If different types of source support radically different interpretations of institutional or regional history (as they do for the East), then which are to be believed? What value do we place on different kinds of evidence and why? These are methodological problems which Jones did not address.

A former student of Jones has suggested to me, rather depressingly, that Jones might have disliked the provisional nature of archaeological results: "To build on archaeology is so often to build on shifting sand". More prosaically, "there was no time" for Jones as he tried to read all of the textual sources thoroughly. I think these two explanations can be reconciled: Jones was trying to produce one of his highly efficient monographs and thus he probably wished to re-use research done for *The Greek City* without re-thinking his general conclusions based on insights from archaeology. He probably also knew what we now appreciate, that his work, based on the massive compilation of textual sources, does not date easily, whilst syntheses based on archaeology do. But in taking this approach Jones produced a general impression of the Late Roman city that even his own allusions to archaeology suggest is wrong.

6. *After Jones*

i) *Sources*

How have 40 years of scholarship altered Jones' vision of late antique cities? The biggest change has undoubtedly been in the sources used for later urban history. Whilst Jones used epigraphy as a source, it

---

[18] Peter Brown's review of Jones shows an appreciation of the relevance of archaeological discoveries, especially in relation to the prosperity of the countryside in the East: Brown (1967) 342. Sadly Brown never really developed his work in this area.

could be said that he leant primarily on the law codes and did not see Late Roman epigraphy as providing an independent and alternative viewpoint for urban political life. Claude Lepelley effectively took up this approach, followed by Charlotte Roueché and Ariel Lewin. Indeed, thanks to the disciplined work of Dennis Feissel and Roueché, late antique epigraphy has now developed something of a self-identity.[19] There has also been progress in the editing and commenting of texts, with Byzantine urban chronicles and saints' lives receiving serious treatment, all of which Jones would surely have welcomed.[20]

The continued growth of archaeology has of course overshadowed these developments. As we have seen, before 1964 late antique urbanism did not really exist as a focus of interest in Mediterranean archaeology. Some individuals had tried to use archaeology to study the urban history of late antiquity in a systematic way, such as Kraeling's work on Gerasa (1938) or Kitzinger (1946) on Stobi, but these were exceptions. The study of the Late Roman city tended to have become lost between classical archaeology and Christian archaeology, both of which focused primarily on 'period architecture'.

In the decades following 1964, however, a late antique urban archaeology gradually began to develop.[21] In Africa, the cities excavated by classical archaeologists contained numerous churches and primarily reflected their condition in late antiquity. These circumstances led to Christian archaeology developing locally into the study of late antique urbanism, with pioneering synthetic articles in 1964 by Février and Duval on the (mainly late) urbanism of Djemila, Setif and Sbeitla. By the 1980s the maturing of Christian archaeology in Gaul and Italy saw the development of a city-wide topographical approach that also spread to the southern Balkans and Israel in the 1980–1990s. With the publication of the acts of the 1987 Christian Archaeological Congress, a holistic urban approach seemed very much the way forward. However, most researchers in this tradition did not adopt this method, and continue to focus on churches alone, providing a very partial view of the late antique city.[22]

---

[19] Lepelley (1979); Roueché (1979), (1984), (1989) and other studies; Lewin (*ca.* 1995 and 2001). Feissel (1985), (1987), amongst very many studies.

[20] To mention just a few: Jeffreys, Jeffreys and Scott (1986) Mango and Scott (1997); Ryden (1963) and (1970).

[21] For bibliography see Lavan (2001b).

[22] AAVV. (1989) esp. vol. 1.

The 1970s and 1980s did of course see a massive expansion in urban excavation in western Europe, driven by rescue archaeology, which revealed striking evidence of the transition from late antiquity to the early Middle Ages. But an increasing interest in the Late Roman period also developed among northern Roman archaeologists in Britain, Serbia, Bulgaria and elsewhere who had never seen any reason to concentrate on the earlier period, resulting in syntheses that included the Late Roman period: such as Frere in Britain, no doubt influenced by his excavation at Verulamium in 1955–61 which had revealed an important late sequence, and Velkov in Thrace and Dacia, where much of the urban evidence was late antique.[23]

Mediterranean classical archaeology was much slower to change, but from the 1970s onwards major excavations also started to focus primarily on late antiquity, especially at Levantine sites such as Apamea, Caesarea Maritima and Scythopolis where spectacular remains from this period were revealed. Changes in priorities were also seen at established sites such as Nicopolis ad Istrum, Delphi, Argos, Aizanoi, Sardis, Ephesus, Aphrodisias, Xanthos and Sagalassos, especially in the 1990s.[24] All this activity meant that by the end of the twentieth century archaeology had become the main source for Late Roman urban history, and that texts alone could no longer be taken to provide reliable indicators for all aspects of city life. Material evidence has begun to appear in multi-regional discussions of the late antique city, as in Liebeschuetz's in his *Decline and Fall of the Roman City* (2001) and most recently Wickham's in his *Framing the Early Middle Ages* (2005), and it seems most unlikely that anyone in the future will attempt a synthesis of the late antique city without bringing archaeology to the fore.

---

[23] Frere (1967) 254–57 and 376–78; Frere (1972–84); Velkov (1977).

[24] Major urban excavations focusing on late antiquity: for Apamea see Balty (1981), for Caesarea Maritima see Holum et al. (1988), for Scythopolis see Tsafrir and Foerster (1997), for Sagalassos see Waelkens et al. (2006), for Nicopolis ad Istrum see Poulter (1995) and subsequent volumes for this site. For changes in priorities see recent reports for Delphi, Argos, Aizanoi, Sardis, Ephesus, Aphrodisias, and Xanthos in *BCH* "*chronique*", *BASOR, ArchAnz, ÖJh, JRA* supplements and *Anatolia Antiqua*. For Delphi see also Petridis (1997) and Weir (2004). For Aphrodisias see also Ratté (2001). The monograph of Frantz (1988) on the Athenian Agora was also influential in this process.

ii) *The development of Jones' interests*

In terms of intellectual content, the forty years since Jones' *Later Roman Empire* have seen many scholars take up Jones' interests in their own research. Some scholars have been so strongly effected by Jones' organisational scheme that their work can be considered almost as "case studies" for Jones. This is obviously true of Liebeschuetz's *Antioch* (1972), and unsurprisingly so from an ex-pupil. Segal's *Edessa* (1970) is very un-Jonesian, and unfortunately so, as his lack of rigour over footnoting makes the work difficult for scholars to use. Ward-Perkins' book on Italy (1984) is strongly marked in both its organisation and especially its feel by the *Later Roman Empire*, though it covers a wider range of topics than Jones' chapters on urbanism. However, scholars as widely spread as Haas on Alexandria (1997) and Lepelley for Africa (1979) also bear the hallmarks of his influence. As I noted earlier, there were undoubtedly other seams of scholarship developing that ran concurrently with Jones' work, which did not coincide directly with his rather conservative interests in administration. Thus the work of Dagron on Constantinople (1974) and other urban topics comes out of a French current of interest in Byzantium (developed notably in the early 20th century by such scholars as Laurent, Grumel and Janin)[25] or in 'late' Classics (from which had emerged the study of Petit in 1955). Bowman's work on Egyptian cities of 1971, though following many of Jones' interests and his style, can be related to earlier papyrological work on administration, as seen in Lallemand.[26] Nevertheless, all scholars coming after Jones cannot help but to have been influenced by him to some degree: the urban landscape that Jones left looked rather like some Balkans cities after the traumas of the 3rd century: demolished and rebuilt anew.

'New' work on civic administration has inevitably brought small changes to Jones' vision of the Late Roman city. Regional studies by Liebeschuetz, Lepelley and Bowman have demonstrated how varied was the relationship between governors and civic councils. A comparison of these works reveals that compulsion was applied only where local initiative was weak—there was no attempt by the government to dominate city councils that were still healthy. These regional studies also reveal great variation in internal institutions: curators and traditional magis-

---

[25] Failler (1995).
[26] Bowman (1971), Lallemand (1964).

trates have a different status in Africa to that in Egypt, with curators not very visible at Antioch.[27] The urban leadership of bishops is better understood especially thanks to Liebeschuetz, although this topic has also attracted work from a number of scholars, with important research done by Brown, Feissel, Lizzi, Rebillard, Sotinel and others.[28] Our knowledge of the civic government of the later period—under the notables—has been refined by Liebeschuetz and Laniado.[29] One area still open to debate is the extent to which palatine officers came to dominate urban administration at the expense of civic and provincial offices during the 6th century, a hypothesis suggested to both Jones and to Dagron by the minutes of the Council of Mopsuestia.[30]

Of outright 'mistakes' Jones can be held as having made few in matters of detail. Much of what he wrote stands the test of time. His surveys of the functions of different magistrates, the constitutional role of the people or the diffusion of urban status need little or no editing. Yet, inevitably, some faults can be found. It was probably wrong to ascribe the decline of athletic training in the East to Christianity (*The Greek City* 253) as this decline occurred too early, being a re-organisation of continuing Greek civic education in the 3rd and early 4th c.[31] The *pater civitatis/pater ths polews* is not the same office as the *curator/logistes* (*The Greek City* 209, *Later Roman Empire* 755).[32] Both the flight to the countryside of the *curiales* and "the massive emigration of urban craftsmen to the countryside" (*Later Roman Empire* 762) now seem very unlikely. Elite residence is easy to detect archaeologically, but there is no evidence for Jones' proposed flight in East or West. Investment in rural villas and the urban *domus* seems to follow broadly similar trends: elites continued to live in towns and retire to their estates, as they had done in earlier centuries, although in both town and country there was

---

[27] Governors and councils: Bowman (1971), Liebeschuetz (1972) and Lewin (*ca.* 1995) 99f. Curators: Bowman (1971) 46–52 and 124–27, Liebeschuetz (1972) 167–74, Lepelley (1979) 168–95.

[28] Urban leadership of bishops: Liebeschuetz (2001) 137–68, Brown (2002), Feissel (1989), Lizzi (1989), Rebillard and Sotinel (1998), amongst others.

[29] The later period: Liebeschuetz (2001) and Laniado (2002).

[30] Imperial offices dominating at the expense of civic offices in Jones (*Later Roman Empire* 760), and at the expense of the provincial administration in Dagron (1980).

[31] On the athletic contests and education in the 4th century: see Liebeschuetz (1972)136–40 and Lewin (1995). Notably, at Antioch in the mid-350s, teaching was focused around the agora, with the best school well-established in the bouleuterion, not in gymnasia: Lavan (2006) 230.

[32] *Pater civitatis*: Roueché (1979), Feissel (1987), Sijpesteijn (1987).

now a tendency towards fewer larger residences.[33] Urban craftsmen do not seem to have retreated either: the east and central Mediterranean saw an increase in the number of well-ordered cellular shops set in the monumental centres of cities during the 5th–7th century, such as those known at Sardis, the tetrastoon and theatre Baths at Aphrodisias, the forum of Sabratha, or the porticoes of Sagalassos.[34]

iii) *New themes*

The main changes in our view of Late Roman cities today compared to that of Jones in 1964 do not come from revising themes that he studied or from pointing out errors. They come from pursuing areas of research which do not seem to have interested him greatly, but which nevertheless strongly affect his vision of the Late Roman city. Some of these areas of research are not new. Church buildings, liturgy, processions and all the manifestations of urban Christianity remain popular themes of research. Such topics have survived Jones' indifference, so that his city of harassed *curiales* has arguably lost ground to those who talk of a dynamic and majestic *Urbs Christiana*. Yet several currents of research are new, and deserve to be described briefly here, though a more thorough listing with references can be found elsewhere.[35]

A stronger interest in urban social history has emerged. Many studies of urban patronage have been undertaken, including Christian evergetism.[36] Text-based research into the poor has also largely been concerned with the urban poor. Work on bishops and the church has gone beyond institutional studies, looking at the social origins and societal impact of the clergy and their allied workers.[37] Archaeologists have had some difficulty responding to this recent interest in matters social. The burgeoning study of (rich) late antique housing is doubtless

---

[33] Elite flight to the countryside questioned: Loseby (2006). Arce, Chavarría and Ripoll (forthcoming), Sfameni (2004).

[34] Urban craftsmen and East Mediterranean shops: Lavan (2006) 225.

[35] For bibliographic details Lavan (2001b).

[36] See evergetism patronage in general and discussion of the poor with references in bibliographic essays in Bowden, Gutteridge and Machado (2006).

[37] Clergy and church personnel: recently Brown (2002) 47–73 and Krause (2006), with a study on *parabalani* being prepared by Bowersock.

an exception: but an effective urban archaeology of either the middle
classes or the poor has proved elusive.[38]

A radically different way of looking at the city not present in Jones is
of course as topography, which appears in his *Cities* as meaning no more
than where cities are located. Thus it was left to Claude to introduce an
empire-wide study of internal urban topography in his *Die byzantinische
Stadt* of 1969, although studies of the topography of Constantinople
based on texts had started to appear in the 1950s, covering both
secular and religious buildings.[39] At both Rome and Constantinople,
our knowledge of topography has steadily increased by the drip-drip
of library-based research.[40] This has included archaeological work at
Rome, though in the Eastern capital most topographical knowledge
still depends on a very few texts; new excavations in the Harbour of
Julian may mark a turning point.[41] Away from the capitals archaeologists have greatly expanded topographical research, mainly by accident,
through the pursuit of very localised research projects, sometimes still
best described as a hunt for monumental architecture.

Yet this archaeological work has produced a great number of site
syntheses, from which urban portraits are emerging.[42] The collective
study of these many 'urban portraits' has also permitted the development of regional studies of urban development, sharpening our focus
and revealing both positive and negative local trends that Jones did
not anticipate.[43] It can also be recognised that imperial capitals such as
Trier, Milan and Ravenna stand out as an urban type regardless of the
region in which they are located. In contrast, provincial capitals, which
Jones suspected to have benefited from their status (765), do not seem
to have been a 'type' of city, but rather reflect regional urban develop-

---

[38] On the poor see the papers in Bowden, Gutteridge and Machado (2006). On
Housing see the bibliographic essays and other papers in Lavan, Özgenel and Sarantis
(forthcoming) and Ellis (2006).

[39] Topography from texts: at Antioch see Downey (1961) 597–679. For Constantinople see Janin (1950), Downey (1952), Mango (1959).

[40] Constantinople: textual works developed further by Guilland (1969), Mango
(1985), Berger (1987) and Bauer (1996), with Müller-Wiener (1977) for first serious
use of archaeology in synthetic accounts of topography of the capital. Rome: Steinby
(1993–99), Fraschetti (1999). New perspectives on both capitals: Bauer (1996), Mayer
(2002).

[41] A survey of standing remains has also produced some new discoveries: for Istanbul
Rescue Archaeological Survey see reports in *BBBS* since no. 25 onwards.

[42] On the development of topographical research: see Lavan (2001b) 18–22, (2003a)
and (2003b).

[43] Lavan (2001b).

ment.[44] Germanic royal capitals seem to show characteristics between the imperial cities (Ravenna) or provincial capitals depending on the extent to which the tax and expenditure structures of each kingdom remained in place. Thus some idea of the late antique urban network is emerging.[45] Along the northern and eastern frontiers archaeologists have revealed a new type of city which Jones did not anticipate: Pollard's compact "fortress cities" with walls and granaries, but no traditional classical buildings.[46]

Within cities, thematic approaches to urban topography have come from the scholars of *Topographie chrétienne*, along with the secular topographies of Brühl and Bauer, while a few scholars have also sought to develop notions of human space or contested topographies.[47] Synthetic studies have also been undertaken on different monument/spatial types, though major omissions still exist, such as in our knowledge of *xenodocheia*, urban monasteries, 6th century elite housing, baths, entertainment buildings and latrines.

7. *Conclusion*

So how can Jones' contribution to our understanding of Late Antique cities be judged in terms of the development of the subject as a whole? His interests were not new and were undoubtedly rooted in the academic tradition out of which he had emerged, as were his research methods and his manner of interpreting the sources. What was new was his familiarity with the evidence, the scale of his ambition, the consistency of his organisation, and his determination to be thorough, in both the topics he covered and in the presentation of the sources he used to support his judgements. Later scholars from both Anglo-Saxon and other traditions have brought different perspectives which he either did not anticipate, felt unable to incorporate, or more likely did not consider important in relation to the available sources and intellectual atmosphere of his time. Nevertheless, Jones' work was of immense importance for

---

[44] Provincial capitals: Lavan (2001d).
[45] Imperial and royal capitals: Ripoll and Gurt (2000).
[46] Pollard (2000) 69–82.
[47] Topography as the study of where buildings are: Gauthier and Duval (1986f), Bruhl (1975, 1990) and Bauer (1996). Human space: Lavan (2003a). Contested topographies: e.g. Lim (1999), Maier (1995), Wharton (1995).

the study of Late Roman urbanism, not so much for the conclusions he drew but for his systematic presentation of the textual evidence, so that his works still serve as essential points of reference today.

Happily, Jones' decision to study the institutions and administrative aspects of Late Roman cities means that less of his work has dated than might have been the case: archaeology challenges the significance of some of the changes he traced, but not most of their details. Even if we might give a different value to different kinds of evidence than he did, his careful presentation of the sources means that we can continue to use his work. Yet from the perspective of 2004, some methodological problems with Jones' account of the cities are clear. With hindsight, it can be said that Jones tended to base his reconstructions too strongly on the law codes, and that he did not relativise the evidence he derived from these and other literary sources sufficiently to understand the transformations of the Late Antique period. He presented too conservative a view of institutional change, unaware of or unsympathetic to the interpretative possibilities offered by comparative institutional history.[48] These limitations must be recognised in order for the subject to develop. Yet they do not greatly diminish Jones' achievement, which over-shadowed everything that came before and has yet to find its equal.

Acknowledgements

I am grateful to Bryan Ward-Perkins, Claude Lepelley, Helen Saradi and Wolfgang Liebeschuetz for reading this text. They are of course absolved from its errors and opinions, with some of which they disagree. I also wish to thank David Gwynn for his work editing the text.

Bibliography

AAVV. (1958a) *La città nell'alto medioevo. Atti del 6o Congresso internazionale di studi sull'alto medioevo* (Spoleto 1958)
———. (1958b) *Studien zu den Anfängen des europäischen Stadtwesens* (Reichenau-Vorträge 1955–56, Vorträge und Forschungen 4) (Sigmaringen 1958)

---

[48] This is of course an approach adopted by Whittow (1990) who sees the institutional changes of the 5th and 6th centuries as the re-arrangement of a continuous urban elite.

——. (1961) *Dikussions Beiträge zum XI Internationalen Byzantinistenkongress (München 1958)* (Munich 1961) 74–102

——. (1966) *Untersuchungen zur Gesellschaftlichen struktur der mittelalterlichen Städte in Europe* (Reichenau-Vorträge, 1963–64, Vorträge und Forschungen 11) (Stuttgart 1966)

——. (1989) *Actes du XIe Congrès international d'archéologie chrétienne. Lyon, Vienne, Grenoble, Genève et Aoste (21–28 septembre 1986)* (Rome 1989)

Abbot F.F. and Johnson A.C. (1926) *Municipal Administration of the Roman Empire* (Princeton 1926)

Arce J., Chavarría A. and Ripoll G. (forthcoming), "The urban domus in late antique Hispania: examples from Emerita, Barcino and Complutum," in L. Lavan, Özgenel and Sarantis (Leiden forthcoming)

Ballu A. (1903) *Guide illustré de Timgad* (Paris 1903)

——. (1926) *Guide illustré de Djemilla* (Alger 1926)

Balty Je. Ch. (1981) *Guide d'Apamée* (Brussels 1981)

Bauer F.A. (1996) *Stadt, Platz und Denkmal in der Spätantike. Untersuchungen zur Ausstattung des Öffentlichen Raums in den Spätantiken Städten Rom, Konstantinopel und Ephesos* (Mainz 1996)

Berger A. (1987) *Untersuchungen zu den Patria Konstantinupoleos* (Bonn 1987)

Bowden W., Lavan L. and Machado C. (2004) *Recent Research on the Late Antique Countryside* (*Late Antique Archaeology 2*) (Leiden and Boston 2004)

Bowden W., Machado C. and Gutteridge A. (edd.) (2006) *Social and Political Life in Late Antiquity* (*Late Antique Archaeology 3.1*) (Leiden 2006)

Bowman A. K. (1971) *The Town Councils of Roman Egypt* (Toronto 1971)

Brown P. (1967) "The Later Roman Empire", *EcHR*, 2nd series, 20 (1967) 327–43, reprinted in *idem* (1972) *Religion and Society in the Age of Saint Augustine* (London 1972) 46–73

——. (2002) *Poverty and Leadership in the Later Roman Empire* (Hanover and London 2002)

Bruhl C.-R. (1975) *Palatium und Civitas, Studien zur Profantopographie Spätantiker Civitates I, Gallien* (Cologne and Vienna 1975)

——. (1990) *Palatium und Civitas, Studien zur Profantopographie Spätantiker Civitates II: Belgica I, beide Germanien und Raetien II* (Cologne 1990)

Chastagnol A. (1960) *La préfecture urbaine à Rome sous le bas-empire* (Paris 1960)

Claude D. (1969) *Die byzantinische Stadt im 6. Jahrhundert* (Munich 1969)

Collingwood R.G. (1993) *The Idea of History*, revised edition with introduction by J. van der Dussen (Oxford 1993)

Dagron G. (1974) *Naissance d'une capitale. Constantinople et ses institutions de 330 à 451* (Paris 1974)

——. (1980) "Two documents concerning mid-sixth century Mopsuestia" in *Charanis Studies*, ed. A.E. Laiou-Thomadakis (New Brunswick 1980) 19–30

Di Segni L. (1999) "Epigraphic documentation on building in the provinces of *Palaestina* and *Arabia*, 4th–7th c.", in *The Roman and Byzantine Near East 2: Some Recent Archaeological Research*, ed. J.H. Humphrey (*JRA* Supplementary Series 31) (Portsmouth, Rhode Island 1999) 149–78

Dölger F. (1962) "Die frühbyzantinische Stadt und byzantinische beeinflußte Stadt (V.–VIII. Jahrhundert)", in *Paraspora* (Ettal 1962) 107–139

Downey G. (1952) "Notes on the topography of Constantinople", *Art Bulletin* 34 (1952) 235–36

——. (1961) *A History of Antioch in Syria from Seleucus to the Arab conquest* (Princeton 1961)

Dunn A.W. (1999) "From polis to kastron in southern Macedonia: Amphipolis, Khrysoupolis, and the Strymon delta", *Castrum 5. Archéologie des espaces agraires méditer-ranéennes au Moyen Age* (Madrid 1999) 399–413

Duval N. (1964) "Observations sur l'urbanism tardif de Sufetula (Tunisie)," *Cahiers de Tunisie* 12 (1964) 87–103

Dyggve E. (1951) *History of Salonitan Christianity* (Oslo 1951)

Elderkin G.W. and Stillwell R. edd. (1934–41) *Antioch-on-the-Orontes I–III* (Princeton 1934–41)

Ellis S. (2006) "Middle class housing in late antiquity", in Bowden, Machado and Gutteridge (2006) 413–37

Failler A. "Le centenaire de l'Institut Byzantin des Assomptionnistes", *Revue des Etudes Byzantines* 53 (1995) 5–40

Feissel D. (1985) "Inscriptions du IVe au VIe siècle", in D. Feissel and A. Philippidis Braat, "Inventaires en vue d'un recueil des inscriptions historiques de Byzance. III. Inscriptions du Péloponnèse (à l'exception de Mistra)", *Travaux et Mémoires* 9 (1985), 267–395

——. (1987) "Nouvelles Données sur l'institution du *pater ths polews*", in G. Dagron and D. Feissel, *Inscriptions de Cilicie* (Paris 1987) appendix 1 215–20

Février P.A. (1964) "Notes sur le developpement urbain en Afrique du Nord. Les exemples comparés de Djemila et Sétif," *Cahiers Archéologiques* 14 (1964) 1–47

——. (1977) "Towns in the Western Mediterranean," in *European Towns. Their Archaeology and Early History* ed. M.W. Barley (London 1977) 315–42

Fraschetti (1999) *La conversione. Da Roma pagana a Roma cristiana* (Bari 1999)

Frantz A. (1988) *The Athenian Agora, vol. 24: Late Antiquity* (Princeton 1988)

Frere S.S. (1967) *Britannia: a History of Roman Britain* (London 1967)

——. (1972–84) *Verulamium Excavations* vols. 1 and 2 (Society of Antiquaries Research Reports nos. 28 and 41) (London 1972 and 1983) vol. 3 (Oxford University Committee for Archaeology Monograph no. 1) (Oxford 1984) vol. 3

Gauthier N. and Duval N. et al. (1986f.) (edd.) *Topographie chrétienne des cités de la Gaule des origines au milieu du VIIIᵉ siècle* several vols (Paris 1986f.)

Gerber W. et al. (1917–39) *Forschungen in Salona I–III* (Vienna 1917–39)

Gregorovius F. (1886f.) *Die Geschichte der Stadt Rom im Mittelalter Vom V. bis XVI. Jahrhundert* (Stuttgart 1886f.)

Grisar F. (1911) *History of Rome and the Popes in the Middle Ages* (London 1911)

Guilland R. (1969) *Etudes de topographie de Constantinople byzantine* (Paris 1969)

Haas C. (1997) *Alexandria in Late Antiquity* (Baltimore 1997)

Holum K.G. et al. (1988) *King Herod's Dream: Caesarea on the Sea* (New York and London 1988)

Janin R. (1950) *Constantinople byzantine: dévelopement urbain et repertoire topographique* 1st ed. (Paris 1950), 2nd ed. (Paris 1964)

Jeffreys E., Jeffreys M. and Scott R. trans. (1986) The *Chronicle of John Malalas* (Byzantina Australiensa 4) (Melbourne 1986)

Jones A.H.M. (1937) *Cities of the Eastern Roman Provinces* (Oxford 1937), 2nd ed. (Oxford 1971)

——. (1940) *The Greek City from Alexander to Justinian* (Oxford 1940)

——. (1957) *Athenian Democracy* (Oxford 1957)

——. (1964) *The Later Roman Empire 284–602: A Social, Economic, and Administrative Survey*, 3 vols (Oxford 1964), reprinted in two volumes with continuous pagination (Oxford 1973)

——. (1970) *A History of Rome through the Fifth Century. Vol. 2 The Empire* (London 1970)

Kelly C. (2004) *Ruling the Later Roman Empire* (Cambridge 2004)

King G.R.D. and Cameron Averil (1994) edd. *The Byzantine and early Islamic Near East II: Land use and settlement patterns* (Studies in late antiquity in early Islam 1) (Princeton 1994)

Kirsten E. (1958) "Die byzantinische Stadt", *Berichte zum XI. internationalen Byzantinisten-Kongress* vol. 3 (Munich 1959) 1–48

Kitzinger E. (1946) "A Survey of the Early Christian Town of Stobi," *DOP* 3 (1946) 81–162

Kraeling C.H. (1962) *Ptolemais: City of the Libyan Pentapolis* (Chicago 1962)

Krause J. (2006) "Überlegungen zur Sozialgeschichte des Klerus im 5./6. Jh. N. Chr.", in J.-U. Krause and C. Witschel (eds.), *Die Stadt in der Spätantike—Niedergang oder Wandel?* (Historia Einzelscriften 190) (Stuttgart 2006) 413–39

Kurbatov G.L. (1971) *Osnovnye problemy vnutrennego razvitiya vizantijskogo goroda v IV–VII vv.* (Leningrad 1971)

Lallemand J. (1964) *L' Administration civile de L'Égypte, de l'avènemente de Dioclétien à la création du diocèse (284–382)* (Mémoires de l'Académie royale de Belgique Cl. des lettres 57.2) (Brussels 1964)

Laniado A. (2002) *Recherches sur les Notables Municipaux dans l'Empire Protobyzantin* (Paris 2002)

Lavan L. (2001a) *Recent research in late antique urbanism* (*JRA* Supplementary Series 42) (Portsmouth, Rhode Island 2001)

——. (2001b) "Late antique urbanism: a bibliographic essay", in Lavan (2001a) 9–26

——. (2001c) "The praetoria of civil governors in late antiquity", in Lavan (2001a) 39–56

——. (2001d) *Provincial Capitals of Late Antiquity* (PhD diss. Nottingham 2001)

——. (2003a) "Late antique urban topography: from architecture to human space", in Lavan and Bowden (2003) 171–95

——. (2003b) "The political topography of the late antique city", in Lavan and Bowden (2003) 314–40

——. (2006) "Fora and agorai in Mediterranean cities: fourth and fifth centuries A.D.," in Bowden, Machado and Gutteridge (2006) 195–249

Lavan L. and Bowden W. (2003) *Theory and Practice in Late Antique Archaeology* (*Late Antique Archaeology 1*) (Leiden 2003) 171–95

Lavan L., Özgenel L. and Sarantis A. (forthcoming) edd. *Housing in Late Antiquity: From Palaces to Shops* (*Late Antique Archaeology 3.2*) (Leiden forthcoming)

Lemerle P. (1945) *Philippes et la Macédoine orientale à l'époque chrétienne et Byzantine. Recherches d'Histoire et d'Archéologie* (Paris 1945)

Lepelley C. (1979) *Les cités de L'Afrique romaine au bas-empire* vol. 1 *La permanences d'une civilisation municipale*, vol. 2 *notices d'histoire municipale* (Paris 1979)

——. (2006) "Hans-Georg Pflaum et l'Afrique romaine. Essai de bilan d'une oeuvre et d'une approche", in *H-G. Pflaum, un historien du XXᵉ siècle*, edd. S. Demougin et al. (Geneva 2006) 19–37

Lewin A. (1995) "Il mondo dei ginnasi nell'epoca tardoantica" in *Atti dell'accademia romanistica costantiniana X convegno internazionale (in onore di Arnaldo Biscardi, Spello-Perugia-Gubbio, 7–10 ottobre 1991) Il tardo impero. Aspetti e significati nei suoi riflessi giuridici* (Napoli 1995) 623–28

——. (ca. 1995) *Assemblee Popolari e Lotta Politica nelle città dell' Impero Romano* (Firenze c. 1995)

——. (2001) "Urban public building from Constantine to Julian: the epigraphic evidence", in Lavan (2001a) 27–37

Liebenam W. (1900) *Stadtverwaltung im römischen Kaiserreiche* (Leipzig 1900)

Liebeschuetz J.H.W.G. (1972) *Antioch: City and Imperial Administration in the Later Roman Empire* (Oxford 1972)

——. (1992) "A.H.M. Jones and the Later Roman Empire" *Institute of Archaeology Bulletin* 29 (1992) 1–8, reprinted in *idem* (2006) *Decline and Change in Late Antiquity: Religion, Barbarians and their Historiography* (Aldershot 2006) XVI

——. (2001) *The Decline and Fall of the Roman City* (Oxford 2001)

Lim R. (1999) "People as power: games, munificence, and contested topography", in *The Transformations of 'Urbs Roma' in Late Antiquity*, ed. W.V. Harris (*JRA* Supplementary Series 33) (Portsmouth, Rhode Island 1999) 265–81

Lizzi R. (1989) *Vescovi e strutture ecclesiastiche nella città tardoantica ("L'Italia Annonaria" nel IV–V secolo d. C.).* (Como 1989)

Loseby S. (2006) "Decline and change in the cities of late antique Gaul", in *Die Stadt in der Spätantike—Niedergang oder Wandel?*, edd. J.-U. Krause and C. Witschel (Stuttgart 2006) 67–104

MacMullen R. (1988) *Corruption and the Decline of Rome* (New Haven 1988)

Maier H.O. (1995) "The topography of heresy and dissent in late-fourth-century Rome", *Historia* 44.2 (1995) 231–49

Mango C. (1959) *The Brazen House. A Study of the Vestibule of the Imperial Palace of Constantinople* (Copenhagen 1959)

——. (1985) *Le développement urbain de Constantinople (IVe–VIIe siècle)* (Paris 1985)

Mango C. and Scott R., with Greatrex G. (1997) trans. *The Chronicle of Theophanes Confessor: Byzantine and Near Eastern History A.D. 284–813* (Oxford 1997)

Mayer E. (2002) *Rom ist dort wo der Kaiser ist. Untersuchungen zu den Staatsdenkmälern des dezentralisierten Reiches von Diocletian bis zu Theodosius II* (Römisch-Germanisches Zentralmuseum. Monographien Bd. 53) (Mainz 2002)

Merlin A. (1911) *Forum et églises de Sufetula* (Paris 1911)

Müller-Wiener W. (1977) *Bildlexikon zur Topographie Istanbuls* (Tubingen 1977)

Ostrogorsky G. (1959) "Byzantine Cities in the Early Middle Ages", *DOP* 13 (1959) 45–66

Petit P. (1955) *Libanius et la vie municipale de Antioch* (Paris 1955)

Petridis P. (1997), "Delphes dans l'antiquité tardive: première approche topographique et céramologique", *BCH* 121 (1997) 681–95

Poinsot C. (1958) *Les ruines de Dougga* (Tunis 1958)

Pollard N. (2000) *Soldiers, Cities, and Civilians in Roman Syria* (Ann Arbor, Michigan 2000)

Poulter A. (1995) *The Roman, Late Roman and Early Byzantine city of Nicopolis A.D. Istrum: the British Excavations 1985–1992* (Monograph of the Society for the Promotion of Roman Studies 8) (London 1995)

Ratté C. (2001) "New research on the urban development of Aphrodisias in late antiquity", in D. Parrish ed., *Urbanism in Western Asia Minor* (Portsmouth, Rhode Island 2001) 117–47

Rebillard E. and Sotinel C. (1998) edd. *L'évêque dans la cité du IVe au Ve siècle. Image et authorité* (Coll. de l'École française de Rome 248) (Rome 1998)

Ripoll G. and Gurt J.M. (2000) edd. *Sedes regiae (ann. 400–800)* (Barcelona 2000)

Rostovtzeff M.I. (1926) *The Social and Economic History of the Roman Empire* (Oxford 1926)

Roueché C. (1979) "A new inscription from Aphrodisias and the title du *pater ths polews*", *GRBS* 20 (1979) 173–85

——. (1984) "Acclamations in the later Roman Empire: new evidence from Aphrodisias," *JRS* 74 (1984) 181–99

——. (1989) *Aphrodisias in Late Antiquity* (London 1989)

Rudakov A.P. (1917) *Očerki vizantijskoj kul'tury po dannym grečeskoj agiografii* (Moscow 1917)

Ryden L. (1963) ed. *Das Leben des heiligen Narren Symeon von Leontios von Neapolis* [Studia Graeca Upsaliensia 4] (Uppsala 1963)

——. (1970) *Bemerkungen zum Leben des heiligen Narren Symeon von Leontios von Neapolis* [Studia Graeca Upsaliensia 6] (Uppsala 1970)

Scranton R.L. (1957) *Corinth*. vol. XVI. *Mediaeval Architecture in the Central Area of Corinth* (Princeton, N.J. 1957)

Segal J.B. (1970) *Edessa 'The blessed city'* (Oxford 1970)

Sfameni C. (2004) "Residential villas in Late Antiquity Italy: continuity and change", in Bowden, Lavan and Machado (Leiden 2004) 335–75

Sijpesteijn P.J. (1987) "The title *pater ths polews* and the papyri", *Tyche* 2 (1987) 171–74

Steinby E.M. (1993–99) *Lexicon topographicum urbis Romae*, several vols (Rome 1993–99)

Tsafrir Y. and Foerster G. (1997) "Urbanism at Scythopolis-Bet Shean in the fourth to seventh centuries," *Dumbarton Oaks Papers* 51 (1997) 85–146

Velkov V. (1977) *Cities in Thrace and Dacia in Late Antiquity (Studies and Materials)* (Amsterdam 1977)

Waelkens M. et al. (2006) "The late antique city in Southwest Anatolia. A case study: Sagalassos and its territory", in *Die Stadt in der Spätantike—Niedergang oder Wandel?*, edd. J.-U. Krause and C. Witschel (Stuttgart 2006) 463–83

Ward-Perkins B. (1984) *From Classical Antiquity to the Early Middle Ages: Urban Public Building in Northern and Central Italy, A.D. 300–850* (Oxford 1984)

Weir R. (2004) *Roman Delphi and its Pythian Games* (BAR IS 1306) (Oxford 2004)

Wharton, A.J. (1995) *Refiguring the Post-classical City: Dura Europos, Jerash, Jerusalem and Ravenna* (Cambridge 1995)

Whittow M. (1990) "Ruling the late Roman and early Byzantine city: a continuous history," *Past and Present* 129 (1990) 3–29

Wickham C. (2005) *Framing the Early Middle Ages: Europe and the Mediterranean 400–800* (Oxford 2005)

CHAPTER NINE

JONES AND THE LATE ROMAN ECONOMY

Bryan Ward-Perkins

Like most scholars today, I belong to a post-Jones generation, whose knowledge of the fourth to sixth centuries was always built on the firm foundations of the *Later Roman Empire*. So, when asked to consider Jones' contribution to our understanding of the late Roman economy, I approached the problem from a position of considerable ignorance—I knew what came after him, but had never read his predecessors, because this had always seemed unnecessary. Jones, as far as I was concerned, had constructed a scholarly edifice so solid that there was really no need to look back beyond 1964—those green (or red) volumes were a reliable starting-point.

My judgement of Jones was therefore a seriously unbalanced one, that examined him only in the light of what came afterwards, in particular in the light of Peter Brown's Late Antiquity, humming with intellectual and spiritual inquiry and with a Holy Man on every street corner. In comparison to this later work, Jones' *Later Roman Empire* is both very institutional, and undeniably bleak, with its overweening bureaucrats and soldiers, and its peasants struggling under fiscal and legal oppression. Therefore, when I agreed to contribute a paper on Jones and the late Roman economy, I thought I would be explaining why his view of it was so pessimistic.

1. *Before Jones*

What I had not realised—but learned after only a few hours in the company of the works of earlier scholars—was quite what a breath of fresh air and quite how cheerful, in the context of scholarship up to 1964, Jones' *Later Roman Empire* really was. Before Jones, the social and economic history (indeed the whole story) of the late Roman empire was predominantly apocalyptic, and almost invariably linked to some Grand Theory of Decline.

A defining work in the field of economic and social history, was undoubtedly Mikhail (or Michael) Rostovtzeff's *The Social and Economic History of the Roman Empire*, published in 1926.[1] Rostovtzeff, an exile since 1918 from Soviet Russia, did not treat the late antique period in any detail, but, famously, he interpreted Roman history as a struggle between the 'bourgeoisie' (exemplifying civilised values) and 'the masses', ending in the third and fourth centuries with the triumph of the latter, when they dragged the educated classes down to their own level. The result was a "simplification of all the functions of political, social, economic, and intellectual life, which we call the barbarization of the ancient world".[2] In economic terms, the late Roman period saw progressive impoverishment, as commercial life died; and, in social terms, it witnessed ever-increasing oppression.

This view of a late empire, already half-way to its own destruction, was by no means exclusive to Rostovtzeff. The great French scholar, Ferdinand Lot, who published his general work on this period in 1927, gave two of his late Roman chapters the following headings: 'A caste-based regime'; and 'Great estates against the State and against the weak'.[3] There were some mildly dissenting voices—for instance, André Piganiol, in his *L'Empire chrétien* of 1947, diagnosed serious problems within the late Roman economy, but did not see it as terminally ill.[4] However, before 1964, the overriding view, present in new work as well as in the 'standard' literature, was of a late Roman economy in the grip of a totalitarian regime, and suffering from systemic failure. Here, for instance, is the German scholar Friederich Oertel, writing about 'The economic life of the Empire' in *The Cambridge Ancient History* Volume XII (of 1939):

---

[1] Rostovtzeff (1926).

[2] The quotation is from page 486, within a final chapter entitled 'The Oriental Despotism and the Problem of the Decay of Ancient Civilization'.

[3] Lot (1927): 'Le régime des castes'; 'La grande propriété contre l'état et les faibles'. Tenney Frank's *An Economic History of Rome* (1927) in effect draws to a close in the third century. But those pages which do deal with the late empire are decidedly pessimistic: e.g. 478–9 (blaming racial degeneration), 501, and 592–644 (by Grenier on late Roman Gaul). Ernst Stein's highly influential *Geschichte des spätrömischen Reiches*, whose first volume was published in 1928, does not deal with economic and social history in detail, but takes a similar line to Rostovtzeff and Lot.

[4] Piganiol (1972) 303–33 and 459–61. Piganiol, who wished to blame the Germanic barbarians for the fall of the empire, attributed its economic problems to the demands of war.

The price paid for the restoration of the Empire [in the tetrarchic period] was twofold. First, the absolute State had come, catering for the population at large, schematic, appealing to mass-intelligence. Secondly, a complete State-socialism was in force, which with its terrorism by officials, its over-emphasised restrictions on the individual, its progressive State-interference, and its burdensome taxation and liturgies, previously not so clearly defined, and its methods of realizing its demands, acted very much as before, except in so far as the union with the Christian Church, from the time of Constantine, gave the system a religious veneer, and stamped subjection as resignation to the will of God.[5]

2. Jones' Contribution in Context

Before looking at the details of Jones' arguments, it should first be noted that one of his principal contributions to scholarship was to banish unreadable and anachronistic language of the kind quoted above, replacing it with terse, crystal-clear prose, solidly rooted in the primary written sources. There is no 'class-struggle' in Jones, though this was to have a later revival in the work of Geoffrey de Ste. Croix, and there are no words like 'state-socialism' and 'bourgeoisie' (the latter a particular favourite with Rostovtzeff).[6] Until I did the preparatory reading for this paper, I had no idea what terrible prose, and anachronistic language, Jones had spared me and all generations of post-1964 students. As Momigliano brilliantly pointed out in a review of the *Later Roman Empire*, "...this book cannot be explained without the English tradition of Royal Commissions, social surveys, Fabian Society pamphlets.... His work deserves to go down to future generations as the Jones Report on the State of the Roman Empire (A.D. 284–602)".[7] The Jones Report is an exemplary civil-service document, exuding common sense, packed with information, and pruned of all verbiage and jargon.

But what was also surprising, when reading Jones in the context of previous scholarship, was to discover that his later Roman empire—when compared to that found in previous work—was quite a cheerful place. It had its problems, fully identified in the Jones Report, which

---

[5] Oertel (1939) 269–70. One can almost hear the groans of the translator, struggling, and failing, under the weight of Oertel's ponderous prose.
[6] For class-struggle, see de Ste. Croix (1981); for Rostovtzeff and the 'bourgeosie' see the index-entry for this word in his *Social and Economic History*, at 642.
[7] Momigliano (1965) 264.

we will look at in some detail below; but it was by no means fatally impaired. Jones' late empire was an austere but powerful structure, brought down only by overwhelming external force. As he expressed it in the very last sentence of his book: "The internal weaknesses of the empire cannot have been the major factor in its decline".[8]

3. *The Role of Trade and Industry*

At first sight, and from the viewpoint of 2007, it can seem paradoxical to argue that Jones saw the late Roman economy in comparatively optimistic terms. For instance, he argued forcefully, in relation to commerce, that it played only a very minor role within the late empire; for Jones, the late Roman economy was basically stagnant, with very little specialised production and very little movement of goods, other than on behalf of the State. In a theory which he first set out in 1955, he claimed he could show (by comparing the revenue raised by different forms of taxes) that the wealth generated by manufacturers and traders was only around a twentieth (5%) of the wealth generated by agriculture and the land. He closed his chapter in the *Later Roman Empire* on 'Industry, Trade and Transport' with the following words about the Roman tax on manufacturers and traders (the *collatio lustralis*): "this terrible tax, which drove the merchants and craftsmen of the empire to desperation...apparently yielded about 5 per cent. of the imperial revenues".[9] The paradox and bathos—of a "terrible tax", that yielded only 5% of imperial revenue—are carefully crafted, and equally carefully positioned. At the very end of a long chapter on merchants and manufacturers, from which one might well form the impression they were important, and after a moving account of how the *collatio* forced traders to sell their children into slavery or prostitution, Jones brings the contribution of trade and manufacture to the ancient economy firmly down to earth, as derisory in comparison to landed wealth.

However, before judging as pessimistic Jones' minimalist assessment of late Roman commerce, we need to view it in a broader context, and be aware of how he described the role of trade in earlier Roman times. Other scholars, like Rostovtzeff and Tenney Frank, had depicted

---

[8] Jones (1964) II, 1068.
[9] *Ibid.*, II, 871–2. Cf. Jones (1955).

the early Roman period as a golden age of specialisation and trade, with ships criss-crossing a peaceful Mediterranean, filled with the agricultural and manufactured products of the different provinces; and, for Rostovtzeff and others, a sharp decline in this network was instrumental in weakening the late empire. For Jones, the whole vision was a fantasy—both the commercial golden age of early imperial times, and its later decline. It is true that commerce plays only a very minor role in the *Later Roman Empire*; but this, Jones argues, is because "...it is very doubtful whether there ever had been any large-scale inter-provincial trade".[10] In the context of the scholarship of his day, Jones' belief in a low-trade late Roman empire was actually a much more up-beat assessment than was generally current. The orthodoxy was that trade had boomed under the early empire, but had collapsed dramatically in the third century. Jones argued that it was never of great significance, and thereby levelled the economic playing field between the early and the late empire.

4. *Taxation, Abandoned Land, and Depopulation*

There were, however, some economic conditions that Jones firmly believed had worsened by late imperial times. In particular, he argued that the burden of the State, in exactions and taxation, was very substantially higher under the late empire than in previous centuries. He believed that, by the fourth century, the army had been roughly doubled in size from its early imperial levels, in order to cope with the threat of Germanic and Persian invasion, and he argued that the number of other unproductive consumers had also substantially increased: bureaucrats, privileged aristocrats, the state-supported poor of Rome and Constantinople, and the clergy of the newly-established Christian Church. These were, to use the splendid phrase he chose to describe them, 'idle mouths', and their demands weighed heavily on those within the economy who were still productive and still tax-paying. This

---

[10] Jones (1964) II, 1039. Unusually, Jones in a footnote (III, 339.n.10) here specifically referred to a work of modern scholarship, with which he disagreed: F.W. Walbank, *The Decline of the Roman Empire in the West* (1946), a short book which argued for dramatic economic decline in the third and fourth centuries. Jones' opinion, that commerce never played much part in the Roman economy, was formed early; it features, for instance, in his *The Greek City* (1940) at 265–9. In 1952 he explicitly questioned Rostovtzeff's enthusiastic estimates of the importance of trade in the Roman world: Jones (1952) 359.

theory was already expounded in Jones' inaugural lecture (as Professor of Ancient History at University College, London), delivered in 1948: "…during the third century the number of idle mouths increased sharply, and their average consumption rose".[11]

In this inaugural lecture, and even more forcefully in an article published in 1959, Jones developed the idea that levels of late Roman taxation were not just heavy, but also progressively damaging economically.[12] He argued that oppressive taxation (necessitated by the increased numbers of soldiers and idle mouths) rendered some agriculture unprofitable, leading to a flight from the land, a fall in population, and the creation of abandoned fields, the *agri deserti* that late Roman law-makers worried about. In developing his theory, Jones was eloquently supported by the testimony of some late antique writers, such as Lactantius, who lamented that under Diocletian "[t]he number of recipients began to exceed the number of contributors by so much that, with the farmers' resources exhausted by the enormous size of the requisitions, fields became deserted and cultivated land was turned into forest".[13] For Jones, a shrinking pool of cultivated land further exacerbated the situation, since it meant raising yet higher the taxes to be paid by the surviving cultivators, thereby creating a vicious cycle of economic and demographic decline. In his 1959 article, "Over-Taxation and the Decline of the Roman Empire", rates of taxation, a shrinking of the Roman economy, and the overall decline of the empire were explicitly and forcefully linked.

However, by the time he came to write the *Later Roman Empire*, Jones had softened his views. While still arguing for a link between 'idle mouths', heavy taxation, the abandonment of some land, and depopulation, he was now careful to state that "[t]he extent of the evil must not be exaggerated", and that it was predominantly marginal land (according to him, seldom more than 20% of the total) that was affected. He even now accepted (on the basis of archaeological work in Syria), that some new and prosperous areas of cultivation were opened up for the first time in late Roman times.[14] In summing up the state of late Roman agriculture, Jones wrote: "It must be emphasised that there was no general agricultural decline; land of good and medium

---

[11] Jones (1948) 18.
[12] *Ibid.*, 16–17; Jones (1959).
[13] Lactantius, *De Mortibus Persecutorum* 7.3 (trans. Creed).
[14] Jones (1964) II, 812–23 and II, 1039–47 (the quotation is from 821).

quality continued to pay high taxes, yield high rents and command high prices."[15] And he concluded that, while "[t]he population fairly certainly sank...the decrease...was not in most areas catastrophic".[16] These are balanced and cautious views, very far from the apocalyptic vision of earlier scholars, and not that far from what many would argue today.

5. *Tied Labour*

As any reader of the *Theodosian Code* must, Jones accepted that tied labour was an important feature of the late Roman period. Large numbers of people were compelled by law to stay in their professions, whether in the army, on the land (as half-free peasants, *coloni*), or in other occupations necessary to the state, such as shipping. Furthermore, not only they, but also their children, were bound to pursue the same hereditary profession. As set out in the *Later Roman Empire*, the story of this compulsion makes undeniably depressing reading. But again, when one examines Jones carefully and views him in the context of what had come before, his position assumes the rosier glow of a distinct softening of the previous orthodoxy.

For scholars like Rostovtzeff, Lot and Oertel, the attempts of the late Roman State to tie people to their professions arose from a combination of willed despotism, and a desperate response to an economy already out of control. For Jones, the phenomenon of tied labour was a much less despotic, more measured, and slowly evolving response to a particular difficulty facing the late Roman State: that it now needed more people to serve it (and pay its taxes), but was finding it hard to get hold of them. In his inaugural lecture of 1948, Jones drew explicit parallels between the restrictions on the mobility of labour enforced by the late Roman government, and the 'Essential Works' and 'Restriction on Engagement' orders which he had helped to administer as a temporary war-time civil servant within the Ministry of Labour. He concluded that:

---

[15] *Ibid.*, II, 1040.

[16] *Ibid.*, II, 1045. As in his discussion of ancient trade, Jones here again breaks his self-imposed silence regarding secondary sources, stating specifically (III, 339.n.14) that he is questioning the arguments for dramatic population decline of A.E.R. Boak, *Manpower Shortage and the Fall of the Roman Empire in the West* (1955).

Historians have been prone to regard the legislation of which I am speaking as due to the insensate passion for regimentation on the part of the
military emperors of the third and fourth centuries, or, more mystically,
as a rather premature attempt to introduce the middle ages. But against
the background of an acute labour shortage, their action becomes at least
intelligible, if not very intelligent.[17]

Because he knew all the evidence so well, Jones was also very careful
in the *Later Roman Empire* not to generalise wildly from the evidence of
the *Codes*, and to argue that all workers were successfully tied down and
oppressed. He accepted that the lot of most workers was unpleasant,
sometimes very unpleasant. But, for instance, in describing the peasantry,
he was careful to state that, outside the *Codes*, there is evidence of free
agricultural labourers and smallholders, and even evidence of *coloni* who
were quite well-off (for example, owning their own slaves).[18] Indeed he
raised important doubts about the evidence of the laws, on which so
much of the image of an oppressive late Roman State depends: "The
laws themselves, by their constant reiteration of the same prohibitions
and their frequent condonation of past offences, show how impossible
it was...to enforce the rules".[19] In 1970, he expressed this same view
in even more forceful terms: "The flood of laws which endeavour to
fix various categories of persons and their descendants in their occupations reveals the volume of the movement which they were intended
to check and goes far to prove that they failed".[20]

Both in the *Later Roman Empire* and his article of 1970, Jones forcefully attacked the notion that the late Roman empire operated a rigid
caste system, with everyone in their hereditary pigeon-hole and with
no movement up or down the social ladder. He pointed out that the
greatly increased army and bureaucracy of late Roman times opened
up opportunities for social betterment within the imperial service, on
a scale that was earlier quite unknown: "I would venture to affirm that
social mobility was greater in the later Roman empire than it had been
under the principate...".[21] Again, in the context of previous scholarship,

---

[17] Jones (1948) 14.
[18] Jones' account of 'The Condition of the Peasantry' is in (1964) II, 808–12, and
very wisely opens with the words: "It would be unwise to generalise on the condition
of the peasantry under the later Roman empire".
[19] *Ibid.*, II, 1052.
[20] Jones (1970), reprinted in Jones (1974) with the quotation at 418.
[21] *Ibid.*, 418.

this was a breath of fresh air within a later Roman empire previously seen as in the grip of 'state-socialism' or a 'caste-based regime'.

6. *Jones the Pessimist*

So far we have examined Jones the (comparative) optimist, saving the later Roman empire from the profound scholarly gloom in which it previously languished. But, interestingly, it takes a careful reading of the *Later Roman Empire* to uncover this more cheerful vision. A rapid assessment of the book leaves the reader with a very different impression, much closer to the dark scholarly consensus that preceded it.

In part, Jones' considered and cautious assessments of the evidence fall victim to his own distinctive scholarly style, and to his particular love of the law-codes. As we have seen in Garnsey's paper earlier in this volume, in researching the *Later Roman Empire* he assembled every scrap of written evidence that he could on a particular topic, and he then set this out in his book in exhaustive detail, often quoting the relevant passages at length.[22] This is the enduring and incomparable strength of the *Later Roman Empire*—it is an encyclopaedic collection of textual material arranged by topic, which is always reliable and which still serves as an invaluable scholarly resource. But, because Jones liked to present all the detail, and in particular liked to quote from most of the relevant laws in the *Theodosian* and *Justinianic Codes*, the sheer weight of his evidence often unbalances the impression that he wished to give.

For instance, as we have seen, a careful reading of Jones on the lot of the peasantry shows him to have been both cautious and balanced, and even to have questioned seriously the effectiveness, and therefore the evidential value, of late Roman legislation. But the laws, which are often highly repressive, are none the less presented in very great detail in his work. To take one example, Jones devoted over seven pages of text in the *Later Roman Empire* to the evidence, primarily legal (and almost invariably grim), for the fate of tied peasants (the *coloni*), and supported his account with four dense pages of notes, in which 86 laws (often quoted *in extenso*), 25 papyri, and five other sources are

---

[22] Garnsey (ch. 2) 26–7.

cited.[23] By contrast, he wrote less than three pages of text on peasant freeholders, supported by only a third of a page of notes, largely because contemporary texts about them are much rarer and they hardly feature in the law codes.[24] The reader can certainly be forgiven for leaving with the impression that freeholders were far less important within the late Roman economy than *coloni*, though in reality it the quantity of evidence cited, and not its absolute value, nor even Jones' overall assessment of it, that gives this impression. At no point does he state that *coloni* were the predominant form of peasant—indeed, when he discusses the relative numbers of different types of tenant farmer, he is very careful to state that we simply cannot tell how many fell into each category: "It is impossible to estimate the relative importance of these...classes of tenant".[25] It is the quantity of evidence he cites, rather than his assessments of it, that leaves the reader with a decidedly bleak view of late Roman social conditions.

It also does not help that Jones kept interrogation of his sources separate, sometimes a long way apart, from the sections where he overwhelmed his readers with data. For instance, the serious questions he raised about the evidential value of late Roman social legislation appear, not in Chapter XX, where he set out the legal evidence for the status of *coloni* in great detail, but in his Introduction and Conclusion.[26] What he wrote in his Introduction is extremely clear:

> My own impression is that many, if not most, laws were intermittently and sporadically enforced, and that their chief evidential value is to prove that the abuses which they were intended to remove were known to the central government. The laws, in my view, are clues to the difficulties of the empire, and records of the aspirations of government and not its achievements.

But the reader will long since have forgotten these wise words by the time they reach Jones' section on *coloni*, some 800 pages later, and the student or scholar, who dips into the *Later Roman Empire* by way of

---

[23] Jones (1964) II, 796–802 with III, 256–60.n.61–76. My figures may not be 100% accurate—but certainly give an accurate impression.

[24] *Ibid.*, II, 779–81 with III, 250.n.25–30. The imbalance in Jones' text and notes is exacerbated by the fact that he liked to quote extensively from the law-codes, but tended to only cite (without quotation) the narrative sources, which are our main evidence for a free peasantry. The 'Jones Report' is full of administrative texts, but low on the anecdotal detail on which, by contrast, Peter Brown's Late Antiquity was built.

[25] *Ibid.*, II, 803.

[26] *Ibid.*, I, viii (Introduction), II, 796–802 (*coloni*), II, 1051–3 (Conclusion).

its excellent index, will miss the caveats altogether. Characteristic of his approach was to lay out the written evidence in exhaustive detail, without much discussion of its absolute or relative value, and only then to attempt some (brief) synthesis and overview—but by this point the reader has probably already formed an opinion, on the basis of the sheer quantity of evidence cited and quoted.

However, it would be wrong to argue that it is just his technique of multiple citation of the evidence, and his style of argumentation, that make the *Later Roman Empire* a rather pessimistic book. Although, compared to previous scholarship, it is an up-beat and cheerful account, none the less, in comparison to most recent work, it is undeniably rather gloomy. Jones does seem to have believed that the Roman empire declined (somewhat) before it fell. This is most apparent in his chapter headings, and in their running-heads. The very last chapter of the *Later Roman Empire* is entitled 'The Decline of the Empire', and the running-heads of this same chapter are: 'The Barbarians'; 'Political Weaknesses'; 'Military Defects'; 'Economic Decline'; 'Depopulation'; 'Idle Mouths'; 'Social Weaknesses'; 'Administrative Abuses'; 'Decline of Morale'; and, finally (and unique in its neutrality), 'East and West'. Much of the text is dedicated to showing that these problems were not terminal; but none the less one has to conclude that Jones' overall vision was more grey than rose-tinted. When he produced an abbreviated version of his book, he entitled it quite simply 'The Decline of the Ancient World'.[27]

7. *Jones and Archaeology*

The minimalist, and predominantly pessimistic, view that Jones had of the later Roman economy was to a large extent possible because he almost completely ignored archaeological evidence. In some ways this position is understandable in the context of the early 1960s. At that date the outpouring of archaeological publications for late Roman times, that we now have available, had not really begun: for instance, it was only in 1968 that the first large-scale and systematic field-survey in the Mediterranean region was published (that of the *Ager Veientanus*, north of Rome); and only in 1972 was the study of the late Roman

---

[27] Jones (1966).

pottery-trade made possible by John Hayes' catalogue of red-slip wares.[28] Without Hayes, for instance, it was still reasonable for Jones to argue in the *Later Roman Empire*, on the basis of textual evidence alone, that "the global demand for manufactured goods was very low".[29]

However, to attribute Jones' reticence over archaeological evidence solely to the period in which he wrote is not a sufficient explanation, if we take 'archaeological evidence' to include dated buildings like churches. There was, when Jones wrote, already plenty of archaeological evidence for an impressive rash of church building within the later Roman empire; indeed Jones himself had published some of it, when, early in his career, he wrote up the inscriptions from excavations at Gerasa (Jerash) in modern Jordan, several of them the dated building-inscriptions from late antique churches.[30] When Kraeling, who directed the project at Gerasa, produced the final report of these excavations in 1938, he drew an obvious economic conclusion from this evidence: "Our best evidence for the nature and brilliance of the new epoch which the late fifth and early sixth century marks in the life of Gerasa is the series of churches built there at this time".[31] In his chapter on 'The Cities', Jones does cite this one example of archaeological evidence for late prosperity, but, as far as I know, none of the hundreds of other churches that he must have seen in his extensive travels merit a mention in the *Later Roman Empire*.[32] As he proudly announced in his Preface: "I have visited 94 of the 119 provinces...have inspected the Roman sites, ruins and still surviving buildings, and have studied the character of the countryside and the contents of the local museums".[33] When Jones discussed the growing wealth of the Church, he did so exclusively from written evidence, with not a single mention of the large and numerous churches of late Roman times.[34]

---

[28] Hayes (1972); Kahane, Murray Threipland and J. Ward-Perkins (1968). Hayes' work was beginning to question Jones' low-trade views; but the Ager Veientanus survey supported his ideas on agricultural abandonment and falling population.

[29] Jones (1964) II, 847.

[30] Jones (1928) and (1930).

[31] Kraeling (1938) 65–6.

[32] Jones' passage on Gerasa ((1964) II, 763) is quoted earlier in this volume by Lavan (ch. 8) 177.

[33] Jones (1964) I, vii. Elsewhere, Jones showed he was well able to observe and describe a building: he contributed the (admittedly dry) descriptions of the buildings of New College, All Souls and Worcester for the *Victoria County History* of Oxfordshire published in Salter and Lobel (1954) 144–54, 183–93 and 301–9.

[34] Jones (1964) II, 904–10.

Jones' silence about buildings in the *Later Roman Empire* is deafening, and is compounded by a total lack of any photographs, or plans of villages, houses, or individual buildings. As far as I am aware, there are only three explicit references to archaeological evidence in all the 1500 pages of the *Later Roman Empire*: the three sentences on Gerasa mentioned above; four sentences dedicated to the extraordinary (and dated) late antique houses of Syria, fully published by Georges Tchalenko in 1953 (a work cited by Jones); and a single paragraph (with no detail), arguing for the wealth of the empire's eastern and southern provinces on the basis of their impressive ruins from earlier Roman times.[35] Of these three references, only the first two (seventeen lines in all) are specific to late Roman times.[36]

Not only did Jones know a great many archaeological sites, he was also very well aware of their potential as evidence. When in 1952 he wrote an assessment of Rostovtzeff's career, it was above all his use of archaeology that he praised: "Perhaps the most striking feature of Rostovtzeff's historical methods is his use of archaeological material"; and, in the same article, Jones lamented the habitual "unhappy divorce between history and archaeology, with loss to both sides, but more especially to history".[37] What is more, when Jones came to write the Preface to the *Later Roman Empire* he was well aware of his own shortcomings: "My most lamentable gap is the archaeological material. I have not read the excavation reports on late Roman sites".[38] Why then, given his extensive knowledge of the empire, the precedent offered by Rostovtzeff, and his own awareness of its potential, did Jones so conspicuously ignore the evidence of archaeology?

---

[35] *Ibid.*, II, 823 (citing Tchalenko (1953)), and II, 1065 (with III, 343.n.57, which proves that Jones had closely observed a large number of churches). Needless to say, I have not re-read all 1500 pages of the *Later Roman Empire*, to check that there is no other passing reference to the physical remains of buildings; but when Jones mentions Justinian's extraordinary St Sophia in Constantinople, the largest building of late Roman times, it is surely significant that he devotes only fifteen words to it, and, as evidence of its cost, cites not the building itself but a written text. Even when referring to *spolia*, which he does in a single line (II, 736), Jones cites no archaeological examples and rapidly switches back to the familiar world of Libanius and the Oxyrhynchus papyri.

[36] To put these seventeen lines in correct perspective, we need to note that there are over 45,000 lines of text in the *Later Roman Empire* (excluding many a thousand of Notes and Appendices).

[37] Jones (1952) 355–7 (the quotations are both from 355).

[38] Jones (1964) I, vii.

The clue to this puzzle lies in Jones' laconic "I have not read the excavation reports of late Roman sites", if we combine this sentence with some phrases from his 1952 assessment of Rostovtzeff. Here he praises the Russian scholar for his ability to penetrate "the jungle of archaeological publications", and he bemoans the tendency of archaeologists "to present their data in a form more and more unpalatable to the historian".[39] Like so many historians, including many active today, Jones felt uncomfortable with archaeology. Although this is speculative, I suspect it was not just its opacity, but also its open-endedness that he found difficult. In the Preface to the *Later Roman Empire* he tells us how systematically and completely he had trawled the written sources: "I have tried to cover completely all historians...I have read and re-read the Codes and Novels...I have read all collections of letters...I have tried to read all contemporary biographies...I can claim to have looked at every published papyrus of relevant date...". The archaeological material was never going to be susceptible to such a meticulous and systematic approach—so Jones excluded it altogether.[40]

8. *After Jones*

The most interesting work on the Roman economy since the *Later Roman Empire* has certainly been in the very field that Jones ignored, archaeology; and over the last four decades a great deal of this work came to be focused specifically on the late Roman period, as scholars realised the richness of information available for this 'poor relation' of classical times. John Hayes' pioneering work on red-slip wares (published in 1972) not only opened up a new field of study, into the production of late Roman ceramics, but also, crucially, provided a reliable chronology for a product that is found all over the Mediterranean, and hence a new and widely-available way of dating sites.

In the countryside, research has taken the form both of excavation of individual sites—still primarily villas (rather than the more typical houses of farmers)—and of systematic field-survey, charting the chang-

---

[39] Jones (1952) 356.
[40] Jones' aversion to archaeology is already apparent in his *Cities of the Eastern Roman Provinces* (1937) and *The Greek City* (1940), which are essentially administrative histories, based on written texts (and some inscriptions), with no discussion of archaeology or topography (and no plans).

ing spread of settlements across time, by the study of their surface remains.[41] Inevitably, all this work has not resolved many important questions to everyone's satisfaction: Was there a fall in the rural population, and if so when? Was the East more prosperous and populous than the West? When did the villa life of classical times disappear? But it has provided a mass of new evidence to argue from, and has rendered debate much more sophisticated than it was in 1964. It is now no longer necessary or fruitful to go round and round the same few scraps of literary evidence.[42]

In the cities of the empire, work has necessarily been much more patchy, because it is never possible at any one time to excavate more than a tiny part of a single settlement. Furthermore, in the case of cities that are still occupied, it is modern circumstances, rather than a research agenda, that determines where it is possible to excavate. Cities are anyway very complex places, and, even when preservation is excellent and excavation extensive (as, for instance, at Pompeii), it is very difficult to show how people were supporting themselves economically, and whether conditions were improving or declining. Consequently, the information that is specifically economic, that has emerged from urban excavation, tends to be very broad-brush in character: an impression that settlement is spreading or contracting, or that building on an impressive scale is continuing or declining.[43]

Specialised production and exchange is an area for which a huge amount of evidence has emerged since 1964. As mentioned above, the pioneer was Hayes, though his strength has always been his genius at identifying typological development, rather than a facility as an economic historian. However, work that started in the late 1970s, pioneered by Italian archaeologists, built on his achievement, and extended the study of late antique pottery into research on amphorae, which of course

---

[41] There is a very useful survey of work up to a few years ago in Chavarria and Lewit (2004), which includes, in an appendix, a list of published field-surveys, arranged by region.

[42] The only area of the empire where there is enough written evidence of rural conditions to allow for fruitful reassessments is Egypt, with its papyri: see, for instance, J. Banaji (2001) and Sarris (2006).

[43] Occasionally a site comes up with more specific economic evidence: for instance the shops excavated at Sardis, which give a wonderful impression of the nature of working and living conditions within one of the many colonnaded streets of the East: Crawford (1990). For an impression of the contribution of archaeology to the study of late Roman urbanism, which goes way beyond the purely economic, see Liebeschuetz (2001) and Krause and Witschel (2006).

were the primary transport and storage containers for liquids in the ancient Mediterranean.[44] Researchers began to quantify accurately the different types of pottery and amphora found on sites at different periods of their history, and, by this method, were able to document changing patterns of trade. The results have been remarkable—in particular, overwhelming evidence for a predominance of eastern and African goods in the northern and western provinces of the Mediterranean under the late empire. Inevitably, because there is so much of it, it is pottery that has dominated discussion of archaeological evidence for production and trade; but other products, such as copper vessels and marble church-fittings, have also been very fruitfully studied.[45] In 1964, Jones was able to ignore almost completely the evidence of archaeology when discussing the late Roman economy, nowadays the boot is more likely to be on the other foot, with material evidence playing by far the preponderant role in any account of ancient economic life.

9. *Jones' Continuing Value*

This does not, however, mean that the *Later Roman Empire* has been pensioned off from all discussion of the late Roman economy. Its overall conclusions have, certainly, become unfashionable, particularly Jones' minimalist views on the role of commerce within the ancient economy—these theories now often assume the unenviable role of the 'straw man' that modern scholars set up, only in order to demolish it.[46] However, despite this, even for economic history (as for so many other fields) the *Later Roman Empire* remains the work that scholars turn to more often than any other book.

It is, quite simply, a wonderful and reliable collection of contemporary written material, above all of the evidence in the law codes. For instance, if one is interested in shippers, Jones' *Later Roman Empire* will point one to the laws one needs to read, quoting (in translation) the crucial passages in his main text, commenting on them tersely but sensibly, and setting

---

[44] A very good impression of this work can be formed from Giardina (1986). A more recent work, in which the archaeological evidence for specialised production and trade is discussed, is Kingsley and Decker (2001).

[45] See, for instance, M. Mango (2001) and Sodini (1989).

[46] See, for example, B. Ward-Perkins (2005) 87. Jones' views of the ancient economy are often (and reasonably) bracketed together with those of Moses Finley.

out much of the Latin in the end-notes. The Jones Report often remains much the best starting point for research. Furthermore, however good and extensive archaeological data have become, for many aspects of the economy (such as prices, taxes, or relations between landlords and tenants), the written record, which Jones knew so well, will always remain the only, or at least the paramount, source of information. Jones can be criticised for ignoring archaeological evidence, but, for the longevity of his book, it was a sensible move. The archaeology is changing all the time; the texts are much more static, so a comprehensive and sensible review of their evidence remains of very great value.

The *Later Roman Empire* is undeniably strongest on administrative sources, as Jones himself admitted, when he stated that he "had read and *re-read* [my emphasis] the Codes and Novels, the Notitia Dignitatum and similar official documents"; but his combing of late Roman texts, of all sorts, was so systematic that he also discovered and published fascinating snippets of information from a wide variety of texts.[47] For instance, in discussing the trade in clothing, Jones quoted the evidence of Diocletian's *Price Edict* in great detail, claiming to show from it that only luxury clothes were sold over long distances within the empire. But he also found a reference, in a saint's *Life* of the early fifth century, to an aristocrat in Rome of ascetic bent, who wore cheap clothes known as "natural coloured Antiochenes".[48] As Jones recognised, this evidence points in a very different direction to the main thrust of his argument—to a world in which cheap garments were perhaps transported for sale over hundreds of miles of sea—but he was much too good a scholar to brush this inconvenient gem under the carpet. His meticulous, scrupulous, and accurate scholarship, which was based in a profound knowledge of the sources, and expressed with extreme clarity and economy of expression, make the *Later Roman Empire* a very great work, of immense value more than forty years after its publication. Of very few scholarly books can this be said.

---

[47] The quotation is from Jones' Preface to the *Later Roman Empire*, (1964) I, vii.
[48] *Ibid.*, II, 848–50.

Bibliography

Banaji J. (2001) *Agrarian Change in Late Antiquity: Gold, Labour and Aristocratic Dominance* (Oxford 2001)

Boak A.E.R. (1955) *Manpower Shortage and the Fall of the Roman Empire in the West* (Ann Arbor and London 1955)

Chavarria A. and Lewit T. (2004) "Archaeological research on the late antique countryside: a bibliographic essay", in *Recent Research on the Late Antique Countryside: Late Antique Archaeology 2* edd. W. Bowden, L. Lavan and C. Machado (Leiden and Boston 2004) 3–51

Crawford J.S. (1990) *The Byzantine Shops at Sardis* (Cambridge, Mass. 1990)

Frank T. (1927) *An Economic History of Rome* (London 1927)

Giardina A. (1986) ed. *Le Merci, gli insediamenti* (= *Società romana e impero tardoantico*, Vol. III) (Rome-Bari 1986)

Hayes J.W. (1972) *Late Roman Pottery: a Catalogue of Roman Fine Wares* (London 1972)

Jones A.H.M. (1928) "Inscriptions from Jerash", *JRS* 18 (1928) 144–78

——. (1930) "Inscriptions from Jerash—Part II", *JRS* 20 (1930) 43–54

——. (1937) *Cities of the Eastern Roman Provinces* (Oxford 1937), 2nd ed. (Oxford 1971)

——. (1940) *The Greek City from Alexander to Justinian* (Oxford 1940)

——. (1948) *Ancient Economic History: an inaugural lecture delivered at University College, London* (London 1948)

——. (1952) "Michael Ivanovitch Rostovtzeff, 1870–1952", *PBA* 58 (1952) 346–61

——. (1955) "The Economic Life of Towns in the Roman Empire", *Recueils de la Société Jean Bodin* 7 (1955) 161–92, reprinted in *idem* (1974) 35–60

——. (1959) "Over-Taxation and the Decline of the Roman Economy", *Antiquity* 33 (1959) 39–43, reprinted in *idem* (1974) 82–89

——. (1964) *The Later Roman Empire 284–602: A Social, Economic, and Administrative Survey*, 3 vols (Oxford 1964), reprinted in two volumes with continuous pagination (Oxford 1973)

——. (1966) *The Decline of the Ancient World* (London 1966)

——. (1970) "The Caste System in the Later Roman Empire", *Eirene* 8 (1970) 79–96, reprinted in *idem* (1974) 396–418

——. (1974) *The Roman Economy: Studies in Ancient Economic and Administrative History*, ed. P.A. Brunt (London 1974)

Kahane A., Murray Threipland L. and Ward-Perkins J. (1968) "The Ager Veientanus north and east of Veii", *PBSR* 36 (1968)

Kingsley S. and Decker M. (2001) edd. *Economy and Exchange in the East Mediterranean during Late Antiquity* (Oxford 2001)

Kraeling C.H. (1938) ed. *Gerasa: City of the Decapolis* (New Haven 1938)

Krause J.-U. and Witschel C. (2006) edd. *Die spätantike Stadt: Niedergang oder Wandel?* (Stuttgart 2006)

Liebeschuetz J.H.W.G. (2001) *The Decline and Fall of the Roman City* (Oxford 2001)

Lot F. (1927) *La Fin du monde antique et le début du Moyen Âge* (Paris 1927)

Mango M. (2001) "Beyond the amphora: non-ceramic evidence for late antique industry and trade", in Kingsley and Decker (2001) 87–106

Momigliano A. (1965) "A.H.M. Jones' The Later Roman Empire", *Oxford Magazine*, NS, 5 (4 March 1965) 264–5, reprinted in *idem* (1969) *Quarto contributo alla storia degli studi classici e del mondo antico* (Rome 1969) 645–47

Oertel F. (1939) "The economic life of the Empire", in *The Cambridge Ancient History XII*, 1st edition, edd. S.A. Cook, F.E. Adcock and M.P. Charlesworth (Cambridge 1939) 232–96

Piganiol A. (1972) *L'Empire chrétien (325–395)*, 2nd ed. (Paris 1972)

Rostovtzeff M.I. (1926) *The Social and Economic History of the Roman Empire* (Oxford 1926)

Salter H.E. and Lobel M.D. (1954) edd. *The Victoria County History of the County of Oxford*, Vol. III (Oxford 1954)

Sarris P. (2006) *Economy and Society in the Age of Justinian* (Cambridge 2006)

Sodini J.-P. (1989) "Le commerce des marbres à l'époque protobyzantine", in (no named editor) *Hommes et richesses dans l'Empire byzantin* (Paris 1989) 163–86

Ste. Croix G.E.M. de (1981) *The Class Struggle in the Ancient Greek World: From the Archaic Age to the Arab Conquest* (London 1981)

Stein E. (1928) *Geschichte des spätrömischen Reiches*, vol. i: *Vom römischen zum byzantinischen Staate (284–476)* (Vienna 1928)

Tchalenko G. (1953) *Villages antiques de la Syrie du Nord*, 2 Vols (Paris 1953)

Walbank F.W. (1946) *The Decline of the Roman Empire in the West* (London 1946)

Ward-Perkins B. (2005) *The Fall of Rome and the End of Civilization* (Oxford 2005)

CHAPTER TEN

IDLE MOUTHS AND SOLAR HALOES:
A.H.M. JONES AND THE CONVERSION OF EUROPE

David M. Gwynn

A.H.M. Jones made no claim to be an ecclesiastical historian. The doctrines and practices of the Christian Church were not subjects that Jones studied or wrote about for their own sake. He was a social and economic historian, and his assessment of the Church in the *Later Roman Empire* must be understood in that light. Yet Jones knew the sources and the controversies of early Christian history considerably better than a superficial reading of his great work might suggest, and his contribution to the history of the Church fully merited the D.D. that he received from Oxford University in 1966.[1] By the standards of contemporary Late Roman historiography Jones was by no means unusual in the limited space that he allowed for the nature and internal conflicts of Christianity, while in the careful attention he devoted to questions of hierarchy, wealth and legal status his work was a watershed in the study of the Church as an organisation within the Later Roman world. The separation between social-political and ecclesiastical-theological history in Late Antique scholarship has still not been satisfactorily closed, and the work of Jones represents an important step forward in bridging the gulf between these fundamental disciplines.

That Jones' priorities were not those of a Church historian is made explicit in the much quoted Preface to the *Later Roman Empire* itself:

> This book is not a history of the later Roman empire. It is a social, economic and administrative survey of the empire, historically treated...I have little to say about doctrinal controversies, but much about the growth of the ecclesiastical hierarchy. I ignore the two major intellectual achievements of the age, theology and law, but discuss the organisation

---

[1] Jones was presented for the degree by Henry Chadwick, to whom I am grateful for this and other personal communications. One of Chadwick's letters to Jones is quoted earlier in this volume by Garnsey (ch. 2) 27.

and finances of the church, the administration of justice, and the social status of the clergy and of lawyers.[2]

Jones does go on to declare that his introductory narrative chapters will nevertheless give an outline of ecclesiastical history, but he then repeats his intention to emphasise social and economic factors.[3] In the following pages I will survey briefly the presentation of Christianity in the *Later Roman Empire*, before I turn to look in slightly more detail at two of Jones' most influential and controversial theories: his characterisation of Constantine, the first Christian Roman Emperor, and his assessment of the impact of Christianity upon the empire as a whole.

I do not intend to comment here upon Jones' personal religious views. In the words of Jones' daughter, Mrs Cordelia Gidney, "although styling himself an atheist he never assumed that believers were necessarily either knaves or fools".[4] Certainly Jones was fully aware of the importance of religious history to the study of Late Antiquity,[5] and also of the potential for personal bias to influence the study of the Church.[6] His own attitude towards the primary sources for Church history is once again made explicit in his Preface, as too are the priorities with which he approached those writings:

---

[2] Jones (1964) I, v.

[3] *Ibid.*, I, vi. Jones' ambivalent attitude towards narrative Church history is already visible in his review of E. Stein, *Histoire du Bas-Empire* (1949) in 1953/4. "The strictly narrative form of presentation somewhat restricts the scope of the book. In ecclesiastical affairs, for instance, a very full account is given of the doctrinal controversies of the age, since they gave rise to events. But such topics as the development of monasticism, or the growing wealth of the church and the consequent evolution of corrupt and simoniacal practices are, because they did not give rise to correspondence and councils, completely ignored" (353).

[4] Quoted in Liebeschuetz (1992) 6.

[5] Crook rightly praised "Jones' ability to appreciate the importance of religiosity in the make-up of the men of late antiquity (paradoxical in one who, in spite of a strong clerical element in his family background—for his mother was the daughter of a clergyman and his father the son of the Revd. Hugh Jones, D.D., minister of the Welsh Wesleyan Methodist Church of Mount Sion in Liverpool—was quite unreligious)" (Crook (1971) 430–1).

[6] In his review of Stein in 1953/4 Jones comments upon the effect of the former's conversion to Catholicism upon his work (353), while in the Preface to *The Decline of the Ancient World* (Jones' abridged summary of the *Later Roman Empire* published in 1966) he explains that "in calling the bishop of Rome the pope I imply no theological overtones, nor do I imply that he was commonly so called in the period of which I write...he was usually styled the bishop, or archbishop, of Rome; to use this title today would, however, savour of aggressive Protestantism" (vii).

As I explored the ancient sources I regretfully came to the conclusion that a lifetime would not suffice to read them all; anyone who surveys only the relevant shelves of Migne's Patrologiae will understand. I soon decided to abandon theological treatises and commentaries on the Scriptures...there are a few grains of wheat in these, but the quantity of chaff (from my point of view) is overwhelming.[7]

I next, after reading a fair sample, abandoned sermons, having discovered that most consisted of exegesis of the Scriptures or of vague and generalised moralisation. . . . I have tried to cover completely all historians, secular and ecclesiastical, in Greek, Latin and (where translated) Syriac. . . . I have read all collections of letters, whether of laymen or churchmen (skipping theological controversy and scriptural exegesis in epistolary form). I have tried to read all contemporary biographies, notably lives of saints, and the hagiographical literature of an anecdotal kind, like the Lausiac History and Gregory's Dialogues. I have read the acts and canons of church councils, omitting purely theological matter.[8]

Whether it is possible to read the letters of the Church Fathers or the records of the councils while "omitting purely theological matter" is perhaps open to doubt, and it is true that Jones only quotes Christian doctrinal texts on extremely rare occasions (he does not, for instance, ever quote the Nicene Creed). However, the impression created by this introduction is one of Jones having read Christian literature widely if somewhat selectively. This impression is reinforced by the comments that Jones makes regarding his sources at the beginning of each of the narrative chapters, where a variety of Christian writers are cited, including the Cappadocian Fathers, Augustine, Jerome and John Chrysostom.[9] Indeed, Brown in his review of the *Later Roman Empire* declares that "Jones has gone on to exploit the immense reserves of the Christian literature of this period, as no other author has done before him".[10] I am not certain I would agree with Brown that "the one serious omission in the LRE is the evidence of the *Talmud*",[11] but it is important that we do not underestimate Jones' knowledge of the primary sources of Christian history in comparison to other literary spheres.

---

[7] Jones (1964) I, vi.

[8] *Ibid.*, vii.

[9] The writings of these Fathers, Jones declares, "are valuable not only for the history of the church, but for the incidental light which they throw on contemporary secular affairs" ((1964) I, 154–5).

[10] Brown (1967, reprinted in 1972 from which all citations here derive) 50.

[11] *Ibid.*, 50.n.3.

There is one essential reason why it is difficult to accurately assess the extent to which Jones did read the theological and ecclesiastical sources to which he refers, and that is due (somewhat ironically in the light of Jones' usual practice) to his citation of secondary sources. As a number of contributors to this volume have commented, Jones in the *Later Roman Empire* almost invariably prefers to avoid referring to the works of other scholars, and at first glance his analysis of the Church would seem to conform to that pattern. The notes to Chapter XXII ('The Church') begin with the famous and slightly barbed comment that "the most useful and comprehensive book of which I know on the organisation and discipline of the church is Joseph Bingham, *The Antiquities of the Christian Church*, London, 1726".[12]

Yet Jones' approach to at least the doctrinal history of the Church directly contradicts his customary method. If we are to trust his footnotes, then it would appear that Jones has taken almost his entire interpretation of the great controversies that divided Late Roman Christianity from modern rather than ancient writers. He cites the studies of W.H.C. Frend on the Donatists and of Stein on the Monophysites,[13] although in neither case does he do so uncritically, but the greatest influence derives from a different source. Jones drew his interpretation of the Arian Controversy, of the Pelagian dispute, of the careers of John Chrysostom and Nestorius, and of almost every other major conflict within the Late Roman Church from a single modern work: the French *Histoire de l'église* of Palanque, Bardy, and de Labriolle edited by Fliche and Martin.[14] That Jones was prepared to follow their authority perhaps reflects the limited importance he placed on these questions as compared to other themes relevant to the Church where he returns to his usual practice and emphasises solely the primary evidence.

When we turn to assess the presentation of Christianity in the *Later Roman Empire* it is necessary to consider both the narrative history chapters of Volume I and a number of the thematic chapters that appear in Volume II. It is in the narrative chapters that we find the short descriptions of the persecution of the Church under the Principate and under Diocletian, and then the equally concise accounts of the major controversies within the Christian Church. These controversies

---

[12] Jones (1964) III, 292.
[13] Frend (1952); Stein (1949).
[14] Fliche and Martin (1947).

are described within the context of Jones' analyses of the religious policies of the different emperors, particularly of Constantine the Great,
whose presentation in Jones I will discuss in more detail below. As I have
already observed the footnotes throughout these sections refer almost
exclusively to the work of Palanque, Bardy and de Labriolle.

Jones' own interests and priorities are better revealed in the presentation of the Church and the clergy in his thematic chapters. The influence of bishops is cited in Chapter XI on 'The Government', although
Jones says very little in his chapters on 'Rome and Constantinople'
(XVIII) or 'The Cities' (XIX) on the new role that bishops came to
play in urban life during this period, which has fascinated later scholars.[15] The evidence for that new episcopal role is cited, particularly the
involvement of bishops in urban decision-making and elections, but
Jones' primary interest in these chapters lies in the role of the Church
as another avenue for the 'flight of the curials' which is the subject of
another paper in this volume.[16]

Chapter XXII, 'The Church', would be better entitled 'The
Constitution of the Church', for this phrase occurs twice in the introduction and more accurately describes the contents of what follows.
Jones' great interest is the developing organisation of the Church and
the clerical hierarchy, including the relationship of episcopal and civic
structures, the emergence of the great sees and their authority, the
wealth of the Church and how that wealth was administered,[17] and the
numbers and social origins of Christians and particularly of the clergy
(focusing once again upon the involvement of the curial class).[18] This
chapter also contains Jones' brief study of asceticism in Late Antiquity
(for which he cites de Labriolle). As Jones explains, "a general history
of the eremitical and monastic movements would lie outside the scope
of this book: here only their social and economic aspects can be briefly

---

[15] This silence is equally true of Jones' earlier work *The Greek City from Alexander to
Justinian* (1940), upon which he draws for these chapters of the *Later Roman Empire*. For
more recent studies of the gradually increasing role of the bishop in the Late Antique
civic environment see Liebeschuetz (2001) 137–68, Rapp (2005) 208–34, and the paper
of Lavan in this volume (ch. 8) 181–2.

[16] Heather (ch. 5).

[17] Jones here expands upon the material he presented in his earlier article, "Church
Finance in the Fifth and Sixth Centuries" (1960).

[18] The social spread of Christianity in the fourth century was another subject
on which Jones in the *Later Roman Empire* could draw upon his own earlier research,
notably "The Social Background of the Struggle between Paganism and Christianity" (1963).

considered".[19] His argument is centred upon the difficulty of estimating monastic numbers and the evidence that monks might have been producers as well as consumers, the latter issue being part of a wider question to which I will return, namely Jones' presentation of the economic burden imposed by the Church on the Later Roman Empire.

Chapter XXII thus presents a detailed and systematic analysis of the emergence of Church organisation in the crucial formative period of the fourth and fifth centuries. What is missing is any discussion of the content of Christian teaching in either doctrine or ethics. For this we might expect to turn to Chapter XXIII, 'Religion and Morals', a chapter which offers perhaps the clearest demonstration of where Jones' interests lie.

The underlying emphasis throughout Chapter XXIII is in fact legal. Jones traces the official status of pagans, Jews, heretics and schismatics within the empire. He says little of the nature of the specific divisions within the Church, preferring simply to separate those who "differed from the catholic church on some purely metaphysical point of theology" from those who "had broken off on disciplinary issues".[20] When he does come to describe the prevailing beliefs of the age, it says much for Jones' approach that he entitled the relevant section of this chapter 'The Growth of Superstition'.[21] First he mourns the increasing belief in demons, magic and miracles not only among the peasants but even among the more enlightened ("such silly stories had no doubt always been believed by the common herd, but it is a sign of the times that a man of the intellectual eminence of Augustine should attach importance to them").[22] Only then does he turn to the heretical and schismatic controversies of Late Roman Christianity.

Jones repeatedly and rightly insists that these controversies were not purely the debates of academic intellectuals, but involved the wider mass of the population. Yet he says nothing in this chapter about the contents of the debates themselves, and the subtitle 'Doctrinal Controversies' here is something of a misnomer. This entire section is actually a repetition of the important article which he wrote in 1959

---

[19] Jones (1964) II, 929.
[20] *Ibid.*, II, 952. Jones does further observe that some sects like the Manichees "differed more radically from the norm" (II, 952) and he also comments that "there certainly were very curious communities on the lunatic fringe of Christianity" (II, 953).
[21] *Ibid.*, II, 957.
[22] *Ibid.*, II, 963.

against the views of certain scholars, notably Frend on the Donatists and Stein on the Monophysites, who attributed those controversies to social or national feeling rather than religious belief.[23] This argument is one of Jones' great contributions to early Christian history, but the study of doctrine was never Jones' primary concern. He does praise the work of certain 'great theologians' in east and west in Chapter XXIV, 'Education and Culture', but his central theme here is the generally low standard of Christian rhetoric and theology ("the sermons of the age show one characteristic which seems to be almost universal: they are mostly very dull").[24] He again says almost nothing regarding the specific teachings of his 'great theologians', and the only individual he actually names is Augustine.

To return briefly to Chapter XXIII, the remainder of that chapter is concerned with 'Morals', and specifically Jones' conclusion that the Church exerted only very limited influence on imperial legislation. Jones cites in particular the laws on marriage and divorce and the evidence that during the great period of Christianisation from Constantine onwards the continuing presence of legal brutality, extortion and corruption suggests that "the general standards of conduct…have remained in general static and in some respects have sunk".[25] This 'Failure of the Church' (which is the subtitle for this section) is attributed in part to the excessive standards demanded by clerical preaching, which Jones believed led many Christians to conclude that as they could not avoid sin "they might as well be hanged for a sheep as a lamb".[26] I will come back to this assertion that Christianity if anything contributed to a decline in public morality and service below.

The three thematic chapters which I have just summarised, and which stand at the end of Volume II immediately before the final chapter on the 'Decline of the Empire', are described by Peter Brown as "the first social history of the established Christian Church".[27] They represent a fundamental advance in the study of the development of the organisation of the Church, of the social and economic position of the clergy,

---

[23] Jones, "Were Ancient Heresies National or Social Movements in Disguise?" (1959). His criticism of the argument of Stein is already stated at some length in Jones' review of the former's *Histoire du Bas-Empire* in 1953/4 (353–4).

[24] Jones (1964) II, 1009.

[25] *Ibid.*, II, 979.

[26] *Ibid.*, II, 984–5.

[27] Brown (1967, 1972) 50–1.

and of the legal status of the different religions within the empire. In
the words of another reviewer, S.L. Greenslade:

> What ecclesiastical historian will not recognise in principle that he can-
> not understand the early church without full regard to its social and
> economic setting—and then sadly confess how thin is his knowledge of
> all that?...I shall not wish, or dare, to put pen to paper without consult-
> ing my "Jones".[28]

It is true that I have highlighted here Jones' omission of any detailed
discussion of the doctrinal controversies of this period or of asceticism.
Yet again it needs to be remembered, as Peter Garnsey has already
observed earlier in this volume, that Jones made no claim to be an
intellectual historian.[29] He was a historian of institutions, and he has
covered in remarkable detail precisely those aspects of the Church which
fall within his sphere. I would also emphasise once more that Jones'
lack of attention to doctrine must not be taken for lack of knowledge.
In the Chapter on 'Education and Culture' in *The Decline of the Ancient
World*, a book he described as an abridged summary of his larger work,
Jones adds a perfectly precise sketch of the major doctrinal questions
of the fourth and fifth centuries, amply demonstrating his grasp on a
complex subject which he specifically chose to omit from the *Later Roman
Empire*. Jones' interpretation of Christianity and the Church continues
to exert influence on later scholars, and in the second half of this
paper I will focus in slightly more detail on two arguments presented
by Jones which illustrate well his methods and his use of primary and
secondary evidence and which remain the subject of debate today:
Solar Haloes and Idle Mouths.

The solar halo refers of course to Jones' famous explanation for the
conversion of Constantine, the first Christian Roman Emperor. As Jones
declares at the beginning of the notes to Chapter III of the *Later Roman
Empire*, this is an argument that he first presented in 1948 in what he
describes as "my popular work",[30] *Constantine and the Conversion of Europe*.
On the subject of Constantine's conversion at least, Jones had not
changed his opinion in the intervening 16 years. Drawing in part on
the work of Norman Baynes,[31] although this influence is not acknowl-

---

[28] Greenslade (1965) 221 and 224.
[29] Garnsey (ch. 2) 39–40.
[30] Jones (1964) III, 10.
[31] Baynes (1929).

edged in the *Later Roman Empire* itself, Jones insists on the genuinely religious motivation of Constantine's adoption of Christianity. Against the argument in particular of Jacob Burckhardt,[32] Jones emphasises that Christians were a tiny minority within the empire at the end of the third century and so of little value for political support. Instead, he defends the attribution of Constantine's conversion to the vision that according to Eusebius of Caesarea in the *Life of Constantine* the emperor saw in A.D. 312, shortly before his victory at the Battle of Milvian Bridge which secured his sole rule over the western Roman Empire.

According to Eusebius, to whom the emperor reportedly described the vision under oath, the emperor saw:

> About the time of the midday sun, when day was just turning...up in the sky and resting over the sun, a cross-shaped trophy formed from light, and a text attached to it which said "By this conquer" (*Life of Constantine*, I.28)

Baynes raised the possibility that the vision was a natural phenomenon, but he refused to debate this question any further, declaring that "a historian...is unable to affirm miracle, but most certainly he cannot deny it".[33] Jones, by contrast, insists on a more scientific approach. To quote from *Constantine and the Conversion of Europe* (from which the shorter account in the *Later Roman Empire* derives):

> What Constantine probably saw was a rare, but well-attested, form of the "halo phenomenon". This is a phenomenon analogous to the rainbow, and like it local and transient, caused by the fall, not of rain, but of ice crystals across the rays of the sun.[34]

The words "in this conquer" were then in turn provided by "Constantine's overwrought imagination".[35] So Jones concludes:

> His conversion was initially due to a meteorological phenomenon which he happened to witness at a critical moment of his career. But this fortuitous event ultimately led to Constantine's genuinely adopting the Christian Faith, to the conversion of the Roman Empire, and to the Christian civilisation of Europe.[36]

---

[32] Burckhardt (1852).
[33] Baynes (1929) 9.
[34] Jones (1948) 85.
[35] *Ibid.*, 86.
[36] *Ibid.*, 90.

Despite certain scepticism, this scientific explanation of Constantine's conversion continues to receive support, notably from a number of German scholars to whom may now be joined T.D. Barnes who in a recent article also approves of the "solar halo" theory.[37] To return to the *Later Roman Empire*, however, the conversion is of course only one element of Jones' presentation of Constantine and his involvement with the Church. I cannot attempt to trace that entire presentation here, but something might briefly be said on two themes that particularly demonstrate the nature and methods of Jones' approach: his interpretation of the Donatist and Arian controversies, and his conception of the relationship of Church and State.

Little needs to be said regarding the first of these topics. According to Jones "it would be tedious to pursue the history of the Donatist controversy in detail",[38] and Constantine's involvement with the Donatists is thus described and dismissed in precisely one page. The Arian Controversy receives slightly greater attention, but the doctrinal content of the debate is not Jones' primary concern and is in fact summarised in a few paragraphs, with three footnotes directing the reader to pages 69–113 of the aforementioned *Histoire de l'église* of Palanque, Bardy, and de Labriolle. The pages in question were written by Gustave Bardy, which also explains the prominence in Jones' brief account of the school of Lucian of Antioch, one of Bardy's central themes.[39]

Rather than doctrine, Jones' great emphasis is on the role of Constantine at the Council of Nicaea, the first ecumenical council of the Church. Most notably, he accepts at face value the apologetic assertion of Eusebius of Caesarea that Constantine himself inspired the adoption of the term *homoousios* into the original Nicene Creed, which Jones attributes in turn to the urging of Constantine's Spanish adviser Hosius of Cordoba. Neither Eusebius' account of Nicaea nor the Western origin of the *homoousion* would now be accepted so readily by the majority of church historians,[40] but Jones is here following the interpretation of Bardy. The sole difference is the far greater prominence that Jones accords to Constantine as an individual, an emphasis that

---

[37] See in particular P. Weiss (1993) and T.D. Barnes (1998) 288–9.
[38] Jones (1964) I, 82.
[39] Cf. Bardy (1936).
[40] Regarding the origins of the Nicene Creed see Kelly (1960), a book that Jones did not apparently consult for the *Later Roman Empire*. The standard modern work on the Arian Controversy is now that of Hanson (1988), to which have recently been added Ayres (2004) and Behr (2004).

reflects one of Jones' principal interests: the relationship of Church and State.

The presentation of Constantine's involvement with the Church in the *Later Roman Empire* offers an interesting comparison and contrast with the presentation of the same theme in *Constantine and the Conversion of Europe*. In both works, Jones rightly places great importance not only on the actions of the first Christian Emperor but also on Constantine's belief that he had a duty to act on religious affairs, and he recognises that the vast majority of the Church welcomed the emperor's involvement. Chapter III on Constantine in the *Later Roman Empire* declares that during his reign "the general principle...that it was the right and duty of the imperial government to suppress heresy and schism was firmly established",[41] and Jones repeats this judgement in the final section of Chapter XXII on 'The Church'.

This emphasis on imperial involvement in the Church, however, in fact represents a marked toning down of Jones' presentation of Constantine. In his earlier book he asserts emphatically that with Constantine "the Church had acquired a protector, but it had also acquired a master",[42] and in his conclusion he returns to that theme.

> Thus was born Caesaropapism, the doctrine that the secular sovereign is by the grace of God supreme governor of the Church within his dominions and is as such divinely authorised to dictate the religious beliefs of his subjects.[43]

Few if any modern scholars would today accept such a conclusion, for no Christian Emperor, even the deeply religious and highly autocratic Justinian in the sixth century, ever succeeded in dictating doctrine to a hostile Church.[44] Jones himself in the *Later Roman Empire* would appear to have recognised the limitations of his own argument, and while he continues (quite reasonably) to emphasise the role of Constantine and his successors in Church affairs he no longer draws the same conclusion of 'Caesaropapism'.

---

[41] Jones (1964) I, 96.
[42] Jones (1948) 107.
[43] *Ibid.*, 205.
[44] The concept of 'Caesaropapism' was already under attack at the time when the *Later Roman Empire* appeared. See Geanakoplos (1965).

A similar toning down can be seen in Jones' final judgement regarding Constantine himself. In the *Later Roman Empire* he concludes with only a brief statement that:

> Constantine has many great achievements to his credit. He firmly established Christianity as the religion of the empire. He built a new capital, which was to outlive the old Rome by nearly a millennium. He organised an efficient mobile army, and laid the foundations of a sound gold currency. But he set a standard of extravagant expenditure and reckless fiscality, which undermined the economic stability of the empire.[45]

This restrained and largely positive judgement can be compared to that of *Constantine and the Conversion of Europe*. "Constantine hardly deserves the title of Great which posterity has given him, either by his character or by his abilities... still less does Constantine deserve the title of saint".[46] Moreover, although he profoundly influenced the history of Christianity:

> The effect on the Church was mainly bad. As converts came in no longer by conviction, but for interested motives or merely by inertia, the spiritual and moral fervour of the Church inevitably waned... and the last remnants of public spirit faded away. Nor is this surprising for the object of the Church was not to reform the empire but to save souls. To contemporary Christian thought the things of this world were of little moment, and the best Christian minds preferred not to touch the pitch of public life lest they be defiled. Men of high conviction and character became bishops or hermits, and government was left in the main to careerists.[47]

No parallel statement of such force is directed against Constantine in the *Later Roman Empire*. Yet the conclusion that the rise of the Church weakened both the spirit and the government of the empire is still visible in the role that Jones attributes to the Church in the final chapter of his great work: Chapter XXV, 'The Decline of the Empire'.[48] The judgement that the Christian clergy represented a body of 'idle mouths', consumers who drained the resources of the empire, is an acutely socio-

---

[45] Jones (1964) I, 111.
[46] Jones (1948) 201.
[47] *Ibid.*, 206–7.
[48] On the broader question of Jones' judgment on the collapse of the Western Roman Empire, which I will not discuss here, see the contribution of Averil Cameron in this volume (ch. 11).

economic conclusion which sheds important light on Jones' general approach to the Late Roman Church.

In the introduction to his explanation of the fall of the West, Jones observes that "rationalists like Gibbon saw religion as a primary cause of its decline...Christianity in his view sapped the morale of the empire, deadened its intellectual life and by its embittered controversies undermined its unity".[49] The flaw with such a judgement, as Jones immediately observes, is that "the East was even more Christian than the West, in theological disputes far more embittered".[50] Yet Jones is not prepared to entirely abandon the idea that Christianity played some role in 'sapping' the empire, and to this extent a Gibbonian influence on Jones can still be seen. Gibbon not only argued that Christianity undermined the intellectual and military virtues of the classical world, he also asserted that through the Church "a large portion of public and private wealth was consecrated to the specious demands of charity and devotion; and the soldiers' pay was lavished on the useless multitudes of both sexes, who could only plead the merits of abstinence and chastity".[51] In Chapter XXII on 'The Church', Jones develops in far greater detail than Gibbon this argument that the Church was an ever-increasing economic burden on the resources of the empire, and he repeats this judgement in a well-known passage in his final chapter:

> The Christian church imposed a new class of idle mouths on the resources of the empire. The pagan gods had, it is true, owned some land, whose revenue helped maintain their temples and to support their cult, but except in Egypt and at a few famous shrines its amount was small, and nowhere outside Egypt did a large body of endowed priests exist. The Christian church from the time of Constantine accumulated ever-growing endowments in land, and from their rents and from the first fruits of the faithful maintained an increasing number of full-time stipendiary clergy. By the sixth century the bishops and clergy had become far more numerous than the administrative officers and civil servants of the empire, and were on the average paid at substantially higher rates. In addition to the clergy there were many thousands of monks and hermits. Not all of these were idle mouths. The inmates of the Pachomian houses of Egypt produced a surplus, and many monks and hermits just earned their keep. But a large number lived on the alms of the peasantry, and as time went on more

---

[49] Jones (1964) II, 1026.
[50] *Ibid.*, II, 1027.
[51] Edward Gibbon, "General Observations on the Fall of the Roman Empire" (attached to ch. 38), *The Decline and Fall of the Roman Empire* (1776–1788) 163.

and more monasteries acquired landed endowments which enabled their inmates to devote themselves entirely to their spiritual duties.[52]

Two objections might be raised against such a conclusion. From the economic perspective of Jones himself, it could be argued that both clergy and monks played a greater role in the redistribution of wealth through welfare and through involvement in trade and agriculture than Jones would allow, although on the balance sheet of consumption over production it seems difficult to avoid the verdict that the Church did take far more than it gave. More importantly, however, it must be open to question whether one can truly judge the role of the Church in the Later Roman Empire solely in economic terms.[53] The very concept of 'idle mouths' is by definition an economic category, as Jones indeed makes clear, and by his socio-economic approach and by his exclusion of the internal life of the Church from his analysis, Jones has made such a judgement on the clergy inevitable. But while that judgement has significant truth according to the viewpoint from which it is made, that viewpoint itself needs to be qualified. Clergy are not expected to be economically productive, any more than are soldiers or bureaucrats, yet all these categories of service were important to the ongoing existence of the Roman Empire.

Here I would turn to another of Jones' famous conclusions from his chapter on 'Decline', the assertion that "the most depressing feature of the later empire is the apparent absence of public spirit".[54] In this regard, Jones goes on to observe, "Christianity has been accused on the one hand of sapping the empire's morale by its otherworldly attitude, and on the other hand credited with giving the empire new spiritual energy and reforming it by its moral teaching. Neither allegation seems to have much substance".[55] Despite this apparently even-handed assessment, however, Jones never discusses the positive interpretation of the spiritual role of Christianity or its sources. Instead, he elaborates on the negative view that he has just questioned. He repeats from Chapter XXIII ('Religion and Morals') his judgement that with Christianity moral standards if anything declined and he then declares:

---

[52] Jones (1964) II, 1046–7.
[53] There is an interesting discussion of this question in Evans (1996) 55–8, who concludes that "the church in Late Antiquity takes us into a realm that cannot be judged in terms of profit or loss for the Gross National Product" (58).
[54] Jones (1964) II, 1058.
[55] *Ibid.*, II, 1062.

There was, of course, a minority who took the Christian message seriously to heart, and regarding the things of the world as of no account, devoted themselves to achieving eternal life in the world to come. Many thousands withdrew into the desert or into monasteries and spent the rest of their lives striving by austerities and prayer to gain salvation; many were drawn, often against their will, into the service of the Church as priests and bishops. Quantitatively the loss to the state was probably not significant. Numerous as the clergy, monks and hermits were, their withdrawal cannot have seriously accentuated the manpower shortage from which the empire suffered, nor can the fact that the majority of them were celibate have contributed much to the shrinkage of the population. Qualitatively the loss was more serious. It was men of high moral character who were drawn to the spiritual life, and were thus lost to the service of the state. In the pagan empire such men had regarded the public service as one of the principal duties of the good man and citizen. Under the new dispensation they were taught that a public career was, if not sinful, so fraught with spiritual danger that it should be eschewed. The service of the state tended to be left to ambitious careerists, and Christianity thus paradoxically increased the corruption of the government.[56]

For Jones, as for Gibbon, the role of Christianity can only be assessed in negative terms. Thus, in his comparison between the eastern and western regions of the empire, he concludes that:

> In some respects the East was at a disadvantage. Christianity prevailed earlier in the Eastern parts and obtained a more thorough hold. Monks and clergy were more numerous and more richly endowed, and thus a heavier burden on the economy. Theological controversy was more widespread and more embittered, and the repression of heresy demanded a greater use of force and provoked more hostility. In so far as the otherworldly attitude which Christianity inculcated weakened public morale, the East should have been more gravely affected.[57]

At no point in the *Later Roman Empire* does Jones even consider the possibility that Christianity might exert a positive effect,[58] and of all his conclusions this I would insist is the judgement that is most in need

---

[56] *Ibid.*, II, 1063–4.
[57] *Ibid.*, II, 1064.
[58] Jones' attitude was already prefigured in 1955 when he informed Edwin Judge that Christianity had made no difference to the empire (a statement discussed further by Cameron in her article in this volume (ch. 11) 242). There is a slightly more optimistic judgement in Jones' earlier *The Greek City from Alexander to Justinian* (1940). Here too he concludes that the Church preached a doctrine of submission and withdrawal, but in the East at least this was transformed in the seventh century "when the onslaught of Islam infused into Christianity a fighting spirit and thus gave the empire in its religion a principle of unity and a motive for survival" (304).

of qualification. Indeed, my own inclination would be to turn Jones' argument around on its head. The survival of that very eastern portion of the Roman Empire in which Christianity had taken the deepest hold by the fourth and fifth centuries suggests that Christianity and the Church did offer strengths which a purely socio-economic interpretation is forced to ignore. The depth of feeling aroused by the doctrinal controversies that divided the early Church is no less visible in the rise of asceticism and the cult of saints that transformed the Late Roman world. At the very least, against the 'balance sheet' of Jones must be set the vibrancy and passion of Christian Late Antiquity in the writings of Peter Brown and his successors.[59] To reduce Athanasius of Alexandria, John Chrysostom or Augustine of Hippo to 'idle mouths' hardly does justice to these men as individuals or to the role that they and their Church played in the Later Roman Empire.

Like all those who have reviewed Jones in the past, however, I do not wish to end my discussion on a negative. As I said at the beginning of this paper, Jones was not a church historian, and many of his omissions or conclusions that I might question are the inevitable and logical consequence of the approach that he has laid down. The *Later Roman Empire* remains beyond question an essential guide for any understanding of the organisation of the Church and of the background against which those of us who study Christian doctrine and asceticism must work. I do not know that I would entirely endorse the judgement of Peter Brown that "any further study of the role of Christianity in Late Roman society must begin with these lucid pages".[60] But I can only agree with Greenslade that within the great work of Jones there is much "to which the ecclesiastical historian must listen even when it hurts".[61]

Bibliography

Ayres L. (2004) *Nicaea and its Legacy: An Approach to Fourth-Century Trinitarian Theology* (Oxford 2004)
Bardy G. (1936) *Recherches sur Lucien d'Antioche et son École* (Paris 1936)
Barnes T.D. (1998) "Constantine and Christianity: Ancient Evidence and Modern Interpretations", *Zeitschrift für antikes Christentum* 2 (1998) 274–94

---

[59] It is difficult to exaggerate the contrast that any reader must feel upon turning from Jones' *Later Roman Empire* in 1964 to Peter Brown's *The World of Late Antiquity* published seven years later in 1971. They might indeed be describing two different worlds.
[60] Brown (1967, 1972) 50.
[61] Greenslade (1965) 222.

Baynes N.H. (1929) *Constantine the Great and the Christian Church* (London 1929)

Behr J. (2004) *The Nicene Faith*, The Formation of Christian Theology, Volume 2 (New York 2004)

Brown P. (1967) "The Later Roman Empire", *EcHR*, 2nd series, 20 (1967) 327–43, reprinted in *idem* (1972) *Religion and Society in the Age of Saint Augustine* (London 1972) 46–73

——. (1971) *The World of Late Antiquity* (London 1971)

Burckhardt J. (1852) *Die Zeit Konstantins des Grossen* (Leipzig 1852), 2nd ed. (1880) translated as *The Age of Constantine the Great* by M. Hadas (London 1949)

Crook J. (1971) "Arnold Hugh Martin Jones, 1904–1970", *PBA* 57 (1971) 425–38

Evans J.A.S. (1996) *The Age of Justinian: The Circumstances of Imperial Power* (London and New York 1996)

Fliche A. and Martin B. (1947) edd. *Histoire de l'église*, volume III: J.R. Palanque, G. Bardy and P. de Labriolle, *De la paix Constantinienne á la mort de Théodose* (Paris 1947), translated as *The Church in the Christian Roman Empire* (volumes I-II) by E.C. Messenger (London 1949 and 1952)

Frend W.H.C. (1952) *The Donatist Church* (Oxford 1952)

Geanakoplos D.J. "Church and State in the Byzantine Empire: A Reconsideration of the Problem of Caesaropapism", *CH* 34 (1965) 381–403

Gibbon, E. (1776–1788) *The Decline and Fall of the Roman Empire* (1776–1788), ed. J.B. Bury, 7 vols (London 1923–38) 163

Greenslade S.L. (1965) "Review: The Later Roman Empire", *JThS*, NS, 16 (1965) 220–24

Hanson R.P.C. (1988) *The Search for the Christian Doctrine of God: The Arian Controversy 318–381* (Edinburgh 1988)

Jones A.H.M. (1940) *The Greek City from Alexander to Justinian* (Oxford 1940)

——. (1948) *Constantine and the Conversion of Europe* (London 1948)

——. (1953/4) "Review of E. Stein, *Histoire du Bas Empire, t. 2. De la disparition de l'empire d'occident à la mort de Justinien (467–565)*", *Historia* 2 (1953/4) 352–59

——. (1959) "Were Ancient Heresies National or Social Movements in Disguise?", *JThS*, NS, 10 (1959) 280–98, reprinted in *idem* (1974) 308–29

——. (1960) "Church Finance in the Fifth and Sixth Centuries", *JThS*, NS, 11 (1960) 84–94, reprinted in *idem* (1974) 339–49

——. (1963) "The Social Background of the Struggle between Paganism and Christianity", in *The Conflict between Paganism and Christianity in the Fourth Century*, ed. A. Momigliano (Oxford 1963) 17–37

——. (1964) *The Later Roman Empire 284–602: A Social, Economic, and Administrative Survey*, 3 vols (Oxford 1964), reprinted in two volumes with continuous pagination (Oxford 1973)

——. (1966) *The Decline of the Ancient World* (London 1966)

——. (1974) *The Roman Economy: Studies in Ancient Economic and Administrative History*, ed. P.A. Brunt (Oxford 1974)

Kelly J.N.D. (1960) *Early Christian Creeds*, 2nd edition (London 1960)

Liebeschuetz J.H.W.G. (1992) "A.H.M. Jones and the *Later Roman Empire*", *Bulletin of the Institute of Archaeology* 29 (1992) 1–8, reprinted in *idem* (2006) *Decline and Change in Late Antiquity: Religion, Barbarians and their Historiography* (Aldershot 2006) XVI

——. (2001) *The Decline and Fall of the Roman City* (Oxford 2001)

Rapp C. (2005) *Holy Bishops in Late Antiquity: The Nature of Christian Leadership in an Age of Transition* (Berkeley, Los Angeles and London 2005)

Stein E. (1949/1959) *Histoire du Bas-Empire*, vol. i: *De l'état romain à l'état byzantin (284–476)*, èdition française par Jean-Rémy Palanque (Paris 1959); vol. ii: *De la disparition de l'empire d'occident à la mort de Justinien (467–565)*, publié par Jean-Rémy Palanque (Paris 1949)

Weiss P. (1993) "Die Vision Constantins" in *Colloquium aus Anlaß des 80. Geburtstages von Alfred Heuss*, ed. J. Bleicken (Kallmünz Opf 1993) 143–69

CHAPTER ELEVEN

A.H.M. JONES AND THE END OF THE ANCIENT WORLD

Averil Cameron

Some autobiographical information is a prerequisite for contributors to this collection, and so I will begin by admitting that I never met A.H.M. Jones. I started teaching the Roman empire at King's College London in 1970, the year when Jones died; furthermore I was based in London and he was in Cambridge, which was not part of my life at that time. On the other hand he had been Professor of Ancient History at University College London before Arnaldo Momigliano, and the chronological period I had to teach was presumably one Jones had influenced, and which he probably inherited from Norman Baynes. At any rate, the Roman empire as defined in the London ancient history syllabus in 1970 covered the period from Augustus to A.D. 641, the death of Heraclius—the same end date as that of Jones' British Academy project, the *Prosopography of the Later Roman Empire*. Soon afterwards the end of the period was cut back in the syllabus to A.D. 400, which did not make much historiographical sense, though it presumably seemed somehow more convenient; shortlived though the experience may have been, having to teach the Jonesian 'long Roman empire' was in retrospect very important in my own formation.

Another piece of autobiography: I came to this long period cold, from having read Greats at Oxford, where the latest Roman history I had studied was the reign of Nero. I left Oxford after 'Schools' (the final examination) in 1962 and did not therefore have the experience of those who read 'Modern History' at Oxford of covering later Roman history from the reign of Diocletian onwards. My experience of Jones was therefore a London experience, and I will say something later about Jones against the London background.

1. *Context*

Looking back at Jones' *Later Roman Empire* today, and at its very curious last chapter, I believe it is important to put Jones back into the context when he actually wrote. In Peter Brown's masterly review of the *Later Roman Empire* we read of Jones' "splendid isolation",[1] and indeed no-one can deny Jones' incredible achievement in producing the *Later Roman Empire*. All the same, when the book appeared in 1964, there had already been a surprisingly large amount of writing in recent years on the subject of the end or decline of the Roman empire, and the change from Principate and High Empire to the Late Empire; indeed, this is amply demonstrated in the footnotes to Brown's review (Jones, of course rarely mentioned modern authors in his own notes to the *Later Roman Empire*), which also reveal how far the scholarship of the day revolved around certain well-worn themes. In his inimitable style, Brown wrote that Jones' book "is like the arrival of a steel-plant in a region that has, of late, been given over to light industries".[2] All the same, it is worth remembering what those light industries actually were.

It is very clear in retrospect that the *Later Roman Empire* was published against a context in which the problems surrounding the end of the Roman empire were attracting a good deal of attention. Only the previous year, Momigliano's collected volume had been published, with the title *The Conflict between Paganism and Christianity in the Fourth Century*; this contained a contribution by Jones on "The social background of the struggle between paganism and Christianity". Other contributors included H.-I. Marrou, P. Courcelle, E.A. Thompson, Herbert Bloch and Momigliano himself.[3] E.R. Dodds' *Pagan and Christian in an Age of Anxiety*, which characterised the rise of Christian asceticism as "madness", and saw the transition from early to late empire in terms of "anxiety", originated as the Wiles lectures in 1963.[4] A few years before, in 1959, Santo Mazzarino had published the Italian version of *The End of the Ancient World*, and this came out in English translation in 1966. The first part surveys the historiography since antiquity and the Renaissance on the reasons for the end of the Roman empire in the west, while the second part discusses the theories of others, such as Otto Seeck's contention that the later Roman empire represented the "elimination of the best";[5] it is interesting that the topic of elites in

[1] Brown (1967, reprinted in 1972 from which the citations here are taken).
[2] *Ibid.*, 49.
[3] See the review by Brown (1963).
[4] Dodds (1990).
[5] Seeck (1897–1921).

this period is again at the top of scholarly agendas.[6] In the same year as Jones' *Later Roman Empire* there appeared a small volume of extracts edited by André Piganiol, with the title *La chute de l'empire romain*, which focused on the sack of Rome by Alaric in 410.[7] This now seems a very French book in flavour, with its references to *la gloire* and to the "flood" (*inondation*) of barbarians. Piganiol wrote of an absence of "esprit militaire", and ended his own essay with the statement that the lesson to be drawn was that the Roman empire in the west existed at all times under the constant threat of invasion.

Not long before Jones' *Later Roman Empire* and rather in the manner of its final chapter, Donald Kagan had brought out a student book of excerpts from earlier publications,[8] including A.E.R. Boak's *Manpower Shortage and the Fall of the Roman Empire in the West* (1955).[9] Jones himself was included, on "the pressure of the barbarians". A similar collection had appeared in 1963 edited by Mortimer Chambers, *The Fall of the Roman Empire—Can it be Explained?*[10] This included Tenney Frank on race mixture and Ellsworth Huntington on climatic change. J.B. Bury and Max Cary also debated the subject, and so did Norman Baynes, who had taught at University College until 1946: the latter's contribution in the *Journal of Roman Studies* for 1943 similarly surveyed a series of current theories only to reject them and opt for the barbarian invasions as the cause.[11] The end of the Roman empire was a classic problem on which every ancient historian had to have a view. Jones' rather dated (to us) complaints about a lack of public spirit[12] may have seemed to Momigliano like the English public schoolboy speaking, but they are also to be understood in the context of the time, against the background of the theories of those who like Otto Seeck, not to mention Spengler or Toynbee,[13] argued for some kind of moral or qualitative decline in the upper classes themselves. It is consonant with this approach that Jones also believed in corruption as a major fault in

---

[6] See Salzman and Rapp (2000); Haldon and Conrad (2004); Lizzi (2006); see also Carrié and Wataghin (2001).

[7] Piganiol (1964).

[8] Kagan (1962, 1978).

[9] Reviewed by Moses Finley in *Journal of Roman Studies* 48 (1958) 156–64.

[10] Chambers (1963).

[11] Baynes (1943); cf. Cary (1935) 771–89.

[12] Jones (1964) II, 1058, "The most depressing feature of the later empire is the apparent absence of public spirit".

[13] Spengler (1919–22); for some remarks on Toynbee see Averil Cameron (2000).

the late Roman bureaucratic system, a view to be taken up after him by Ramsay MacMullen.[14]

Jones does not venture much in the *Later Roman Empire* into literary matters, but the inferior quality of late Latin literature had been a theme in the argument about whether the 'Bas-Empire' represented *décadence*.[15] Wolfgang Liebeschuetz has dared to return to the theme of literary quality in *The Decline and Fall of the Roman City*.[16] By the time the *Later Roman Empire* was published Marrou had famously recanted,[17] and his essay on Synesius in Momigliano's *Conflict between Christianity and Paganism* of 1963 (based on a conference held several years before), may have been an influence in the development of Peter Brown's positive view of late antiquity.[18] Jones however was not impressed. He writes in his chapter in *Later Roman Empire* on 'Education and Culture' that "the literary output of the age was large, but on the whole not distinguished" (II, 1008), and a little earlier on the same page that the educational system provided in sum merely "a jumble of miscellaneous lore". Other words which he applied to late Roman literature include "vapid and turgid", "very jejune and artificial" (II, 1009) and "repetitive and derivative" (II, 1011). This is interesting, since while admittedly in 1940 in *The Greek City* he had also written of mediocrity (284), he writes favourably of the Greek culture of the age for its diffusion over a remarkably wide area (284–85). Moreover while he believes that 'Byzantine' literature is even less often read (he seems to call Byzantine anything from the later fourth century), "it does not entirely deserve its ill repute" (284), even though theology is "not congenial to the modern mind".[19]

In answer to the question 'Why did Rome Fall?' the last chapter of the *Later Roman Empire* plumps for the external explanation, blaming the barbarian invasions. In effect Jones denies decline, even while calling his last chapter 'The Decline of the Empire', and giving to his abridgement of the *Later Roman Empire* the title *The Decline of the Ancient*

---

[14] Jones (1964) II, 1053–53; MacMullen (1998).

[15] See for example Marrou (1938).

[16] Liebeschuetz (2001) chs. 7, 'Transformation of Greek literary culture under the influence of Christianity', 223–48 and 10, 'Transformation of literary culture in the west under the influence of Christianity', 318–41.

[17] See Marrou (1949).

[18] See the discussion by Vessey (1988).

[19] See now Johnson (2006); Averil Cameron (1997), for the need to include theological writing when considering late antique literary output. Hagiography continues to pose problems for some scholars, but no-one now would exclude hagiographical texts as completely irrelevant to history.

World (1966).[20] Blaming the barbarians had also been the strategy of André Piganiol, in his book *L'Empire chrétien*, first published in 1947, which famously ends "the empire did not die a natural death, it was assassinated". J.B. Bury, in contrast, in his *History of the Later Roman Empire*, of 1923, denied both assassination and inevitability, and argued for contingency, or a series of accidents. Others had focused on the supposed internal collapse, for instance Frank Walbank, in a small book first published in 1946 as *The Decline of the Roman Empire in the West*, then again in 1953, and finally with the title *The Awful Revolution* (Gibbon's phrase) in 1966: this gave a prominent role to slavery, and the internal contradictions and conflict which this caused, and traced the beginnings of its bad effects to the fifth century B.C. Walbank's preface is dated 1944, and one of his expressed objects was to consider whether a similar collapse was inevitable for the civilisation of his own day. He termed the 'bureaucratic' late Roman state a "Frankenstein's monster", and equated what he called the "corporative state" of the late empire, which he believed came into being between A.D. 270 and 337, with modern-day fascism.[21] The flight of industry from towns to the estates of the rich, and a conception of the peasantry as "virtually enslaved" were important themes, as was the assumed decline of Roman literature and the overall "mental atmosphere".[22] Jones' pupil, Geoffrey de Ste. Croix, returned to the theme of the decline of the Roman empire in 1981 in *The Class Struggle in the Ancient Greek World*, which consists partly of didactic sections on Marx and Marxism and their importance for ancient history; like Walbank, de Ste. Croix saw the corrosive effects of slavery as continuing from classical Greek polis up to the end of the later Roman empire, to a date not far removed from Jones' own stopping point of A.D. 602. Croix explains that his own book goes up to the Arab conquests, "not much later than the great book of my revered teacher".[23] In contrast with Jones, however, de Ste. Croix's main argument is that the Roman empire (or rather, "the ancient Greek world") came to an end through its own internal contradictions, above all as a result of internal class struggle.

[20] The choice seems odd, given that the *Later Roman Empire* itself is called a 'Survey'. The preface to the shorter volume states that the *Later Roman Empire* is "a very long book (three volumes) and correspondingly dear (14 guineas)".
[21] Walbank (1946), 46, 76.
[22] *Ibid.*, 58, 62.
[23] See also the further essays published in Ste. Croix (2006).

Rostovtzeff's *The Social and Economic History of the Roman Empire* also belongs to this background, even though the original had come out as early as 1926. The *The Social and Economic History of the Roman Empire* was heavily influenced by the author's Russian origins; in 1919, having left revolutionary Russia, he published a pamphlet on "proletarian culture", and one of the main arguments of the book was the thesis that the bourgeois elite of the high empire was destroyed in the third century by the rise of the peasant element. As Wolfgang Liebeschuetz has pointed out, the influence of Rostovtzeff on Jones seems to have begun early.[24] 1926, the year of the *The Social and Economic History of the Roman Empire*, was the year in which Jones took Greats at Oxford, and the unusual habit which Jones later developed of writing long books dealing with the provinces and with cities and administration surely had much to do with Rostovtzeff's example. The second English edition of Rostovtzeff's *The Social and Economic History of the Roman Empire* by P.M. Fraser came out in 1957, not so long before Jones' *Later Roman Empire*. It does not cover the period which Jones tackled, but Rostovtzeff makes clear enough his negative view of the late empire, and his theme that the successful bourgeoisie of the High Empire was destroyed by the rise of the masses in the third century 'crisis' brings us back to the 'internal' explanation and to the notion of the failure of the elites. Jones' debt to Rostovtzeff was selective; he did not echo Rostovtzeff's view of the Roman empire as succumbing to "Oriental" influences which brought it "nearer to the masses" and which "accelerated barbarization". But he was not himself very impressed by the late Roman empire.

Decline and fall were therefore in the air while Jones was writing, and so were competing explanations. Jones seems to have felt it incumbent on him to pay lip service to this 'problem' in his final chapter, and like Kagan and Chambers, he runs through one 'explanation' after another, if only to reject them. The explanations thus listed do indeed seem limited or unconvincing; nevertheless by adopting this approach Jones rather surprisingly also located himself in this final chapter within this rather sterile contemporary way of thinking. The two modern works he actually mentions in the footnotes to Chapter XXV (in each case in order to disagree with them) are Walbank's *Decline of the Roman Empire in the West* (1946), whose contention that there was a reduction in trade in the late empire he rejects as an explanation of economic decline, and

---

[24] Liebeschuetz (1992) 2.

Boak's *Manpower Shortage* (1955), on which he cites the critical review by Moses Finley. It is interesting to note that Jones might have found already in Walbank a version of the theory of an excess of 'idle mouths' which in his view were choking the late Roman economic system.[25] Despite naming only Walbank and Boak, Jones' chapter reads like a survey of the range of current explanations. It is curious then that it rejects nearly all of them, and all the more curious because Jones did not leave it there. Later essays like that on ancient empires of 1965,[26] repeat the theme from the *Later Roman Empire* of the burden of a top-heavy superstructure, and use phrases such as "contributing to decline". In the 1965 essay we read that "the crushing burden of taxation was probably also the main cause of the progressive abandonment of cultivated land" (133), and "the heavy weight of taxation may also have contributed to the depopulation of the empire" (134); the words 'probably' and 'may have' introduce a note of uncertainty, but the prevalence of *agri deserti* at least is taken as given, and Jones accepts that there must have been depopulation, even if Boak's argumentation is defective.[27] Jones' paper on "Over-taxation and the Decline of the Roman Empire" was published in *Antiquity* in 1959; he concludes there that high taxation "was [probably] a major factor in reducing the man-power of the empire, and thereby contributed directly to its military collapse". It is as though he could not make up his mind: his paper on the "caste-system" of the later empire (1970) argues against excessive rigidity and for social mobility.[28] But this is contrasted with his stress on the size of the army and the weight of taxation. He accepted the figure of 650,000 for the army by the end of the fourth century in "Ancient Empires" (129),[29]

---

[25] 'Too few producers supported too many idle mouths'; see Jones (1964) II, 1045–48. Like Jones, Walbank argued that the late Roman state suffered from a decline in productivity; Jones criticises his contention that trade and industry had declined, *Later Roman Empire*, 1038–39, and argues for structural and religious factors, too many Christian ascetics and others living off the rest of the population.

[26] Jones (1965).

[27] Jones (1964) II, 1042.

[28] Jones (1970); the theme of social mobility in the later empire was current in the 1960s: cf. MacMullen (1964), and Hopkins (1961) and (1965).

[29] Cf. Jones (1964) I, 60: "Diocletian certainly increased the size of the army so substantially as to put a strain on the manpower of the empire", with 683–84. The paper figure of 645,000 is given by Agathias, *Hist.* V.7–8; the large size and effectiveness of the late Roman army is currently argued by some, e.g., though with caution, Michael Whitby (1995) 73–75, but it is not easy to square this with the retreat from forts on the eastern frontier, or the very small numbers fielded during the Gothic war in Italy under Justinian, for which see Liebeschuetz (1996).

and talks of a massive increase in the army and the civil service, which in turn led to the crushing weight of taxation.

2. *Jones in London*

We also need to put Jones back into the London context. Jones was Professor of Ancient History at UCL after the war until 1951 when he moved to Cambridge. When did he start writing the *Later Roman Empire*? Or have the idea of writing it? As has been noted, he was suspicious of ideology (though he was a Labour supporter). But the ancient historians in London in the post-war years were an interesting group. They included John Morris, for one. E.A. Thompson left King's College London for a chair at Nottingham in 1948 but had already published his book on the late Roman historian Ammianus Marcellinus the year before. These were years when the Historians' Group of the Communist Party flourished; one member of it was Robert Browning, also at University College London in that period. Browning and others had become Marxists before the war at Balliol, and several had been in Cairo in intelligence during the war and then (in Browning's case) in Yugoslavia. In contrast, though Jones had also spent some time in Cairo, but in a teaching post at the University in the 1930s; he spent the war as a civil servant in the Ministry of Labour.

Edward Thompson was also a member of the Communist Party until 1956 and his later books on the later empire showed his Marxist perspective. Geoffrey de Ste. Croix was a solicitor who had come to ancient history through Jones; he had been a member of the CP before the war, though he had difficulties with it in 1939. To quote the editors of *Crux*, "it has been aptly observed that Ste. Croix is in a way almost as much a Jonesian as he is a Marxist, and some might say he has been a more orthodox follower of Jones than of Marx".[30] Still, his brand of Marxism found its full expression when he turned to the late empire in his *Class Struggle*, where, as we saw, Croix referred to Jones as his "revered teacher"; he had also dedicated the *Origins of the Peloponnesian* War to him in 1972. Robert Browning, also at University College London, stayed in the Party even after the events of 1956 in Hungary. All these were much further to the left than Jones. The end

---

[30] Cartledge and Harvey (1985).

of the Roman empire, and the collapse of Greco-Roman antiquity as a slave-owning society, were of course key elements in the Marxist view of history, and were sharply expressed by Walbank and de Ste. Croix. Jones explicitly rejects Walbank in his Chapter XXV, and puts the blame on the barbarian outsiders, not on inevitable internal collapse. But his interaction with these colleagues and pupils must have been crucial to his thinking, even though he is said to have avoided engaging with political argument. Among the students who encountered Jones in London were the Roman archaeologists John Mann and John Wilkes, and in particular Wolfgang Liebeschuetz, who has written so well about the genesis of the *Later Roman Empire*.[31] Liebeschuetz is very far from being a Marxist, but the influence of Jones is clearly visible in his writing, not least in the extent to which he has continued to be occupied with Jones' problems, and has put back decline (the 'internal explanation') onto the academic agenda.[32]

Marxist views of the end of the Roman empire were alive and well in Britain when I started teaching it in 1970; for instance, Perry Anderson's influential *Passages from Antiquity to Feudalism* came out in 1974.[33] Such British Marxist views were very different from the more nuanced and theoretical Italian versions, with their archaeological emphasis;[34] they focused on internal decline, and interestingly, Perry Anderson says of Jones' conclusion in *Later Roman Empire* Chapter XXV that "the belief that "the internal weaknesses of the empire cannot have been a major factor in its decline" is clearly untenable" (97). In a perspicacious note Anderson adds, in a reference to the "greatness and the narrowness of Jones as a historian" that this last sentence of Jones' *Later Roman Empire* is "contradicted by the burden of his own evidence".

3. *London in the 1970s, post-Jones*

The influence of Jones' *Later Roman Empire*, especially his model of an increased bureaucracy and army, was very strong on anyone teaching the later Roman empire in the 1970s. Jones starts the *Later Roman Empire* with a chapter which covers the period from the Antonines to

---

[31] Liebeschuetz (1992).
[32] Cf. Liebeschuetz (2001a), (2001b), (2001c) and (2006).
[33] Anderson (1974).
[34] For which see Wickham (1988).

the late third century, seeming to take for granted the third century as the hinge, and what was in those years routinely referred to as the 'third-century crisis' continued to loom very large. Interestingly, the recent collection by Simon Swain and Mark Edwards returns to this third-century 'hinge', as do Peter Garnsey and Caroline Humfress in *The Evolution of Late Antiquity*.[35] Swain and Edwards define their period as "approximately A.D. 200 to A.D. 400", and do not engage with the issue of why the eastern empire survived. The earlier and negative picture of tied *coloni* and *agri deserti* in the third century depended to a large extent on the interpretation of legal evidence, which has since been challenged, and which is still under discussion.[36] Jones himself argued against social rigidity, and saw that late Roman legislation often had little effect in practice, but only gradually was the model challenged, as the complexities of the Codes as evidence were realised; characteristically, Jones called his chapter on law simply 'Justice', whereas in fact it deals mainly with organisation.[37] Few can match Jones' amazing grasp of the legal evidence, but this is an area where scholarship has moved on since he wrote.

Estimates of the size of the late Roman army are still disputed today. But in the decade after the publication of the *Later Roman Empire* came Moses Finley's *The Ancient Economy* (1973), and in London Finley's pupil Keith Hopkins was introducing quantitative methods and sociological models which were a long way away from the massiveness of Jones' *Later Roman Empire*.[38] As Liebeschuetz notes,[39] Finley's model of the ancient city as consumer was similar to Jones', but it had been reached by a very different route. An emphasis on the role of trade crept back as time went on, and Finley himself modified his position, but this was an emphasis on trade very different from the early Rostovtzeffian approach which Jones had rejected.[40] These were also the years following Peter Brown's *World of Late Antiquity* of 1971. The Jones model

---

[35] Swain and Edwards (2004); Garnsey and Humfress (2001).

[36] See in particular Carrié (1982), arguing for the primacy of fiscal motivation behind the legislation, and for recent discussion, Sarris (2006) ch. 8, 'The historiography of the great estate', 131–48.

[37] For a survey of the present state of discussion cf. Honoré (2004), which begins with a section tracing the demise of the idea of 'decline' as applied to late Roman law.

[38] Hopkins (1978) and (1983); cf. Runciman (1986).

[39] Liebeschuetz (1992) 3; (2006) 475.

[40] Cf. Garnsey, Hopkins and Whittaker (1983), with the second edition of Finley (1973) in 1985.

was being challenged simultaneously from several directions, including the impact of the enormous boom in late antique archaeology from the 1970s on, and the study of late antique urbanism which followed. Women's studies, deconstruction, rhetorical criticism and the discovery of Christian texts by ancient historians and classicists also followed, and it was soon clear that however fundamental, Jones' *Later Roman Empire* would not be enough.

4. *East and West*

Chapter XXV of the *Later Roman Empire* seems all the more strange because while it is really about the fall of the western empire in the fifth century, which is also the subject of many of the publications which preceded it, Jones in fact chose to end the work at A.D. 602, and points out that the east survived, even though many of the same conditions applied. Thus the *Later Roman Empire* ends before the reign of Heraclius (610–641) and before the Arab conquests. Jones' source book of 1970, *A History of Rome through the Fifth Century*, ended earlier. His *Greek City*, published in 1940, ended with the reign of Justinian. But the *Prosopography of the Later Roman Empire*, on which John Martindale began work as Jones' assistant in 1960,[41] takes the *Later Roman Empire* to A.D. 641, the end of Heraclius' reign, and the end-date of the London syllabus until the 1970s. There was thus some fluidity. The *Prosopography* was originally planned to start at 284, the same starting date as the *Later Roman Empire*. But then Jones and John Morris, who was also closely involved in the planning, decided that it had to start in A.D. 260. Jones' pupil de Ste. Croix's *Class Struggle in the Ancient Greek World* is subtitled *From the Archaic Age to the Arab Conquests*, though it does not in fact cover the conquests; de Ste. Croix justified this departure from Jones' model by saying that that was as far as his knowledge went. Current 'late antiquity', for instance in the recent volume edited by Peter Brown, Glen Bowersock and Oleg Grabar, takes in the first century or so of Islam, up to the end of the Umayyads.[42]

---

[41] For the genesis of the *Prosopography of the Later Roman Empire* see Martindale (2003).

[42] Bowersock, Brown and Grabar (1999). There is a very large recent bibliography about this periodisation: see for the 'long' view Averil Cameron (2002). Wickham (2005)

Jones does not have much to say about the question of the connection between or separation of east and west in the reign of Justinian or later, though in the chapter on his successors he talks about 'collapse' and of the 'calamitous years' (I, 317) of the Arab conquests. Apart from these brief sentences he avoided writing about the Arab conquests in the *Later Roman Empire*, but had provocatively ended *The Greek City* with these words: "The east received a new lease of life only when the onslaught of Islam infused into Christianity a fighting spirit and thus gave the empire in its religion a principle of unity and a motive for survival."[43] He did not follow this opinion up in more detail. But he already thought in 1940 that the church not only produced 'idle mouths' but also (304) that "it had no positive political doctrine to offer and propounded no ideal of civic duty. Rather it despaired of the republic." This opinion was reinforced in 1955 when Edwin Judge was applying to be a doctoral student at Jesus College, and told Jones he wanted to find out what difference Christianity had made in the empire. Jones said he already knew the answer: "None". Judge wrote about this himself, and in 1984 Ramsay MacMullen cited the story[44] and made it the opening question of his article "What difference did Christianity make?"[45] While a chapter of the *Later Roman Empire* is devoted to the church, the following chapter, headed 'Religion and Morals', concludes with a section headed 'The Church's Failure', in which Jones expresses the view that the church was entirely unsuccessful in its aim of raising the general standards of morality.[46] This dismissive view was in sharp contrast to the opinions of Momigliano expressed in *The Conflict between Paganism and Christianity in the Fourth Century*, who in Peter Brown's view asserted in his introduction "the decisive role of religious factors in the fall of the Western Empire", and showed that "the argument cannot be so easily avoided".[47]

---

identifies a series of trends which can be seen across the whole Mediterranean world, without the need to postulate a break between 'ancient' and 'medieval'.

[43] Jones (1940) 304.
[44] Judge (1980) 10; MacMullen (1984) 154 n. 25.
[45] MacMullen (1986) 322 ff.
[46] Jones (1964) II, 979–85; in contrast the recent much-discussed book by the sociologist Rodney Stark (1996) makes the opposite assumption, namely that one can assume that the church's moral teachings had a direct effect on the general behaviour of Christians.
[47] See Brown (1963, reprinted in 1972 from which the citations here are taken) 148; for the importance of Christianity also for Marrou see Liebeschuetz (2006) 477. Liebe-

Like the *Later Roman Empire*, *The Decline of the Ancient World* ends with the question of why the empire fell; here however the question posed is 'Why did the *Western* Empire Fall?' The theme of inertia is as strongly emphasised: "this apathy was not peculiar to the western part; instances of self-help are as rare in the east" (368). Nevertheless, the eastern empire "survived for centuries as a great power" (370). But Jones did not seriously address the issue of why the eastern empire continued and in what form, and he seems unsure what he thought about it. If his choice of end-date varied in his different works, I think this had less to do with any ideological notion of when the ancient world ended than with the pragmatic question of where his preferred evidence lay.

5. *Jones and Today*

Whatever answers we may now give, Jones' questions still have to be tackled. As I have argued, he has very little to say on why the East was in fact richer than the west and better able to support his idle mouths and fend off barbarians; in contrast the material resources and urban life of the Eastern Mediterranean are one of the major themes in current publications. Jones' interest in and experience of archaeology did not (and could not at that time) lead him to the kind of argument with which we are nowadays familiar, or to the amassing of quantitative and comparative evidence on a modern scale. Nor is it only archaeology that is missed: the *Later Roman Empire* of course has no pictures. There are not very many pictures in the Swain and Edwards volume either, except in an important chapter by Jas Elsner on late antique art which also deals with models of decline.[48] Visual art was not part of Jones' conception of what to include. The use now made by virtually all late antique historians of archaeological and artistic evidence marks a vast change even from when I started teaching the Roman empire, and one that happened in parallel with the development of the Brownian cultural model of 'late antiquity'. Indeed it has been argued that the

---

schuetz's own view follows that of Jones in tending to the negative: see the discussion in Liebeschuetz (1990) 236–52.

[48] Elsner (2004).

'Brownian model' began with discussion from within the field of art history.[49]

Similarly, Jones' model of Romans and barbarians contrasts with the current scholarship that works in terms of change, transformation, ethnogenesis and hybridity. Significantly, he places his discussion in a chapter headed 'The Fall of the Western Empire and the Barbarian Kingdoms'. He does not resort to the rhetoric of exaggeration used, for instance, by Perry Anderson, who writes of "the collapse of the whole imperial system" in the west "before barbarian invaders" and of a "darkening world of sybaritic oligarchs, dismantled defences and desperate rural masses" encountered by the Germanic barbarians when they crossed the Rhine in 406.[50] But again, Peter Brown was one who already saw the one-sidedness of Jones' model, and its acceptance of the attitudes expressed in the late Roman sources. Perhaps unexpectedly, he also saw that for all its exhaustiveness, Jones' piling up of evidence did not allow for regional variation or the economic micro-history of different areas;[51] it is a narrow sort of economic history in comparison with later historiography in this field.

Brown quite rightly makes the point in his review that not even Jones could encompass all the available evidence, and that for all its massive size, the evidence he does amass is not necessarily going to tell the whole story.[52] In a way then, the conclusion Jones reaches follows from his choice of evidence. Other kinds of material might have led to different kinds of conclusions. Brown also rightly says that Jones' conclusions, for example about the survival of the east, can be rather simplistic.[53]

Brown's footnotes give a very good indication of how people other than Jones were looking at the period and the problem in the 1960s, and show that that the 'fall of the western empire' was then one of the major contemporary issues. The case was argued not just by the historians mentioned but also in terms of a culture of 'pagan reaction' among the Roman senatorial class, and their historiography, for instance in the problem of the supposed senatorial reaction to Christianity,

---

[49] Specifically from Riegl (1901), see Elsner (2004) 275–76, and cf. Mazzarino (1966) 183 for Riegl on late Roman aesthetic values ("'Decadence', said Riegl, 'does not exist'"); see also Liebeschuetz (2004).
[50] Anderson (1974) 96, 107.
[51] Brown (1967) 70.
[52] *Ibid.*, 51–52.
[53] See Jones (1964) II, 1025–27.

and in M. Wes' book of 1967 on the historiography of the end of the western empire.[54] Alan Cameron is currently returning to the question of the literary culture of the late fourth century in this tradition. For all his phenomenal grasp of detail, Jones emerges from Brown's review as a kind of early Byzantine historian, "viewing Roman society from the standpoint of the central government, like the great historians of the early Byzantine period".[55] It was an authoritative—and authoritarian—view from which it was very hard to escape.

There is far less theorizing in Jones' *Later Roman Empire* than other people were prone to at the time, but his set of possible reasons for internal decline does now seem dated. Listing and dismissing in turn possible monocausal explanations is a way of understanding historical process which I doubt would now appeal. Nor would Jones' use of the legal evidence, impressive though it is. It was indeed the acceptance of the evidence of the Codes more or less at face value, and, I would say, his computations about army size based on figures in the sources, that led directly to the Jonesian model of a top-heavy late Roman state which then in turn suggested the internal explanation which Jones paradoxically rejects.

6. *Jones and Empire*

Jones does not concern himself with current issues of imperialism and identity. His is a top-down view of the late Roman state when contrasted with current attempts to understand colonialism and empire, to hear the voices of the ruled and to understand how much the ethnogenesis of barbarian peoples depended on their interaction with the rulers. To dismiss the influence of Christianity as he does, even while contributing such a detailed analysis of the organisation of the church,[56] sets the Jones of the early 1960s very far apart from historians of the present day trying to understand the development of Islam in the context of the Christian world of the eastern Mediterranean. Such questions cannot be answered if one follows Jones' precedent and reads only those parts of the religious sources which are deemed to contain nuggets of

---

[54] Wes (1967).
[55] Brown (1967) 73.
[56] For his interest in ecclesiastical matters see also Jones (1960).

historical detail. The *Later Roman Empire* also seems a very English book for its time in its overtly non-theoretical approach (as was indeed noted by Momigliano), when compared with books by others writing about the period such as Marrou, Momigliano and Lellia Ruggini. He even chose to divide the chapters into two parts—narrative and 'descriptive',[57] and for me at least he is much less good when he tries to argue a case, as opposed to when he is indeed describing.

Finally, Jones does after all seem to have believed in decline. He did not accept the logic of his own arguments in the *Later Roman Empire*, but if they are put together with statements in his other writings, and indeed with other passages in the *Later Roman Empire*, they point clearly towards decline. It is certainly not easy to isolate causal factors; for instance, Simon Swain says both that "failures to repel incursions by Sassanians or northern barbarians are in the end about internal weaknesses" and "the collapse of the (western) Empire was ultimately a military matter".[58] Why was change not allowed for? Why did Jones not expand on his views about the east in contrast to the west? And why did he feel he had to opt for one or the other and not some combination of both?

I have tried to argue that giant though he was, Jones was also a historian who belonged to a particular time. The *Later Roman Empire* must also be set in the context of Jones' other works, and it should not seem surprising that some uncertainty emerges on the key questions of decline and causation even within Jones' own corpus. Like all of us, Jones belonged to a specific time and context, and this is reflected in his work and in his ideas. But at the same time, Jones' *Later Roman Empire* was a huge milestone in the rehabilitation of the later Roman empire as a major field of study. Its sheer power and monumentality gave it a fundamental role in the formation and thinking of the generation which followed. Historians of the later Roman empire and late antiquity generally must still use Jones' *Later Roman Empire* even while they may react against it, and that is the measure of its greatness.[59]

---

[57] A division also followed in the fourteen volumes of the second edition of the Cambridge Ancient History.

[58] Swain and Edwards (2004) 2, 8.

[59] For a valuable recent assessment of the influence of Rostovtzeff and Momigliano on Late Antique studies, which unfortunately appeared too late for discussion here, see Marcone (2006).

Bibliography

Anderson P.L. (1974) *Passages from Antiquity to Feudalism* (London 1974)

Baynes N.H. (1943) "The decline of the Roman power in western Europe: some modern explanations", *JRS* 33 (1943) 29–35

Boak A.E.R. (1955) *Manpower Shortage and the Fall of the Roman Empire in the West* (Ann Arbor and London 1955)

Bowersock G.W., Brown, P. and Grabar, O. (1999) *Late Antiquity, a Guide to the Post-Classical World* (Cambridge Mass. and London 1999)

Brown P. (1963) "Review of A. Momigliano (ed.), *The Conflict Between Paganism and Christianity in the Fourth Century*", *Oxford Magazine* (16 May 1963) 300–301, reprinted in *idem* (1972) *Religion and Society in the Age of Saint Augustine* (London 1972) 147–50

——. (1967) "The Later Roman Empire", *EcHR*, 2nd series, 20 (1967) 327–43, reprinted in *idem* (1972) *Religion and Society in the Age of Saint Augustine* (London 1972) 46–73

Cameron Averil (1998) "Education and literary culture, A.D. 337–425", in *Cambridge Ancient History XIII*, 2nd ed., *The Late Empire: A.D. 337–425*, edd. Averil Cameron and P. Garnsey (Cambridge 1998) 665–707

—— (2000) "Bury, Baynes and Toynbee", in *Through the Looking Glass. Byzantium through British Eyes*, edd. R. Cormack and E. Jeffreys (Aldershot 2000) 163–76

—— (2002) "The 'long' late antiquity: a twentieth-century model", in *Classics in Progress*, British Academy Centenary Series, ed. T.P. Wiseman (Oxford 2002) 165–191

Carrié J.-M. (1982) "Le colonat du Bas-Empire; un mythe historiographique?", *Opus* 1 (1982) 351–70

Carrié J.-M. and Wataghin G.C. (2001) edd. *La "démocratisation de la culture"dans l'antiquite tardive, Antiquité tardive* 9 (2001)

Cartledge P. and Harvey F.D. (1985) edd. *Crux. Essays in Greek History presented to G.E.M. de Ste. Croix on his 75th Birthday* (London 1985)

Cary M. (1935) *History of Rome* (London 1935)

Chambers M. (1963) *The Fall of the Roman Empire. Can it be Explained?* European Problem Studies (New York 1963)

Dodds E.R. (1990) *Pagan and Christian in an Age of Anxiety. Some Aspects of Religious Experience from Marcus Aurelius to Constantine* (Cambridge 1990)

Elsner J. (2004) "Late antique art: the problem of the concept and the cumulative aesthetic", in Swain and Edwards (2004) 271–309

Finley M. (1973) *The Ancient Economy* (London 1973), 2nd ed. (London 1985)

Garnsey P., Hopkins K. and Whittaker C.R. (1983) edd. *Trade in the Ancient Economy* (London 1983)

Garnsey P. and Humfress C. (2001) *The Evolution of Late Antiquity* (Cambridge 2001)

Haldon J. and Conrad L.I. (2004) edd. *The Byzantine and Early Islamic Near East VI. Elites Old and New in the Byzantine and Early Islamic Near East*, Studies in Late Antiquity and Early Islam (Princeton 2004)

Honoré T. (2004) "Roman Law A.D. 200–400: From Cosmopolis to Rechtstaat?", in Swain and Edwards (2004) 109–132

Hopkins K. (1961) "Social mobility in the LRE: the evidence of Ausonius", *CQ*, NS, 11 (1961) 239–48

——. (1965) "Elite mobility in the Roman Empire", *Past and Present* 32 (1965) 12–26

——. (1978) *Conquerors and Slaves* (Cambridge 1978)

——. (1983) *Death and Renewal* (Cambridge 1983)

Johnson S.F. (2006) ed. *Greek Literature in Late Antiquity. Dynamism, Didacticism, Classicism* (Aldershot 2006)

Jones A.H.M. (1940) *The Greek City from Alexander to Justinian* (Oxford 1940)

——. (1960) "Church Finance in the Fifth and Sixth Centuries", *JThS*, NS, 11 (1960) 84–94, reprinted in *idem* (1974) 339–50

——. (1966) *The Decline of the Ancient World* (London 1966)

——. (1965) "Ancient Empires and the Economy", *Troisième Conférence Internationale d'Histoire Économique* (first published Paris 1970) 81–104, reprinted in *idem* (1974) 114–39

——. (1970) "The Caste System in the Later Roman Empire", *Eirene* 8 (1970) 79–96, reprinted in *idem* (1974) 396–418

——. (1974) *The Roman Economy: Studies in Ancient Economic and Administrative History*, ed. P.A. Brunt (London 1974)

Judge E.A. (1980) *The Conversion of Rome. Ancient Sources of Modern Social Tensions* (North Ryde, Sydney 1980)

Kagan D. (1962) *The Decline and Fall of the Roman Empire: Why did it Collapse?* Problems in European Civilization (Lexington, Mass. 1962), 2nd ed. *The End of the Roman Empire. Decline or Transformation?* (Lexington, Mass. 1978)

Liebeschuetz J.H.W.G. (1990) *Barbarians and Bishops. Army, Church, and State in the Age of Arcadius and Chrysostom* (Oxford 1990)

——. (1992) "A.H.M. Jones and the *Later Roman Empire*", *Institute of Archaeology Bulletin* 29 (1992) 1–8, reprinted in *idem* (2006) *Decline and Change in Late Antiquity: Religion, Barbarians and their Historiography* (Aldershot 2006) XVI

——. (1996) "The Romans demilitarised: the evidence of Procopius", *Scripta Classica Israelica* 15 (1996) I, 230–39, reprinted in *idem* (2006) *Decline and Change in Late Antiquity: Religion, Barbarians and their Historiography* (Aldershot 2006) XI

——. (2001a) *The Decline and Fall of the Roman City* (Oxford 2001)

——. (2001b) "The uses and abuses of 'decline' in later Roman history", in *Recent Research in Late-Antique Urbanism*, ed. L. Lavan (Portsmouth, Rhode Island 2001) 233–38

——. (2001c) "Late antiquity and the concept of decline", *Nottingham Medieval Studies* 45 (2001) 1–11

——. (2004) "The birth of late antiquity", *Antiquité tardive* 12 (2004) 253–61, reprinted in *idem* (2006) *Decline and Change in Late Antiquity: Religion, Barbarians and their Historiography* (Aldershot 2006) XV

——. (2006) "Transformation and decline: are the two really incompatible?", in *Die Stadt in der Spätantike—Niedergang oder Wandel?*, edd. J.-U. Krause and C. Witschel (Stuttgart 2006) 463–83

Lizzi R. (2006) ed. *Le trasformazioni delle* Élites *in età tardoantica* (Rome 2006)

MacMullen R. (1964) "Social mobility and the Theodosian Code', *JRS* 54 (1964) 49–53

——. (1984) *Christianizing the Roman Empire (A.D. 100–400)* (New Haven 1984)

——. (1986) "What difference did Christianity make?", *Historia* 35 (1986) 322–43, reprinted in *idem* (1990) *Changes in the Roman Empire: Essays in the Ordinary* (Princeton 1990) 142–155

——. (1988) *Corruption and the Decline of Rome* (New Haven 1988)

Marcone A. (2006) "Un treno per Ravenna. Riflessioni sulla tarda antichità", in *Arnaldo Momigliano nella Storiografia del Novecento*, ed. Leandro Polverini (Rome 2006) 219–33.

Marrou H.-I. (1938) *Saint Augustin et la fin de la culture antique* (Paris 1938)

——. (1949) *Saint Augustin et la fin de la culture antique: Retractatio* (Paris 1949)

Martindale J.R. (2003) "*The Prosopography of the Later Roman Empire*, Volume I: A Memoir of the Era of A.H.M. Jones", in *Fifty Years of Prosopography: The Later Roman Empire, Byzantium and Beyond*, ed. Averil Cameron (Oxford 2003) 3–10

Mazzarino S. (1959) *La Fine del Mondo Antico* (1959), translated as *The End of the Ancient World* by G. Holmes (London 1966)

Piganiol A. (1964) *La chute de l'empire romain* (Paris 1964)

——. (1972) *L'Empire chrétien (325–395)*, 2nd ed. (Paris 1972)

Riegl A. (1901) *Spätrömische Kunstindustrie* (Vienna 1901)

Runciman W.G. (1986) "The sociologist and the historian", *JRS* 76 (1986) 259–65

Salzman M.R. and Rapp C. (2000) edd. *Elites in Late Antiquity* (Baltimore 2000)

Sarris P. (2006) *Economy and Society in the Age of Justinian* (Cambridge 2006)

Seeck O. (1897–1921) *Geschichte des Untergangs der antiken Welt* (Berlin 1897–1921)

Spengler O. (1919–22). *Der Untergang des Abendlandes*, 2 vols (Munich: Beck), translated as *The Decline of the West* by C.F. Atkinson (London 1926–9)

Stark R. (1996) *The Rise of Christianity. A Sociologist Reconsiders History* (Princeton 1996)

Ste. Croix G.E.M. de (2006) *Christian Persecution, Martyrdom and Orthodoxy*, edd. Michael Whitby and J. Streeter (Oxford 2006)

Swain S. and Edwards M. (2004) edd. *Approaching Late Antiquity. The Transformation of Early to Late Empire* (Oxford 2004)

Vessey M. (1988) "The demise of the Christian writer and the remaking of Late Antiquity, from Marrou's *Saint Augustin* (1938) to Peter Brown's *Holy Man* (1968)", *JECS* 6 (1988) 377–411

Walbank F.W. (1946) *The Decline of the Roman Empire in the West*, Past and Present. Studies in the History of Civilization (London 1946)

Wes M.A. (1967) *Das Ende des Kaisertums im Westen des Römischen Reichs* ('s-Gravenhage 1967)

Whitby Michael (1995) "Recruitment in Roman armies from Justinian to Heraclius (*ca.* 565–615)", in *The Byzantine and Early Islamic Near East III. States, Resources and Armies*, Studies in Late Antiquity and Early Islam, ed. Averil Cameron (Princeton 1995) 61–124

Wickham C. (1988) "Marx, Sherlock Holmes and late Roman commerce", *JRS* 78 (1988) 183–93

——. (2005) *Framing the Early Middle Ages, Europe and the Mediterranean, 400–800* (Oxford 2005)

AFTERWORD

A.H.M. JONES AND THE LATER ROMAN EMPIRE*

Wolfgang Liebeschuetz

As the writer of its Afterword I must, of course, try to give an idea of what this work is about, but I cannot avoid making some subjective comments. Thus, for example, while Alexander Sarantis provides a striking record of Jones' enormous ability and achievement, his formation—that which made Jones precisely the kind of historian he was—remains obscure.[1] Likewise, while Averil Cameron draws attention to the fact that in the years after the war there was in London an interesting group of ancient historians with left-wing political views,[2] we have no direct evidence of any intellectual interaction between them and Jones. He obviously recognised the very considerable qualities of John Morris, though they were very different from his own. We know just as little about the influence of friends and contemporaries during Jones' earlier years.

There is one aspect of Jones' personality which perhaps deserves notice. He had a very clear conception of the limits to what even he could do. Several chapters of this book draw attention to what Jones left out. He was not an historian of ideas, or of art and architecture, nor did he keep up with modern scholarly literature or read, at least not systematically, archaeological research.[3] Now there is evidence that Jones' interests were considerably wider than his writings would suggest. He had taken part in the excavation of Jerash and of the imperial palace at Constantinople. He wrote about the buildings of New College,

---

* This Afterword owes a great deal to John Drinkwater (who was examined by Jones) and Robert Markus. The failings are my own.
[1] Sarantis (ch. 1).
[2] See Averil Cameron above (ch. 11) 238–9.
[3] It is perhaps worth remembering that archaeology only achieved full academic status in Jones' lifetime, and that the cooperation between text-based historians and archaeologists is even now sometimes problematic.

Oxford. He had some knowledge of Arabic.[4] But he evidently was well aware that if he widened the scope of his writings he would not be able to complete his projects. So he limited his field. This is brought out by various contributors here.[5] Jones' planning of the *Prosopography of the Later Roman Empire* exemplifies his realism. He certainly knew about the sad fate of the project of the Prussian Academy, here described by Stefan Rebenich,[6] so he decided that in the British Prosopography there would be a minimum of references to secondary literature. The work would consist basically of references to sources and short citations of text. Articles on emperors would be cut down to essentials. There would be no discussion of problems. This can be frustrating. But it meant that the first volume came out in 1971, and the whole immense work was completed by 1992. We all have reason to be grateful.

Jones' major books are awe inspiring, but they are easy to read. His style is spare and lucid, his argument logical, and the reader always knows exactly on what evidence a particular historical reconstruction is based.[7] Jones' lectures and seminars required greater concentration. For he was never content just to tell a story or develop a theory, but was invariably determined to show precisely how whatever he said was derived from ancient sources. Peter Garnsey was lucky to find a cardboard box full of the notes that Jones made as he read the ancient texts, and has used it to draw a fascinating picture of how he worked.[8] To a hearer who was already interested in their subject matter, the lectures offered a fascinating and impressive insight into Jones' masterly handling of texts. Someone who was not must have found them very hard-going! While his lectures were not particularly accessible, Jones was certainly concerned to make the results of his scholarship widely available, and a number of his books were written for students and interested readers rather than scholars.[9] He did indeed achieve one triumphant success in this field: *Constantine and the Conversion of Europe*, first published in 1948, which both constitutes an advance in scholar-

---

[4] Acquired during Jones' time at the University of Cairo. Richard Duncan-Jones was told that Jones had had an Indian nanny, and that at the age of seven he was equally fluent in English and Hindi though he claimed that he had eventually forgotten all of it.
[5] See Sarantis (ch. 1) 14–16 and Garnsey (ch. 2) 33–6.
[6] Rebenich (ch. 3) 56–9.
[7] Sarantis (ch. 1) 13.
[8] See Peter Garnsey (ch. 2) 26–9, also Caroline Humfress (ch. 6) 125–6.
[9] Sarantis (ch. 1) 6–7.

ship and is extremely readable. There are remarkably few books of which that can be said.

Jones' Roman studies mark an enormous advance in our knowledge of the structure and the functioning of the Empire and of its economy. This is brought out very strongly by Peter Heather, who at the same time shows that Jones' attempt to produce a large scale, fully documented analysis of the late imperial world had no forerunner in Britain.[10] Jones' immediate forerunners were continental. He is notorious for his apparent disregard of secondary literature, but this was less extreme than his footnotes might suggest. Rebenich shows that Jones was well aware of the writings of his great predecessors, and that the careful reader of the *Later Roman Empire* will notice that Jones quite frequently seems to be responding—sometimes positively, often negatively—to the writings of Otto Seeck, Ernst Stein and, above all, Michael Rostovtzeff.[11] Continental reviewers were immediately able to place Jones in a historiographical succession.[12]

The emperor, his officials and his legislation are at the centre of many chapters of the *Later Roman Empire*. Michael Whitby informs us how the treatment of that theme by historians has developed since Jones' time.[13] He notes that such characteristics of Late Antiquity as rhetoric, ceremonial, public spectacles, art and architecture are actually more prominent in Bury's *History of the Later Roman Empire* than they are in the work of Jones.[14] He goes on to show that in the last forty years interest has shifted from constitution, law and administrative structures to precisely these areas, that is the less formal and less easily described instruments of power. That is true, and this change of direction can be observed in much modern work on Late Antiquity.[15] The shift is surely linked to changes in the way the general public, which for this purpose includes historians, perceives politics. Ceremony has always been a

---

[10] See Heather (ch. 5) 104–10; Averil Cameron (ch. 11) 231–3 shows that while the Late Empire and its fall were being discussed, and in interesting and stimulating ways, there was nothing even approaching the scale and depth of Jones' *Later Roman Empire*.

[11] Rebenich (ch. 3). On this see also Garnsey (ch. 2) 28–32 (perhaps overly severe on Jones' narrative chapters), also David Gwynn (ch. 10) 216–17 on Jones' use of Fliche and Martin (1947).

[12] Rebenich (ch. 3) 43–4.

[13] Whitby (ch. 4).

[14] Whitby (ch. 4) 67. Bury employs evocative descriptions. Jones aimed at clarity and sharpness of outline. He did not try to evoke the past.

[15] See introductory chapters and articles in Bowersock, Brown and Grabar (1999).

conspicuous feature of public life, particularly in England. People have taken it for granted and enjoyed it. They did not ask themselves what precisely the ritual meant, and how it manipulated their own ways of thinking. There was even casual talk of 'empty show' and 'mere rhetoric'. Judging by the topics he selected for discussion, Jones too did not take public ceremony and display very seriously, referring to "flowery and uninformative panegyrics".[16] A certain suspicion of ostentatious display in public life, and indeed elsewhere, may have been part of his Protestant heritage. As we now recognise, those who did give careful thought to what could be achieved through ceremony and rhetoric were the dictators. Since then, everybody has learnt to take rhetoric and the symbolic communication in politics, 'spin' and 'image', extremely seriously, and the interest of historians has changed in parallel.

Historians, like most people who were not sociologists or political scientists, used to assume that the word 'power' was more or less self-explanatory. If it needed a closer definition, it could be adequately explained in terms of constitutional rules. There was little awareness that power does not exist by itself, but has to be perpetually constructed and reconstructed. Failure to exercise power was most easily explained as a consequence of a ruler's feeble personality. Jones, as a pupil of Hugh Last, had been trained in the centrality of constitutional history in the tradition of Mommsen, and he sometimes seems to suggest that the position of the emperor could be adequately defined in terms of constitutional law. So he asserts, without any qualification, that "both in theory and in practice the emperor was absolute", citing Ulpian's *quod principi placuit legis habet vigorem.*[17] This represents a gross simplification of the scope of the emperor's power as revealed in the *Later Roman Empire*. The reader very quickly becomes aware that a Roman emperor could not do whatever he wanted, and the descriptive chapters provide abundant insight into the factors, bureaucratic and otherwise, that limited the emperor's freedom of action. Jones repeatedly points out that though emperors could legislate, they were only to a very limited extent able to enforce their laws, and shows that the actual power of the emperor fluctuated in line with the exigencies confronting his Empire. By the time he wrote the *Later Roman Empire* Jones' objectives as a historian

---

[16] On the recent revaluation of this genre see Whitby (ch. 4) 71–4.
[17] Jones (1964) I, 321.

had moved from adopting Last's 'model' of constitutional history to
the production of "a social, economic and administrative survey of the
Empire historically treated".[18] But the actual process of the continuous
construction of power was not one of his themes.

Jones was the first historian to reconstruct more or less the whole
structure, including the conditions of employment, of the Late Antique
bureaucracy.[19] He was of course extremely critical of many aspects
of imperial officialdom.[20] Heather points out that Jones' criteria are
those applicable to a modern western civil service. This says more
about Jones' approval of the British civil service, and of contemporary
political culture in Britain, than about the circumstances under which
officials operated in a totally different society. Heather notes that "any
comparison with large medieval states...underlines that the key issue
in imperial longevity is keeping constituent local elites 'interested' in
the enterprise".[21] The Late Roman civil service similarly had to satisfy
the expectations of local elites. Kelly has shown how the apparent corruption, inefficiencies and inconsistencies in the functioning of the Late
Roman bureaucracy were closely bound up with the social conditions
in which the administration was operating, and that in many cases they
actually helped to keep the system running.[22] A society so very different
from that of 20th century Britain necessarily gave rise to a different
kind of civil service, whose members had a different view of what was
required of them. It is a mistake to think that one model is applicable
to no matter what society.

Jones was always very much interested in problems of the dispensation
of justice. At the time of his death he was working on the criminal courts
of the Republic and Principate, and he left a fragmentary manuscript
which was edited and published by J.A. Crook.[23] In the *Later Roman
Empire*, the Theodosian and the Justinianic Codes are cited by Jones
much more often than any other source. They provide a large part
of the evidence for his reconstruction of the administrative machine
of the Empire. Caroline Humfress provides a full discussion of Jones'

---

[18] *Ibid.*, I, v (Preface). On the influence of Hugh Last see Sarantis (ch. 1) 16–17.
[19] More recent work: Weaver (1972), Delmaire (1995), Haensch (1992) and (1994).
[20] See also Noethlichs (1981) and MacMullen (1988).
[21] See Heather (ch. 5) 117.
[22] See Kelly (2004).
[23] Jones (1972).

account of the late Roman legal system.[24] She finds that Jones is interested in Roman law as action, not abstraction. So he does not discuss its substance but describes the machinery available for the dispensing of justice. He was also interested in problems of access to justice, and in the quality of the justice available. Jones noted that the same laws were repeated again and again in only slightly changed form and concluded that their chief evidential value was that "the abuses which they were intended to remove were known to the government". According to Humfress, though Jones' primary focus was on efficacy and equity (or otherwise) in so far as they are exposed by official legal documents, he was so thoroughly acquainted with other sources that his account also throws light on the working of the system from the user's point of view.[25] The user's—and the victim's—points of view have interested more recent scholars. Work on the way law impacts on society, on the effect of penalties, on the way society copes with violence, and on the settlement of disputes in or out of court, has influenced research on Late Antiquity.[26] In addition scholars have gone behind the Codes in researching the history of the laws themselves. Honoré has identified individual legal draftsmen. Matthews has investigated the circumstances that instigated legislation, the manner in which laws were promulgated, and the processing individual laws underwent prior to being fitted into one of the Codes. Liebs has thrown new light on the state of jurisprudence in the western provinces. Jones' Chapter XIV remains a formidable achievement, but scholarship is now offering a more nuanced view of the making and functioning of law in Late Antiquity.

Chapter XVII of the *Later Roman Empire*, in which Jones deals with the army, comprises two sections, concerning the fourth century and the sixth century, respectively. In this volume, Roger Tomlin discusses only the first of these.[27] His assessment is that, by and large, Jones' reconstruction is confirmed by more recent research. For instance, Jones was right to insist that there was no difference as regards fighting quality between *comitatenses* and *limitanei*. Jones' definitions of *laeti* and *federati* are still valid. Scholars have still not found any case of a German enrolled

---

[24] Caroline Humfress (ch. 6) with references to the writings of Honoré, Matthews and Liebs in her bibliography.

[25] Caroline Humfress (ch. 6) 132–3.

[26] J. Harries (1999), also (2006). For a more favourable view of Roman justice see J-U. Krause (2004).

[27] Tomlin (ch. 7).

in a regular Roman army, as opposed to a federate unit, having proved disloyal. However, Tomlin also corrects some views which have been superseded. *Comitatus* describes the whole body of men—soldiers and civilians—who accompanied the emperor: it is not a term for the field army alone. The Diocletianic *Ioviani* and *Herculiani* did not originate as legionary detachments, but were raised as full legions. *Calcarienses* are not workers in imperial boot factories, but lime burners. Tomlin considers evidence relating to the creation of mobile field armies in the third century, and argues that Diocletian distributed much of the mobile cavalry which he had inherited, the 'Dalmatian cavalry' of the sources, among the frontier armies as *equites Dalmatae*. He notes that Jones does not cite any archaeological reports to confirm his statement that there is ample archaeological evidence for Diocletian's activity in building roads and forts.[28] Indeed he does not, but he did advise his students to read Poidebard's, *La trace de Rome dans le desert de Syrie*.[29] Jones probably read more archaeology than he lets on. He certainly had seen a great many archaeological sites.[30] This knowledge underpins his confident assertion that the Eastern Empire was richer than the Western Empire.[31] But again he does not present the evidence. The most important section of Tomlin's chapter concerns the size of military units. On the basis of a discussion of two Beatty papyri and the small size of the legionary camps at Augst and elsewhere, Tomlin concludes that both legions and auxiliary units were much smaller than Jones had thought, in fact only around one fifth of their strength under the Early Empire. It follows that the whole army was significantly smaller and less expensive than Jones had assumed.[32]

Cities have always been central to Ancient History. Athens and Rome were city states, and the combination of city and territory was the core element of ancient civilisation. Scholars have taken it almost for granted that the self-governing city state was the fundamental institution of the ancient world, and that the survival of ancient civilisation was closely linked with the well being of its cities. This in turn was thought to depend on the prosperity of the urban elite, which under the Empire came to be more or less identical with the ruling caste, the decurions

---

[28] Tomlin (ch. 7) 144.
[29] Poidebard (1934).
[30] Sarantis (ch. 1) 14–15, Ward-Perkins (ch. 9) 203–6.
[31] Jones (1964) II, 1065–66.
[32] Tomlin (ch. 7) 159–62, developing Duncan-Jones (1990b).

or *curiales*.[33] The Roman Empire can be seen as a confederation of cities under the overwhelming leadership of Rome. The history of the ancient city includes two dramatic developments. First the spreading of the institution into all the lands surrounding the Mediterranean, and later, strongly encouraged by the Roman administration, into western Europe and the Balkans; and second, the decline of the classical city, sometimes to the point of leaving nothing more than spectacular ruins. Both developments have long been known and registered by historians. Cities always were a central interest of Jones. *The Cities of the Eastern Roman Provinces* (1937) and *The Greek City from Alexander to Justinian* (1940) were his early masterpieces. In these Jones greatly increased our understanding of both, though he gave much more attention to the spreading of the classical model of city state over the Near East than to its decline. The chapter on 'The Cities' in the *Later Roman Empire* is largely based on these earlier works, as Luke Lavan notes.[34]

The nineteenth century saw the start of the great collections of Greek and Latin inscriptions, which continue to grow as new inscriptions are found in excavations. Numerous and lengthy excavation reports have been published, though until comparatively recently excavators were chiefly interested in classical remains, and tended to neglect those of Late Antiquity. The epigraphic researches of L. Robert produced a great deal of information about the cities of Asia Minor.[35] The founding of cities and the relations between cities and the reigning power figure in all accounts of the Hellenistic period. Some cities received monographs, and different aspects of urban development received attention from scholars.[36] But there seems to have been no overall synthesis of the history of the city after Alexander since Liebenam's book of 1900.[37] Perhaps scholars thought that once they had lost their independence cities ceased to have a history and were no longer of interest to historians. In any case the task was difficult, because the evidence was very fragmentary, with numerous brief references scattered over very many literary texts, and with the need to search for inscriptions and papyri through a great many collections, some of them difficult to find.[38]

---

[33] See Heather (ch. 5) 105.

[34] Lavan (ch. 8) 170–1.

[35] On Jones' relations with L. Robert see Caroline Humfress (ch. 6) 124–5.

[36] See even the minimalist bibliographies of Jones' two city books ((1937) and (1940)).

[37] Not to mention Kuhn (1865).

[38] See Caroline Humfress (ch. 6) 124–5.

Of course Jones read all the inscriptions, which was a great many, and he was actually the first to compile a history of the Hellenistic and post Hellenistic city. Characteristically, he took a long term view by making his subject the city from Alexander to Justinian, and made the task manageable by restricting himself to Greek cities. In the earlier book the subject is essentially a comprehensive account of urbanisation and of the progressive diffusion of the city, which was of course closely associated with the cultural revolution of Hellenisation.[39] In the later volume he concerns himself with urban activities: 'relations with the suzerain', 'internal politics', and 'civic services'. He then proceeds to sum up the economic, political, administrative, and cultural achievements of the city. It is probably fair to say that Jones' central interest was the evolution of constitutional government, first in the undoing of popular participation under Roman rule, and then of the decline of curial government. He was writing at a time when the evolution of parliamentary government was considered a fundamental theme in English history. Since then urban history has evolved into a recognised sub-section of historiography, and students of the ancient city are now concerning themselves with aspects of urbanisation which Jones did not consider part of his remit.[40]

Jones was not an economist, but when the *Later Roman Empire* was published it provided by far the most complete and thorough synthesis of the evidence about the economy of Late Antiquity to date. The book contains an enormous amount of information about currency, inflation, taxation, great estates and their management, the condition of the peasantry, prices, trade, demography and so on. It significantly modified accepted doctrines. Jones shows that the economy did not decline disastrously as a result of the crisis of the third century, though it was weakened.[41] The emperors tried to make essential occupations hereditary, but could not enforce their legislation. In Jones' opinion this policy was a response to a shortage of manpower. He argued that the

---

[39] Since then scholars have gone further into the significance of Hellenisation, and the relationship between the known Greek and Greco-Roman culture of the Near Eastern cities and what came before. See Millar (1983) and (1987), both reprinted in Millar (2006).

[40] See Lavan (ch. 8) 183–5.

[41] Fewer shipwrecks: Hopkins (1980) 105–6, Parker (1992). The decline of metal extraction and production in the west: McCormick (2001) 42–53, Wilson (2002a) 26–7 (evidence of Greenland ice cores). People smaller: Kron (2005).

tied colonate was essentially a fiscal measure,[42] anticipating the views
put forward by J.-M. Carrié.[43] Not least among Jones' achievements
in the economic field was the research he inspired in his pupils, who
went on to develop the Jonesian heritage in quite different directions.
Richard Duncan-Jones has done important work on quantifiable evidence about the Roman economy as well as on coinage.[44] Keith Hopkins
has used 'model building' and comparative evidence from other societies to compensate for the fragmentary nature of evidence for Late
Antiquity.[45] He in turn inspired Walter Scheidel[46] and Willem Jongman.[47]
Jones' pupil, John Kent, produced two important volumes of the *Roman
Imperial Coinage* series.[48]

Jones' treatment of the Late Roman economy is discussed by Bryan
Ward-Perkins.[49] Jones' views on trade are still controversial.[50] As is
well-known, he emphasised the relative unimportance of trade in the
Ancient World in general and in Late Antiquity in particular.[51] This
view certainly has to be qualified. Ancient civilisation could not have
continued without trade in certain materials, especially metals. Moreover
progress in archaeology and in the recognition and dating of different kinds of pottery,[52] as well as greater understanding of the minting
and distribution of coinage and of the abundant information bearing
on the economy in papyri, have greatly increased our knowledge of
economic exchanges.[53] It is clear that there was extensive trading in

---

[42] Jones (1964) I, 58; II, 796.

[43] Carrié (1982) and (1993).

[44] See Duncan-Jones (1974), (1990) and (1994), and also personal communication:
"The main pattern of what I have worked on over the decades has probably been in
areas of interest which Jones mapped out to some extent".

[45] For example see Hopkins (2002); for Hopkins' life and works: Harris (2005).

[46] See references in the bibliography of Scheidel (2001) 229–30.

[47] Jongman (1998) and (2002).

[48] Kent (1981) and (1994).

[49] Ward-Perkins (ch. 9).

[50] See Ward-Perkins (ch. 9) 196–7.

[51] Jones (1948b), but the unimportance of trade and manufacture is implied in all
his works.

[52] The pioneering work of J.W. Hayes, starting with Hayes (1972), has been of
outstanding importance and has led to very much greater knowledge of the extent and
duration of Late Roman trade, see Ward-Perkins (ch. 9) 203–4 and 207–8; Wickham
(2005) 693–824.

[53] Horden and Purcell (2000) emphasise the importance of small scale, short distance trade, which brought the objects of trade to their final destination over a large
number of stages. They may be right, but such trade is very difficult to observe, and
their theory therefore very difficult to prove.

the Roman world, and that manufacturing played an important part in the economy of some cities.[54] The need to supply troops and the major cities required transport of goods, especially of food products, on a very large scale. Jones' short cut to a quantitative estimate of the magnitude of trade in the Roman Empire is not very conclusive, since it is calculated from the alleged yield of the traders' tax from the single city of Edessa.[55] But all this does not necessarily refute Jones' view that, relatively speaking, and especially in comparison with the situation in post-renaissance Europe, trade and manufacture claimed a very small proportion of the available resources, and that manufacturers and traders occupied a relatively humble place in society. Manufacturers and merchants as such did not figure among the late Roman elite, either at civic or at imperial level. The houses of merchants and the halls of guilds were not conspicuous in Late Antique cities, as they were to be in the medieval trading cities of Italy or Flanders, or the Hanseatic cities of northern Europe.[56] Moreover, it looks as if much of the trade of the Late Antique world was not self-sustaining, but depended on the subsidised transport which supplied the needs of the government, and above all of the two capital cities.[57]

Jones can be said to have done for the history of the Late Roman Church the same as he did for the history of the Empire, in that he put the study of its organisation and social basis as an institution on a solid basis. David Gwynn notes that the work of Jones represents an important step towards bridging the gap between social-political and ecclesiastical-theological history, though the gap (which is actually as old as ecclesiastical history itself)[58] remains. Gwynn also feels that the *Later Roman Empire* remains an essential guide to the organisation of the Church and to the background against which those who study Christian doctrine and asceticism must work—and that "within the great work of Jones there is much to which the ecclesiastical historian must listen even when it hurts".[59]

---

[54] Wilson (2001), (2002a), (2002b); Bagnall (1993) 78–91.

[55] Jones (1964) I, 465.

[56] The preceding might, of course, also be said of the views of Moses Finley, Jones' colleague and close neighbour for many years at Jesus.

[57] Convincingly argued by Wickham (2005) 708–20, see also Jongman (2002), Bang (2002).

[58] Gwynn (ch. 10) 213; see Momigliano (1963).

[59] See Gwynn (ch. 10) 228, quoting Greenslade.

Prominent among matters that might hurt an ecclesiastical historian must be Jones' apparent belief that Christianity made very little difference. In *The Greek City* Jones had already proposed that "the Church had no positive political doctrine to offer, and propounded no ideal of civic duty. Rather it despaired of the republic; the world was evil, and if a man would save his soul he had better withdraw from it".[60] In the *Later Roman Empire* his judgment seems to be even more negative, for he claims that to the ordinary man the moral teaching of Christianity made little practical difference, while it actually increased the corruption in the government: for by emphasizing the spiritual danger of carrying out the routine duties of a Roman official or soldier, it discouraged all but the selfishly ambitious from public service.[61] These assertions are not altogether wrong. A religion which focuses on the community of believers and aims at the saving of individual souls is *a priori* less likely to encourage civic and military virtue than one which is focused on the well-being of city and Empire. Furthermore, long established customs such as those concerned with marriage and divorce are very difficult to change and Christianity was very slow to change them.[62] But these generalisations are also far from the whole truth. They raise many questions about the actual influence of Christianity, and the whole process of Christianisation, that Jones might have investigated, and his successors are investigating.

Why is Jones' summing up of the influence of Christianity on the Empire so oversimplified? He was certainly not motivated by hostility to Christianity.[63] He assessed the effect of paganism in similar terms: "There is little to show that pagan worship promoted public spirit... [the gods] do not seem to have inspired patriotic devotion".[64] But such scepticism as to the power of religion to influence behaviour requires further comment. Of course to make a generalisation is always also to simplify, especially if the generalised statement employs paradox and is intended to raise eyebrows. Jones showed that he understood perfectly well that religion can affect human action in many areas which have nothing directly to do with religion when he asked the question,

---

[60] Jones (1940) 304; See also the anecdote in Averil Cameron (ch. 11) 242.
[61] Jones (1964) II, 1063–64.
[62] *Ibid.*, II, 974–75; Bagnall (1995); also the balanced assessment of Clark (1993) 139–41.
[63] Liebeschuetz (1992) 6. Note that in the preface he bracketed theology with law as "the two major intellectual achievements of the age" (Jones (1964) I, v).
[64] Jones (1964) II, 1062–63.

"were the ancient heresies national or social movements in disguise?" and answered it negatively.[65] But theology and religious belief and their social effects lay outside the area that Jones chose to explore. His is a very 'scientific' history. He investigated institutions and processes which could be observed and described exactly, and he drew conclusions which, in theory at least, could be proved or disproved.[66] Religious belief, philosophy, custom, legal thought as opposed to legal institutions, visual art, rhetoric and the like cannot be treated in this way, and so Jones avoided them. But that is not quite all. I suspect that deep down he felt that human activities that cannot be grasped 'scientifically' are less significant than those that can. Chris Wickham, whose *Framing the Early Middle Ages* is in respect of its subject matter a very Jonesian book, seems to share this outlook, which is indeed widespread today, not only among historians. But it is essentially this important area that Jones left vacant which has been colonised in the recent boom in Late Antique studies, associated especially with Peter Brown and Averil Cameron but involving many others.[67]

In her contribution, Cameron concentrates on Chapter XXV, the concluding chapter of the *Later Roman Empire*, 'The Decline of the Empire'.[68] She notes that this is overwhelmingly concerned with the end of the Western empire.[69] Jones' discussion of the reasons for the fall of the Empire is compact and clear, but Cameron rightly feels that the argument does not have the solidity that characterises the rest of the book.[70] The *Later Roman Empire* is not really about why the Empire fell. As John Crook observed,[71] what Jones attempts to show throughout the book, and what really interested him, is how the Empire kept going. But he could not avoid the reasons for its disappearance. The question has always been discussed.[72] It was discussed by his contemporaries,[73]

---

[65] Jones (1959).

[66] See Peter Brown's exceptionally perceptive review (1967, reprinted in 1972 from which all citations here derive) on 51; also Collingwood (1946) 126–133 on 19th century Positivism.

[67] See the contributors to Bowersock, Brown and Grabar (1999), also Robert Markus (1990) and numerous others all over the world.

[68] Averil Cameron (ch. 11).

[69] Averil Cameron (ch. 11) 243.

[70] See Averil Cameron (ch. 11) 236–8.

[71] Crook (1971).

[72] See Demandt (1984), and *idem* (1989) for Demandt's own full account of Late Antiquity.

[73] See Averil Cameron (ch. 11) 231–6.

and it is a reasonable assumption that as long as people are impressed by the achievements of the Empire they will want to discuss why it ever ended. Given his theme, Jones had to provide an answer. This he proceeded to do, but within the parameters of the scholarship of his day, and not at the deeper level made possible by his own research.

As has been noted, his focus is very much on the West. The obvious reason for that is that the Eastern Empire did not finally fall until 1453. Jones knew that unlike Gibbon he could not write a book long enough to cover that story. But the Eastern Empire also 'declined', losing its oriental provinces as early as the mid-seventh century. Jones did not try to explain that either, even though chronologically his book stops only just short of the Arab expansion. Cameron remarks that Jones has very little to say about why the East was richer than the West, and plausibly explains this omission as a consequence of the sources that he used.[74] The prosperity of the East in the fifth and at least the first half of the sixth century remains a puzzle even now,[75] though archaeology has provided much more evidence than was available to Jones. There is another point. Although the book covers the reign and the reforms of Justinian in some depth, the *Later Roman Empire* is basically a survey of the Empire in the fourth and fifth centuries. Though the descriptive chapters generally have a separate section on the sixth century, Jones did not try to work out systematically in what ways the Empire of the sixth century differed from that of the fourth. But the sixth century was significantly different. Jones considered writing a book on Justinian, but never did. A pity!

Jones' view of the relations between Romans and barbarians differs significantly from that of most scholars today.[76] The *Later Roman Empire* has some acute remarks about the barbarian invaders, but like most writers on this topic at that time Jones considered the various barbarian tribes to be stable groups, which kept the same ethnic composition, characteristics and traditions over centuries, like the European nation-states.[77] But in 1961 Wenskus had published a book which argued that this was not so.[78] According to Wenskus, the typical history of these

---

[74] Averil Cameron (ch. 11) 243.

[75] Banaji (2001) offers an interesting explanation which will stimulate discussion.

[76] Averil Cameron (ch. 11) 244.

[77] E.A. Thompson, a younger contemporary of Jones and the leading expert on the peoples of the Age of Migrations, sometimes seems to have seen the relationship between Goths and Romans as something like that between Irish and English.

[78] Wenskus (1961).

warrior bands was one of continuous transformation, or 'ethnogenesis'. The *gentes* lost or gained new members, according to the success or failure of their operations. Those that eventually settled in the Empire had acquired much of their character in the course of their efforts to enter the Empire, and from interaction with its inhabitants. Wenskus' reassessment of the character of the *gentes* has been profoundly influential and has given rise to a wave of research which has transformed the historiography of the Age of Migrations.[79]

Jones found fault with Late Antiquity, making derogatory remarks about Late Antique literature.[80] It is clear that, having been brought up on classical literature, he judges later writings by a standard which is not theirs, and that in doing so is unjust to some great and original writing. But it is a fact that in Late Antiquity the subject matter of literature was becoming increasingly narrow. Jones might perhaps have tried to understand why that happened, and how the role of literature in society had changed. But he did not set out to be a literary critic, and in any case it is very difficult to assess that development as anything other than retrograde.

As for the state of the Empire, Jones registers the widespread lack of public spirit among its citizens, and obviously thought that these, especially the upper classes, were less public spirited and less willing to fight to defend their society than those of the Early Empire and Republic. Something has been said about this already. Here it must suffice to plead that an historian must be allowed to make judgments of this kind. Such changes of mentality do happen, and do make a difference. Attitudes towards warfare have changed dramatically in all the nations of western Europe since 1918, and even more since 1939—or 1945, after the A-bomb. Similarly, observers of modern elections cannot fail to notice apathy among voters. Jones also decided that the imperial government spent too much, and that this led to over-taxation. This, he thought, hit the peasants, who in many regions of the empire could no longer afford to raise children, with the result that there was a significant fall in population. Jones reached this assessment on what he thought was the evidence. It now looks as if he may have significantly

---

[79] H. Wolfram, W. Pohl and many other contributors to the European Science Foundation project, *The Transformation of the Roman World*.

[80] Averil Cameron (ch. 11) 234.

overestimated the rate of Late Roman taxation, at any rate in Egypt,[81] and government expenditure, since as argued by Tomlin, his estimate of the size of the Late Roman army appears to have been considerably too large.[82] He was also wrong about depopulation, at least as far as the East is concerned. He may well have been right about depopulation in the West, though even this remains a matter of debate.[83]

Cameron feels that Jones did not particularly like the Later Empire.[84] That is surely right. As a classicist,[85] as a humanist and, not least, as a democrat he could not be enthusiastic about the direction in which classical civilisation evolved in Late Antiquity.[86] Nevertheless his overall judgment is positive. As we have seen, he censured corruption and numerous other failings in the administration and policy of the Empire, and took a more negative view of the condition of the Empire than more recent researchers have done. However, he did not think that these failings were what caused the demise of the Empire in the West. His final assessment is that if it had not been for the barbarians the Empire would have survived.[87] Moreover, he repeatedly observes that the possession of a civil service strengthened the Empire, and that it was thanks to its civilian administration that the Eastern Empire endured.[88] The reader understands that the elaborate administrative machinery of the Later Empire, not least its system of taxation, was, whether one likes it or not, a very considerable achievement.

In Late Antiquity it was thought that all new philosophy must take the form of commentary on the philosophy of Plato and Aristotle. It

---

[81] See Bagnall (1985), Carrié (1993), Duncan-Jones (1994). Rowlandson (1996) 247–52 argues for an average yield of 12 artabas per aroura, considerably higher than Jones' estimate. The rate of taxation may have been considerably higher in the West (Ravenna), Wickham (1994) 15. Neither CAH² XIII nor XIV has a chapter on Late Roman taxation.

[82] See Roger Tomlin (ch. 7) 159–62.

[83] Scheidel (2001a) and (2001b).

[84] Averil Cameron (ch. 11) 236.

[85] The traditional classical education did not include either Hellenistic Greek or post-Silver Age Latin or, needless to say, Late Antique writing.

[86] It is, I think, significant that Jones was quite unsentimental also in his assessment of the Republic and Early Empire. It may be that a certain lack of sentimentality with regard to traditional institutions, such as the Grammar Schools, or the House of Lords, or indeed the Empire, is part of the English political culture.

[87] The majority of contemporary historians would probably agree with Jones that the Western Empire was brought down by 'the incomers', but they have become more reluctant to uncover weaknesses in the imperial system, lest they be thought to be upholders of 'decline'.

[88] Jones (1964) I, 406.

might similarly be proposed that most of recent work on Late Antiquity has been a commentary on the work of Jones.

Bibliography

Bagnall R.G. (1985) "Agricultural production and taxation in Later Roman Egypt", *Transactions of the American Philological Association* 115 (1985) 289–308, reprinted in *idem* (2003) XVII

———. (1993) *Egypt in Late Antiquity* (Princeton 1993)

———. (1995) "Women, law and social realities in Late Antiquity", *Bullletin of the American Society of Papyrologists* 32 (1995) 65–86, reprinted in *idem* (2003) II

———. (2003) *Later Roman Egypt, Society, Religion, Economy and Administration* (Aldershot 2003)

Banaji J. (2001) *Agrarian Change in Late Antiquity: Gold, Labour and Aristocratic Dominance* (Oxford 2001)

Bang P.F. (2002) "Romans and Mughals:. Economic Integration in a Tributary Empire", in edd. de Blois and Rich (2002) 1–27

Bowersock G.W., Brown, P. and Grabar, O. (1999) *Late Antiquity, a Guide to the Post-Classical World* (Cambridge Mass. and London 1999)

Brown, P. (1967) "The Later Roman Empire", *EcHR*, 2nd series, 20 (1967) 327–43, reprinted in *idem* (1972) *Religion and Society in the Age of Saint Augustine* (London 1972) 46–73

Carrié J.-M. (1982) "Le colonat du bas-empire, un mythe historiographique?", *Opus* I (1982) 351–70

———. (1993) "Observations sur la fiscalité du IVᵉ siècle pour servir à l'histoire monétaire", in *L'inflazione nel quarto secolo D.C.* (Rome 1993) 115–54

Clark G. (1993) *Women in Late Antiquity* (Oxford 1993)

Collingwood R.G. (1946) *The Idea of History* (Oxford 1946)

de Blois L. and Rich J. (2002) edd. *The Transformation of Economic Life under the Roman Empire* (Amsterdam 2002)

Delmaire R. (1995) *Les institutions du Bas—Empire romain de Constantin à Justinien*, vol.1, *Les institutions civiles palatines* (Paris 1995)

Duncan-Jones R. (1974) *The Economy of the Roman Empire: Quantitative Studies* (Cambridge 1974)

———. (1990a) *Structure & Scale in the Roman Economy* (Cambridge 1990)

———. (1990b) "Pay and numbers in Diocletian's armies", in *idem* (1990a) 105–17, 214–21

———. (1994a) *Money and Government in the Roman Empire* (Cambridge 1994)

———. (1994b) "Taxes and tax cycles: the case of Egypt", in *idem* (1994a) 47–59

Finley M. (1973) *The Ancient Economy* (London 1973)

Fliche A. and Martin B. (1947) edd. *Histoire de l'église*, volume III: J.R. Palanque, G. Bardy and P. de Labriolle, *De la paix Constantinienne á la mort de Théodose* (Paris 1947), translated as *The Church in the Christian Roman Empire* (volumes I–II) by E.C. Messenger (London 1949 and 1952)

Haensch R. (1992) "Das Statthalterarchiv", *ZRG* 109 (1992) 209–317

———. (1994) "Die Bearbeitungsweisen von Petitionen in der Provinz Aegyptus", *ZPE* 100 (1994) 487–546

Harries J. (1999) *Law and Empire in Late Antiquity* (Cambridge 1999)

———. (2006) "Violence, victims and the legal tradition in Late Antiquity", in *Violence in Late Antiquity*, ed. H.A. Drake (Aldershot 2006) 85–102

Harris W.V. (2005) "Morris Keith Hopkins 1934–2004", *PBA* 130 (2005), Biographical Memoirs of Fellows IV, 80–105

Hayes J. (1972) *Late Roman Pottery* (London 1972)

Hopkins K. (1980) "Taxes and Trade in the Roman Empire (200 B.C.–A.D. 400)", *JRS* 70 (1980) 101–25

——. (2002) "Rome, taxes, rents and trade", in W. Scheidel and S. von Reden (2002) 190–230

Horden P. and Purcell N. (2000) *The Corrupting Sea* (Oxford 2000)

Jones A.H.M. (1937) *Cities of the Eastern Roman Provinces* (Oxford 1937), 2nd ed. (Oxford 1971)

——. (1940) *The Greek City from Alexander to Justinian* (Oxford 1940)

——. (1948a) *Constantine and the Conversion of Europe* (London 1948)

——. (1948b) *Ancient Economic History: an inaugural lecture delivered at University College, London* (London 1948)

——. (1959) "Were Ancient Heresies National or Social Movements in Disguise?", *JThS*, NS, 10 (1959) 280–98, reprinted in *idem* (1974) *The Roman Economy: Studies in Ancient Economic and Administrative History*, ed. P.A. Brunt (London 1974) 308–29

——. (1964) *The Later Roman Empire 284–602: A Social, Economic, and Administrative Survey*, 3 vols (Oxford 1964), reprinted in two volumes with continuous pagination (Oxford 1973)

——. (1972) *The Criminal Courts of the Roman Republic and Principate*, with a preface by John Crook (Oxford 1972)

Jongman W. (1998) *The Economy and Society of Pompeii* (Amsterdam 1998)

——. (2002) "The Roman economy: from cities to Empire", in edd. de Blois and Rich (2002) 28–47

Kelly C.M. (2004) *Ruling the Later Roman Empire* (Cambridge, Mass. 2004)

Kent J. (1981) *Roman Imperial Coinage*, vol. 8, A.D. 337–364 (London 1981)

——. (1994) *Roman Imperial Coinage*, vol. 10, A.D. 395–491 (London 1994)

Krause J.-U. (2004) *Kriminalgeschichte in der Antike* (Munich 2004)

Kron G. (2005) "Anthropometry, physical anthropology, and reconstruction of ancient health, nutrition and living standards", *Historia* 54 (2005) 68–83

Kuhn E. (1865) *Die städtische und bürgerliche Verfassung des römischen Reiches bis auf die Zeiten Justinians* (Leipzig 1865)

Liebenam W. (1900) *Städteverwaltung im römischen Kaiserreiche* (Leipzig 1900)

Liebeschuetz J.H.W.G. (1992) "A.H.M. Jones and the *Later Roman Empire*", *Bulletin of the Institute of Archaeology* 29 (1992) 1–8, reprinted in *idem* (2006) *Decline and Change in Late Antiquity: Religion, Barbarians and their Historiography* (Aldershot 2006) XVI

——. (2006) "Transformation and decline: are the two really incompatible?", in *Die Stadt in der Spätantike—Niedergang oder Wandel*, edd. J.-U. Krause and C. Witschel (Stuttgart 2006) 463–83

MacMullen R. (1988) *Corruption and the Decline of Rome* (New Haven 1988)

McCormick M. (2001) *The Origins of the European Economy: Communication and Commerce* (Cambridge 2001)

Markus R.A. (1990) *The End of Ancient Christianity* (Cambridge 1990)

Millar F. (1983) "The Phoenician cities: a case-study of Hellenisation", *Proceedings of the Cambridge Philological Society* 209 (1983) 54–74, reprinted in *idem* (2006) 32–50

——. (1987) "The problem of Hellenistic Syria", in *Hellenism in the East*, edd. A. Kuhrt and S.M. Sherwin White (London 1987) 110–33, reprinted in *idem* (2006) 3–31

——. (2006) *Rome the Greek World and the East*, vol. 3, *The Greek World, the Jews and the East* (Chapel Hill 2006)

Momigliano A.D. (1963) "Pagan and Christian historiography in the fourth century A.D", in *The Conflict between Paganism and Christianity in the Fourth Century A.D.*, ed. *idem* (Oxford 1963) 77–99

Noethlichs K.L. (1981) *Beamtentum und Dienstvergehen: zur Staatsverwaltung in der Spätantke* (Wiesbaden 1981)

Parker A.J. (1992) *Ancient Shipwrecks of the Mediterranean and the Roman provinces* (Oxford 1992)

Poidebard A. (1934) *La trace de Rome dans le desert de Syrie* (Paris 1934)

Rowlandson J. (1996) *Landowners and Tenants in Roman Egypt* (Oxford 1996)

Scheidel W. (2001a) ed. *Debating Roman Demography* (Leiden, Boston and Cologne 2001)

———. (2001b) "Progress and Problems in Roman demography" in *idem* (2001) 9–81

Scheidel W. and von Reden S. (2002) edd. *The Ancient Economy* (Edinburgh 2002)

Ste. Croix G.E.M. de (1954) "*Suffragium*: from vote to patronage", *British Journal of Sociology* 5 (1954) 33–48

Weaver P.R.C. (1972) *Familia Caesaris* (Cambridge 1972)

Wenskus R. (1961) *Stammesbildung und Verfassung, das Werden der frühmittelalterlichen gentes* (Cologne and Graz 1961)

Wickham C. (1994) *Land and Power* (London 1994)

———. (2005) *Framing the Early Middle Ages, Europe and the Mediterranean* (Oxford 2005)

Wilson A. (2001) "Urban economies of Late Antique Cyrenaica", in *Economy and Exchange in the East Mediterranean during Late Antiquity*, edd. S. Kingsley and M. Decker (Oxford 2001)

———. (2002a) "Machines, power and the ancient economy", *JRS* 92 (2002) 1–32

———. (2002b) "Urban production in the Roman world: the view from North Africa", *PBSR* 70 (2002) 231–74

Wolfram A.H. (1998) (first published in Germany 1979) *History of the Goths* (tr. T.J. Dunlap) (Berkeley, Los Angeles and London 1998)

APPENDIX

THE WRITINGS OF A.H.M. JONES

(1928) "The Inscriptions" and "The Coins", in *Preliminary report upon the excavations carried out in the Hippodrome of Constantinople in 1927 on behalf of the British Academy* (London 1928) 43–50

(1928) "Inscriptions from Jerash" *JRS* 18 (1928) 144–78

(1930) "Inscriptions from Jerash—Part II" *JRS* 20 (1930) 43–54

(1931) "The Urbanization of Palestine", *JRS* 21 (1931) 78–85

(1931) "The Urbanization of the Ituraean Principality", *JRS* 21 (1931) 265–75

(1935) *A History of Abyssinia*, with E. Monroe (Oxford 1935)

(1936) "Another interpretation of the 'Constitutio Antoniniana'", *JRS* 26 (1936) 223–35, reprinted and significantly revised as "The Dediticii and the Constitutio Antoniniana" in *idem* (1960) 127–40

(1937) *The Cities of the Eastern Roman Provinces* (Oxford 1937), 2nd ed. (Oxford 1971)

(1938) "The election of the metropolitan magistrates in Egypt", *JEA* 24 (1938) 65–72

(1938) *The Herods of Judaea* (Oxford 1938)

(1940) *The Greek City from Alexander to Justinian* (Oxford 1940)

(1940) *A Silver Find from South-West Asia Minor*, with P. Jacobsthal (Society for the Promotion of Roman Studies 1940)

(1941) "In Eo Solo Dominium Populi Romani Est Vel Caesaris", *JRS* 31 (1941) 26–31, reprinted in *idem* (1960) 141–49

(1942) "Egypt and Rome", in *The Legacy of Egypt* ed. S.R.K. Glanville (Oxford 1942) 283–99

(1948) *Constantine and the Conversion of Europe* (London 1948)

(1948) *Ancient Economic History: an inaugural lecture delivered at University College, London* (London 1948)

(1949) *Documents Illustrating the Reigns of Tiberius and Augustus*, with V. Ehrenberg (Oxford 1949), 2nd ed. (Oxford 1955), 2nd ed. reprinted with addenda (Oxford 1976)

(1949) "The Roman civil service (clerical and sub-clerical grades), *JRS* 39 (1949) 38–55, reprinted in *idem* (1960) 151–75

(1950) "The Aerarium and the Fiscus", *JRS* 40 (1950) 22–29, reprinted in *idem* (1960) 99–114

(1951) "The Imperium of Augustus", *JRS* 41 (1951) 112–19, reprinted in *idem* (1960) 1–17

(1952) *The Athens of Demosthenes* (Cambridge 1952)

(1952) "The Economic Basis of the Athenian Democracy", *Past and Present* 1 (1952) 13–31

(1952) "Michael Ivanovitch Rostovtzeff, 1870–1952", *PBA* 58 (1952) 347–61

(1952/3) "Two synods of the Delian and Peloponnesian league" *Proceedings of the Cambridge Philological Society* 2 (1952/3) 43–46

(1953) "The Athenian Democracy and its Critics", *Cambridge Historical Journal* 11 (1953) 1–26

(1953) "I appeal unto Caesar", in *Studies presented to David Moore Robinson*, Vol. II, edd. G.E. Mylonas and D. Raymond (Saint Louis 1953) 918–30, reprinted in *idem* (1960) 51–65

(1953) "Inflation under the Roman Empire", *EcHR*, 2nd series, 5 (1953) 293–318, reprinted with additions in *idem* (1974) 187–227

(1953) "Census Records of the Later Roman Empire", *JRS* 43 (1953) 49–64, reprinted in *idem* (1974) 228–56

(1953) "St. John Chrysostom's Parentage and Education", *HThR* 46 (1953) 171–73

(1953) "Military Chaplains in the Roman Army", *HThR* 46 (1953) 239–40

(1953/4) "Review of E. Stein, *Histoire du Bas Empire, t. 2. De la disparition de l'empire d'occident à la mort de Justinien (467–565)*", *Historia* 2 (1953/4) 352–59

(1954) "Notes on the Genuineness of the Constantinian Documents in Eusebius" Life of Constantine", *JEH* 5 (1954) 196–200, reprinted in *idem* (1974) 257–62

(1954) "The Date and Value of the Verona List", *JRS* 44 (1954) 21–29, reprinted in *idem* (1974) 263–79

(1954) "Cities of the Roman Empire: Political, Administrative and Judicial Functions", *Receueils de la Société Jean Bodin* 6 (1954) 135–73, reprinted in *idem* (1974) 1–34

(1954) "New College (The Buildings)", in *The Victoria County History of Oxford. Volume iii: The University of Oxford*, edd. H.E. Slater and M.D. Lobel (Oxford 1954) 144–62

(1954) "All Souls", in *The Victoria County History of Oxford. Volume iii:*

The University of Oxford, edd. H.E. Slater and M.D. Lobel (Oxford 1954) 183–93

(1954) "Gloucester Hall and Worcester College (The Buildings)", in *The Victoria County History of Oxford. Volume iii: The University of Oxford*, edd. H.E. Slater and M.D. Lobel (Oxford 1954) 301–309

(1954) "The Date of the *Apologia Contra Arianos*", *JThS*, NS, 5 (1954) 224–27

(1955) *A History of Ethiopia*, with E. Monroe (Oxford 1955), 2nd ed. (Oxford 1978)

(1955) "The Social Structure of Athens in the Fourth Century", *EcHR*, 2nd series, 8 (1955) 141–55

(1955) "The Elections under Augustus", *JRS* 45 (1955) 9–21, reprinted in *idem* (1960) 27–50

(1955) "The Economic Life of the Towns in the Roman Empire", *Recueils de la Société Jean Bodin* 7 (1955) 161–92, reprinted in *idem* (1974) 35–60

(1955) "Imperial and Senatorial Jurisdiction in the Early Principate", *Historia* 3 (1955) 464–88, reprinted in *idem* (1960) 67–98

(1956) "Slavery in the Ancient World", *EcHR*, 2nd series, 9 (1956) 185–99

(1956) "Numismatics and History", in *Essays presented to Harold Mattingly*, ed. R.A.G. Carson (London 1956) 13–33, reprinted in *idem* (1974) 61–81

(1957) *Athenian Democracy* (Oxford 1957)

(1957) "*Capitatio* and *Iugatio*", *JRS* 47 (1957) 88–94, reprinted in *idem* (1974) 280–92

(1957) "The authenticity of the '*Testamentum S. Remigii*'", with P. Grierson and J.A. Crook, *Revue Belge de philologie et d'histoire* 35 (1957) 356–73.

(1958) "The Roman Colonate", *Past and Present* 13 (1958) 1–13, reprinted in *idem* (1974) 293–307 and in *Studies in Ancient Society*, ed. M.I. Finley (London 1974) 288–303

(1959) "Over-Taxation and the Decline of the Roman Economy", *Antiquity* 33 (1959) 39–43, reprinted in *idem* (1974) 82–89

(1959) "Were the ancient heresies national or social movements in disguise?", *JThS*, NS, 10 (1959) 280–98, reprinted in *idem* (1974) 308–29

(1959) "The Origin and Early History of the Follis", *JRS* 49 (1959) 34–38, reprinted in *idem* (1974) 330–38

(1960) *Studies in Roman Government and Law* (Oxford 1960)

(1960) "Church Finance in the Fifth and Sixth Centuries", *JThS*, NS, 11 (1960) 84–94, reprinted in *idem* (1974) 339–49

(1960) "The Cloth Industry under the Roman Empire", *EcHR*, 2nd series, 13 (1960) 183–92, reprinted in *idem* (1974) 350–64

(1962) "The Constitutional Position of Odoacer and Theoderic", *JRS* 52 (1962) 126–30, reprinted in *idem* (1974) 365–74

(1963) "The Social Background to the Struggle between Paganism and Christianity", in *The Conflict Between Paganism and Christianity*, ed A. Momigliano (Oxford 1963) 17–37

(1963) "The Greeks under the Roman Empire", *DOP* 17 (1963) 1–19, reprinted in *idem* (1974) 90–113

(1964) *The Later Roman Empire 284–602: A Social, Economic, and Administrative Survey*, 3 vols (Oxford 1964), reprinted in two volumes with continuous pagination (Oxford 1973)

(1964) "The Hellenistic Age", *Past and Present* 27 (1964) 3–22

(1964) "Collegiate Prefectures", *JRS* 54 (1964) 78–89, reprinted in *idem* (1974) 375–95

(1965) "Ancient Empires and the Economy", *Troisième Conférence Internationale d'Histoire Économique* (first published Paris 1970) 81–104, reprinted in *idem* (1974) 114–39

(1966) *The Decline of the Ancient World* (London 1966)

(1967) *Sparta* (Oxford 1967)

(1968–1970) *A History of Rome through the Fifth Century* (London 1968–70)

(1970) "Asian Trade in Antiquity", in *Islam and the Trade of Asia*, edd. D.S. Richards and B. Cassirer (Oxford 1970) 1–10, reprinted in *idem* (1974) 140–50

(1970) "The Caste System in the Later Roman Empire", *Eirene* 8 (1970) 79–96, reprinted in *idem* (1974) 396–418

(1970) *Augustus* (London 1970)

(1971) "Rome and the Provincial Cities", *Tijdschrift voor Rechtsgeschiederis* 39 (1971) 513–51

(1972) *The Criminal Courts of the Roman Republic and Principate*, with a preface by John Crook (Oxford 1972)

(1974) *The Roman Economy: Studies in Ancient Economic and Administrative History*, ed. P.A. Brunt (Oxford 1974)

(1971–1992) *The Prosopography of the Later Roman Empire*, with J.R. Martindale and J. Morris (Cambridge 1971–1992)

INDEX

ii) *General Index*